Creatures

of

Darkness

*Raymond Chandler,
Detective Fiction,
and Film Noir*

GENE D. PHILLIPS

THE UNIVERSITY PRESS OF KENTUCKY

Publication of this volume was made possible in part by a grant from the National Endowment for the Humanities.

Editorial and Sales Offices: The University Press of Kentucky
663 South Limestone Street, Lexington, Kentucky 40508–4008

07 06 05 04 03   5 4 3 2 1

Library of Congress Cataloging-in-Publication Data

Phillips, Gene D.
    Creatures of darkness : Raymond Chandler, detective fiction, and film noir /
Gene D. Phillips.
        p.   cm.
    Filmography: p.
    Includes bibliographical references (p.   ) and index.
    ISBN 0-8131-9042-8 (paper : alk. paper)
    1. Chandler, Raymond, 1888–1959—Criticism and interpretation. 2.
Detective and mystery stories, American—History and criticism. 3. Chandler,
Raymond, 1888–1959—Film and video adaptations. 4. Chandler, Raymond,
1888–1959—Motion picture plays. 5. Detective and mystery films—History
and criticism. 6. Motion picture plays—History and criticism. 7. Chandler,
Raymond, 1888–1959—Influence. 8. Film noir—History and criticism. I.
Title.
PS3505.H3224 Z836   2000
813'.52—dc21   00–028306

For
Bryan Forbes

Tolerated by the studios rather than welcomed,
screenwriters have never enjoyed the acclaim
so lavishly bestowed on actors and directors.
For required reading on the subject,
I recommend the series of articles that
Raymond Chandler wrote on the studio system.

—Bryan Forbes

Contents

Photographs follow page 136

Preface

Billy Wilder Speaking

I went to Hollywood in 1943 to work with Billy Wilder on *Double Indemnity*. . . . This experience has probably shortened my life, but I learned from it as much about screen writing as I am capable of learning, which is not very much.
—Raymond Chandler

Script writing in Hollywood, when I came here in the mid-1930s, was a field for novelists on their way down or for successful novelists and playwrights who came here from the East during the rainy and the snowy seasons in New York in order to steal some money writing for films; and then as quickly as possible they would get back on the Super Chief and get out of town. Screenwriters had to build up a place of some standing in the industry over a long period of time, thanks largely to the eventual emergence of a strong Screen Writers' Guild.

In all my years in Hollywood, when some interviewer has asked me about the people I have been connected with, one individual whom everyone is interested in is Raymond Chandler. It is not surprising that people are fascinated with him, because he was an enigma. Raymond Chandler worked on the script of *Double Indemnity*, and I think that he did the best work on that film that he ever did on a movie. As I have said on another occasion, distinguished novelists have frequently made the trip to Hollywood and left disillusioned. No one doubted their writing ability. The problem was that too often the writer, not trained to the film medium, made the script a thing to read instead of a blueprint for the camera. Still, many fine films have resulted from the collaboration of writer and director. Mr. Chandler and I worked well together, except for the fact that this was the first picture he ever wrote. He had no idea of what a script looked like. But he wrote like an angel.

When it came to putting the screenplay on film, I filmed *Double Indemnity* on location partially around Los Angeles; I went on location to get away from the Hollywood back lot. Nevertheless, Von Stroheim had shot a lot of *Greed* on the streets of San Francisco in 1923, so I don't claim to be an innovator in that regard.

In serious films like *Double Indemnity,* which was based on the James M. Cain novel, I strove for a stronger sense of realism in the settings in order to match the kind of story we were telling. I wanted to get away from what we described in those days as the white satin decor associated with MGM's chief set designer, Cedric Gibbons. Once the set was ready for shooting on *Double Indemnity,* for example, I would go around and overturn a few ashtrays in order to give the house in which Phyllis (Barbara Stanwyck) lived an appropriately grubby look because she was not much of a housekeeper. I worked with the cameraman, John Seitz, to get dust into the air to give the house a sort of musty look. We blew aluminum particles into the air and when they floated down in to a shaft of light it looked just like dust. Real dust is invisible to the camera's eye. Shortly afterwards MGM made another James M. Cain novel into a picture, *The Postman Always Rings Twice,* with Lana Turner as the wife of the proprietor of a hot dog stand. She was made up to look glamorous instead of slightly tarnished the way we made up Barbara Stanwyck for *Double Indemnity,* and I think *Postman* was less authentic as a result.

Our script for *Double Indemnity* clearly did not have a happy ending because there was simply no other ending possible. It was inevitable that Phyllis and Walter, her partner in crime (Fred MacMurray), would have a falling out, and the picture was designed that way. Of course, in those days, when you dramatized evil, your protagonists had to pay for their wrongdoing. Still, no other ending would have worked in the film, and the studio at no point questioned this. So, you see, it is vastly exaggerated that happy endings were expected in Hollywood pictures until recent years.

Double Indemnity has quite a reputation as an example of film noir. But I really don't like all of these categories for pictures. For me there are only two types of movies: interesting movies and boring movies. It's as simple as that. Does a film rivet my attention so that I drop my popcorn bag and become part of what is happening on the screen or doesn't it? If the film engages my interest only sporadically, the picture just hasn't got it.

As to *Double Indemnity,* it was well received, but frankly I have never been interested in what the critics say of my films. A good review means much less to me than, for instance, a comment made by Mr. Chandler about *Double Indemnity* a few years after we made it. He said it was his favorite among all the films he had ever been associated with. That means a great deal more to me than anything a critic has ever said of one of my films.

Acknowledgments

First of all, I am most grateful to the filmmakers who were willing to discuss their Chandler films with me in the course of the long period in which I was engaged in remote preparation for this study. I interviewed Billy Wilder in Hollywood, Sir Alfred Hitchcock in New York City, and Edward Dmytryk and Bryan Forbes in London. In addition, I talked with Howard Hawks at the Chicago International Film Festival and with Robert Altman and Bob Rafelson at the New York International Film Festival.

I would also like to single out the following for their assistance: novelist-screenwriter Graham Greene for sharing his thoughts about fiction on film; screenwriter Ernest Lehman for talking to me about working with Alfred Hitchcock; actor Fred MacMurray for discussing his working with Billy Wilder on *Double Indemnity;* Tim Zinnemann, production manager and assistant director on *Farewell, My Lovely;* and Patricia Hitchcock O'Connell, who played a supporting role in *Strangers on a Train,* for examining an early draft of the material on the film directed by her father.

Many institutions and individuals provided research materials; I would like to specifically mention several: the Film Study Center of the Museum of Modern Art in New York; the Raymond Chandler Collection in the Department of Special Collections of the Research Library of the University of California at Los Angeles; the Paramount Collection in the Margaret Herrick Library of the Academy of Motion Picture Arts and Sciences in Los Angeles; the Wisconsin Center for Film and Theater Research in Madison; the Collected Papers of Howard Hawks at the Howard Lee Library of Brigham Young University; the Warner Brothers Collection in the Archive of the Library of the University of Southern California; the Theater and Film Collection of the New York Public Library at Lincoln Center; the Helga Greene Private Collection of Chandler's files; the Roy V. Huggins Private Collection of Chandler's Papers; the Script Repositories of Warner Brothers, Metro-Goldwyn-Mayer/United Artists, and Avco Embassy; the Federal Bureau of Investigation, Freedom of Information Section; William Luhr and Katherine

Restaino of St. Peter's College in Jersey City; film scholars Michael Oliker and Curtis Brown, and film expert Robert Schmidt; and Lorna Newman of the Cudahy Library of Loyola University.

Some material in this book appeared in a different form in the following publications and is used with permission: *The Movie Makers: Artists in an Industry* (Chicago: Nelson-Hall, 1973), copyright © 1973 by Gene D. Phillips; and Billy Wilder's account of working with Raymond Chandler on *Double Indemnity*, which appears as the preface of this book, is reprinted from "Billy Wilder," *Literature/Film Quarterly* 4, no. 1 (Winter 1976), copyright © 1976 by Salisbury State University.

Chronology

Prologue

Trouble in Paradise

Isn't Hollywood a dump—in the human sense of the word? A
hideous town, full of the human spirit at a new low of
debasement. . . . This is no art, this is an industry.
                                        —F. Scott Fitzgerald

This isn't a business, it's a racket.
                                  —Harry Cohn, studio executive

Novelist James M. Cain (*Double Indemnity*) once remarked that he had rarely
gone to see the screen version of one of his novels: "People tell me, don't
you *care* what they've done to your book? I tell them, they haven't done
anything to my book. It's there on the shelf. They paid me and that's the end
of it."[1]

Like Cain, Raymond Chandler acknowledged that the sale of the film
rights of his books was a source of income. As a matter of fact, nearly all of
Chandler's novels were filmed, some more than once. Novelist Graham
Greene (*Brighton Rock*) conceded, however, that the monetary gain carried
with it some degree of sacrifice on the author's part: "Now when you sell a
book to Hollywood you sell it outright. The long Hollywood contracts . . .
ensure that you have no 'author's rights.' The film producer can alter everything."[2] Consequently, Raymond Chandler observed, serious novels may
be transformed into "cheap, gun-in-the-kidney melodramas . . . with wooden
plots, stock characters."[3] Greene accordingly concluded that the novelist
was well advised not to involve himself in the production of a film derived
from one of his works: "No, it is better to sell outright, and not to connive
any further than you have to at the massacre."[4]

Even when a filmmaker wants to do justice to his literary source, the
fact remains that a movie adaptation can never be a literal transcription of

a fictional work. "The achievement of even partial fidelity to the text of the novel poses major problems." The scope of a lengthy novel must be reduced, resulting in the surgical removal of substantial portions of the original work. "Scenes are omitted or rearranged," and even if dialogue from the original is included, "new dialogue must also be written for added or modified scenes."[5]

In fact, Vladimir Nabokov never had anything but good comments to make about Stanley Kubrick's 1962 film of his novel *Lolita*, precisely because he realized the necessity of altering a fictional work for the screen. Despite the fact that Kubrick extensively revised Nabokov's own screenplay, the novelist commented cheerfully, "Infinite fidelity may be the author's ideal, but can prove the producer's ruin."[6] Nabokov's challenging remarks indicate the rich lode that can be mined by examining the Chandler films.

To put it simply, the scriptwriter is composing a kind of paraphrase of the fictional work he is adapting to the screen. The resulting film, therefore, can never be a replica of the literary source on which it is based; for a work of art that was originally conceived in terms of the techniques of one medium always resists, to some extent at least, being converted into another medium.

Accordingly, Alfred Hitchcock, with whom Chandler collaborated on *Strangers on a Train*, stated that adapting fiction for film involves translating ideas from one creative medium to another. "The screenwriter," he noted, "does not have the same leisure as the novelist to build up his characters."[7] The novelist can spend paragraphs describing what is going on in the mind of his hero, but it is difficult for the screenwriter to take the filmgoer inside the mind of a character in the same way that a novelist can.

And therein lies a fundamental problem in bringing Chandler's fiction to the screen. In most of his fiction Chandler employs the first-person point of view, "in which events are seen through the eyes and mind of a single individual."[8] As a result, "the voice-over flashback strategy" used by filmmakers in the movie adaptations of his novels "clearly seems an effort to approximate this narrative style."[9]

Avrom Fleishman describes how filmmakers try to approximate this kind of first-person narration when adapting a novel for film. "Some films," he writes, accompany their images "with the words of a narrator who exudes the implication that this speaking is the source of what we see and hear." The narrator in these monologues recounts "the past as it later seems to a reminiscing participant."[10]

This voice-over narration comes out of the conscious recall of the narrator, whose voice, therefore, functions as the source of all that we see. Still, these attempts to recreate on the screen Chandler's monologues, in which the hero expresses his subjective thoughts and feelings about his experiences, are not always effective. The reason is that "those words spoken in voice-over accompany images which necessarily take on an objective life of their own. One no longer has the sense of everything being filtered through the consciousness of the protagonist-speaker." This is because "one now sees everything the camera 'sees,' not just what impressed itself" on the hero-narrator's consciousness, as reported in the novel's first-person narration.[11] In short, in the film the camera *shows* us what happens, while in the novel the narrative prose *tells* us what happens.

It is a truism that the filmmaker should attempt to be "faithful to the original text" on which the film is based.[12] Nonetheless, it is a practical impossibility for a film to include all, or even most, of the events a novel presents. A work of fiction must admittedly undergo many superficial alterations in plot and dialogue when it is transformed into a movie. The director's only constraint is to be true to the author's personal vision, that is, the latter's fundamental conception of the human condition as it is embedded in the literary work.

The faithful adaptation is one that captures the author's personal vision—the spirit and theme of the original work. The faithful adaptation of a Chandler work to the screen must consequently be designed to capture on film the thematic meaning—the essential spirit—of the source story.

Despite the fact that Chandler never pretended to present a coherent religious philosophy in his work, his characters operate in a Judeo-Christian environment; and many of them—regardless of their personal shortcomings—represent a genuine concern for ethical and moral values. It is precisely by striving to live up to their ideals that Chandler characters can redeem themselves. "In everything that can be called art there is a quality of redemption," Chandler affirmed in "The Simple Art of Murder"; and this is certainly true of his fiction.[13]

Chandler's words reflect his "hope for a better day to come for some of the characters—and implicitly for the society—of his fiction."[14] As we shall see later, both the novel and the film version of *The Big Sleep* conclude with Chandler's private eye Philip Marlowe hoping that Carmen Sternwood, a disturbed young woman addicted to drugs, can find some degree of redemption in the sanatorium to which he consigns her.

Philip Marlowe, the detective who appears most often in Chandler's fiction, is really a modern knight who is engaged in a quest for justice, whereby he strives conscientiously to protect the innocent and even the not-so-innocent from suffering injustice in the rough, corrupt world he inhabits. Marlowe may speak in a modern voice, but he is no less heroic than the chivalrous knights of old.

"Down these mean streets a man must go, who is not himself mean, who is neither tarnished nor afraid," Chandler states in "The Simple Art of Murder." He envisioned the ideal private detective as such a man: "He must be, to use a weathered phrase, a man of honor"; as such, "he must be the best man in his world."[15] Commenting on this passage, John Cawelti says in his authoritative study of detective fiction that the hard-boiled detective, as conceived by Chandler, bears "more than a little resemblance to the chivalrous knights of Sir Walter Scott." In short, a detective of Marlowe's heroic stamp views a case not merely as a problem to be solved but also as a crusade to hunt down and destroy the evils that have vitiated modern society. As a matter of fact, Chandler explicitated the link between his detective-hero and the knights of yore by actually naming the Scotland Yard detective in "English Summer," a late short story published posthumously, Inspector Knight.

Chandler "sought to create a hero" who is unswerving in preserving a traditional code of honor while living in a disordered and tarnished environment. Chandler's sleuth-knight acts with remarkable consistency in Chandler's fiction. He is "a man of honor and integrity who cannot be made to give up his knightly quest for justice" once he has accepted a mission from a client.[16]

It is not by chance that Chandler named the private investigator in his very first short story Mallory. The name, after all, is associated with Sir Thomas Mallory, author of *Morte D'Arthur* (1485), the story of King Arthur and the Knights of the Round Table. From the outset, then, Chandler implicitly identified his detective-heroes with the legendary Arthurian knights of the past, who were committed to rescuing the oppressed and vanquishing the wicked. In fact, Chandler later recalled that when he introduced Philip Marlowe to the reading public, he initially named him Marlowe, after Marlowe House at Dulwich Preparatory School, which he had attended, then changed his mind and was "going to call my detective Philip Mallory." His wife Cissy convinced him to stick to Marlowe.[17]

Robert Baker and Michael Nietzel, who coauthored *Private Eyes*, a study of American detective fiction, acknowledge the knightly virtues in Chandler's gumshoe-protagonist. They cite E.R. Hagemann's deft description of Marlowe as a "virtuous knight in Corruption City. His charger is an out-of-style Plymouth; his lance, a well-oiled Luger. . . . Forty dollars a day and expenses—Marlowe's fee for knighthood. He'll take twenty-five and he's been known to take less."[18]

That Marlowe will reduce his fee for a client who cannot afford it indicates that beneath his tough exterior is a humanity that can be reached. He is "the tough-but-tender hero cracking wise to cover up his soft spots," hiding his vulnerability behind the shield of his "tough-guy" mannerisms. Chandler's quixotic sleuth is an immortal creation, "a private eye and public conscience, sitting behind his pebbled-glass door with an office bottle and a solitary game of chess." Marlowe is not a genius like Sherlock Holmes; he is "just an underpaid drudge, with a habit of making other people's worries his own, and a gift for walking in on corpses he knows just well enough to mourn."

Marlowe's constant adversary is California. No writer has ever caught so well "the treacherous lights and crooked streets of Los Angeles. . . . And the unrelenting sun of California only intensifies the shadiness" of the depraved, soulless world of violence and duplicity in which Marlowe, the white knight, operates.[19] Indeed, Chandler adroitly reduces the sunny California setting to a gray atmosphere of despair: bourbon for breakfast, bloody corpses, and shadowy streets lit by garish neon lights. Underneath the golden glitter is a sleazy underworld peopled with gangsters, psychos, and con artists. Little wonder that the novelist found the seedy side of Los Angeles a fertile soil for Marlowe's investigations. In fact, Chandler is "often considered to be that city's epic poet."[20] Like any epic poet, Chandler's thematic vision reflects a deep concern for moral and ethical values.

In the chapters to come I shall explore the extent to which the film adaptations of Chandler's work have succeeded in capturing the dark, implacable vision that emerges from his fiction. I shall first consider each short story or novel as a literary work in its own right, independent of the fact that it was later filmed; for it is only by understanding the significance of each story as Chandler conceived it that we can judge the relative artistic merits of the subsequent screen version and consequently come to a firmer grasp of the relationship of fiction to film.

The basic aim of this book, then, is to examine the relationship of film and fiction as reflected in the screen versions of the work of one novelist, Raymond Chandler. That this is a fruitful venture is proved by the fact that what one learns about the integration of literature and film as complementary media enhances one's appreciation of both media. As film scholar Bernard Dick has written on the relationship of fiction and film, the director who translates a novelist's words into images is really doing what a composer does when he combines lyrics with a tune: "He shapes them into art."[21]

I am confident that it will become clear that, despite Chandler's feelings to the contrary, every one of these movies retains at least some moments that are true to his original work, and that at least some of them rank as examples of superior cinema, just as the novels and short stories on which they are based rank as superior fiction. After all, as Somerset Maugham once quipped, "if your characters are well conceived, they can withstand anything—even Hollywood."[22]

Indeed, writers on the order of Chandler, "brandishing incredibly laconic prose and razor-strop dialogue, wrote books that had almost the skeletal structure and style of a script." Movies such as *Murder, My Sweet* and *The Big Sleep* capitalized on the filmic qualities of Chandler's tough detective fiction: "Crisp, clever plotting; locales where light and shadow could disport themselves; characters short on talk and big on action."[23]

Besides analyzing the screen adaptations of Chandler's fiction, we will also examine Chandler's own work as a screenwriter in order to ascertain how successful he was in composing screenplays based on the work of other authors. Chandler said more than once that he never became an accomplished screenwriter; there are those who might disagree.

Introduction

Dead of Night

The characters lived in a world gone wrong, a world in which the streets were dark with something more than night.
> —Raymond Chandler

It's a dark and dirty world out there; don't expect a bed of roses.
> —Mrs. Fortescue, a widow in the film
> *A Soldier's Daughter Never Cries*

Raymond Chandler once observed that American writers of hard-boiled detective stories like himself had taken murder out of "the vicar's rose garden" and dropped it in the alley.[1] His tough, hard-edged crime fiction was a departure from the more refined, genteel detective stories of British writers such as Agatha Christie (*The Murder of Roger Ackroyd*) and Sir Arthur Conan Doyle (*The Adventures of Sherlock Holmes*).

Christie's armchair supersleuth, Hercule Poirot, for example, can find the solution to any mystery with his ingenious faculties of deduction. After he solves the case, everyone breathes a sign of relief while the butler pours a round of sherry. Satirizing the British school of mystery fiction, Chandler wrote, "Heigh ho, I think I'll write an English detective story, one about superintendent Jones and the two elderly sisters in the thatched cottage, something with . . . period furniture and a gentleman's gentleman."[2]

On a more serious note, Chandler dismissed the classic English detective story churned out by Christie and company as merely an exercise in puzzle solving.[3] By contrast, he was less interested in the solution of a mystery than in portraying his detective-hero's encounters with the evils of modern society in a vivid and compelling fashion. "The solution of the mystery," Chandler insisted, "is only the olive in the martini."[4]

Chandler's gumshoe may solve the mystery at hand, but the story inevitably concludes with an abiding sense of dissatisfaction. For the detective-protagonist is aware that his best efforts are ultimately futile, to the extent that the corrupt urban environment will inevitably undercut and outlast his heroic attempts to see justice done. When the case is closed, the city remains essentially lawless.

Significantly, as early as 1912 Chandler wrote an essay for the *Academy*, a British literary weekly, in which he asserted that he could relate easily to "those shop-soiled heroes . . . with unflinching courage" who stoically accept the disappointments and reversals life visits upon them.[5] It seems that, if the hard-boiled detective story had not already existed when Chandler began his writing career, he would have had to invent it. For he very much preferred the forbidding cityscapes and underworld types associated with hard-boiled detective fiction to the baronial country estates and the upper-class gentry familiar to classic mystery fiction.

Hard-Boiled Detective Fiction

With the emergence of hard-boiled detective fiction in the 1920s, the mystery story shed its refined manners and went native. Hard-boiled detective fiction "reached its full flower in the 1930s with the diamond-hard prose of such geniuses as Dashiell Hammett, James M. Cain, and the great Raymond Chandler. . . . They all but reinvented American prose before the war by somehow desentimentalizing it." They saw the city not as a neon-lighted, glittery world, but as a squalid sewer, "where death was hiding in the alley." Hammett, Cain, and Chandler are considered "the central pantheon of hard-boiled fiction," as they helped make this kind of detective fiction both respectable and popular in the 1930s, but Chandler occupies a canonized position among twentieth-century detective novelists.[6] Even more than Hammett and Cain, he helped raise perishable pulp fiction to the lofty level of permanent literature.

It should be emphasized at the outset that the hard-boiled, "tough private eye" school of detective story at which Chandler excelled is not a separate genre of fiction, as it is carelessly referred to by some literary critics. More precisely, it is a subgenre of detective fiction, as J.K. Van Dover correctly terms it when he declares Chandler the master of this "important sub-genre of detective fiction."[7] Hard-boiled fiction was so named because the tough detective-hero developed a shell like a hard-boiled egg in order to protect his feelings from being bruised by the calloused and cruel criminal types he often encountered.

The hard-boiled detective story first began appearing in the pages of the pulp detective magazine *Black Mask* in the spring of 1923. (Pulp fiction got its name from the "cheap, rough, wood-pulp paper" on which it was printed, a paper far less costly than the smooth paper typical of slick magazines like the *Saturday Evening Post*.)[8] Carroll John Daly is generally considered to have penned the first hard-boiled detective stories for *Black Mask*. Daly's stories featured a gumshoe named Race Williams, a violent, somewhat sadistic, wise-cracking loner who was far removed from Christie's gentlemanly sleuth Hercule Poirot. Race Williams was unquestionably the prototype of the tough private eye associated with hard-boiled fiction. "In spite of his popularity," Daly was "cursed with a tin ear for dialogue," and all of his characters "seemed hewn from the same block of wood."[9] Daly was the sort of cookie-cutter hack who "couldn't rise above formula with the aid of a hydraulic lift," quips crime novelist–screenwriter Donald E. Westlake (*The Bank Shot*).[10]

In short, Daly's stories were primitive and crude compared with those of Dashiell Hammett, whose detective stories were first published in *Black Mask* in the fall of 1923, shortly after Daly's began to appear. Hammett was a much more literate and polished writer. He had himself been an operative for the Pinkerton Agency, the first private detective agency in the United States, which had been established in 1850. In fact, Pinkerton's trademark, an all-seeing eye coupled with the motto "We never sleep," was the genesis of the term *private eye*.[11]

Hammett's classic hard-boiled novel *The Maltese Falcon*, which featured his celebrated gumshoe Sam Spade, was serialized in *Black Mask* before its book publication in 1930. In the novel, Hammet minted the prototypical private investigator, a cynical, tough individual who maintains his code of honor in a world tarnished by deception and betrayal at all levels of society. It was this pivotal novel that firmly established the vogue of hard-boiled detective fiction.

Chandler always maintained that Hammett, not he, deserved "most of the credit" for bringing the hard-boiled detective story into prominence.[12] "Hammett gave murder back to the kind of people who commit it for reasons," and not just to provide a gentleman detective with a mystery to puzzle over, Chandler wrote in "The Simple Art of Murder." "He put the people down on paper as they were, and he made them talk and think in the language they customarily used." Hammett, Chandler concluded, proved once and for all that detective fiction could be important writing.[13]

Still, Matthew Bruccoli feels that Hammett is somewhat overrated. "Hammett did it first," he comments, "but Chandler did it better."[14] Chandler himself confessed that, although he much admired Hammett's work, he was not blind to Hammett's faults. He thought that at times a Hammett story lurched too close to lurid melodrama. In an October 13, 1945, letter to Charles Morton, editor of the *Atlantic Monthly*, Chandler observed that Joseph "Captain" Shaw, the renowned editor of *Black Mask*, "may have put his finger on the trouble when he said Hammett never really cared for any of his characters." By contrast, Chandler wanted to be a bit more humane, to be a bit more concerned with the characters than with violent death.[15]

As for James M. Cain, the third member of the triumvirate of hard-boiled mystery writers, Edmund Wilson, who called the practitioners of hard-boiled fiction "the boys in the back room," found some merit in Cain's work. He characterized Cain as preeminent among novelists who could vividly portray the sorts of criminals involved in "those bizarre and brutal crimes" that figure in the tabloids."[16] In fact, Cain often drew his inspiration from front-page news stories about sensational crimes.

For his part, Chandler did not like to be linked with Cain as a fellow author of hard-boiled tales. In a letter to his publisher on October 22, 1942, Chandler compared Cain to "a dirty little boy with a piece of chalk," scrawling obscenities on a board fence when no one is looking. Chandler disapproved of authors like Cain, "not because they write about dirty things, but because they do it in a dirty way."[17] Chandler seems to have been too harsh on Cain. Admittedly, Cain's later stories sometimes take on the flat, matter-of-fact tone of a coroner's report, offering little psychological insight into the characters he draws so graphically, but at his best, Cain's work is well-crafted and entertaining, and he deserves to be in the company of Chandler and Hammett.

Wilson was one of the first literary critics to note that Chandler, Hammett, and Cain all "stemmed originally from Hemingway."[18] And rightly so. Ernest Hemingway's terse, brittle, vernacular prose, which was similar to that of a journalist's on-the-spot reportage, plus his economical, colloquial dialogue, impressed the writers of hard-boiled fiction; and they honed their own writing styles to achieve a similar effect. In fact,

Chandler praised the author of *The Sun Also Rises* as "the greatest living American novelist."[19]

In the last analysis, Wilson believed that Chandler was a cut above other mystery writers. He said as much in an essay entitled "Who Cares Who Killed Roger Ackroyd?" (the title is a satirical thrust at Agatha Christie's mystery, *The Murder of Roger Ackroyd*). Chandler wrote serious novels, imbued with psychological depth and rich, vivid detail: "To write such a novel successfully, you must be able to invent character and incident and generate atmosphere; and all this Mr. Chandler can do."[20]

Chandler's fiction was far removed from the sort of routine detective thrillers with wafer-thin plots, devoted primarily to solving a mystery, that are little more than "private eye-wash." "Inveterate readers of Chandler well know that it is no longer for the solution to the mystery that they re-read him, if indeed the solution ever solved anything in the first place." It is for the finely wrought characterizations and gripping human conflicts "that one rereads."[21] Although Chandler, like most mystery writers, was at first given the back-of-the-bus treatment by book reviewers, he eventually came into his own and was treated not as a hack but as a serious novelist.

Chandler was not only acknowledged as a major novelist in America but also praised by the British literary establishment. In his influential essay on detective stories novelist Somerset Maugham (*The Razor's Edge*) declared that Chandler was a more accomplished writer than Hammett, whom he considered Chandler's closest competitor. Chandler's "pace is swifter," he explained, and his stories are more plausible than Hammett's. He concluded by lauding Chandler for creating in Philip Marlowe, not only a private investigator, but "a vivid human being."[22]

The distinguished British poet W.H. Auden echoed Maugham's praise of Chandler when he wrote in his important essay on detective fiction, "I think Mr. Chandler is interested in writing, not detective stories, but serious studies of the criminal milieu. His powerful but extremely depressing books should be read and judged, not as escape literature, but as works of art."[23]

In a similar vein, R.W.B. Lewis recognizes Chandler as one of the premier writers of American detective fiction of the twentieth century, whose work set the standard for those who have followed after. Chandler "is the first mystery writer to be honored by the Library of America," a literary Hall of Fame established by the National Endowment for the Humanities. The Library published a two-volume edition of Chandler's novels and short stories in 1995. By including Chandler's work in their Literary Classics series, the Library not only acknowledged that crime writing can have literary worth but also "made the right choice for its representative."[24] As a novelist writing within the conventions of the detective genre, Chandler is unsurpassed: "At his best Chandler used the detective story; he was not used by it."[25]

It is not surprising that film director Billy Wilder turned to a major crime novelist like Chandler to be his partner in composing a screenplay derived from Cain's novelette *Double Indemnity*. Cain made a point of seeing the film, although he sometimes ignored movies made from his work, and he liked what he saw. The fact that the film of *Double Indemnity* (1944) is the creative product of two major crime writers, Cain and Chandler, brings into relief the observation that "American hard-boiled novelists" like Cain and Chandler "helped cinema develop its interest in squalid subjects and a hard-hitting style."[26]

Furthermore, *Double Indemnity* is generally considered one of the very best examples of film noir, a style of filmmaking with which Chandler became closely associated. So it is appropriate to examine film noir and Chandler's connection with it.

Film Noir

Raymond Chandler was an "intelligent, hard-hitting crime writer, whose highly cinematic novels had a direct influence on the emergence of film noir."[27] Indeed, Chandler was central to the development of the trend in the American cinema in the 1940s known as film noir (dark cinema), both in terms of films such as *Double Indemnity*, which he coscripted, and the movies adapted from his books by other screenwriters, such as *The Big Sleep*.

In fact, film noir provided the perfect pictorial complement for Chandler's hard-boiled fiction. As captured on film, Chandler's bleak world was pictured in terms of "shadows, darkness, and rained-on streets," with flickering neon signs piercing the night.[28] Because the novels of Chandler and other writers of hard-boiled crime fiction influenced the development of film noir, their work became known as American noir fiction.[29]

It has been said that film noir has lived in greater intimacy with its literary sources than any comparable trend in cinema. Hard-boiled fiction, especially the works by "its most respectable figures such as Dashiell Hammett and Raymond Chandler," had a great impact on the movies "by maintaining a constant supply of subject matter for the film noirs of the 1940s and 1950s." Thus, just as Dashiell Hammett's *Maltese Falcon* was the founding novel of hard-boiled detective fiction, so John Huston's film version of *The Maltese Falcon* (1941) was a milestone in the development of film noir. In the movie, writer-director Huston presents two prominent character types that would become staples of film noir: the "noirish lone wolf private detective," Sam Spade (Humphrey Bogart), and the crafty, malevolent femme fatale Brigid O'Shaughnessy (Mary Astor). With *Falcon* a new kind of detective film had arrived—leaner, tougher, and darker than the crime movies of the 1930s.[30]

Raymond Chandler supplanted Dashiell Hammett as the detective writer whose work was a major source of noir films in the 1940s. Chandler's private eye Philip Marlowe appeared in several major noirs, beginning with *Murder, My Sweet* (1945). More obliquely, Chandler's influence as a screenwriter marked noir films such as Billy Wilder's *Double Indemnity*.

Noir films were frequently shot on the double and on the cheap, that is, on a tight shooting schedule and a stringent budget. Still, many superior examples of film noir, including *Murder, My Sweet* and *The Big Sleep*, were turned out under these conditions. Furthermore, the low-budget, high-quality thrillers that surfaced in the 1940s had a profound influence on the crime film throughout the 1940s and 1950s. Indeed, the term *film noir* has continued to be applied to a body of films that has been influenced by the noir tradition in succeeding decades.

This trend in American cinema was in full flower by the time Chandler began his professional association with Hollywood during World War II. French critics christened films that fit this category film noir in 1946, when they were at last able to view the backlog of American movies made during World War II, which the war had prevented them from seeing until then. The French reviewers noticed "the new mood of cynicism, pessimism, and darkness that had crept into American cinema," writes Paul Schrader in one of the most influential essays on film noir in English. Never before had Hollywood films "dared to take such a harsh, uncomplimentary look at American life."[31]

A seminal essay on film noir was written for the *French Screen* (*L'Écran Français*) in 1946 by French critic Nino Frank, who coined the term *film noir* and was the first critic to use it in print. In the essay Frank singles out *Double Indemnity*, which Chandler coscripted, and *Murder, My Sweet*, based on Chandler's *Farewell, My Lovely*, as being in the vanguard of the new movement.[32]

The very phrase *film noir* is a variation on the French term *roman noir* (dark novel), which referred to a tough sort of fiction dealing with low-life criminals turned out by certain French novelists. This term, in turn, was related to the phrase *série noire* (dark series), which denoted "a Parisian publisher's new line of grim thrillers and violent detective stories, most of them American in origin. These novels were French translations of the works of such writers of hard-boiled fiction as Chandler, Hammett, and Cain, and were easily identifiable by their standard black covers. "The initial delineators of film noir saw at once . . . the kinship between noir fiction and film noir."[33] And so, many of the noir films were derived from these grimly naturalistic stories, such as Hammett's *Maltese Falcon,* Cain's *Double Indemnity,* and Chandler's *Big Sleep.* Film noir, then, was the cinematic extension of hard-boiled fiction. The work of Hammett, Cain, and Chandler became "the source of some of the most trenchant films of the next decade."[34]

The term *film noir* was not in common use in the film industry itself at the time. It was not until the 1960s that the term "gained widespread currency."[35] Film actress Marie Windsor (*The Killing*) has since said, "I think after a great collection on the screen of film noir pictures" the term became generally known. At the time, "I just thought . . . it was a job."[36]

Schrader rightly maintains that film noir is not a separate movie genre, since it depends on the conventions of established genres, such as the gangster film and the murder mystery. Hence, it is necessary to "approach the body of films made during the noir cycle as . . . expressions of pre-existing genres."[37]

Stephen Holden describes the standard ingredients of film noir in a nutshell: "A world-weary private eye finds himself trapped in a decadent, crime-ridden society. Even when he solves a case," good doesn't necessarily triumph over evil. "The evil is simply mopped up."[38] The milieu of film noir is a stark night world of dark angles and elongated shadows, where rain glistens on windows and windshields and faces are barred with shadows that suggest some imprisonment of body or soul. This dark, brooding atmosphere, coupled with an equally somber view of life, mark a movie as film noir.

The pessimistic view of the human condition exhibited in such movies was an outgrowth of the disillusionment spawned by World War II, with its "massive casualties, genocide, torture, and atomic clouds."[39] Moreover, this disillusionment would continue into the cold war, that period of uncertainty that was the war's aftermath. Indeed, the cold war, which followed the hot war, spawned Senator Joseph McCarthy's witch hunt for Communists, which was carried on by the hearings of the House Unamerican Activities Committee. "The world was gloomier and more complicated than it had been before."[40]

Also in keeping with the conventions of film noir is an air of spare, unvarnished realism, typified by the stark, documentary-like quality of the cinematography, especially in the grim scenes that take place at night. In essence, the sinister nightmare world of film noir is one of "seedy motels, boarding houses, and roadside diners," shabby bars and cafés.[41]

It is a world in which a woman with a past can encounter a man with no future in the insulated atmosphere of a tawdry cocktail lounge. The heroine, is usually discovered "propped against a piano, singing an insolent dirge. The hero is a cynic who has been pushed around once too often" by life.[42] As the seductive temptress Mona Stevens in the 1948 noir film *Pitfall* observes, "If you want to feel completely out of step with the rest of the world, sit around a cocktail lounge in the afternoon."

Foster Hirsch, in his exhaustive study of film noir, writes that the trend prospered between the early 1940s and the late 1950s. To be more precise, the outer limits of the cycle stretch from *The Maltese Falcon* (1941) to *Touch of Evil* (1958), which Orson Welles adapted from Whit Masterson's hardboiled novel *Badge of Evil*. Welles's grim study of the ignominious downfall of a corrupt cop named Quinlan (played by Welles) appeared just when film noir was on the wane. Welles's film "gathered many of the noir trademarks" (paranoia, double-dealing, darkness, and danger) into a summary statement of the genre's conventions and thus serves as a "convenient demarcation" for the end of the classic noir cycle.

Nevertheless, he adds that the impulse that fueled noir "did not suddenly stop after *Touch of Evil*."[43] Although film noir has ceased to exist as a distinct movement in American cinema, its influence survives in the tough, uncompromising crime movies that Hollywood continues to turn out from time to time. For example, films made from Chandler's fiction in the 1970s, like *Farewell, My Lovely* and *The Long Goodbye*, still bear the unmistakable earmarks of classic film noir.

Regarding the strong influence Chandler's screenplays had on the development of film noir, Monaco's *Encyclopedia of Film* notes, "Though often written in collaboration, Chandler's screenplays bear all the trademarks of his books, from lightning-quick dialogue to labyrinthine plots."[44] Schrader adds that Chandler's screenplay for *Double Indemnity*, coscripted with Billy Wilder, "was the best written and most characteristically noir of the period. *Double Indemnity* was the first film that played film noir for what it essentially was: small-time, unredeemed, unheroic."[45] In turning to the film version of Chandler's own fiction, we shall see to what extent other movie writers and the directors involved in transfiguring his works to film created motion pictures worthy of his fictional works.

Part One

Knight and the City

The Films of Chandler's Fiction

2

Paint It Black

Chandler as Fiction Writer

I concentrated on the detective story because it was a popular form, and I thought the right and lucky man might finally make it into literature.

—Raymond Chandler

As I saw it, the thriller had nowhere to go but up.

—Eric Ambler

Tennessee Williams often said that a writer's life is his work and his work is his life. This book does not purport to be a full-scale biography of Raymond Chandler; nevertheless, it is appropriate, before going on to analyze his fiction and the films made from it, to take a brief look at the private world in which he lived, in order to survey the experiences that helped to shape the outlook of the budding artist.

Portrait of the Artist as a Young Man

Raymond Thornton Chandler was born in Chicago on July 23, 1888. (The usually reliable Richard Schickel mistakenly places Chandler's birthplace in Nebraska.)[1] His father, Maurice Chandler, was of British descent, while his mother, Florence Thornton, was of Irish stock. Since both of Chandler's parents were Protestant, he was the product of Anglo-Irish Protestant parentage.

Chandler's father, a railroad engineer, was an unregenerate alcoholic and an unfaithful husband, so the marriage foundered. His parents were divorced in 1895. His father then deserted his family, without even providing support for his ex-wife and baby son. That same year Florence Chandler and young Raymond sailed for England, when Raymond was seven years old, to live with his mother's relatives in suburban London. Raymond never again saw his father, whom Raymond ever after resented for turning his mother into a "drink widow."[2]

In 1900, when Raymond was twelve, he entered Dulwich Preparatory School in London. At Dulwich, Jerry Speir emphasizes, Chandler received "solid instruction in the craft of writing," instruction that would stand him in good stead in the years ahead.[3] Chandler had no immediate plans to return to the United States after he graduated from Dulwich in 1904, so in due course, on May 20, 1907, he officially became a naturalized British subject. In 1908 Chandler decided to explore a career as a professional writer; for the next four years he contributed essays and reviews to the *Westminster Gazette,* a liberal newspaper, and the *Academy,* a literary weekly.

In the fall of 1912, at age twenty-four, Chandler at last decided to return to America. Because he had been born in the United States, he had retained his American citizenship while living in Britain and therefore maintained a dual nationality after he went back to his native country. After he arrived in America, Chandler went to visit friends on the West Coast and eventually took up permanent residence in Los Angeles. Chandler arrived in Los Angeles, he recalled years later, with a British accent, no prospects for obtaining employment, "and a contempt for the natives which, I am sorry to say, has in some measure persisted to this day."[4] He had trouble finding work and at first was reduced to stringing tennis rackets for the Spaulding sporting goods company, but he ultimately got an office job as a bookkeeper.

On August 14, 1917, at the outbreak of World War I, Chandler enlisted in the Canadian army at Victoria, British Columbia. Because of his dual citizenship, Chandler was still acknowledged to be a naturalized British subject; he was accordingly permitted to join the Canadian army. He chose to do so because he still felt some loyalty to England, where he had spent his formative years.

Chandler was assigned to the Seventh Battalion of the Canadian Expeditionary Force and was shipped to France in March 1918. He saw action in France, and in June was knocked unconscious by one of the German shells bombarding the trenches. He was transferred back to England and in July was accepted as a cadet in the Royal Air Force and ordered to learn to fly fighter planes. The war ended in November, though, spelling the end of Chandler's short term in the service, which had lasted little over a year. On February 20, 1919, after the Armistice, he was demobilized, and he returned to Los Angeles.

In later years Chandler was sometimes asked if the war had had the kind of strong effect on him as it had on his fellow novelist Ernest Hemingway, who turned his experiences in World War I into *A Farewell to Arms*, one of the best novels to come out of the war. Chandler would reply with a shrug that the only significant fallout he experienced as a result of his military service was that, during his four-month training program in the RAF, he developed a decided taste for alcohol. He had never been a serious drinker before the war, but he regularly spent his evenings while in the RAF drinking with his mates. As a matter of fact, the postwar disillusionment common to many veterans who were wounded in both body and soul by their war experiences affected Chandler to the extent that in the years ahead his drinking would steadily increase, so his problem with alcohol was clearly traceable to his military service. Later on he would say heavy drinking was the only discernible legacy he brought home with him from the service. Since, unlike Hemingway, Chandler did not become a professional writer for another ten years, he produced no war novel like *A Farewell to Arms*, then or later. In fact, he set his sights on a career in business when he returned to Los Angeles.

Chandler's settling in Los Angeles "coincided with the discovery of oil in the city," according to the narrator of David Thomas's 1988 television documentary, *Raymond Chandler: Murder He Wrote*. "It was one of the biggest oil booms America had ever seen. In 1920, at the age of thirty-two, his friend Warren Lloyd got Chandler a job in the new industry," specifically with the Dabney Oil Syndicate.

Chandler in due course fell in love with and married a divorcée, Cecilia "Cissy" Pascal. He was thirty-six years of age when he wed Cissy on February 6, 1924. Cissy was, at age fifty-four, eighteen years her husband's senior; nevertheless, she had a youthful appearance and a lively manner and, therefore, the age differential did not seem to matter much at the time. As the years wore on, however, the gap between their ages became apparent, especially when Cissy's health began to fail, and Chandler's aging wife became a source of embarrassment to him in later life. Billy Wilder remembered that after the first sneak preview of *Double Indemnity* in Westwood Village, "Chandler sneaked out because he did not want to be seen with his wife. . . . People would turn to him and say, 'Oh, this is your mother.' She *looked* like a mother."[5] Withal, Cissy continued to be a source of stability and encouragement for her husband throughout their married life.

Meanwhile Chandler spent the prosperous Roaring Twenties becoming a successful executive in the oil business, but he grew to hate business life and began to turn to alcohol for solace. Speir states that the increasing pressures of his responsibilities as a vice-president of the Dabney Oil Syndicate, plus some domestic difficulties with his aging wife, provided further incentives for Chandler to hit the bottle—"a reaction to adversity that would recur throughout his life."[6] In the course of one binge Chandler even made a halfhearted attempt at suicide. His drinking inevitably led to philandering. He began spending weekends with young women from the office, since they were closer to his own age than his wife, and sometimes he did not return from a "lost weekend" until Tuesday or even Wednesday. Consequently, in 1932, Chandler was inevitably fired by Dabney Oil for alcoholism and absenteeism.

Ironically, by neglecting his wife and drinking to excess, Chandler was repeating the reprehensible behavior of the father he despised, but Cissy never thought of divorcing her hard-drinking husband, as Chandler's mother had done. Given her age and declining health, Cissy had no choice but to forgive and try to forget. For his part, Chandler's emotional attachment to his wife always led him back to her, "no matter how many secretaries he chased around the filing cabinets at the Dabney Oil Syndicate" or, later on, at Paramount, as Al Clark wryly points out.[7]

Pulp Fiction

Fired at the age of forty-four, Chandler found himself out of a job and with no prospects of reemployment in the midst of the Great Depression. He therefore decided to devote himself once more to becoming a professional writer, specifically, to try his hand at writing fiction. Moreover, since his business career had been sabotaged to some degree by his drinking, he made a serious effort to taper off from his heavy consumption of alcohol while pursuing his new career.

As already indicated, Chandler admired the tough, hard-edged prose of Ernest Hemingway and Dashiell Hammett, and he was familiar with *Black Mask,* the pulp detective magazine in which Hammett's hard-boiled stories regularly appeared. "It suddenly struck me," he said, "that I might be able to write this stuff and get paid while I was learning."[8] Perhaps he was aware that Rex Stout, author of the Nero Wolfe whodunits, had quipped that "only two kinds of books could earn an American writer a living: cookbooks and detective novels."[9] Furthermore, Chandler concentrated on detective fiction because it was a popular form of writing that he thought he could raise to the level of literature.

Chandler set his sights on *Black Mask,* the leading pulp detective magazine, which would assure him of a wide audience. In composing his very first detective story, which was really a miniature novel, Chandler was aware that he must cloak his British sophistication, the result of his English education, with a brash American slang that would be acceptable to *Black Mask* readers. He revised his first story, a novella entitled *Blackmailers Don't Shoot,* no less than five times before submitting the eighteen-thousand-word novelette to Joseph "Captain" Shaw, *Black Mask'*s renowned editor. Shaw paid Chandler the going rate for pulp fiction, a paltry penny-a-word, so Chandler's first detective story netted him $180 when it hit the streets in the December 1933 number of *Black Mask.*

Chandler's second novelette, *Smart Aleck Kill,* appeared the following July. Chandler was a slow writer and therefore not prolific, so his income from *Black Mask* was meager. He recalled later on, "I never slept in the park; but I came damn close to it. I went five days without anything to eat but soup once."[10]

Significantly, Chandler's first two stories both feature a Hollywood setting, and this was a decade before he went to work there as a screenwriter. In the first novella Mallory, a private detective who hails from Chandler's hometown of Chicago, is hired by Rhonda Farr, a fading movie queen, who claims she is being blackmailed. The supposed blackmail is merely a publicity stunt, however, engineered with the aid of a local gangster, in an attempt to resuscitate her ailing career. In the second novelette Mallory is working on a case at Eclipse Studios, where the career of a washed-up movie director named Derek Walden is totally eclipsed when he is slain. Mallory's investigation shows that Walden was exterminated by a ruthless racketeer with whom he had had a falling out.

A second killing occurs in the story when a vengeful woman ices her unfaithful husband. This femme fatale is the first of a long line of homicidal females in Chandler's fiction. "Chandler is known for creating murderous females as the antagonists of his novels," Charles Smith points out. In fact, the female murderers outnumber the male killers in Chandler's stories and novels by a wide margin.[11]

Chandler experimented with several private detectives in his short fiction before finally settling upon Philip Marlowe as the sleuth-hero of his novels. Thus Mallory, Ted Carmady, and John Dalmas were among the prototypes of Marlowe, who ultimately developed into a complex character. For the record, after Philip Marlowe became a popular figure in detective fiction, Chandler published an anthology entitled *Trouble Is My Business: Philip Marlowe Stories* (1950), containing four of his early novellas. In each case the name of the detective in the story as originally published was changed to Philip Marlowe, although none of his detective stories for the pulps originally featured a detective named Philip Marlowe.

From the outset of his career, Chandler's stories were constructed with painstaking care. In the course of composing the twenty-one novelettes Chandler published between 1933 and 1938, his work steadily improved, as Baker and Nietzel point out in *Private Eye*. He advanced from writing merely competent novellas like *Blackmailers Don't Shoot,* his first story, to works of genuine craftsmanship like *Killer in the Rain,* his fourth. The latter story showed a marked improvement in the delineation of character and demonstrated that Chandler was beginning to feel at home with the detective genre. His conscientious efforts at mastering his trade are also reflected in the background research in which he engaged while writing his stories. Chandler not only read widely in books on crime and police procedures but also actually visited places that figured in his stories in order to soak up atmosphere. "If he wanted to write about a seedy hotel," Baker and Nietzel note, he would go visit one "and sit in the lobby for half a day and observe the details around him."[12]

Killer in the Rain (January 1935) is important because Chandler used it, along with *The Curtain* (September 1936), as the basis for his first novel, *The Big Sleep* (1939). He took to "cannibalizing" his novelettes (his term) for material for his novels because Chandler, like Hemingway, whom he much admired, always conceived of a novel as an extended short story. As Tuska explains, in order to combine two or more of his stories into a seamless narrative, he had to interweave the plots of the original stories carefully and finally "try to bring them together at the conclusion."[13] Be that as it may, the plotting of the novels, which were constructed in part from various earlier stories, tended to be decidedly episodic in nature, precisely because the plots of the books in question were stitched together from preexisting works.

Chandler never apologized for revamping old material and reusing it in his novels. "This gave a book body," he later said in a letter to Hamish Hamilton on November 10, 1950, "but it didn't make it any easier to write."[14] In addition, Chandler felt that the novellas he had written for the pulps were "as extinct as the dodo" by the time he incorporated them into his novels, because these novelettes were largely unknown to a generation of readers who never knew *Black Mask* in its heyday. Furthermore, by reworking these earlier stories for his longer, more ambitious novels, he was convinced that he was recreating them in a different form and turning them into enduring fiction in the bargain.

As we know, Chandler found it difficult to fashion the kind of long, intricate plot required for a novel-length mystery story. Indeed, he freely admitted that it was hard for him to maneuver a large group of characters throughout a long, complicated novel. "A crowded canvas just bewilders me," he said.[15] Accordingly, Chandler decided that at least for his first few novels he would give himself a running start on a given book by combining and expanding material he had ready to hand. Nevertheless, he would still jokingly refer to himself at times as "a fellow who had jacked up a few pulp novelettes into book form."[16] In reality, the process of cannibalizing and recycling earlier material gave him the chance to improve it, Ralf Norrman contends. "This material was now refined into a final perfection."[17]

Killer in the Rain and *The Curtain* are also significant because they are among the first of his stories to be narrated by the detective-hero in the first person. Chandler ultimately decided to have Marlowe be the first-person narrator of all of his novels. As a matter of fact, Marlowe's first-person narration became the trademark of Chandler's novels.

R.W. Lid explains that Marlowe's voice reflects his "combativeness, his slow-burning but explosive personality," and his sardonic wit, along with the weariness he experiences as he engages in the never-ending battle with crime.[18] In brief, Chandler learned that having a first-person narrator gives the writing "a personality" that could not be achieved by third-person narration. MacShane affirms that Joseph Conrad (*Heart of Darkness*) discovered this when he employed the seaman Marlow [*sic*] to tell his tales about mariners like himself. "So did Chandler," McShane adds, "when by coincidence he used a man with the same name" to narrate his novels.[19]

As Chandler moved on from being a successful author of detective stories for the pulps to being an even more successful novelist, he was not ready to admit his age. He wrote to his publishers, "I'd rather my age were kept confidential. I'm not ashamed of it, but I look a good ten years younger; and I think it's bad publicity to be middle-aged and a beginner."[20] By the time he published his second novel, *Farewell, My Lovely* (1940), certainly one of his best books, he could hardly be considered a beginner.

3

The Lady Is a Tramp

The Falcon Takes Over; Murder, My Sweet; and *Farewell, My Lovely*

I've hitched and hiked and grifted too from Maine to
  Albuquerque. . . .
Hate California, it's cold and it's damp,
That's why the lady is a tramp.
> —Words and music by
> Lorenz Hart and Richard Rogers

All the society dames talk like tramps nowadays. Probably
some of them *are* tramps.
> —Philip Marlowe,
> in the novel *Farewell, My Lovely*

Because Raymond Chandler wanted to give his crime novels the authentic flavor of real life, he studiously read books on law enforcement and crime detection. He also did his homework by keeping abreast of press reports on crime and criminals in Los Angeles, his adopted city.

Los Angeles in those days was still something of a "frontier town, rough, corrupt, and teeming with immigrants in search of the American Dream," the narrator of David Thomas's television documentary, *Raymond Chandler: Murder He Wrote,* states. "Southern California, with its climate and rich farm lands, acted like a magnet for the disadvantaged all over America."

Indeed, six hundred thousand new citizens flocked to Los Angeles in the 1920s alone. The successive waves of Americans from other parts of the country to California at that time created the greatest internal migration in U.S. history. And, as Victor Hugo reflected in *Les Misérables,* when the city grows, crime grows with it.

"Lawlessness in 1930s Los Angeles was a fact," Hiney declares. "Even before the start of the Depression" the crime rate in L.A. had risen alarmingly. "The metropolis had simply grown too quickly to be controlled." A steady stream of news stories in the local Los Angeles papers documented the rise of organized crime, which went hand-in-hand with police corruption in the city. John Cloud writes that "bad cops of that era took bribes of French champagne from madams and cash from bootleggers and gamblers."[1]

Meanwhile, nearby Santa Monica, which was generally considered a wide-open town, allowed gambling ships to operate illegally off its shores. One of them, the *Monte Carlo,* was owned by L.A. racketeer Tony Cornero. "Chandler made Santa Monica into 'Bay City,' and the *Monte Carlo* into 'Montecito' for *Farewell, My Lovely,*" as William Marling observes; while Tony Cornero became the model for gambler-gangster Laird Brunette in the same novel.[2] Yet Chandler was criticized in some quarters, when the novel was published, for painting an exaggerated picture of Los Angeles and its environs as a corrupt, crime-ridden neon slum; such criticism, he rightly contended, was manifestly unjustified.

Farewell, My Lovely: The Novel

In his notebook Chandler has a "Plan of Work," dated March 16, 1939, in which he says that he plans to write a detective novel "about the corrupt alliance of police and racketeers in a small California town, outwardly as fair as the dawn."[3] The town was Bay City, and the novel was eventually—against his publisher's wishes—entitled *Farewell, My Lovely.*

Chandler recalled that his publisher "howled like hell" about the book's title because it did not sound like the title of a mystery.[4] Chandler, however, consciously avoided titles beginning the "The Case of" or "The Mystery of," such as Sir Arthur Conan Doyle employed for his Sherlock Holmes stories. Chandler's reason was that he wanted the title of each of his books to suggest a serious novel, and not a mere run-of-the-mill whodunit.

Chandler cannibalized three of his short novels to provide material for *Farewell, My Lovely* (1940): two from *Black Mask, The Man Who Loved*

Dogs (March 1926) and *Try the Girl* (January 1937); and a third, *Mandarin's Jade,* from *Dime Detective* (November 1937).

In *Try the Girl* Steve Skalla, an apelike ex-convict asks private eye Ted Carmady to find his old flame, Beulah. Carmady interviews Violet Shamey, a miserable old alcoholic who knows Beulah. Following her lead, Carmady discovers that Beulah is singing on the radio and having an affair with her boss. Carmady has a mordant sense of humor, which will likewise characterize Philip Marlowe in the novel. During Carmady's interview with Violet, she stands up at one point, and her bathrobe falls open. Violet wags her finger at him and warns, "No peekin'." Carmady is amused, since he has no intention of leering at the wretched woman's withered body. That little incident survives not only in the novel but also in *Murder, My Sweet,* the 1944 film version of the novel.[5]

Mandarin's Jade centers on Mrs. Prendergast, a woman with a shady past, who has acquired a wealthy, respectable husband. She hires shamus John Dalmas to ransom an Oriental jade necklace that she claims has been stolen from her. *The Man Who Liked Dogs,* the third novella Chandler ransacked for material for the novel, revolves around Dr. Sundstand, a crooked physician who runs a phoney clinic that in reality is a hideout for criminals on the lam. Carmady stumbles across Sundstand's shady operation and, with the aid of alcohol and morphine, is temporarily held hostage at the clinic by the doctor and his cohorts. Nevertheless, Carmady is eventually able to make good his escape. The climax of the novelette occurs when Carmady has a showdown with Sundstand's gang aboard the gambling ship *Montecito.* This entire episode was transplanted, with only minor elaboration, to the novel.

Chandler expanded the material he lifted from the three previously published novellas and integrated it into a single ongoing narrative. *Try the Girl* yielded the Moose Malloy–Velma Valento relationship (Steve Skalla and Beulah in the novelette) and minor characters like Jessie Florian (Violet Shamey in the story). *Mandarin's Jade* supplied the theft of the jade necklace of Helen Grayle (Mrs. Prendergast in the novella). Finally, *The Man Who Liked Dogs* provided the sinister private clinic of Dr. Sondeborg (Dr. Sundstand in the novelette) plus the novel's climax aboard the gambling ship.

Chandler is able to mesh adroitly the recycled material from the novellas into a unified novel primarily because he amalgamated private investigator Ted Carmady from *Try the Girl* and *The Man Who Liked Dogs* with private eye John Dalmas from *Mandarin's Jade* in order to create Philip Marlowe in the book.

In brief, in the course of *Farewell, My Lovely* Marlowe becomes enmeshed in a line of investigation that in fact originated in *Try the Girl.* This line of investigation leads to a dead end, so he takes on another case, which is actually derived from *Mandarin's Jade.* Initially this case seems to have no apparent connection with the other one. "When the novel reaches its climax," John Cawelti points out, "the solution is seen to lie in the intersection of the two lines of investigation."[5] Moreover, the climax is staged aboard the floating casino from *The Man Who Liked Dogs.*

In the draft of a letter dated July 6, 1951, Chandler cites from his notebook a diary that he kept of his progress (or lack thereof) on various writing projects from 1939 to 1943.[6] This record indicates that he began *Farewell, My Lovely* in mid-April 1939 with the working title of *The Girl from Florian's,* a reference to a dive that figures in the novel. Chandler composed his novels on half-sheets of paper in order not to waste words and to ensure that each half-page contained a bit of magic, an apt metaphor or a snatch of pungent dialogue. On May 22, when he had reached page 233, he noted in his diary, "This is a flop. It smells to high heaven. Think I'll have to scrap it and try something new." He then moved on to other projects, devoting himself mostly to short fiction.

On July 1 he went back to *The Girl from Florian's.* He proceeded "more or less steadily" until September 15, 1939, when he completed the rough draft on page 638. Sorely disappointed with the first draft, Chandler "rewrote the entire thing in 1940." Finally, he recorded that he "actually finished *Farewell, My Lovely,*" as the book was now called, "on April 30, 1940."[7]

The novel begins with Philip Marlowe crossing the path of Moose Malloy, a hulking, gargantuan ex-con, outside Florian's, the seedy nightclub where Moose's beloved, Velma Valento, had been a two-bit entertainer and a good-time girl. Moose had lost touch with Velma during the eight-year stretch he did for bank robbery, but he is confident that "little Velma," as he calls her endearingly, has waited for him. He enlists the aid of Philip Marlowe in locating her. Marlowe, who is not so sure that Velma has been true to Moose, nevertheless agrees to take the case. They enter Florian's, which had been a burlesque house with a white clientele but is now a bar for black patrons exclusively.

Moose tries to strong-arm the manager in to revealing the whereabouts of Velma. The frightened manager, who of course knows nothing of Velma, pulls a gun on Moose; the big ape, who does not know his own strength, knocks the man dead with one blow. Moose's killing of the manager is arguably self-defense, but as an ex-con he thinks it best to flee the scene before the police arrive. Marlowe is intrigued by the case of the missing Velma and decides to continue his search for her. He visits Jessie Florian, the widow of the owner, and plies the sodden old drunk with booze in order to get her to talk. Jessie insists that Velma is now dead, and she will say no more about Velma.

Since this investigation is getting him nowhere, Marlowe turns his attention to another case. A Lindsay Marriott, whose effete mannerisms and strong scent of perfume imply that he is homosexual, hires Marlowe to accompany him to Purissima Canyon, an isolated area near Malibu off the Pacific Coast Highway. Marriott purportedly is to ransom a jade necklace that has been stolen from a lady who has retained him to get it back. He feels that he needs a gumshoe for protection, so he enlists Marlowe as backup. When they arrive at the remote rendezvous, though, Marlowe is sapped with a blackjack and wakes up only to find that Marriott has been beaten to death.

It is an index of Marlowe's professional integrity that he does not dismiss the slaying of Marriott as just another L.A. "homo-cide." He believes that since he was engaged to protect his client and bungled the job, he owes it to Marriott to bring his killer to justice. Later on, Anne Riordan, a freelance journalist who is interested in the case, informs Marlowe that the missing jade necklace is the property of Mrs. Helen Grayle, so Marlowe pays a call to Mrs. Grayle and her wealthy, aging husband, Lewin Grayle, who is devoted to her. (Chandler inadvertently calls him Mr. Merwin Grayle on page 223, an oversight that has never been corrected in subsequent printings of the text.)

Helen explains that she asked Marriott to retrieve the necklace because he was experienced in dealing with the underworld, but she admits that she had no illusions about Lindsay Marriott, whom she describes as a wily piranha, a high-class homosexual dandy who preys upon rich women.

Helen is an alluring, promiscuous young woman, yoked to a sexually used-up older man, so she becomes coquettish with Marlowe after her husband leaves them alone. But Marlowe is wary of responding to her overtures, for fear of offending her rich and powerful husband. "I got to watch my step," he reflects afterward. "This Grayle packs a lot of dough in his pants. And law is where you buy it in this town" (139). This is a reference to the crooked police officials and rogue cops he has encountered in his line of work. As a matter of fact, Chandler initially had considered entitling the novel *Law Is Where You Buy It.*[9]

Marlowe eventually finds out that Jessie Florian has been receiving financial aid from Lindsay Marriott, money Marlowe assumes is a payoff of some sort. Suddenly there is a link between his two cases: Lindsay Marriott was somehow associated with Jessie Florian, who is involved in the Moose Malloy–Velma Valento case, and he was likewise involved with Helen Grayle and her stolen necklace. The two cases are beginning to mesh.

Marlowe had found a calling card for Jules Amthor, a psychic consultant, on Marriott's corpse, so he arranges to see Amthor. Marriott and Amthor seem to be cut from the same cloth. Like Marriott, Amthor comes across as an upper-class homosexual fop who ingratiates himself with wealthy women in order to con them. In short, Marriott and Amthor stack up as the kind of homosexuals who give homosexuality a bad name.

Marlowe dares to suggest to Amthor that Amthor was Marriott's silent partner in a racket to exploit wealthy women. These rich ladies would discuss their private lives with Amthor in his role as psychic consultant. As Speir puts it, Amthor, "with his knowledge of the habits of wealthy women" and of their guilty secrets, very likely set up some of his clients so that Marriott could blackmail them.[10] Amthor responds to Marlowe's veiled allegations with cold fury and has one of his minions, who happens to be a rogue cop, beat Marlowe unconscious. Just before he loses consciousness, Marlowe says, "A pool of darkness opened at my feet and was far, far deeper than the blackest night. I dived into it. It had no bottom" (165).

Marlowe winds up in a private clinic, where he awakens in a stupor as a result of the drugs and alcohol he was fed upon his arrival. The dizzy Marlowe then experiences a hallucinatory vision in which he is enveloped in a cloud of smoke. After he regains consciousness, he figures out that he has been sequestered in the clinic to short circuit his efforts to carry his investigation any further. He confronts Dr. Sondeborg, who presides over this bogus sanitorium, which is really a front for illegal drug traffic. Marlowe snatches the gun from the doctor's desk and makes good his escape.

Next Marlowe revisits Jessie Florian, but discovers that she has been strangled to death. She was murdered accidentally by Moose, who sought to squeeze further information about Velma from her; once again Moose did not know his own strength and exterminated someone whom he had intended only to intimidate.

Marlowe is advised by the local police that Laird Brunette, the racketeer who operates the *Montecito*, a gambling ship off shore, may know of

Moose's whereabouts because of Brunette's underworld connections. Accordingly, Marlowe sneaks aboard the vessel with the assistance of Red Norgaard, a huge, husky ex-cop, whom Marlowe meets accidentally on the waterfront. With Red as backup, Marlowe gets the drop on Brunette's bodyguards and gains entrance to the gambler's private office. Brunette, with sublime inconsistency, at first denies knowing Moose Malloy, then relents and promises to pass on a message to him for Marlowe.

Moose gets the message, for he soon after appears at Marlowe's apartment. Marlowe has also invited Helen Grayle to visit him, but before she arrives he hides Moose in the closet. He then has a conference with Helen, in which he rehearses for her the history of her wrongdoing as he has been able to reconstruct it. In essence, the lady is a tramp. To begin with, Marlowe has deduced that Helen Grayle is Velma Valento; she was Moose's partner in the bank robbery, and she turned him in to the police for the reward. But Moose's devotion to Velma was such that he was willing to take the rap for the robbery and allow her to go free.

She had, during Moose's eight years in prison, carved out a new life for herself and had been accepted as a respectable socialite, once she had married into Lewin Grayle's social circle. "Apparently the distance from the gutter to the house on the hill is not as great as one might suspect," comments Leahna Babener.[11] Jessie Florian knew enough about Helen's dubious past to extort hush money from Helen, who employed Marriott as her go-between. It was Jessie who warned Helen that Marlowe was trying to track her down for Moose. Helen panicked at the thought of Moose reappearing and, however unwittingly, resurrecting her sordid past as a full-time entertainer and part-time trollop at Florian's tawdry cabaret—not to mention her part in the bank robbery.

It so happened that Marriott knew all about Helen's past, probably by way of Amthor, since Helen at one point had been one of Amthor's clients. Consequently, Marriott, with Amthor's help, had been blackmailing Helen for some time. Helen accordingly was afraid that Marlowe would eventually persuade Marriott to tell him what he knew about her.

As Marlowe explains it to Helen during their final interview, Helen was afraid that Marriott might eventually spill the beans to Marlowe if she could not meet his exorbitant demands for bigger sums of money. Helen could not afford to have Marlowe learn that she had been Moose's partner in the bank robbery. Even Helen's indulgent husband might not have been able to countenance being married to the former gun moll of a gangster—

even if he could swallow the discovery that she had once been a floozy and a grifter working at Florian's.

In Speir's words, Marriott was unreliable; as such, he "was the weak link" in the chain of her efforts to keep her past a secret, and "Velma (Helen) had to silence him."[12] Helen devised a ruse, whereby she pretended that her jade necklace was stolen and then dispatched Marriott, who asked Marlowe to accompany him to the Purissima Canyon rendezvous, ostensibly to ransom the stolen jewelry. But Helen got there first, knocked Marlowe cold, and savagely clubbed Marriott to death. The root of the word *Purissima,* by the way, is pure—an ironic reference to the impure, corrupt Helen and the crime she committed at the canyon.

The redoubtable Marlowe continued on the case, however, until he could bring Helen-Velma together with Moose in his apartment, so that Moose could at last grasp what a heartless bitch she has always been. Helen shows her true colors when Moose emerges from the closet. In what Wolfe calls "the supreme example of treachery in all of Chandler," Helen shrieks at Moose, "Get away from me, you son-of-a-bitch" and brutally empties her revolver into his stomach (282). So ends Moose Malloy's eight-year vigil for his "little Velma," who is the "lovely" of the title, to whom Moose bids farewell before he expires. "She was afraid of him," Marlowe says to Anne later. "But he wouldn't have hurt her. He was in love with her." After eight years "she pumped five bullets into him, by way of saying hello," Anne replies. "What a world" (286).

"Helen Grayle," the name Velma Valento assumed, becomes significant at this point. "Helen" is an implied reference to Helen of Troy, whom Christopher Marlowe termed the legendary beauty with the face that launched a thousand ships, who precipitated the Trojan War. Helen Grayle, like Helen of Troy, is a bewitching beauty associated with violence and death. "Grayle" is a reference to the Holy Grail, the cup which Christ used at the Last Supper. The medieval knights made their search for the grail into a sacred quest. Wolfe says that Moose's knightly quest to find Velma "has been mocked and smirched by the foulness of the quest's object"; Helen Grayle is no Holy Grail.[13]

At all events, after eradicating Moose Malloy, Helen disappears, but she later surfaces as a thrush singing torch songs in a smokey Baltimore café. When the police inevitably catch up with her, she commits suicide before she can be taken into custody. On hearing of Helen's death, Marlowe expresses his compassion for her sickly, aging husband. Like Othello,

Marlowe muses, Lewin Grayle was a man "who loved not wisely but too well" (292). Grayle, like Moose, is forced to bid farewell to his lovely.

Marlowe at times seems to manifest a streak of homophobia; for example, he characterizes Lindsay Marriott as a pansy—a condescending term implying that homosexuals are weak sisters. Some critics have hazarded that Marlowe's derogatory references to homosexuals are the result of his attempt to mask his own repressed homosexuality. Indeed, an ongoing controversy has been waged about whether or not Marlowe's friendship with Red Norgaard is subliminally homoerotic in nature. Norgaard is a former policeman, a straight-arrow type who has always played by the rules. As a result, Fredric Jameson opines that Marlowe feels an affinity for Red, which really reflects the sort of "homoerotic male bonding sentimentalism" that is aroused in Marlowe whenever he encounters a man of honor like himself.[14]

Gershon Legman goes further by emphasizing Marlowe's susceptibility to masculine charm. As evidence, Legman points to Marlowe's description of Red, whom he encounters on the Bay City dock and asks to help him get aboard the *Montecito*. "He had deep-set eyes of the sort that you never see, that you only read about," Marlowe muses. "His voice was soft, dreamy, so delicate for a big man that it was startling. . . . His skin was as soft as silk" (245, 247).

Legman goes on to recall how Marlowe steadfastly maintains that he avoids getting romantically involved with his female clients because, as a man of honor, he finds such behavior unprofessional. Legman disagrees with Marlowe's self-estimate, in the light of the passage just cited. "Marlowe moons over these big men," he contends. Therefore, "the true explanation of Marlowe's temperamental disinterest in women is not 'honor,' but his interest in men. . . . Chandler's Marlowe is clearly homosexual."[15]

Legman's assertions are patently open to question. Joanna Smith is convinced that Marlowe views Red as a kindred soul, a man of principle like himself, and he accordingly makes a bid for "Red's companionship," for the kind of relationship which is not sexual in nature at all.[16] Furthermore, Marlowe expresses an interest in the opposite sex in the novel. Indeed, he is undeniably attracted to Helen when she flirts with him during their first meeting. Very likely Chandler had Legman's allegations in mind later on, when he wrote "The Pencil," his very last short story, which was published posthumously. In it Marlowe confesses that he has known many girls, but has yet to find a true blue young woman he wanted to marry.[17] Perhaps Chandler said it best when he explicitly responded to Legman's theory this way: "Mr. Legman seems to me to belong to that rather numerous class of American neurotics which cannot conceive of a close friendship between a couple of men as other than homosexual."[18] He likewise bristled, we remember, when the relationship of Buzz and George in *The Blue Dahlia* was thought by an associate at Paramount to be homosexual.

After all is said and done, Chandler seems to have meant his portrayal of Red in *Farewell, My Lovely* as a private tribute to Ralph "Red" Barrow, an old friend from his days in the oil business. Chandler stayed in contact with Red (!) Barrow after Red moved to the East, writing to him at one point, "I wish you weren't so damn far away. I miss you."[19] Surprisingly, no previous commentator on Chandler's work has connected Red Norgaard with Red Barrow.

Farewell, My Lovely enjoyed respectable sales, though it was hardly a best-seller; still, the word continued to spread in literary circles that Chandler was at the very least a better-than-average crime novelist. Some reviewers already considered him among the best writers in his chosen genre. Novelist Morton Thompson (*Not as a Stranger*) wrote in the *Hollywood-Citizen News* that Chandler's work shows "intense effort, constant polishing, never-ending creative activity."[20]

Chandler agreed that he had composed the novel with great care and effort. "I will never again achieve quite the same combination of ingredients," he wrote to Dale Warren on September 15, 1949, nearly a decade after *Farewell, My Lovely* was published. Chandler believed that the plot complications were worked out within the framework of a solid narrative structure in a "less forced and more fluent" fashion than was true of some of his other books.[21] With the reviews praising *Farewell, My Lovely* as a top-drawer hard-boiled detective novel, it seemed inevitable that some enterprising producer would snap up the picture rights, and soon one did.

The Falcon Takes Over: The First Film Version

During the period when Chandler was establishing himself as a mystery writer in the late 1930s and early 1940s, Philip French notes, private detectives were becoming popular with film audiences. As noted before, the detective film had a mass appeal because filmgoers delighted in these spare, tough, fast-moving pictures. Crime movies of this sort recommended themselves to the paying customers because of their engrossing, melodramatic plots, and because viewers could easily relate to their sharply drawn characters. As one critic put it, these films presented the gripping conflict of Good and Evil—in terms of smoking gun barrels.

Each studio had a detective series "on the conveyor belt."[22] There were, for example, the Falcon series at RKO and the Michael Shayne series at Twentieth Century Fox. The majority of these private-eye series were given low-budget status by the studios, which means that each entry in a given series was produced quickly and cheaply. In 1941 RKO contributed to Hollywood's list of "B" sleuths Michael Arlen's Falcon.

The first film of this series was based on Michael Arlen's only tale about the Falcon, a short story entitled "The Gay Falcon." The movie, which starred George Sanders as Gay Lawrence, better known as the Falcon, was produced in 1941 with the same title. The adjective *gay* in the title of both story and film was a reference to Lawrence's first name, not to his sexual orientation, which is decidedly heterosexual.

Since there were no other Falcon stories, the studio was on the lookout for mystery stories which could be adapted to the series format. In the subsequent films in the series, all that was retained of the source stories "was the Falcon's fondness for the ladies and the smoothness with which he moved in high society," writes William Everson.[23] In due time RKO acquired *Farewell, My Lovely* to serve as the basis of the third film of the series, *The Falcon Takes Over* (1942).

Since Chandler needed the movie sales of his books to supplement the meager earnings he derived from his novels, he was chagrined that his agent, Sydney Sanders, sold the screen rights of the novel to RKO in July 1941 for a measly two thousand dollars. Chandler's disappointment is understandable, since Michael Arlen received twenty-two hundred dollars simply for the use of his character in the film and screenwriters Lynn Root and Frank Fenton were paid seven thousand dollars for their script.

The film was directed by Irving Reis, who had also directed the first two entries in the Falcon series. By now Reis had the standard ingredients of the formula down pat. The debonair Falcon, an amateur sleuth, nonchalantly solves a complex mystery which the plodding police fail to unravel.

Since the cut-rate films in the series were meant to fill the lower half of double features in neighborhood theaters, they were designed to run about an hour apiece. Consequently, Root and Fenton could do little more than recycle Chandler's fundamental plot, with the Falcon standing in for Philip Marlowe. Although their script retained the broad outline of Chandler's convoluted novel, they altered some of the characters. For example, although Jules Amthor, psychic consultant (Turhan Bey), appears in the movie as Marriott's fellow con artist, he has been inexplicably retooled into an Oriental swami straight out of *The Arabian Nights,* complete with turban and crystal ball.

Then too the screenwriters perforce took liberties with the novel's story line in order to make it fit the Falcon formula. Since Gay Lawrence moves in upper-class circles, Moose Malloy (Ward Bond) would never have bumped into him anywhere near a sleazy gin joint like the Florian's bar of the novel. So the night spot where Moose meets Lawrence, while Moose is looking for Velma, his erstwhile sweetheart, is upgraded in the film to Club 13. It is just the kind of swanky Manhattan nightclub frequented by Lawrence and his sophisticated social set—but totally foreign to Marlowe's seedy haunts (or Moose's hangouts) in the book. By the same token, Lawrence is attired in evening clothes, complete with top hat, tuxedo, and walking stick, items which are a far cry from Marlowe's wrinkled, lived-in business suits.

It so happens that the Falcon appears at Club 13 on the very night that Moose gets into a scuffle with the manager about Velma's whereabouts and rubs him out, just as he does in the book. The police encourage the Falcon to help them out, hence "the Falcon takes over" the case. The film continues to follow the novel in its essentials, if not in its subtleties, as the Falcon questions Jessie Florian (Anne Revere), Lindsay Marriott (Hans Conreid), and others implicated in the case. The Falcon is aided and abetted in his investigation by Goldy Locke (Goldie Locks?), his chauffeur and stooge (Alan Jenkins), who is on hand to supply broad comic relief.

The Falcon diligently follows the clues until the trail eventually leads to Diana Kenyon (Helen Grayle in the novel), and he astutely reasons that Diana and Velma are one and the same. The movie further matches the novel by including the scene in which the Falcon arranges a showdown with Diana (Helen Gilbert) and Moose. Before she is aware that Moose is eavesdropping on her conversation with the Falcon, Diana confesses that she arranged Marriott's death because he was blackmailing her. "He was weak; it would only be a matter of time till he talked under pressure," despite the money he had extorted from her, she explains.

When Moose makes his presence known, Diana does not hesitate to gun him down on the spot. But Diana is immediately arrested by the police, whom the Falcon has tipped off in advance about his meeting with Diana and Moose. Therefore there is no question of her taking her own life, as in the novel. As Diana is taken away, the Falcon sardonically quips that Diana had declared open season on Moose, "and without a license."

Chandler, sure that the low-budget picture was pretty far removed from the serious novel he had written, steadfastly ignored the film when it was released in May 1942. But the fact that *The Falcon Takes Over* departed significantly from his original story was due at least in some measure to Joseph Breen, the industry film censor. (We will see that Breen was initially reluctant even to consider a film version of *Double Indemnity*.) In the present instance, his objections to this film's script are clear from the documentation available at the Library of the Motion Picture Academy. The censor drew the studio's attention to the fact that nearly every character in the movie possesses a gun, and seems willing to use it at the least provocation. "Such a suggestion is completely unacceptable," Breen declared.

The censor also warned that there should be no overt suggestion that the weakling Marriott is in fact "a pansy," since homosexuality was a forbidden subject for American films.[24] So director Reis implied Marriott's sexual orientation by having Hans Conreid play Marriott with a silky smooth manner and an artificial pencil moustache, and let it go at that. As Lily Tomlin says in narrating *The Celluloid Closet*, the 1995 television documentary about homosexuality in the movies, "The film censor didn't erase homosexuals from the screen; he just made them harder to find." The censor also took exception to Jessie Florian being pictured as a hopeless dipsomaniac. Reis got around the objection to Jessie's excessive drinking in a humorous way. When Jessie is miffed by the Falcon's intrusive questions about Velma, he beats a hasty retreat to the nearest exit, just as Jessie hurls one of her many empty whiskey bottles at him. The bottle just misses him and smashes against the wall. The Falcon retorts, "Now you won't get your deposit back."

The Falcon Takes Over has been treated rather benignly by the critics, ever since its initial release. Everson commends Irving Reis's fast-paced direction, which enabled him to cram much of the book's complex plot into the movie's one-hour running time. In addition, Leonard Maltin's *Film Guide* singles out Ward Bond's "memorable performance" as Moose Malloy.[25] Actually, Bond's portrayal of Moose was no more than adequate, and certainly no match for Mike Mazurki's performance in the second adaptation of *Farewell, My Lovely*, released just three years later.

Murder, My Sweet: The Second Film Version

The second time around *Farewell, My Lovely* was filmed by Edward Dmytryk (*Crossfire*) as *Murder, My Sweet* (1945), "with the care it deserved, introducing Marlowe officially to the movies," Everson affirms.[26] Indeed, Leslie Halliwell goes so far as to term the movie "a revolutionary crime film, in that it was the first to depict the seedy milieu suggested by its author."[27]

Adrian Scott, a former writer who had just become a producer at RKO, stumbled onto the property on the discard pile in the Story Department. "Scott saw the virtues of the original novel," Dmytryk recalled, "and since most of them had been jettisoned in the *Falcon* film, decided that it could be remade immediately, and nobody would be the wiser."[28] The studio gave Scott the green light because RKO still held the screen rights to the book. This is because Chandler had been forced to sell the movie rights of the novel outright, if he was to sell them at all. The studio consequently did not have to pay him an additional fee for filming the book a second time. Another factor contributing to the studio's desire to film the book a second time was the advance word around town about *Double Indemnity*, which Chandler had recently coscripted. The movie promised to be a hit, and that, in turn, boded well for the commercial success of another gritty crime movie associated with Chandler. As things turned out, both *Murder, My Sweet* and *Double Indemnity* were to be numbered among the first major noir films of the period.

"I looked at *The Falcon Takes Over* before making *Murder, My Sweet*," Dmytryk said in conversation after a screening of *Murder, My Sweet* at the British Film Institute in London. "I thought Chandler's novel had been gutted by forcing it to conform to the Falcon formula. After all, I directed a Falcon picture myself, *The Falcon Strikes Back* (1943). The whole tone and feel of *The Falcon Takes Over* was different from the book. The attempt to superimpose another writer's detective on Chandler's plot simply had not worked." In making *Murder, My Sweet*, Dmytryk concluded, he tried his best "to be faithful to the spirit of the novel." Dmytryk met Chandler around this time, and described him in terms similar to those employed by Billy Wilder: "He was a dour type of man who drank a lot, as many writers in Hollywood do."[29]

Chandler, who was at the time under exclusive contract to Paramount, RKO's neighboring studio, could not work on the screenplay at RKO. So Scott commissioned John Paxton, a New York journalist whose work he was familiar with, to write his very first screenplay. Paxton took one look at the novel and decided that "this is too complex to handle in ninety-odd minutes of film."[30] Accordingly, Paxton eliminated Laird Brunette, Red Norgaard, and all of the scenes on Brunette's floating casino, in order to get a "straighter storyline," he explained. (Laird Brunette appeared as a gangster in *The Falcon Takes Over*, but without his gambling boat.) Paxton also wanted to make Moose Malloy more sympathetic, "so he doesn't kill the proprietor of Florians" in the movie.[31]

Paxton consulted with Scott while he was preparing the script. They agreed that to remain as close as possible to the spirit of Chandler's novel, they should retain Marlowe's first-person narration from the book. They were aware that two of Chandler's principal assets were his hard-boiled dialogue, which at times seemed to be dipped in battery acid, and his adroit use of first-person narration, which had become a trademark of the Marlowe novels. Consequently, *Murder, My Sweet* capitalizes on Chandler's skill with language by presenting Marlowe's running narration on the sound track, thereby employing in the picture, as much as possible, Chandler's crisp, colorful language verbatim. In this fashion the film foregrounds Marlowe not only as the principal character but also as a presence, someone whose comments, presented voice-over on the sound track, color the viewer's perception of events.

For example, when Marlowe is knocked flat, just prior to Marriott's murder at Purissima Canyon, Marlowe says in a voice-over, "I caught a black jack right behind my ear. A black pool opened up at my feet. I dived in. It had no bottom." This remark accompanies an image of inky blackness, which spreads across the screen and fills the entire frame. James Griffith comments that Marlowe acts as both the "hero and the narrative filter" throughout the film. Hence we view "Southern Californian corruption" from Marlowe's point of view, much as we did in the novel.[32]

"Once we decided on the first-person narration," Paxton remembered, "there had to be a frame in which to tell it."[33] The story proper is therefore framed by opening and closing sequences in the police station, as Marlowe (Dick Powell) recounts his experiences to the police and, by extension, to the audience. In the opening prologue Marlowe is sitting at a table in the shadowy interrogation room at the police station, being grilled by Lieutenant Randall (Don Douglas) and some other cops. A naked light bulb overhead and a gooseneck table lamp provide the scant illumination in the room.

Marlowe, who has been temporarily blinded, wears a bandage over his eyes. We learn subsequently that he got his eyeballs scorched accidentally by the flash from a gun's muzzle, just as the revolver was fired—at someone else—while the pistol was near his face. Both the blindfold and the murky room, taken together, symbolize that Marlowe inhabits a dark, disturbing nightmare world in which evil thrives and people are seldom what they seem. In one of the most laconic bits of dialogue ever spoken from the screen, Marlowe says to Randall, "The boys say I did a couple of murders. Anything in it?" Then Marlowe proceeds to explain how he wound up in the tight spot that he is now in. The plot unfolds in flashback, accompanied by Marlowe's retrospective narration.

It all began with Marlowe sitting in his darkened office, which is illuminated solely by a flickering neon sign outside his window. Marlowe relaxes at his desk, gazing out of his window at the Los Angeles skyline. Suddenly the towering figure of a man appears behind him and he sees the sinister stranger's reflection in the window pane. "The glass reflects a stolid, brutish face," says the screenplay. "The massive features are carved by the dim lights."[34] Dmytryk commented, "The effect of size and menace was more than we had hoped for."[35] Indeed, when Moose Malloy (Mike Mazurki), the gigantic, slow-witted ex-convict, materializes out of the shadows in Marlowe's office, he resembles a creature of darkness, one who will lead Marlowe into a threatening night world.

Moose prods Marlowe into helping him hunt for Velma Valento, his lost love. The first stop is Florian's, where Velma worked as a tatty showgirl. Moose "was supposed to tower above Marlowe," whenever they appear together on the screen, Dmytryk recalled. "But Dick was 6'2" while Mike Mazurki was 6'4½". So Dick walked in the gutter while Mike walked on the cub, or Dick stood in his stocking feet while Moose stood on a box."[36]

Although in *Murder, My Sweet* Florian's is not a snazzy New York night-club it is in *The Falcon Takes Over*, it is still not the low-down bar for black patrons only that it is in the Chandler novel because race was still a touchy topic in forties Hollywood films. At least it is a tavern located in the mean streets of Los Angeles, the setting of Chandler's novel.

At any rate, Moose loses patience when the manager fails to provide him with information about Velma. Moose does not kill the proprietor, as he does in the book and in the previous film; he only roughs him up by hurling him against the nearest wall. The search for Velma then leads Marlowe to Jessie Florian, the widow of Florian's former owner (Esther Howard, in a flawless performance). The censor no longer objected to Jessie Florian being portrayed as a lush, as he did in the case of *The Falcon Takes Over*. In the present film the pathetic old drunk is obviously tipsy as she responds to Marlowe's queries with answers that are at best misleading, at worst confusing.

When the trail to Velma grows cold, Marlowe takes on another assignment. It is extended to him by Lindsay Marriott (Douglas Watson), a rather mannered dilettante, decked out in a camel hair coat and silk scarf, who appears to be homosexual. As we know, Marriott asks Marlowe to be his bodyguard when he delivers ransom money to some thieves, in exchange for the jade necklace they supposedly stole from Helen Grayle. But Marriott does not return alive from the rendezvous, and Marlowe himself makes it home only after he has been bashed with a blackjack and rendered unconscious for some time.

In a scene that is not in the book, a female reporter calls at his office the next day, on the pretext of filing a story about the stolen necklace and Marriott's murder. Marlowe astutely suspects that she is bluffing and forces her to admit that she is actually Anne Grayle (Anne Riordan in the book), the stepdaughter of Helen Grayle, who is married to her father, Llewellyn Grayle (Lewin Grayle in the book). It was Scott's idea to make Anne (Anne Shirley) a member of the Grayle family because that gives her a personal interest in the case. Anne is also able to give Marlowe entrée to Helen and her father, Lew Grayle (Miles Mander).

When Marlowe calls on the Grayles, he informs Helen (Claire Trevor) that he knows that Marriott was acting on her behalf when he attempted to buy back her jade necklace. Jules Amthor (Otto Krueger), a self-styled psychic consultant and charlatan, unexpectedly appears on the scene to see Helen. Marlowe later divines that Amthor advised Marriott which of his female clients in high society to cultivate as their potential targets for blackmail. These two opportunists, says Barton Palmer, are depicted as "superficially respectable parasites" who beguile members of the opposite sex for their own personal gain.

The industry censor would not permit Dmytryk to represent Marriott and Amthor in the film as obvious homosexual types since homosexuality was a forbidden subject in American films in those days. As screenwriter Jay Presson Allen (*The Prime of Miss Jean Brodie*) says in *The Celluloid Closet*, a clever director could get around this restriction by broad hints that a character was homosexual. Hence Dmytryk implied that Marriott and Amthor were homosexual by artistic indirection. Thus when Amthor shows up in the scene just described, his "polished and . . . somewhat effeminate manners" immediately suggest his affinity with Marriott as a classy homosexual, as Palmer shrewdly points out.[37] So does his fancy tie and boutonniere. Moreover, Dmytryk directed the actors how to play their roles in a subtle fashion which would imply their sexual orientation. As screenwriter Gore Vidal (*Ben-Hur*) says in the same documentary, "It was perfectly clear" to the cognoscenti "who were on the right wave length" that the characters were homosexual.

Dmytryk emphasized that "Paxton incorporated whole chunks of dialogue from the book into the screenplay," in an effort to be faithful to Chandler. There is, for example, the scene in which Marlowe has a confrontation with Amthor in the latter's Sunset Towers penthouse in order to ascertain the nature of his involvement with Helen Grayle. Amthor expresses his disdain for the honest private eye in lines lifted from the novel (157). "I could teach you," Amthor says with a sneer, "but to what purpose? You're a dirty little man in a dirty little world."

Amthor makes it clear that he fears that Marlowe may jeopardize his lucrative criminal activities. So he decides to have the meddlesome private investigator incarcerated in the asylum operated by Dr. Sondeborg, a quack doctor, to scare him off the case. Dmytryk describes the situation in the following terms: Marlowe is knocked out and "carried away to a phoney sanitorium and drugged to the gills. After two days of DTs, he awakens to find himself literally befogged. As he struggles to dispel his hallucinations," he envisions a "web of smoke that overlays the scene."[38]

Marlowe's voice-over comments in this sequence are patterned after his first-person narration in the corresponding scene in the novel (167–71). In this scene in the film, as he lies on a cot in a gloomy cell, Marlowe perceives a curtain of smoke surrounding the cot and reflects, "It didn't move; it was a grey web woven by a thousand spiders." Dmytryk explains, "I managed the effect by means of a superimposition. I had still photos of cigarette smoke blown up in size and magnified them over the image of Marlowe returning to consciousness."[39] The web of smoke gradually evaporates, Dmytryk concludes; and when it disappears entirely, the filmgoer knows that Marlowe's mind is finally clear. This is a fine example of a director employing cinematic sleight-of-hand in a most inventive way. In fact, Everson remarks that this depiction of drug-induced delirium, "though simple in design and conception, is among the most convincing ever filmed."[40]

As Marlowe endeavors to shake off the last vestiges of his delirium, he gives himself a pep talk which is derived from the novel. I reproduce this monologue here as it appears in the book (170–71) in order to give its flavor, and indicate by brackets the part that Paxton judiciously pruned when Marlowe speaks it in the movie in order to condense the lengthy speech for film: "Okay, Marlowe. You're a tough guy. [Six feet of iron man. One hundred and ninety pounds stripped and with your face washed. Hard muscles and no glass jaw. You can take it.] You've been beaten half silly. . . . You've been shot in the arm [full of hop and kept under it] until you're as crazy as two waltzing mice. [And what does it all amount to? Routine.] Now let's see you do something really tough, like putting on your pants."

With that, Marlowe rouses himself to action, manages to elude Sondeborg's malevolent orderlies, and escapes from the clinic. When he goes to see Anne, his disheveled state arouses her pity, which she expresses in lines that are, like the speech just quoted, almost a direct quotation from the book (288): "Everybody bats you down, smacks you over the head, and fills you full of stuff; and you just keep right on hitting between tackle and end, until they're all worn out. I don't think you even know which side you're on." Marlowe replies in words contributed to the scene by Paxton: "I don't know which side anybody is on. I don't even know who's playing to-day."

Marlowe is undaunted by the reversals he has suffered, however, and he continues his investigation until he is in a position to declare that Helen Grayle, an archetypal femme fatale, is at the bottom of the whole mystery. The movie's highly charged climax is staged in the Grayle beach house, a scene that brings together not only Moose and Helen but also Llewellyn Grayle, who is not present at the final confrontation between Moose and Helen in the novel. This is one of the adjustments of the novel's story line in the film's climactic scene, and it indicates that the movie is a faithful, but not a slavish, adaptation of the book.

Marlowe first arranges to talk with Helen one-on-one, before her husband and former lover make their presence known. He begins by advising Helen that her obsessive efforts to wipe out her tarnished past have come to nothing. She had been paying blackmail money to Marriott, Amthor, and Jessie Florian. But Marriott made the mistake of pressuring her for ever more exorbitant payoffs, so she murdered Marriott.

Helen hears him out and then pulls a gun on Marlowe, who whips out his own pistol. Llewellyn Grayle, followed by Moose Malloy, rushes into the room at precisely this moment. Lew grabs Marlowe's revolver and kills Helen with one bullet. Still holding the smoking gun, he whimpers, "I couldn't let her go. I loved her too much." To be precise, Lew could not let Helen go to jail and thereby lose her completely. Thus, in the film Helen is murdered by her own husband, and does not go to a suicide's grave, as in the book.

Moose is inconsolable when he looks upon Helen's corpse. "You killed my Velma!" he shouts at Grayle as he tries to wrest the revolver from Grayle's grip. Marlowe also lunges for Grayle's pistol; his face is only inches from the muzzle when the gun goes off, and the blazing blast scorches Marlowe's eyeballs. Marlowe says stoically on the sound track, "The black pit opened up again right on schedule, only it was blacker and deeper this time." The black pool flows across the screen once more, and engulfs the entire frame.

We return to the narrative frame, as the movie ends where it began, in the police interrogation room, where Marlowe sits blindfolded. Since Marlowe was blinded by a gunshot, he does not yet know the outcome of the exchange of gunfire in the Grayle beach house. In the screenplay, when Marlowe hears that Grayle is dead, he inquires if Llewellyn Grayle killed himself. "He did it himself?" he asks. But that line of dialogue is not in the film. Instead, Lieutenant Randall explains how both Grayle and Moose died. They both struggled for Grayle's gun; Grayle mortally wounded Moose, who nevertheless managed to turn the revolver on Grayle and fatally shoot him before he himself expired.

"There is no reprieve in film noir," Martin Scorsese notes in his documentary, *A Personal Journey Through American Movies.* "You pay for your sins." *Murder, My Sweet* proves the rule: Helen pays with her life for murdering Marriott, Lew Grayle receives instant retribution for killing his wife, Moose pays for rubbing out Jessie Florian. Commenting on the multiple deaths at the end of the movie, William Phillips says that the interests of justice are clearly served when "the three who commit murder have murdered each other."[42]

Anne, who inexplicably seems not the least bit bothered by the death of her father, much less of her stepmother, endorses Marlowe's version of the facts when she talks to the police; he is accordingly released from custody. To cite Foster Hirsch, a beleaguered protagonist like Marlowe represents an entire gallery of noir heroes. In such films as *The Blue Dahlia* and *Strangers on a Train,* both treated later, "characters are accused of crimes they did not commit, their lives subjected to wild reversals and inversions. Cornered, framed, set up as the patsy and the fall guy, these victims are the playthings of a malevolent noir fate."[43] Marlowe certainly fits this pattern in the present film. After he is exonerated, Anne escorts Marlowe out of the police station, and they embrace at the fade out. So *Murder, My Sweet* has an old-fashioned Hollywood ending, with the hero winning the heroine. Marlowe has no such luck in the novel.

Dmytryk, who had earned his spurs making low-budget programmers, was not discouraged by the film's frugal $450,000 budget and by the stringent forty-four-day shooting schedule, which were rather modest for a top-level production. He was accustomed to making movies quickly and inexpensively. Because most of the scenes took place at night, Dmytryk photographed many scenes in deep, jarring shadows. He therefore was often able to get by with simple settings, because they were shrouded in shadows. In this manner he was spared the cost of building elaborate sets and was able to stay within his budget.

At the time he made the picture, Dmytryk did not think in terms of film noir at all. "We didn't think of *Murder, My Sweet* as film noir. It was a picture that simply demanded that dark mood from beginning to end," Dmytryk remembered. "It wasn't for another year or so that the French decided to call it film noir."

In the documentary short about the making of *Murder, My Sweet*, which was appended to the film when it was released on videocassette in 1996, Dmytryk recalls his initial misgivings about casting Dick Powell as Marlowe. Powell had spent most of his career making lightweight musicals such as *Forty-Second Street* (1932); he wanted to move on to serious dramatic roles, since the heyday of the movie musical was over for the time being. Not long before, Powell had futilely campaigned to secure the lead in *Double Indemnity*. "Adrian Scott and I decided to meet him," Dmytryk continued. "He was a lot taller than we thought and huskier and more masculine than he looked in the musicals. We decided to try him. That was the best thing we ever did." Powell seemed a surprising choice for the part, to some, says Geoffrey Macnab, "but from the moment he strikes a match off the backside of a stone cupid" on the Grayle estate, "it's clear that he's a natural in the role."[44]

Dmytryk was sure that *Murder, My Sweet* would be a success, but when the movie, with the novel's title, played its preliminary engagements in New England and in Minnesota, audiences stayed away. "After some speedy market analysis" by Audience Research Incorporated, Frank Miller explains, "the executives at RKO realized that, by employing Chandler's title, *Farewell, My Lovely,* they had given the public the impression that this was just another Dick Powell musical."[45] When RKO hastily recalled the film and changed the title to *Murder, My Sweet,* the movie took off, and so did former crooner Powell's career as a tough guy in pictures.

That the title change occurred at the eleventh hour is plain from the copy of the script on file in the RKO archive: *Farewell, My Lovely* is printed on the title page of the screenplay, and *Murder, My Sweet!* [*sic*] is handwritten above it. (The film retained the novel's title, however, in Britain, where Powell's former screen image apparently was not a problem.)

For the record, Dick Powell would prove to be the only actor ever to play Philip Marlowe in all the media: besides his appearance in the present film, Powell also played Marlowe on radio in a 1945 Lux Radio Theater version of *Murder, My Sweet,* and on television in a 1954 dramatization of Chandler's novel *The Long Goodbye.*

Chandler affirmed later on that Powell came closest to his own conception of Marlowe (though he had once pictured Cary Grant in the role). Dmytryk concurred. Powell played Marlowe "as Chandler visualized him," Dmytryk noted, "with a patina of toughness only skin deep."[46] Beneath Marlowe's tough exterior, Powell neatly implies in his superbly underplayed performance, is a humanity that can be reached. He is the tough-but-vulnerable hero, tossing off the biting Chandler wisecracks to cover up his tender spots. Then, too, Claire Trevor, as the bewitching platinum blonde temptress who is deadlier than any male, played the dangerous noir siren Helen Grayle to perfection.

Spencer Selby correctly labels *Murder, My Sweet* "the first full-fledged noir version of a Raymond Chandler detective novel."[47] What's more, *Murder, My Sweet* was an influential film that set the standard for many noir detective thrillers to come. Noir films pictured a brutal and corrupt society, and *Murder, My Sweet* with uncompromising realism exposed the underside of glamorous Los Angeles, scarred by violence and moral decay and populated with desperate degenerates. Chandler was quite satisfied with the film and sent John Paxton a congratulatory letter, stating that he had "considered the book untranslatable to the screen."[48]

As a matter of fact, Paxton produced such a nearly perfect screenplay on this, his first time out, that it required very few last-minute revisions, as is clear from examining the copy of the screenplay, dated April 21, 1944, which is in the RKO files. The few revisions in the script, dated between April 25 and May 18, are really negligible.

Chandler also lauded Dmytryk's direction of the movie, in a letter to literary critic James Sandoe: "Whenever you see a well-cut picture, for example, *Murder, My Sweet,* . . . you can be sure that either the director was once a cutter himself" or that the cutter consulted with the director.[49] As it happened, Dmytryk had in fact been a cutter, or a film editor, before graduating to directing films, so Chandler's hunch proved true. In fact, as a former cutter, Dmytryk saw to it that the scenes were edited exactly as he had envisioned them. At any rate, Chandler did not live to see the third film of this novel.

Farewell, My Lovely:
The Third Film Version

Filmmaker Dick Richards (*March or Die*) was a Chandler aficionado who had for a long time nursed the ambition of making a film from one of his books that would preserve the flavor of Chandler's original novel. Therefore, when producer Elliott Kastner offered him a script for *Farewell, My Lovely* (1975) that had been updated to the present, "I turned it down. I thought it was sacrilegious to screw around with that book," he declared flatly. So screenwriter "David Goodman and I rewrote the whole thing, making it a period piece. . . . I tried to stay true to Chandler." They both screened *The Falcon Takes Over* and *Murder, My Sweet*. "I wanted Los Angeles to be seedy in my film, the way it had been when Chandler described it."[50] This meant that his film would have none of the plush decor associated with Gay Lawrence, the bon vivant-turned-amateur-detective in *The Falcon Takes Over*, but rather the grimy, gritty atmosphere of *Murder, My Sweet*.

As for the cast of characters, the director and screenwriter opted to include Laird Brunette (Anthony Zerbe) and his gambling boat, which were left out of *Murder, My Sweet*. Conversely, they dropped Anne Riordan from the film as a source of love interest for Marlowe, which she certainly was in *Murder, My Sweet*. They did so because Robert Mitchum was fifty-seven when he donned Marlowe's trench coat and fedora. He seemed too old to be romancing a girl in her mid-thirties like Anne. By contrast, Dick Powell was nearly twenty years younger than Mitchum when he played Marlowe, so filmgoers found his romantic interest in Anne in the film appropriate.

It was Richards's idea to conflate the characters of Dr. Sondeborg and Jules Amthor into Frances Amthor (Kate Murtagh), the butch-lesbian madam of the brothel where Marlowe is imprisoned temporarily. Asked why he substituted a cat house for Dr. Sondeborg's asylum and a crude lesbian (whose first name is sexually ambiguous) for the suave psychic, Jules Amthor, Richards replied, "I didn't like Jules Amthor as a villain." Amthor did not seem a credible character to Richards, though he declined to say why.[51]

It is worth noting that Dmytryk was not permitted to portray either Marriott or Amthor as explicitly homosexual in *Murder, My Sweet*. Moreover, Alfred Hitchcock, we shall see, had to skirt the issue of homosexuality in *Strangers on a Train*. Those were "different days," as Alfred Hitchcock said in conversation. Indeed they were, since by the time the present film was made, Richards was able to portray Lindsay Marriott (John O'Leary), as well as Frances Amthor, as homosexuals in *Farewell, My Lovely*. Still, amalgamating two complex and intriguing characters like Dr. Sondeborg and Jules Amthor into Frances Amthor—a grotesque caricature never imagined by Chandler—seems well nigh indefensible, especially since Richards contended that he wanted his film to be faithful to Chandler's book.

Having decided to place the film's action in the early 1940s, the same period as the novel, Richards assembled a sterling production crew with the help of production manager–first assistant director Tim Zinnemann (son of filmmaker Fred Zinnemann) in order to recreate the Los Angeles of the period. "We were lucky enough to attract some A-list production people," Zinnemann remembers, "like Oscar-winning production designer Dean Tavoularis (*The Godfather*) and cinematographer John Alonzo (*Chinatown*)."[52]

Zinnemann assisted Tavoularis in choosing location sites for the movie. Zinnemann continued, "We used the S.S. *Catalina,* a gambling boat that was in mothballs, for the exterior shots of the *Lido,* Brunette's gambling ship. The budget for the production was modest for the time, $2.3 million; so we couldn't afford to build elaborate interior sets in the studio." Consequently, with Tavoularis's approval, "I chose the *Queen Mary,* which had long since been retired to dry dock at Long Beach, to stand in for the lavish interiors of Brunette's floating casino." The scenes set in the Grayle mansion were shot in the opulent home of the late screen comedian Harold Lloyd (*Safety Last*).

All in all, the period settings reflect a genuine homage to Chandler. So does David Shire's background music, which recalls the kind of music played in vintage noir films, complete with a wailing saxophone and a bluesy piano. Royal Brown observes that Shire's score has a "classical-jazz elegance" that reflects the influences of George Gershwin.[53]

To photograph the picture Alonzo relied on Fujicolor, a special film stock that enabled him to photograph the movie in drab grays and pastels, in order to evoke the haunting atmosphere of gloom and doom called for by the story. "It is a credit to Alonzo," comments Robert Bookbinder, that he truly captured on film Marlowe's "dark, shoddy, nocturnal world."[54] That bleak, shadowy atmosphere is evoked in Marlowe's opening remarks, which are part of his voice-over narration, which recalls Marlowe's retrospective voice-overs in *Murder, My Sweet*. "Mitchum intones the litany according to Chandler," Bruce Crowther writes, but it is "neatly adjusted by Goodman to accommodate an older Marlowe."[55]

"This past spring was the first time that I'd felt tired and realized that I was growing old," Marlowe begins. "Maybe it was the rotten cases I've had. . . . Or maybe it was the plain fact that I'm tired—and growing old." It is patent from Marlowe's opening narration that Richards and Goodman wanted Marlowe's first-person narration to approximate the tough-guy phrasing so resonant of Marlowe's narration in the novel.

Goodman's final shooting script, dated February 10, 1975, is preserved in the files at Avco-Embassy, which released the film. Goodman's script contains some significant additions to the dialogue. These additions were apparently made at the very last minute, since they are not in typescript like the rest of the screenplay; instead, they are written by hand in the margins of the existing pages of the script. Evidently Goodman made these additions on his personal copy of the screenplay and then Richards had the pages, as emended, photocopied and distributed to cast and crew because there was not enough time to have this new material typed up by a secretary. This indicates that these emendations were made at the eleventh hour. Most of these handwritten passages of dialogue are additions to Marlowe's from the novel and consequently bring the script closer still to the film's literary source.

For example, when Marlowe recounts his first meeting with the hooligan Moose Malloy (Jack O'Halloran), this remark from the novel (5) is inserted in the margin of the script at this point: "A hand I could have sat in took hold of my shoulder."[56] This is a reference to the 1933 movie *King Kong*, in which the giant ape holds the heroine in the palm of his huge paw. This line "rhymes" with Marlowe's later comment in the film, when he explains why he complied with Moose's request to find his former sweetheart: "Ever since I saw the movie *King Kong*, I've been a sucker for any gorilla who falls in love with a girl." The devotion of the ape-like Moose Malloy for his beloved Velma Valento, then, recalls the classic beauty-and-the-beast theme of *King Kong*.

When Malloy cajoles Marlowe into coming with him to Florian's, the tavern turns out to be the self-same all-black bar in skid row pictured in the novel, not the all-white bar of *Murder, My Sweet*. Moose, in fact, observes disdainfully that Florian's has become a "shine bar." He wipes out the proprietor, as he does in the novel, when the terrified manager pulls a gun on him. So Moose must lie low for the time being.

Marlowe stays on the case, however, and talks with the blowsey, drunken hag, Jessie Florian (Sylvia Miles, in an Oscar-nominated performance). Jessie makes a pathetic attempt at one point to seduce Marlowe, while she is decked out in a glitzy cocktail dress that has seen better days. So, of course, has Jessie.

As the film unreels, it continues to have much in common with the novel; thus Lindsay Marriott is slain, as he is in the book. In another snatch of dialogue added in the margin of the final shooting script in longhand, Marlowe says in a voice-over that he feels obligated to find Marriott's killer because "Marriott had hired me to protect him; and I'd let him down. As far as I was concerned, I was still working for him."[57] Following the book, Marlowe is ashamed for having failed to save his client's life and accordingly assumes responsibility for tracking down Marriott's slayer.

Marlowe has a conference with Helen Grayle (Charlotte Rampling) and her desiccated, elderly husband, Judge Baxter Grayle (Lewin Grayle in the novel); Judge Grayle is played by crime novelist Jim Thompson (*The Grifters*). Marlowe is suspicious of this sly, seductive female, and he determines to dig up Helen's past. His investigations disclose that Helen not only worked as a clip joint cutie in Florian's honky-tonk but also as a hooker in Frances Amthor's whorehouse. Amthor's bordello, which we recall does not figure in the novel or the two previous pictures, is rife with kinky sex and drugs and hence represents the depths of depravity and perversity; to that extent Helen's past is revealed to be more sordid and shocking in this movie than in the novel or the earlier films.

Before Marlowe can make much headway with the case, he is knocked unconscious and kidnapped by a couple of Amthor's hoodlums. He wakes up amid the squalor and degradation of Amthor's brothel. Cruel, obese Frances Amthor intends to hold him hostage until she can bully him into divulging just how much he knows about her racket and Helen Grayle's association with it. When Marlowe refuses to cooperate, she barks at him, in a piece of dialogue that is a variation on Jules Amthor's sarcastic remark to Marlowe in *Murder, My Sweet:* "You look stupid; you're in a stupid business; and you're on a stupid case." Then her thugs overpower him and she injects him with a heavy dose of drugs.

Amthor gets what is coming to her, however, when she catches Jonnie, her bouncer (a young Sylvester Stallone), making love to her own personal favorite among her girls. The jealous Amthor pounces on Jonnie, who reacts by shooting her point blank. Little wonder that Carl Macek scolded Richards by writing, "The use of prostitution, vice, and corruption, which is only hinted at in the earlier Marlowe films, is developed with a vengeance in *Farewell, My Lovely.*"[58] Meanwhile, Marlowe snaps out of his woozy torpor and makes his getaway in the ensuing chaos and confusion precipitated by Amthor's murder.

Moose eventually resurfaces and accompanies Marlowe to the *Lido*, since Brunette is rumored to know all about Velma. Therefore in the present film Moose replaces Red Norgaard from the novel as Marlowe's companion-in-arms aboard the *Lido*. In the course of their meeting with Brunette, Helen quite unexpectedly makes her entrance. Marlowe then discloses the he knows that Helen and Brunette have been partners in crime for some time. Moose, of course, is most gratified to be reunited with his sweetie. But Helen shoots him in cold blood, as she does in the book. So much for Moose's eight-year vigil for "my Velma," as he has affectionately referred to her throughout the movie.

Marlowe snaps, "Okay, Dragon Lady, who's next?" They exchange gunfire, and this time it is Helen who bites the dust. "There was simply no one else to shoot her; Marlowe had to do it," Richards explained.[59] After all, her husband was not on hand to kill her, as he did in *Murder, My Sweet*. Gazing on Moose's corpse, Marlowe eulogizes Moose. His observations represent still another passage of dialogue appended to the final shooting script in longhand, and once again it is derived directly from the novel. "Moose wouldn't have hurt her. It didn't matter to him that she hadn't written for six years," Marlowe muses. "The big lug loved her." He adds a sardonic comment that is actually spoken by Anne in the novel: "What a world."[60] In sum, none of the three films drawn from the novel use Chandler's ending, in which Helen commits suicide.

Principal photography commenced on February 18, 1975, and lasted for thirty-seven days. Richards employed wide-ranging location shooting throughout the greater Los Angeles area. John St. John, an experienced L.A. homicide detective, acted as technical adviser during the shoot. When it was all over, Richards said, "Chandler wrote what critics call the classic detective story. We have tried to be faithful to his legacy and his style by creating the basic classic detective movie."[61] It is difficult to reconcile this statement with the introduction into the picture of Frances Amthor, a sadistic lesbian brothel keeper, since there is no genuine analogue for her in the book.

Edward Dmytryk found Robert Mitchum's Marlowe something of a disappointment because "he looked his age." Mitchum was actually the oldest actor to portray Marlowe (just as George Montgomery, who played Marlowe in *The Brasher Doubloon*, was the youngest). After all, Chandler never portrayed Marlowe as aging, even in the later novels. Several critics agreed with Dmytryk, as did, surprisingly, Mitchum himself. Mitchum described the film as "a museum piece" and said he was "all worn out" when he played the role—although that did not deter him from playing Marlowe a second time three years later in a remake of the 1946 version of Chandler's *Big Sleep*.[62]

Richards strongly disagreed that Mitchum was miscast. "The role of Philip Marlowe had been waiting thirty years for Robert Mitchum to claim it," he asserted.[63] Richards too had several critics on his side, who were convinced that Mitchum's rumpled, dog-tired appearance seemed just right for Chandler's resigned, world-weary rogue knight. Philip French insists that Mitchum is "an authentic forties Marlowe," traversing the mean streets of Los Angeles, "a Camel cigarette between his lips and a wide-brimmed hat on his head."[64] Significantly, when Mitchum died on July 1, 1997, his obituary in the *London Times* saw Mitchum's presence in *Farewell, My Lovely* as hearkening back to the great noir films of the 1940s in which he appeared, such as Dmytryk's *Crossfire* (1947). Although he was "a good deal too old for the role of Raymond Chandler's detective," the obituary noted, Mitchum played it with total conviction.[65] Nevertheless, Mitchum's performance was no match for Dick Powell's carefully honed work in *Murder, My Sweet*.

By the same token, Charlotte Rampling's Helen Grayle was not in the same league with Claire Trevor's, nor was Jack O'Halloran's Moose Malloy the equal of Mike Mazurki's. In the last analysis, if one can forget all about Dmytryk's movie while watching Richards's remake, the latter picture is a fairly estimable thriller. But this is a tall order, because *Murder, My Sweet* is quite simply unforgettable and remains the definitive screen adaptation of the book.

4

Knight Moves

Two Films of *The Big Sleep*

They call Los Angeles the City of Angels. I didn't find it to be that.
    —The Stranger, in the film *The Big Lebowski*

The life of a private eye means prying into other people's problems, picking at the scabs. . . . It's a bit odd, earning money from other people's misery.
    —A suspect, in the telefilm *Sacrifice*

Frank Krutnik describes the universe of pulp fiction as "a shadow realm of crime and dislocation, in which benighted individuals do battle with implacable threats and temptations."[1] This is certainly the world in which Philip Marlowe functions in *The Big Sleep*. Marlowe keeps his moral footing in this world, says Paul Skenazy, because he is a man of conviction who can "withstand and overcome the forces of social disruption and personal greed."[2]

The Big Sleep: The Novel

Like *Farewell, My Lovely, The Big Sleep* is based on material Chandler cannibalized from some of his earlier short fiction. Chandler composed *The Big Sleep*, which was in fact his first book-length detective story, in three months. The framework of the novel, Hiney notes, was "a collage of the best *Black*

Mask plots."[3] The book was derived essentially from the novellas *Killer in the Rain* (January 1935) and *The Curtain* (September 1936).

Some of the characters in Chandler's novellas for the pulps, in turn, were based on individuals he had met during his years of living and working in Los Angeles. Thus the wealthy oil baron in *The Curtain,* Gen. Dade Winslow, was modeled on an executive Chandler had known in the oil business, very likely E.L. Doheny. Chandler's oil tycoon in *The Curtain* "built his mansion above the stench of his wells and his business methods," the authors of *Raymond Chandler's Los Angeles* pointed out. Similarly, Doheny built Greystone, a magnificent estate from which "the Dohenys could look toward their oil fields."[4]

Hiney wryly observes that "Chandler would never quite forgive the oil industry" for firing him, even though, we recall, he got what he deserved.[5] Chandler made the following sardonic comment about a rich oil baron and his family in *The Curtain,* probably with Doheny's estate in mind: "Beyond the estate the hill sloped down to the city and the old oil wells of La Brea. . . . Some of the wooden derricks still stood. These had made the wealth of the Winslow family; then the family had run away from them up the hill, far enough to get away from the smell of sumps, not too far for them to look out of the front windows and see what made them rich." This passage is repeated virtually verbatim in *The Big Sleep.*[6]

Killer in the Rain is the first Chandler story to be narrated by the detective-hero in the first person. The nameless gumshoe is hired by another oil baron, Anton Dravec, to extricate his adopted daughter Carmen from her sordid association with a homosexual named Harold Steiner, a pornographer and drug peddler. Steiner runs a bookstore that deals in pornography and plans to blackmail Carmen in return for hushing up the fact that she poses for him while zonked out on drugs. Chandler named Carmen after the title character of Bizet's opera, for she occasions the same kind of misfortune and tragedy in the course of the novelette as her namesake does in the opera.

In *The Curtain* General Winslow engages Ted Carmady, a private eye who figures in several of Chandler's pulp stories, to find his missing son-in-law Dud O'Mara. Carmady has reason to believe that Dud has been murdered and a curtain has been dropped over the deed. It emerges that Dud was shot and killed by his emotionally disturbed eleven-year-old stepson Dade, whose mother has connived to cover up the crime.

Like *Farewell, My Lovely, The Big Sleep* is a salient example of how skillfully Chandler reworked material from his novellas into a single narrative. Chandler stated that in composing the novel, he drew a significant portion of the first half of the book from *Killer in the Rain;* this phase of the book features Carmen's association with the pornographer Arthur Geiger (Harold Steiner in the novelette). With chapter 20, however, Chandler brought to bear the plot of *The Curtain* by having Marlowe search for Rusty Regan (Dud O'Mara in the novella), who is married to General Sternwood's older daughter Vivian.

In some instances, Chandler combined a character from one story with a similar character from the other story to create a single character for the novel. The most obvious example, of course, is Philip Marlowe, who is an amalgam of the two sleuths in the two novellas: the nameless private detective in *Killer in the Rain* and Ted Carmady in *The Curtain.* In a similar fashion, Carmen Sternwood in the novel is a composite of Carmen Dravec in *Killer* and the psychopathic Dade in *Curtain.* Carmen, then, like Marlowe, "is a common denominator of the two old plots," writes Peter Rabinowitz.[7]

"But despite the impression of labyrinthine complexity given by fusing the two cases, the join between them . . . is very discernible," Martin Priestman affirms. After the solution of the murder of Arthur Geiger halfway through the novel, Marlowe then turns his attention to the disappearance of Rusty Regan. "Chandler has just stuck the two stories end-to-end," the glue chiefly provided by Marlowe as "the unifying factor."[8]

As the plot of the novel unwinds, General Sternwood (General Winslow in *Curtain*) commissions Marlowe to deal with the homosexual Arthur Geiger, the extortionist who is blackmailing his daughter Carmen. Marlowe camps in his car outside Geiger's house on a rainy night, after he has spied Carmen going inside. He hears a sudden scream from inside and decides to break into Geiger's house, but before he can make it to the front porch, shots ring out, and someone flees into the rain. When he goes inside, Marlowe finds Carmen naked and deep in a drugged state, from a mixture of ether and laudanum that she has been imbibing from a flagon by her side. She had just posed naked for the pornographer's camera, and Geiger lies dead on the floor nearby.

Commenting on this scene, Gershon Legman opines that *The Big Sleep* involves "a pornographic lending library business operated by a homosexual who is murdered for taking nude photographs of a drugged debutante. . . . Mr. Chandler seems to be sold on the proposition that homosexuals have the pornography business tied up."[9]

Legman, as we saw earlier, can usually be counted on to miss the point. Actually his observation about Chandler is based on a misreading of the text, since Marlowe discovers later that a heterosexual named Joe Brody has been involved with Geiger's porno racket all along and is carrying on the business, now that Geiger is dead. So Chandler does not imply that homosexuals have cornered the market in porn, as Legman maintains. Moreover, Brody is in possession of the negative of the lewd picture that Geiger had taken of Carmen on the fateful night Geiger was eradicated. Marlowe goes to Brody's apartment for a showdown. While Marlowe holds Brody at gunpoint, he forces Brody to admit that he planned to blackmail Carmen with the candid photo, and he turns over the negative to Marlowe. Before Marlowe can leave, however, Brody answers the doorbell, only to be shot dead by an assassin.

Marlowe later pieces together the facts. Brody was slain by Geiger's homosexual lover, Carol Lundgren, who acted on the mistaken assumption that Brody had killed Geiger—when in fact it was the Sternwood chauffeur, Owen Taylor; he was the killer in the rain that Marlowe saw fleeing from Geiger's house. The distraught Owen Taylor thought that murdering Geiger was the only way to release Carmen, to whom he was devoted, from Geiger's clutches. Owen's corpse is subsequently discovered floating in the Pacific Ocean, off the Lido fishing pier. Although Owen apparently committed suicide, there is a lingering suspicion that he was murdered. Still the police never officially accuse anyone of liquidating him.

With the Geiger case wrapped up, Marlowe devotes himself to searching for the General's missing son-in-law, Rusty Regan. A former bootlegger, Regan is looked upon by the General as a surrogate son, since Regan offered the aging patriarch a degree of companionship that he received from no one else. Regan has supposedly vanished in the company of Mona Mars, the wife of gambler-gangster Eddie Mars; the ruthless Mars is aptly named after the god of war. Marlowe finds Mona ensconced in a house in a desert hamlet, where she is hiding out. Mona confesses that her disappearance was a subterfuge, designed to keep the police from finding out that Regan was not with her at all, but had been murdered. Vivian had asked Mars to arrange the coverup, in order to keep the police from investigating the Sternwoods and exposing any of the family secrets.

When Lash Canino, Mars's trigger-happy henchman, finds Marlowe in Mona's hideaway, he wants to put the meddling Marlowe out of commission for good. With Mona's help Marlowe gets the drop on Canino and outguns him, making Canino the only person Marlowe slays in the entire Chandler canon.

The whole case comes to a head when Carmen asks Marlowe to help her practice her marksmanship on the grounds of the Sternwood estate. She attempts to kill him, but Marlowe, who does not trust the emotionally unstable Carmen, has had the foresight to load her gun with blanks before the "practice" session. It is at precisely this juncture that Marlowe deduces that Carmen, a confirmed nymphomaniac, killed Regan for resisting her advances, and she wanted to exact the same revenge on Marlowe for likewise rejecting her. After Carmen killed Regan, Vivian arranged to have Mars dump the body in an abandoned sump in the Sternwood oil fields, and Mars has been blackmailing Vivian ever since. Ironically, the first time Marlowe surveyed the Sternwood oil fields, he was unwittingly looking upon the burial ground of Rusty Regan, whose putrefied corpse was interred in a rusty, unused pump.

Marlowe agrees to keep Regan's death a secret; in return, Vivian agrees to send Carmen off to a drug rehabilitation clinic. Marlowe's real purpose for suppressing Regan's murder is to shield General Sternwood from the ugly truth about his younger daughter. Marlowe wishes to "protect what little pride a broken and sick old man has in his blood, in the thought that his blood is not poisoned" (229). Besides, in a little while, the General too, "like Rusty Regan, would be sleeping the big sleep" (231). As a metaphor for death, "the big sleep" was such a felicitous phrase that Eugene O'Neill used it in his play *The Iceman Cometh* (1946), possibly without knowing that it had been invented by Chandler and was not a time-honored metaphor for death.

It is in the newly written portions of the novel that Chandler really distinguished himself from the average writer of pulp detective fiction, especially by adding depth to the characterization of Marlowe. Chandler was at pains to portray Marlowe in the novel, not just as a hard-boiled private eye, but as a knightly hero. As mentioned earlier, Marlowe views a case as a crusade, whereby he aims to protect the innocent and helpless, and not merely solve a mystery. "Like a knight in shining armor," says Geherin, Marlowe is ready to risk his life for those in distress, "and, if need be, to remove the dragons that lie in the way of their happiness."[10]

To be more precise, "*The Big Sleep* testifies to Marlowe's knight errantry," states Robert Merrill, by portraying how Marlowe does his best "to bring order to the rather foul world of the Sternwoods."[11] Chandler establishes Marlowe's symbolic link with the knights of yore at the very outset of *The Big Sleep*.

As Marlowe enters the Sternwood residence, he notices a stained-glass panel, depicting a medieval knight "in dark armor, rescuing a lady who was tied to a tree and didn't have any clothes on." The knight was not making much headway in freeing the lady, so Marlowe reflects that "if I lived in the house I would sooner or later have to climb up there and help him. He didn't seem to be really trying" (3–4). This scene foreshadows how Marlowe, the knight errant, will rescue Carmen, the naked damsel in distress, from Geiger's lair, after Geiger is murdered.

In order to function in his knightly role, Geherin adds, Marlowe must be vigilant against temptation. Therefore celibacy is an important element in his purity of character. So, when Carmen comes to his apartment unbidden and seeks to seduce Marlowe, he unceremoniously throws her out. Afterward Marlowe, who plays solitaire chess, studies his chessboard. "There was a problem laid out on the board," he muses; "I couldn't solve it, like a lot of my problems" (154). He is at a loss where to move his knight: "Knights had no meaning in this game. It wasn't a game for knights" (156).

"Maintaining his values in a world that largely flouts them," says LeRoy Panek, makes Marlowe's stance as a medieval knight seem out of fashion in the modern world.[12] The milieu in which Marlowe carries on his crusade, Wolfe reminds us, is one in which the forces of good never win a decisive victory over the forces of evil. Thus Marlowe's success in unmasking Carmen as a murderess is undercut by the fact that Eddie Mars, the ruthless racketeer and blackmailer, remains "as firmly entrenched in his power and villainy as ever." Nonetheless, the fact remains that Marlowe has identified Carmen as Regan's killer, and he accordingly has had her institutionalized; to that extent his crusade against crime has succeeded.[13]

The sales of *The Big Sleep* were remarkably good, but Chandler was distressed by the notices that expressed disapproval of the book's unsavory subject matter, dealing as it does with nymphomania, pornography, homosexuality, and drug addiction, as well as murder and mayhem. "I do not want to write depraved books," Chandler wrote to his publisher, Alfred Knopf, on February 19, 1939. "I was aware that this yarn had some fairly unpleasant citizens in it." He had learned his craft in the "rough school" of the hard-boiled pulp magazines, however, and consequently was accustomed to dealing with moral decay.[14]

Durham questions those critics of the novel who contended that Chandler's depiction of crime and corruption in southern California was any more grisly than that offered by James M. Cain in his books. Durham declares that, after all, "Cain was a master of portraying degeneracy in Southern California," as exemplified by Cain's novella *Double Indemnity,* which is surely more lurid than any of Chandler's books and more lurid than the script Chandler cowrote for the film version of Cain's novelette.[15] In addition, Chandler himself insisted that novels like *The Big Sleep* were true-to-life, as evidenced by the heavy press coverage of actual crimes committed in 1930s Los Angeles. Organized crime was on the rise in southern California throughout that period. Indeed, Hiney affirms that "on a daily basis local newspapers were full of real-life dramas" similar to those Chandler concocted in his crime fiction.[16]

Still, no movie studio ventured to acquire the film rights of *The Big Sleep* at the time, precisely because of the book's sensational subject matter. So Chandler was delighted that the review in the *Los Angeles Times* saw that the novel could be the basis of a good movie. In the same letter to Knopf cited above, Chandler declared that the *Times* critic thought Humphrey Bogart should play Marlowe, and he very much agreed: "It only remains to convince Warner Brothers."[17]

The Big Sleep: The First Film Version

As a matter of fact, filmmaker Howard Hawks convinced Warner Brothers to make the film, with Humphrey Bogart as Marlowe, some five years later. Hawks took the occasion to sell Jack Warner, the studio chief, on the idea the night they attended a sneak preview of Hawks's film version of Ernest Hemingway's *To Have and Have Not* (1944), the first film to costar Bogart and Lauren Bacall. Warner, riding in his limousine with Hawks after the preview, had told the director that he was so pleased with the audience reaction to the picture that he wanted to pair Bogart and Bacall in another movie immediately. It was then that Hawks advised Warner that he already had a project in mind for them, a murder mystery by Raymond Chandler entitled *The Big Sleep.* Hawks thought of Bogart as Marlowe and Bacall as Vivian, Carmen's older sister.

Hawks was aware that Warner Brothers was among the studios who had been wary of purchasing the screen rights to *The Big Sleep* when it was published. After all, Joseph Breen, the film censor, had discouraged the studios in the 1930s from filming hard-boiled fiction like *Double Indemnity,* and he had only rather recently relented by allowing *Double Indemnity* and *Farewell, My Lovely* to be filmed. And so Hawks assured Warner that he would see to it that a screenplay was devised for *The Big Sleep* that would pass muster with Breen. "The next day," Hawks recalled, "I bought the screen rights to *The Big Sleep,*" with the help of his agent, Charles Feldman.[18] Chandler was content to receive twenty thousand dollars for the screen rights, since he had no other offers and this sum was ten times what he had received for the rights to *Farewell, My Lovely.*

Hawks much admired Chandler's work; in fact, he believed that Chandler was a real standout among mystery writers. The director thought Chandler's dialogue in particular "was awfully good." Moreover, the film of *Double Indemnity,* which Chandler had coscripted, had been an enormous success when it opened earlier that same year; therefore Hawks wanted to hire Chandler to do the screenplay for *The Big Sleep* (1946). As Chandler was at the time under exclusive contract to Paramount, however, that was out of the question. Consequently, Hawks engaged the distinguished novelist William Faulkner (*Sanctuary*) to work on the script. Like Chandler, Faulkner disliked having to work in Hollywood, because he preferred writing fiction to collaborating on screen work. But, like Chandler, he found it necessary to write for the movies because his earnings from his books were never large. Be that as it may, *The Big Sleep* is a significant film in that it is the creative product of a Nobel Prize–winner, Faulkner, and a premier mystery novelist, Chandler.

Hawks chose Leigh Brackett to be Faulkner's partner on the screenplay of *The Big Sleep,* because he was favorably impressed with her first mystery novel, *No Good from a Corpse,* recently published. Brackett remembered that when Hawks met her, he was somewhat chagrined to discover that it was Miss, and not Mister, Brackett he was hiring; "but he rallied and signed me anyway." Brackett was understandably daunted by the prospect of collaborating with Faulkner, whom she revered as a great literary light. How, she wondered, could she work with him? She need not have worried.

The morning that she checked in at Warners, Faulkner handed her a copy of the novel and said, "We will do alternate sets of chapters. I have them marked. I will do these and you will do those." And so it went. The two screenwriters labored alone in their separate offices; Brackett never saw what Faulkner wrote, and he never saw what she wrote. "Everything went in direct to Mr. Hawks," Brackett recalled. "Beyond a couple of conferences, we never saw him."[19]

In one of these story conferences, they decided to make Shawn Regan (Rusty Regan in the novel) General Sternwood's employee rather than Vivian's husband. Vivian instead was said to have an ex-husband named Rutledge. In this manner Vivian Sternwood Rutledge would be free to fall in love with Marlowe in the course of the picture, long before Regan's death is revealed.

Hawks told Faulkner and Brackett in one of their script conferences to revise Chandler's tough detective story wherever necessary, in order to provide the picture with plenty of action. "It won't be a great work of art," he told them; "just keep it moving."[20] And so they did. Moreover, the writing team proved adept at approximating in the script the clipped, understated, sardonic quality of Chandler's own dialogue.

"It was basically an entertaining story, even though I could never figure out who killed who," Hawks told me in conversation. "When I was asked who killed Owen Taylor, the man whose car is fished out of the river, I said, 'I don't know; I'll ask Faulkner.' But Faulkner didn't know either. So I asked Chandler."[21] Hawks wired Chandler; the novelist, humorously invoking an old cliché from stage melodrama, replied, "The butler did it." "And I said, 'Like hell he did; he was down at the beach house at the time.'" Chandler fended off Hawks's query with a quip, because he was too embarrassed to admit that he himself had by this time lost track of Owen Taylor's murderer. He subsequently wrote to Hamish Hamilton, his British publisher, about Hawks's inquiry, "Dammit. I don't know either. Of course, I was hooted at."[22] In any case Jack Warner, who saw Chandler's return wire, reproved Hawks for wasting money on an unnecessary telegram. In point of fact, the cost in those days for sending a telegram from Hollywood to La Jolla, Chandler's home, was seventy cents.

As a result of the Owen Taylor incident, a legend grew up in Hollywood that actually is reported as gospel by Fredric Jameson. Jameson pictures Bogart and Hawks "very late at night, after much drinking," arguing about the fate of Owen Taylor: murder or suicide? "They finally phone Chandler himself, still awake and drinking at that hour; he admits he can't remember either." Actually, Leigh Brackett testified that the discussions about Owen took place on the set and principally involved Hawks, Faulkner, and herself, with Hawks finally telegraphing Chandler when they could not come up with a solution to the problem that satisfied him. The Owen Taylor discussion did not involve late-night boozing on the part of any of the parties involved but took place during the working day.[23] "The picture was a success; so I never worried about logic again," Hawks stated. "But I have always been concerned about the overall structure of a film, since the audience has to be able to follow that, whether or not some of the details get lost along the way."

Chandler himself once observed about writing crime fiction, when the author is in doubt about what to do next, "have a man come through a door with a gun in his hand."[24] Faulkner and Brackett relied on that solution to the plot complications of The Big Sleep more than once. For example, in both book and film, Joe Brody opens his front door at one point and finds Carol Lundgren taking a dead aim at him.

Because the cowriters were working simultaneously and separately on different portions of the screenplay, they were able to complete their first draft, dated September 11, 1944, in record time—a little over a week. They then revised and expanded their work into a second draft, dated September 29; that was the version of the screenplay Hawks used as the shooting script, when principal photography commenced on October 10. Both the preliminary draft of the screenplay by Faulkner and Brackett and their revised version are among the papers of Howard Hawks at the Harold Lee Library of Brigham Young University.

Like Chandler, Faulkner had a serious drinking problem, but that did not deter Hawks from retaining his services as a screenwriter on several films. After all, there were other heavy drinkers on the Story Department's payroll; Hawks believed that as long as writers did their job, their drinking habits were their own business. Hawks continued to ask Faulkner for rewrites as shooting progressed, but Faulkner eventually tired of making endless revisions in the script. Moreover, Faulkner's drinking began to increase as time wore on, and eventually Hawks honored Faulkner's request to leave the production.

Faulkner's last contribution to *The Big Sleep* consisted of revisions he made in the shooting script in mid-December, on his way back to Oxford, Mississippi, his home, by train for a break from film writing. In forwarding these additional pages to Warner's Story Department, he attached a humorous note, wryly thanking the studio for arranging for him to have a seat in the day coach rather than a berth in the sleeping car, because otherwise he might have wasted some time during the journey "in dull and profitless rest and sleep" and would not, therefore, have used the time to make the revisions in the screenplay that he was now sending on to the studio.[25]

Before Faulkner departed, Hawks invited Chandler to the set to meet his fellow novelist; Bogart and Bacall were on hand as well. Lauren Bacall remembered Chandler as looking like "a professor: very quiet, rather shy, quite pleasant."[26] Chandler later allowed that he was satisfied with Bogart's portrayal of Philip Marlowe. "Bogart, of course, is so much better than any other tough guy" in pictures, he later wrote to Hamish Hamilton. "As we say here, he can be tough without a gun. . . . Ladd (*The Blue Dahlia*) is hard, bitter, and occasionally charming; but he is after all a small boy's idea of a tough guy. Bogart is the genuine article. . . . All he has to do to dominate a scene is to enter it." In fact, Michael Sragow affirms that, by the time Bogart played Marlowe, he had already honed his screen persona as the tough guy with a battered trench coat, a worn suit, "and a look of hard-boiled melancholy," an individual with a manly code "tested in action and connected to trust and honor"—an image which certainly fit Chandler's shamus perfectly.[27]

"Hawks had a great habit of shooting off the cuff," Brackett remembered; he would sometimes make additions to a scene based on suggestions made by the actors, as they rehearsed it with him on the set. These give-and-take sessions at times yielded some memorable moments in the film. In one early scene, for example, Marlowe quizzes a clerk in the Acme Bookstore (Dorothy Malone) about Geiger's rival bookstore across the street. Hawks had Bogart and Malone embroider their dialogue with sexual innuendo. "That wasn't the way the scene was written at all," Hawks recalled. "We just did it that way because the girl was so damned good looking." The upshot was that, by scene's end, the clerk seduces Marlowe in record time.

Marlowe enters Geiger's bookstore later on, in an effort to gather more information about the disreputable operation that Geiger is running behind the facade of a respectable business. While working out this scene on the set before the cameras rolled, Hawks and Bogart engaged in the same sort of improvisation they had employed in the scene just described. They decided that Marlowe should disguise his true identity as a gumshoe, in order that Agnes, the bookstore clerk (Sonia Darrin), will not suspect his true purpose. "Can you play a fairy?" Hawks asked Bogart, who replied, "Start your cameras." Bogart walked up to the store, Hawks recalled, put his sunglasses on the bridge of his nose, "pushed the brim of his hat up, and went in as quite an effeminate character."[28]

Hawks apparently forgot that the basis of Marlowe's adopting a prissy air in this scene was actually suggested by the corresponding scene in Chandler's novel, where Marlowe says that Agnes approached him "with enough sex appeal to stampede a business men's lunch. . . . I had my horn-rimmed glasses on. I put my voice high and let a bird twitter in it." He then addresses Agnes in "a polite falsetto" (23–24).

Sometimes this kind of improvising notably lengthened a given scene, as in the scene in the Acme bookstore. As a result, Hawks "eventually wound up with far too much story left than he had time to do on film," Brackett said.[29] So Hawks brought in Jules Furthman, with a view to shortening the remaining portion of the screenplay, still to be shot, in order that the finished film would be a manageable length. Furthman was a regular Hawks standby and worked on several Hawks films, including *To Have and Have*

Not. He accordingly condensed and revised the last twenty-eight pages of the script. The cutter's script, which was employed by Christian Nyby while he was editing the film, is preserved in the Film and Theater Collection of the New York Public Library at Lincoln Center; it is dated March 16, 1945, and contains Furthman's revisions of the screenplay.

Joseph Breen, the industry censor, had rejected the ending of the Faulkner-Brackett script, so Furthman had to provide a different conclusion for the movie. In the original screenplay Marlowe has a final confrontation with Carmen Sternwood (Martha Vickers) in the house of Arthur Geiger (Theodore von Eltz), the deceased pornographer-extortionist. Marlowe knows that Eddie Mars (John Ridgely) and his hoods are waiting outside to ambush him when he emerges onto the front porch, in retaliation for Marlowe's having exterminated Mars's right-hand man, Lash Canino (Bob Steele), in an earlier shootout.

Meanwhile, Carmen makes a play for Marlowe, and he spurns her advances. She then pulls a gun on him and fires, in revenge for his rejecting her—just as she had liquidated Regan for the same reason. But Marlowe, who had guessed that Carmen had killed Regan, anticipated just such an eventuality and had surreptitiously filled her revolver with blank shells.

Before departing, Carmen taunts Marlowe with the fact that he will never turn her over to the authorities for Regan's murder, because the ensuing scandal would break her father's heart. Marlowe knowingly allows her to go out the front door—and to walk right into the trap that had been set for him; Carmen thereby stops a bullet meant for Marlowe. But Breen would not sanction the movie's hero taking the law into his own hands in order to punish the depraved Carmen—a murderess, nymphomaniac, and drug addict—for her crime, even to save his own life.[30]

In Furthman's rewrite of this scene, it is Vivian Rutledge, Carmen's older sister (Lauren Bacall), who is with Marlowe in Geiger's house, where Marlowe faces off with Eddie Mars, while Mars's gunmen wait outside to blow Marlowe away. The authors of *Great Detective Pictures* succinctly summarize how Marlowe spells out for Mars what he has learned about the mobster's sinister involvement with the Sternwoods: "Regan was killed by crazy Carmen when he refused her advances; and to protect her sister, Vivian got Mars to spread the rumor that Regan had run away with his wife, whom he then kept hidden. In return, he blackmailed Vivian and ordered Canino to kill . . . Marlowe," who already suspected what Mars was up to.[31]

Marlowe nevertheless gets the drop on Mars and forces him to open the front door, while the gangster's men, assuming that it is Marlowe who is coming out, let loose a hail of bullets. Marlowe then phones the police and says that Eddie Mars has just been gunned down by his own mob; he adds that Mars had killed Regan. Bruce Kawin comments that Marlowe is therefore "making Mars out to be the principal villain" in the picture, not Carmen.[32]

On the contrary, Stephen Pendo rightly maintains that Marlowe is "protecting Carmen" by pinning the murder rap on Mars, who is now conveniently dead and cannot deny the charge.[33] To be specific, Marlowe lies to the police in order to shield General Sternwood (Charles Waldron, in a peerless performance) from ever finding out the truth about his perverse and rapacious daughter Carmen. Marlowe is convinced that justice is served by his having Carmen taken away to a sanatorium, instead of going to her death, "the big sleep" of the title, as a convicted murderess. Moreover, the notion that Mars, rather than Carmen, actually murdered Regan simply contradicts Marlowe's whole explanation of the case, which he delivered to Mars.

Elizabeth Cowie totally corroborates the fact that Carmen, not Mars, is the ultimate villain of the piece: "The key to the story is Carmen; it is she who is the principal cause of the events in the film. She killed Regan, leading Vivian to seek Eddie Mars's help in covering it up, opening herself to his blackmail; and it is Carmen's drug habits which give rise to demands for money and prompt General Sternwood to engage Marlowe's services."[34]

That Marlowe and Vivian had reached a mutual understanding with each other in the course of the picture is clear from the fact that at the final fadeout they gaze trustingly into each other's eyes, as they speak the closing lines of the film. "What's wrong with you?" Marlowe asks her; Vivian replies, "Nothing that you can't fix." Then they listen together to the sirens, which signal the arrival of the police Marlowe has just summoned.

Chandler was pleased that the film version of *The Big Sleep* preserved the cynical, hard-boiled flavor of his fiction. Chandler's sole regret about the movie was that the original ending of the script, about which he had been consulted, had not been used in the picture. "I don't know what happened to this scene," he said in a letter to his English publisher. "Perhaps the boys wouldn't write it or couldn't. Perhaps Mr. Bogart wouldn't play it. You never know in Hollywood. All I know is, it would have been a hair-raising thing if well done. I think I'll try it myself some time." Interestingly enough, Chandler mentioned in the same letter that he was especially happy with the first half of the film—the portion that Hawks had Furthman leave pretty much as Faulkner and Brackett had written it.[35]

Breen called for other alterations in the screenplay, besides the revised ending. The issue of the portrayal of homosexuals in a Hollywood film surfaced again, as it had in the case of earlier adaptations of Chandler's fiction, already treated. For a start, Breen allowed Bogart's caricature of a homosexual sissy in the scene set in Geiger's bookstore to get by. On this point, film scholar Vito Russo, who wrote the book *The Celluloid Closet*, on which the television documentary of the same title was based, said in discussing homosexuality in the movies with me that the sissy was one of Hollywood's homosexual stock characters. "They were always a cliché, a joke, and hence were not to be taken seriously," he said. Consequently, the censor allowed them to be depicted—or in this instance lampooned—on film.

Still Breen insisted that the restrictions of the industry's censorship code prohibited Hawks from depicting an overtly homosexual relationship, such as that of Arthur Geiger and Carol Lundgren (Tom Rafferty), as explicitly homosexual. As a result, Hawks had to portray their relationship in a more muted manner than Chandler did in the book. Hawks implied that Geiger was homosexual by way of his overdecorated residence, with its Oriental decor, all beaded curtains and sculptured vases, suggesting the exotic East; and by the florid silk dressing gown Geiger is wearing when he is murdered. As Foster Hirsch put it, audiences understood what decor and costuming of this kind meant in the existing codes by which movies expressed themselves in that period. Geiger thus embodied the popular notion that homosexuals were "dandified, affected, . . . and concerned excessively with fashion and appearance."[36]

In addition, when Marlowe enters Geiger's bookstore, he affects an effeminate manner by which he implicitly associates Geiger's store with the effete image of the man himself, as represented by his dress and home. What's more, Geiger's housemate, Carol, whose name is sexually ambiguous, dresses in a rugged style and sports a leather jacket, so he comes across as a tough, butch-type of homosexual; indeed, Carol nurtures a devotion to Geiger fierce enough to drive him to murder, in order to avenge the death of the man to whom he was devoted. So Carol's dress and behavior testify to the homosexual nature of his liaison with Geiger.

Oscar Wilde called homosexuality the love that dare not speak its name, and the film censor wanted to keep it that way. Yet Hawks was able to suggest that the relationship of Geiger and Carol was homosexual in the code of the time by which homosexuals were identified in films and thereby sneak it by the censor.

Joseph McBride mentioned to Hawks that Hawks occasionally slipped a veiled homosexual relationship past the industry censor in one of his movies, despite the censor's policy that homosexuality was too strong a subject for motion pictures. Hawks looked askance at McBride and answered that that was a "god-damned silly statement to make."[37] Hawks must have forgotten about the partnership of Geiger and Carol in *The Big Sleep*, which is certainly depicted as being well outside the buddy-buddy variety of male friendships in the general run of Hawks's films like *Rio Bravo*.

By the same token, nymphomania, pornography, and drug addiction were likewise taboo subjects for Hollywood films in that period, but Hawks manages to imply them all in the film, if in less explicit terms than Chandler did in the novel. There is, for example, the scene in which Marlowe finds Carmen in Geiger's living room, wearing a sultry Oriental robe and striking a provocative pose for Geiger's camera, seemingly unaware, in her drugged state, that Geiger is lying dead on the floor. Asked if he thought that Carmen came across as a nymphomaniac in Martha Vickers's performance, Hawks replied baldly, "I thought she played a nympho."[38] On this point Charles Gregory argues, "In the minds of viewers with the requisite imagination, the spirit of the book's censorable content remains." Although the movie eschewed explicit allusions to sex, dope, and pornography, "somehow the film reflects all this to the sophisticated viewer."[39] Putting it another way, Andrew Sarris remarks that *The Big Sleep* proves that "a director of Hawks's unusual intelligence can control the most lurid materials" without descending into sensationalism.[40]

Hawks completed principal photography on January 12, 1945. The movie was then scored by Max Steiner (*Gone with the Wind*). Steiner's score, writes Tony Thomas, is one of the film's major assets: "The music punctuates the action as vividly as gunshots and cleverly comments on the characters, particularly with its jaunty theme for Marlowe." In short, the score represents the sort of "genuine film craftsmanship" that characterized the contributions of all of the production artists who worked on the picture.[41]

When postproduction was finished, Hawks decided to have the movie shown at American military bases overseas before its official release in this country, as a favor to American servicemen—a common practice during World War II. But Hawks also wanted to employ these advance screenings of the picture to test audience reaction to the film. *The Big Sleep*, as originally shot, was exhibited to American fighting men throughout the Pacific theater of war in the fall of 1945, starting in Luzon, in the Philippine Islands.

Meanwhile, Jack Warner put Lauren Bacall into *The Confidential Agent*, adapted from the Graham Greene novel. Warner chose to release *Confiden-*

tial Agent in October 1945, ahead of *The Big Sleep*'s official American pre-
miere. *Agent* received a decidedly negative critical reception when it opened,
with many reviewers expressing disappointment in what they termed Bacall's
wooden performance. Graham Greene told me that he thought that one of
the reasons Bacall's performance was generally disliked was that she "was
thought to be unconvincing as the daughter of an English aristocrat" because, as an American, she was woefully miscast.[42]

At this juncture, Charles Feldman, a prestigious talent agent who numbered both Hawks and Bacall among his clients, entered the picture. Feldman
advised Warner with Hawks's support that, if Bacall got the same kind of
negative notices for *The Big Sleep* that she had received for *Confidential
Agent*, her career might well be aborted. He therefore urged Warner, after he
had viewed the film, to give Bacall "three or four additional scenes with
Bogart, of the insolent and provocative nature that she had had in *To Have
and Have Not*."[43] Jack Warner responded on November 2, 1945, that he was
in complete agreement and immediately commissioned screenwriter Philip
Epstein (*Casablanca*) to provide the needed scenes. Epstein contributed
twelve pages of new material for the required retakes.

These pages are appended to the copy of the cutter's script on file at
the New York Public Library at Lincoln Center; it is the only known copy of
the screenplay that contains these additional pages.

The cutter's script includes, among other additions, a couple of scenes
between Marlowe and Vivian Rutledge that are freighted with sexual innuendo. One of these occurs when they meet in a cocktail lounge in
midafternoon. The conversation is typical of the brand of teasing badinage
that Epstein brought to the script. While a tinkling piano plays "I Guess I'll
Have to Change My Plans" and other cocktail tunes, the pair have a discussion ostensibly about horse racing. Marlowe quips that Mrs. Rutledge looks
like a slow starter, and she responds in kind that it all depends on who is in
the saddle. By this point in the conversation it is abundantly clear that they
are no longer talking about horses or racing—if they ever were.

Hawks said that he suggested the context of horse racing for this interchange because he was himself fond of the sport of kings. But Pauline
Kael reported that this particular "passage of double-entendre dialogue"
was actually inspired by a similar spicy interchange between Richard Arlen
and Ethel Merman in a long-forgotten 1938 horse-racing farce entitled
Straight, Place, and Show.[44]

Another important addition to the film composed by Epstein was a
rewrite of the scene in the hideout of Mona Mars, who was originally played

by Pat Clark. Clark was replaced by Peggy Knusden in the retakes of this scene because Clark's performance was thought to be too harsh. Mona is, after all, fairly cooperative in discussing the case with Marlowe, prompting him to say to Vivian, who is also present, "She's alright, I like her." In the redraft of this scene Vivian is given more closeups, in order to beef up Bacall's role still more, as Feldman had asked.

But Epstein's most crucial addition to the film was a scene in the office of Assistant District Attorney Bernie Ohls (Regis Toomey). In it Bernie tells Marlowe to lay off the Sternwood case, presumably at the behest of Vivian, who fears that Marlowe is bringing too many of the family skeletons out of the closet. This scene was substituted for a longer scene in which Marlowe compares notes with Bernie's superior, District Attorney Wilde (Thomas Jackson), about the various crimes that have been committed. It so happened that, when the movie was shown to GIs overseas in the prerelease version, this lengthy, eight-minute scene of nonstop expository dialogue had made many of them restless. David Thomson records that this "ponderous" scene required that the audience remember all of the names of the characters and make diagrams of the plot in their heads. Consequently, when the picture was screened for the troops abroad, some members of the audience "went to the bathroom and never came back."

When Jack Warner got wind of this reaction to the scene in question, he declared that he too thought it slowed down the pace of the picture. He therefore personally ordered that this "boring clearing-up sequence" be replaced by the much briefer scene between Marlowe and Bernie, which Epstein accordingly supplied.[45] With that, Thomas Jackson's only appearance in the movie as the district attorney was left on the cutting room floor.

The original scene between Marlowe and Wilde is printed in the published edition of the Faulkner-Brackett screenplay (which does not include the revisions made in their script either by Furthman or by Epstein). The exposition contained in this scene neatly settled the question of who killed Owen Taylor, mentioned above. In it Wilde sums up the case to this point in the following manner: "So Taylor killed Geiger because he was in love with the Sternwood girl [Carmen]. And Brody followed Taylor, sapped him and took the photograph [of Carmen], and pushed Taylor into the ocean. And the punk [Carol] killed Brody."[46]

McCarthy assumed that, because this speech of Wilde's is in the Faulkner-Brackett script, it is likewise in the scene as shot. Yet a careful examination of this scene in the 1945, prerelease version of the film, as it is available on videocassette, shows that this is not the case. Since Wilde's speech, in which he positively identifies Brody as Owen's killer, was deleted from the scene as Hawks shot it, it seems that Hawks did not buy Faulkner and Brackett's solution to the mystery of Owen's slaying. Instead, he asked the screenwriters and even Chandler himself for an acceptable explanation of Owen's death, as we know. Perhaps that is what Sonia Darrin, who played Agnes, meant when this topic was bandied about on the set: "It must have been Hawks" who killed Owen, since he would not accept any of the explanations offered by the screenwriters and others, when the question was discussed on the set; nor was Chandler any help.[47]

Nevertheless, there is a basis in the novel for thinking that Joe Brody murdered Owen, which Faulkner and Brackett most probably picked up on when they named Brody as Owen's murderer in their script. In the novel, when Marlowe interrogates Brody in the racketeer's apartment, he catches Brody in one implausible lie after another. Finally, Brody admits to Marlowe that he followed Owen from Geiger's house, after Owen had rubbed out Geiger. Brody caught up with him, after Owen recklessly drove the Sternwood limousine into a ditch in his haste to escape from the crime scene.

Brody further confesses that he zapped Owen with a blackjack and took the negative of the compromising photograph of Carmen, which Owen had snatched from Geiger's camera. Owen had planned to destroy it, but Brody, of course, planned to blackmail Vivian Rutledge with it. Nevertheless, Brody insists that Owen suddenly came to and delivered a Sunday punch that "knocked me off the car." Owen, in despair over the murder he had committed, then headed for the Lido pier and drowned himself (95).

Still Chandler leaves the possibility open in this passage in the book that Brody is telling yet another lie. In fact, Marlowe intimates that it is much more plausible that Brody knocked Owen out, grabbed the negative, and drove the limo to the Lido pier while Owen was still unconscious. Brody, in Marlowe's version of the incident, then pushed the car off the pier before Owen regained consciousness and left him to drown.

By contrast, in *Killer in the Rain* Chandler indicates that Owen did in fact drown himself. Chandler even has a police detective exonerate Joe Brody by explicitly asserting that "Joe couldn't have known Owen was dead" because Owen committed suicide.[48]

Nevertheless, in the novel, as we have seen, Chandler left the question as to whether Owen killed himself or was murdered by Brody unresolved, for the book ends with Owen's death left on the police blotter as an unsolved crime. Little wonder, then, that Chandler candidly admitted to Hawks that he did not know Owen's ultimate fate when Hawks inquired about it, since both murder and suicide are presented as possible explanations of Owen's demise in the novel and the question is never settled. More specifically, in the book, when Marlowe visits the Lido pier, after Owen's corpse turns up awash in the Pacific Ocean, one plainclothesman states, "Ask me, and I'll call it murder." Another cop asserts, "Ask me, I say suicide" (47).

Still, if Owen was murdered, then Brody does surface as the most likely suspect in both novel and film. The scene in which Marlowe questions Brody in his apartment, just before to Brody's own death, is brought over into the film just as Chandler wrote it. Brody (Louis Jean Heydt), after all, admits that he was actually the last person to see Owen alive. Nevertheless, once Brody, the prime suspect in the Owen Taylor murder case, has himself been slain by Carol, his guilt becomes a moot point. And so the police are willing to let the matter drop in both in book and movie.

Neither Hawks nor anyone involved in the production seemed to remember the district attorney's unshot speech, which explicitly targeted Brody for slaying Owen, and hence ruled out the possibility of suicide altogether. As a result, whenever Hawks recounted the anecdote about determining how Owen died, he accordingly forgot to mention that Faulkner and Brackett had in fact settled the question of Owen's death once and for all in their shooting script, and that this speech was never filmed. Hence, Owen's fate remains in doubt in the version of the movie that was released. Consequently, Kawin remarks that in the movie, as in the novel, "it is suggested, but not proved, that Joe Brody killed the chauffeur."[49]

I have examined the mystery surrounding Owen's fate in some detail because most commentators on this film have failed to notice that the Faulkner-Brackett script had answered the question and that their solution to the crime was inexplicably deleted from the scene in the district attorney's office as Hawks shot it. Yet Hawks always maintained that no viable solution to the mystery had ever been presented to him. This is not the only example of one of Hawks's favorite anecdotes being proved to be at least partially apocryphal, but it is a salient one.

Hawks, we know, actually filmed the scene in the district attorney's office, "and it was included in the original cut of the picture that was shown only to the GIs in 1945," writes McCarthy. He emphasizes that the elimination of this expository scene from the final cut, when the movie finally went into general release a year later, was a substantial loss to the finished film, regardless of Thomson's opinion to the contrary. For this scene in Wilde's office, as Hawks shot it, still offered a handy resumé of the Geiger and Brody murder cases by tying up the loose ends about both cases. Hence some plot details are left unclarified in the film as released. As a result, McCarthy concludes, the film has gained the reputation of having a labyrinthine plot that is well-nigh incomprehensible.[50]

At all events, the cast and crew reconvened on January 21, 1946, to shoot Epstein's revised scenes, and the production finally wrapped once and for all on January 28. Both Hawks and Warner were confident that the retakes represented a marked improvement in the final cut of the movie. In February Warner wired his New York office, "In my opinion, we have a one hundred percent better film."[51] *The Big Sleep* was at long last released on August 23, 1946. In retrospect, nobody really cared who killed Owen Taylor, according to Leigh Brackett. "Hawks's fast-paced direction, crisp and unerring, raced the story along from one exciting moment to the next." It was great fun, she concludes, all done with professional expertise.[52]

Nearly half a century later, the original 1945 cut of the film was located in the Warner vaults and fully restored by Robert Gitt of the UCLA Film and Television Archive. It was given a limited theatrical release in the U.S. in 1997 and released on videocassette shortly afterward. All in all, the original version of the movie was trimmed of about twenty minutes of footage to accommodate the eighteen minutes of new footage, giving the final 1946 version of the film a final running time of 114 minutes.

The videocassette containing the 1945 prerelease cut of the film, of course, includes twenty minutes of original footage never before seen by the general public. It also includes, as an appendix, the eighteen minutes of footage added to the film for its release in 1946, in order to indicate to the viewer the vast differences between the original sequences that were cut and the scenes that were substituted for them. The 1946 final cut of the movie, released on videocassette in 1992, also remains in circulation.

On the one hand, McCarthy rightly argues that the 1945 prerelease cut of *The Big Sleep* possesses a richness of narrative detail "that was sacrificed in the reshooting and cutting."[53] On the other hand, the 1946 release version of the movie is admittedly highly entertaining as well and contains substitute scenes, absent from the earlier version, in which Bogart and Bacall really strike cinematic sparks. Both versions of the film have their champions, therefore; perhaps Andrew Sarris said it all when he concluded, "*The Big Sleep* is socko in both versions."[54]

In *Newsweek's* special issue on film, screenwriter-director Curtis Hanson (*L.A. Confidential*) maintains that "movies which take us to the dark side can be among the richest emotionally and thematically. That's what makes us want to see them again and again, long after the plot no longer keeps us guessing." Hanson seems to have films such as Hawks's *Big Sleep*, with its convoluted story line, in mind, since appended to his essay is a list of the top ten Hollywood thrillers ever made. Leading the list are two Chandler-related films, *Double Indemnity* and *The Big Sleep*, the latter described as "still the Chandler flick to beat."[55] Michael Winner's 1978 remake of *The Big Sleep* offers the Hawks version scant competition as the Chandler flick to beat.

The Big Sleep: The Second Film Version

Perhaps the greatest compliments ever paid Hawks's *Big Sleep* came with the release of the 1978 remake. Several reviewers declared that when the later version is measured against the 1946 film, the earlier movie takes on even greater stature than before.

Two significant differences between the remake, which was scripted and directed by Michael Winner (*Death Wish*), and Hawks's version of the same novel are immediately obvious. First of all, the time frame of the novel has been moved forward from the late 1930s to the 1970s; by contrast, the remake of *Murder, My Sweet* as *Farewell, My Lovely* was set, like the novel from which it was derived, in the 1940s. Second, the locale of the story has been transferred from Los Angeles to London. The picture was shot in England, although it was made by American producer Eliott Kastner for United Artists, because Winner was a British director whose base of operations was in London. When Winner was asked why he set the film in Britain, he replied, "Why not?" and added, "Chandler was educated in England, you know."[56] As if that settled the matter.

On the contrary, Bruce Crowther sees that transplanting the film's setting to London as a cardinal error. Chandler made the mean streets of Los Angeles Philip Marlowe's stamping grounds, and Marlowe seems out of place in London and its environs. Furthermore, says Crowther, it is not even "seedy dockland London," which might have approximated the gloomy urban landscapes of Los Angeles, but "chintzy suburbia."[57] Suburban London, all lush lawns and rolling hills, is miles away from the mean streets that Chandler conjured up in the book.

On the credit side of the ledger, Winner was largely free of the censorship restrictions that dogged Hawks. The industry's censorship code had prohibited Hawks from explicitly portraying drug addiction and homosexuality, whereas Winner graphically renders both of these elements of Chandler's plot in his film. It so happened that between Hawks's film and

Winner's film of the same novel, Geoffrey Surlock (who had by this time replaced Joseph Breen as industry censor) had, in concert with his advisory board, amended the censorship code so that both drug addiction and homosexuality were no longer outlawed as legitimate subjects for American motion pictures.

For the record, film director Otto Preminger was largely responsible for getting both drug addiction and homosexuality removed from the code's list of taboo topics for Hollywood films. Preminger first petitioned the film censor, on behalf of his film *The Man with the Golden Arm* (1955), to remove the code's prohibition against treating drug addiction. The censor ultimately granted his petition.

Perhaps following the old adage that a winner never quits, Preminger later petitioned the censor, in the case of his film *Advise and Consent* (1962), that the code be amended to allow the depiction of homosexuality on the American screen. Preminger could point to the precedent established in England by John Trevelyan, the British film censor, in 1958, when he had decreed that films with homosexual themes would not be banned in England, provided that the subject was treated "responsibly." Once again the censor acceded to Preminger's request. The official press release on this occasion read: "In keeping with the culture, the mores, and values of our time, homosexuality . . . may now be treated with care, discretion, and restraint" in American films.[58] Accordingly, homosexuality, as we have already seen, was depicted explicitly in *Farewell, My Lovely* (1975).

In the present instance, the remake of *The Big Sleep* deals openly with both drug addiction and homosexuality. Thus when Philip Marlowe (Robert Mitchum) breaks into Geiger's house, he discovers Camilla (Carmen in the novel and first film) clearly under the influence of narcotics, with a hypodermic needle close at hand. By the same token, the homosexual relationship of Geiger (John Justin) and Karl (Carol in the book and first film) is firmly established early on. Hence, when Marlowe accuses Karl (Simon Turner) of terminating Joe Brody (Edward Fox), he does not mince words: "You shot the wrong man, kid; Joe Brody didn't kill your boyfriend."

Still, the relaxation of censorship restrictions was not a particular advantage to Winner. Charlotte (Vivian in the novel and first film) is married to Rusty Regan in this film, as in the novel; but that does not stop her from attempting to seduce Marlowe in the present film in the most blatant fashion, even though her husband at this point is thought to be missing, not dead. Charlotte Sternwood Regan (Sarah Miles) shows Marlowe a pornographic photograph of her sister Camilla naked (Winner in turn shows the

photograph to the filmgoer in closeup). Commenting on the photo of
Camilla, Charlotte says lasciviously, "Camilla has a beautiful little body, hasn't
she? You ought to see mine sometime." Griffith reminds us that at the time
Hawks made his film, the censorship code would not have countenanced
Vivian making Marlowe in Hawks's film the tantalizing proposition that
Charlotte extends to Marlowe in Winner's movie so brazenly. Nor would
Hawks have been permitted to exhibit to the filmgoer in closeup the compromising photo of Camilla naked; the viewer, of course, never sees the
pornographic photo of Carmen in Hawks's movie.[59] On the one hand, Winner cannot be faulted for taking advantage of the increased freedom of the
screen at the time he made this movie to portray graphically the behavior
of the lowlifes in the story. On the other hand, this lurid film wallows too
long in the sleazy, voyeuristic world of these characters.

One definite plus for Winner's film is that, unlike Hawks, Winner leaves
absolutely no doubt as to the fate of Owen Taylor. Owen is shown driving
the Sternwood limousine off the pier near Ramsgate and straight into the
ocean. In a subsequent sequence at police headquarters Inspector Carson
(John Mills) and Commissioner Barker (Richard Todd) officially pronounce
Owen's death a suicide. "We don't suspect foul play," one of them says. Winner seems to be hearkening back to Chandler's novella *Killer in the Rain* at
this juncture, for, as we have seen, in this novelette the police officially rule
Owen's death a suicide, whereas Chandler leaves the question—murder or
suicide—open in the novel.

The scene at the police station just described, of course, parallels the
scene in Hawks's film in which the district attorney summarized for
Marlowe—and for the audience—the essential facts of both the Geiger and
Brody murder cases. That scene, we remember, was excised from the Hawks
film, but an equivalent scene is included in Winner's remake and goes a
long way in tidying up the loose ends of the plot up to that point.

Winner also depicts in his film the scene from the novel in which
Carmen futilely attempts to kill Marlowe for resisting her advances. This
scene figured in the Faulkner-Brackett screenplay for Hawks's film, but it
was jettisoned by Furthman in his rewrite of some of the later scenes in
their screenplay. In Winner's film Camilla (Candy Clark) attempts to shoot
Marlowe when he rejects her; this incident is immediately followed by a
flashback of Camilla actually shooting Rusty Regan (Shawn Regan in Hawks's
film) for the same reason.

As in the novel and the previous movie, Camilla is soon relegated to a
mental institution rather than turned over to the police, so that the sickly,

aging General Sternwood (James Stewart, in one of his last roles) can retain what little pride he has left in his family. Both Owen and Regan are phantom characters in Hawks's movie, since Owen appears only briefly in the film and his face is never seen, while Regan does not appear at all. By contrast, both Owen (Martin Potter) and Regan (David Savile) appear in flashbacks in the remake, in order to flesh out their characters and clarify their respective roles in the action.

Nevertheless, aside from clearing up the confusion that marked Hawks's perplexing film, Winner's remake has little else to recommend it. The critical consensus is that Winner's screen adaptation of *The Big Sleep* pales in comparison with the Hawks original. The 1946 version, the authors of *The Motion Picture Guide* declare, is a sharp, sprightly movie that never flags for a second, whereas Winner's soporific remake gives new meaning to the title, *The Big Sleep,* which should have been changed, in the case of Winner's film, to *The Big Snooze.* Admittedly, they continue, some very good American actors (Robert Mitchum, James Stewart) and British actors (John Mills, Richard Todd) are among the cast, but they are "hamstrung by the turgid screenplay (Winner) and mediocre direction (Winner again)."[60]

Michael Winner himself felt, in retrospect, that he did not adapt the film with sufficient freedom. "I was so riveted by Chandler, I found it such incredible writing," he explained. "So I didn't want to disturb it with too much trickery in the photography or too much atmosphere. A couple of American critics did say it was the most faithful Chandler ever. . . . Most of my films I'm rather pleased with, however conceited that may seem."[61]

To be fair, it would be hard for any remake to come within striking distance of Hawks's movie. "After all," Barry Norman points out, "where today could you find a team to equal Hawks, Bogart, the young Bacall, and William Faulkner?"[62] Remaking a classic film is a risky business under the best of circumstances, and Dick Richards demonstrated that it could be worth the effort when he remade Edward Dmytryk's *Murder, My Sweet* as *Farewell, My Lovely.*

On the other hand, Michael Winner's crude craftsmanship was simply no match for Hawks's assured artistry in the case of *The Big Sleep.* In fact, a singular honor was bestowed on Hawks in 1997 when the 1946 *Big Sleep* was selected by the Library of Congress in Washington as a film worthy to be preserved in the permanent collection of the National Film Registry at the Library, as a historically and aesthetically important motion picture.

When Winner's remake was released in 1978, many fans of Hawks's film were riled that it had to compete with a later reincarnation of the same story. On this point, Tom Leited remarks that there is one question "that remakes always raise," and it has never been asked more pointedly than in the case of Winner's remake of *The Big Sleep:* If the Hawks original is an acknowledged classic, why was it remade at all?[63]

Why, indeed? Despite Winner's competent direction and serviceable cast, the remake lacks the panache and verve of Hawks's tough, affectionate treatment of the same material. The movie sags after a while, largely because the direction lacks the brisk pacing Hawks brought to his film. Winner's *Big Sleep* has therefore not superseded the Hawks original.

5

Down among the Rotting Palms

Time to Kill and *The Brasher Doubloon*

Phil Marlowe, the shop-soiled Galahad.
     —Dr. Carl Moss, in the novel *The High Window*

Everybody lives by chiseling everybody else.
     —A crooked millionaire, in the film *The Great McGinty*

Raymond Chandler tapered off from writing short fiction for the pulps after the publication of his first novel, *The Big Sleep,* in 1939. Of the five crime stories he penned between 1939 and 1941, "Pearls Are a Nuisance," published in *Dime Detective* (April 1939), later figured in his novel *The High Window.*

The High Window: The Novel

In "Pearls Are a Nuisance," a tough, hard-drinking shamus named Walter Gage is commissioned to find an invaluable pearl necklace that has been stolen from the aging, crotchety Mrs. Penruddock, a wealthy dowager, whom Walter refers to as "the old crow."[1] Ironically, when Walter tracks down the necklace, the pearls turn out to be fake.

In Chandler's notebook, in his plan of work dated March 16, 1939, he notes that he plans to write a novel with the working title of *The Brasher Doubloon* that will encompass "some stuff from 'Pearls Are a Nuisance,' but mostly new plot." To this entry, Chandler later added a notation that *The Brasher Doubloon* was completed in April 1942, "but as a novel with Philip Marlowe, to be published under the title *The High Window*."[2]

The tie-in between "Pearls Are a Nuisance" and *The High Window* is the fundamental situation that sets the plot of both tales in motion. A rich dowager in each story engages a private investigator to retrieve a family heirloom: in the pulp story the object is a pearl necklace; in the novel it is a precious coin known as the Brasher Doubloon.

The previously mentioned draft letter dated July 6, 1951, in which Chandler quotes a diary in which he tracked the progress of his various writings from 1939 to 1943, indicates that by June 5, 1940, he had embarked on a novel with the working title of *The Brasher Doubloon*. Although "this work went very slowly," he completed the first draft of the manuscript on September 9, 1941. He mailed it immediately to his literary agent, Sydney Sanders, who rejected it out of hand. Chandler accepted Sanders's verdict as reasonable. Indeed, he saw, in retrospect, that *The Brasher Doubloon* was not up to snuff because he had been too anxious to get another book in print and therefore had hurried to get it finished. Chandler devoted himself to rewriting the manuscript with great care. His diary states on January 3, 1942, that he was laboring assiduously on the novel. He actually completed it on March 1 "and mailed the finished manuscript on March 3" to Sanders.[3]

Chandler wrote to Blanche Knopf on March 15 that he was frankly dissatisfied with *The Brasher Doubloon* because, as he states with some exasperation, it contained "no likeable characters." Even Marlowe seemed unpleasant. He explained that he submitted the book for publication anyway because he had done his best; "I suppose I would have kept tinkering at it indefinitely otherwise."[4] Blanche Knopf responded on March 30 that she judged the novel "a magnificent yarn, beautifully done." She did, however, question the appropriateness of the title, since she was worried that booksellers were apt to mispronounce "Brasher" as "brassiere."[5]

In Chandler's return letter of April 3, 1942, he conceded her point. He went on to explain that "Brasher, more commonly Brashear, is an actual name." There was an Ephraim Brasher who "actually did make a coin for the State of New York in 1787. It is not the most valuable coin," but it possesses "sufficient value to be of . . . use for my purposes."[6] Chandler rejected the alternate titles that had occurred to him so far, such as *The Stolen Coin Mystery* or *The Lost Doubloon Mystery* because he consistently avoided using the word *mystery* in the title of any of his novels. He always maintained that his books were not mere pulp mystery stories but full-scale novels of some literary merit. Each of his novels, he once said, could "stand on its own legs as a novel, with the mystery a few drops of tabasco on the oyster."[7]

As a felicitous afterthought, Chandler sent Blanche Knopf a brief follow-up letter on April 5, saying that he had finally settled upon *The High Window* as the book's title: "It's simple, suggestive, and points to the ultimate essential clue."[8] The title he finally chose refers to a crucial event that happened in the past, before the action of the story proper begins; that is, the first husband of a key character, Mrs. Murdock, fell to his death from a high window under suspicious circumstances, as we shall shortly see.

The plot gets rolling when Mrs. Elizabeth Bright Murdock summons Philip Marlowe to her mansion in Pasadena. She desires to enlist his services in finding the Brasher Doubloon, an invaluable gold coin that has disappeared from the collection of rare coins bequeathed to her by her deceased second husband, Jasper Murdock. Mrs. Murdock, Marlowe observes, is a strong-willed, domineering woman; in fact, her sharp beak of a nose betokens that she is like a bird of prey, ruthlessly using and abusing those who are in her power. Marlowe also notices that Mrs. Murdock is addicted to alcohol. As a matter of fact, she incessantly sips port during their initial interview, while grandly claiming that she imbibes it solely for medicinal purposes.

While talking with Marlowe, Mrs. Murdock reclines magisterially on a chaise lounge in a darkened, cheerless room. It is a sun porch "which she has dimmed with heavy drapes. Despite her middle name (Bright) and her sunny hometown (Pasadena), she exudes darkness," writes Peter Wolfe.[9] As Chandler puts it, Mrs. Murdock receives Marlowe on a "sun porch that has been allowed to get completely overgrown outside" with wild vegetation.[10] Indeed, the grounds of Mrs. Murdock's estate are a jungle of palm trees and untamed vegetation, typifying the savage nature of the ruthless woman who lurks inside the house in semidarkness, ruling "her petty and crumbling fiefdom," as Speir comments.[11]

Understandably, Marlowe is not favorably impressed by Mrs. Murdock in the course of their discussion. But he is immediately sympathetic to Merle Davis, her bashful, inhibited personal secretary, who is totally dominated by her overbearing employer. Moreover, he observes that when he happens to touch Merle casually, she recoils from him; he therefore infers that she is pathologically shy of men. Marlowe further discovers that Mrs. Murdock has a son named Leslie, whom his mother has spoiled rotten. Leslie, in fact, is an irresponsible ne'er-do-well who owes twelve thousand dollars to gambler Alex Morny, the owner of the Idle Valley nightclub.

Marlowe resents the fact that Mrs. Murdock treats him with condescension because he is a mere private eye, nothing more than a keyhole peeper and a snoop. For his part, Marlowe, as always, has small respect for the idle rich, so he responds in kind by addressing Mrs. Murdock in a sarcastic manner. Mrs. Murdock snaps at him at one point, "I don't like your tone," to which Marlowe replies, "I don't blame you; I don't like it myself." He continues, "I don't like this house or you or the air of repression in this joint, ... or that twerp of a son you have" (169). Nevertheless, Mrs. Murdock grudgingly overlooks his insolence and keeps him on the case because he is known to be a competent private investigator.

For a start, Marlowe pays a visit to Elisha Morningstar, a numismatist who had informed Mrs. Murdock that the Brasher Doubloon had been brought to him for appraisal. The old coin dealer is a grotesque character straight out of Dickens; he plays his cards close to the vest, so Marlowe gets nowhere in his inquiry. As Marlowe departs, however, he overhears Morningstar phoning a gumshoe named George Anson Phillips. He accordingly goes to see Phillips in a musty rooming house in the tawdry Bunker Hill section of Los Angeles and finds the hapless sleuth shot to death.

Marlowe follows up this turn of events by going back to question Morningstar again, only to discover the coin dealer likewise dead. In the wake of discovering two dead bodies, Marlowe feels that his investigation has reached a dead end—until he receives a parcel in the mail containing what appears to be the Brasher Doubloon. The package has no return address.

Marlowe's next stop is the Idle Valley Club, where he grills Alex Morny, the slick and sleazy gambler who holds Leslie's marker for twelve thousand dollars. The racketeer urges Marlowe to investigate one Louis Vannier, a slippery, sinister con artist who has been noticed visiting the Murdock estate. Marlowe subsequently contacts Mrs. Murdock, who insists that she has nothing to say about Vannier but informs him that the Brasher Doubloon has inexplicably been returned to the Murdock coin collection. The coin that was delivered to Marlowe's office, then, must be a fake; in any case, he reclaims it from the pawn shop.

Marlowe decides to check out Vannier, as Morny suggested; when he arrives at Vannier's house, he discovers Vannier shot in the head. Marlowe in due course pressures Leslie into admitting that he borrowed the Brasher Doubloon from the coin collection as part of a money-making scheme that would enable him to pay off Morny. He turned the coin over to Vannier, who made a counterfeit copy of it; Leslie then returned the genuine doubloon to the Murdock Collection. The two partners in crime hired Phillips, an inexperienced PI, to front for them by taking the coin to Morningstar for an appraisal, in order to ascertain if the bogus doubloon could pass for the genuine article. Phillips regretted being implicated in this shoddy affair, and he therefore mailed the counterfeit coin to Marlowe anonymously, so that the fraudulent coin could not be traced to him by the police.

As Marlowe assembles the facts of the case, he realizes that Vannier had become obsessed with repossessing the counterfeit coin so he could peddle it for big bucks. He therefore liquidated Phillips and searched his premises for the counterfeit coin; when he failed to locate it, Vannier then wiped out Morningstar and futilely searched the coin dealer's office for the counterfeit doubloon. It never occurred to Vannier that Marlowe was in possession of the coin.

At this point Marlowe comes to the conclusion that Leslie had decided to eliminate Vannier before his trigger-happy accomplice could wipe him out. After putting a bullet into Vannier's skull, Leslie arranged the crime scene to look as if Vannier had shot himself. The official police verdict in the case is that Vannier took his own life, supposedly in despair after the whole conspiracy had gone awry. But Marlowe does not feel obligated to accuse Leslie of murdering Vannier, a double murderer and an extortionist, since he has no hard evidence that would compel the authorities to reopen the case. Like Eddie Mars in *The Big Sleep*, Leslie has managed to elude the long arm of the law.

Marlowe has reason to believe that Vannier's disreputable dealings with the Murdock family went beyond the scheme he had worked out with Leslie to vend the counterfeit doubloon. He accordingly turns his attention to Merle Davis, in order to ascertain what she knows about Vannier's unsavory connection with the Murdocks.

To Marlowe's surprise, Merle informs him that Mrs. Murdock had been paying blackmail money to Vannier on her behalf. To begin with, Merle explains, she had been the secretary of Mrs. Murdock's first husband, Horace Bright, back in the 1930s. When Bright made sexual advances toward her on one occasion, she resisted him; in the ensuing struggle he fell out of his office window. Vannier, a professional photographer, happened to be covering a traffic accident on the street below at the time; a confirmed opportunist, Vannier snapped a picture of Bright plummeting to his death. Bright's death was ruled a suicide, since he had gone bankrupt during the Depression.

Nevertheless, Elizabeth Murdock managed to convince the naïve Merle that Vannier's photo proved that Merle was responsible for Bright's fatal fall, which occurred while Merle was fending him off. Mrs. Murdock therefore had Merle deliver hush money to Vannier at regular intervals; she told Merle that she was paying the extortionist blackmail money for Merle's sake, in order to keep Vannier from turning over the incriminating photograph to the police. Vannier, the blackmailing photographer, represents a cross reference with *The Big Sleep*, since he recalls Geiger, that other extortionist-photographer. In consultation with Dr. Carl Moss, Merle's physician, Marlowe figures out that Merle's neurotic fear of men originated with Horace Bright's attempt to seduce her, followed by his untimely death.

In searching Vannier's apartment after his murder, Marlowe turns up the compromising photograph of Horace Bright falling to his death. But the photo clearly reveals none other than Elizabeth Murdock herself shoving her lecherous husband through the high window, with a view to punishing his philandering once and for all and to collect on his insurance policy. So the blackmail money that Mrs. Murdock was doling out to Vannier was meant to hide her own guilt, not Merle's.

In brief, Chandler interweaves the two main strands of the plot through Vannier: He is revealed to be both the culprit who counterfeited the Brasher Doubloon as well as Mrs. Murdock's blackmailer. Marlowe posthaste gives Merle the news that she has been unequivocally exonerated of any part in Bright's death and need no longer shoulder Mrs. Murdock's burden of guilt for the crime. He hereby liberates Merle from the clutches of her fearsome and obdurate employer.

Marlowe emphasizes to Merle that Mrs. Murdock is an unscrupulous, remorseless harridan, who shamelessly manipulated her "without mercy or pity." She used Merle "as a scapegoat" to conceal her own crime (259). He then volunteers to drive Merle back to her parents' home in Wichita, Kansas, which the hapless girl should never have left.

Horace Bright's death has been officially declared a suicide and the case closed for some years, so Marlowe feels that it would be futile to endeavor to reopen the case by accusing Mrs. Murdock of slaying her first husband. Moreover, Marlowe cannot finger Mrs. Murdock for exterminating Bright without involving the fragile, neurotic Merle in a scandalous trial, during which her traumatic experience of Bright's attempt to molest her would inevitably be raked up.

Furthermore, Peter Sandgren states that Marlowe, according to his lights, believes that his credibility as a private investigator largely depends on his ability to protect his client's interests by maintaining confidentiality. "Hence Marlowe's professional loyalty to his client spares the old lady from the law," but not from her own conscience.[12] In explaining to Leslie why he does not intend to turn Leslie's mother over to the police for Vannier's slaying, Marlowe states, "I've been working for your mother, and whatever right to my silence that gives her, she can have. I don't like her. I don't like you. . . . But I do like Merle" (254). Marlowe retains the crucial photograph and the negative, however, in order to use them against Mrs. Murdock, should she ever try to make trouble for Merle again.

The law likewise cannot touch Leslie, we remember, because the authorities have also ruled Vannier's death a suicide. So in the end Marlowe must stand by while two murders, those of Horace Bright and Louis Vannier, are officially classified as suicides; he accordingly leaves the murderers to their fates. When we last see Elizabeth Murdock, she is cheating at solitaire. This is a telling image, since it implies that the solitary old hag cannot be honest even with herself. In essence, Mrs. Murdock, with her ever-present glass of port, is pictured as a pathetic woman driven into alcoholism by loneliness and advancing age. What's more, her sole companion at novel's end is her wayward son, whom she suffocates with her possessive love.

Leslie, her weak-willed son, in turn, nurtures a neurotic dependence on his domineering mother, which leads him to submit to her control. They are both shut in with the life they have elected to lead; perhaps the punishment they endure for their crimes consists in their being imprisoned together in their dead-end lives. In short, they deserve each other.

Dr. Moss calls Marlowe a "shop-soiled Galahad" (209), and the epithet fits. For The High Window reflects Chandler's ongoing theme, namely, that Marlowe is a knight errant, striving to bring justice to "a wronged and fallen universe," as R.W. Lid puts it. He endeavors to correct injustices and to stand up for the underdog, even though the cards are usually stacked against him.[13] Marlowe is all too often confronted with unsatisfactory resolutions to his cases. In the present instance, he has liberated Merle from Mrs. Murdock, but she and her son have escaped the law. Indeed, Chandler suggests that despite Marlowe's best efforts, the corrupt urban environment in which he functions will undermine and outlast his noble endeavors to bring order and justice to a chaotic world. And all he receives in return for his best efforts is his meager fee. "It is the struggle of a fundamentally honest man to make a decent living in a corrupt society," said Chandler. "It is an impossible struggle; he can't win."[14]

"The theme of the individual's weakness in the face of evil is reinforced by Marlowe's surname," Peter Rabinowitz points out. Marlowe's last name is the same as that of Joseph Conrad's narrator-hero in his novella

Heart of Darkness, which is about the exploitation of the African natives by European traders in the Congo. Both Marlowes are "idealists whose adventures seem destined to bring them in contact with some kind of truth, but who in fact find only a hollowness and a horror."[15] Yet, Speir observes, Chandler's Marlowe will continue to make the attempt to fight for right, despite his nagging awareness of the frequent "futility of such efforts."[16]

MacShane adds, "The seriousness of Chandler's theme shows how ambitious he was for the detective story. Chandler's anger at a world in which innocent people are made to suffer by the unscrupulous rich is expressed mainly" in Mrs. Murdock's cruel exploitation of Merle Davis.[17] In a letter to Charles Morton on January 7, 1945, Chandler himself explained that "Marlowe and I do not despise the upper classes because they take baths and have money; we despise them because they are phoney." Mrs. Murdock's brainwashing Merle into accepting responsibility for Harvey Bright's death while all the time pretending to nurture a maternal solicitude for the girl certainly proves that she is a phoney—to put it mildly. "There are people who think I dwell on the ugly side of life," Chandler concluded. "God help them! If they had any idea how little I have told them about it!"[18]

The High Window was published on August 17, 1942, and was greeted with favorable, though not enthusiastic, notices. "Some people liked it better than my other efforts; some people liked it much less," Chandler told Blanche Knopf on October 22. As far as the author was concerned, the novel was not a "striking and original job of work," but in the last analysis he was pleased with it.[19] The book sold a total of 18,500 copies in America and in Britain, well above average for the hardcover edition of a mystery. Moreover, it was Billy Wilder's admiration for *The High Window,* we shall see, that clinched his decision to hire Chandler to coscript *Double Indemnity.*

The novel's critical reputation has been upgraded since its first appearance. Fredric Jameson lauds Chandler's unvarnished portrait of Los Angeles, the "centerless city. . . . As an involuntary explorer of society," Marlowe visits the garish haunts of the wealthy, epitomized by Mrs. Murdock's decaying, shuttered mausoleum, with its retinue of servants and secretaries, and "the various institutions that cater to wealth," like Morny's private gambling club. The other side of urban life that "Marlowe comes into contact with is the reverse of the above," namely, those parts of the city that are "as seedy as public waiting rooms": from Morningstar's dingy office to George's shabby furnished rooms.[20]

Nicholas Freeling is impressed with Chandler's ability "to draw a character in a few lines (how instantly do Mrs. Murdock and Merle Davis come to life, inside that horrible house in Pasadena. . . . In his California world he could produce ever-memorable people in three lines. *The High Window* is full of them."[21] Along the same lines, Pendo remarks that the book exemplifies how a Chandler novel is like a well-cast movie: the reader not only can appreciate "the major characters, but also the minor ones as well."[22] Thus minor characters, like Morningstar, the eccentric old numismatist, and George, the bumbling young gumshoe, are vividly sketched.

The High Window is an angry monograph about the crass greed and depravity that flourish in the realms of the degenerate rich. As such, it is just what Chandler intended it to be: a serious work of fiction, with the ingredient of mystery supplying the olive in the martini. Hollywood rightly saw the book as a promising property for filming, and like some other Chandler novels, it would be filmed more than once.

Time to Kill: The First Film Version

By the 1940s low-budget private-eye movies were becoming a staple of the Hollywood output. The Falcon series was being churned out at RKO, for example, while the Michael Shayne series was being manufactured at Twentieth Century Fox. Sydney Sanders, Chandler's agent, had sold the screen rights of *Farewell, My Lovely* to RKO, and it was retooled into *The Falcon Takes Over* as a vehicle for series star George Sanders. Sanders likewise sold the film rights of *The High Window* to Fox around the same time as an entry in the Shayne series. The studio purchased the rights for thirty-five hundred dollars, five hundred more than Chandler netted in royalties from the first edition of the novel, so he could hardly refuse the offer.

As with the Falcon series, so too the Michael Shayne series drew its plot lines from various hard-boiled detective writers. Hence *The High Window* was acquired by Fox to be reshaped into a cut-price film featuring Lloyd Nolan as Shane, the creation of mystery writer Brett Halliday. *The High Window* was forthwith converted into a cheaply produced quickie entitled *Time to Kill* (1942; not to be confused with the 1996 film *A Time to Kill*). *Time to Kill* utilized the plot of Chandler's novel, but not its sleuth-hero Philip Marlowe, who was, of course, replaced by Michael Shayne. Shayne was portrayed in the series, according to William Everson, as "a refreshingly realistic type, played with self-confidence and good humor by Lloyd Nolan."[23]

Screenwriter Clarence Young was given the unenviable task of compressing the plot of Chandler's book into one hour of screen time. Although Chandler's Marlowe was perforce masked as Halliday's Shayne, Young otherwise managed to paste together a scenario that stuck reasonably close to the overall premise of *The High Window*. The Brasher Doubloon is missing from the Murdock coin collection, and crusty, reclusive Elizabeth Murdock (Ethel Griffes) wants Shayne to get it back. Shayne eventually pins the theft of the doubloon on Leslie Murdock (James Seay), who was involved in a plot to counterfeit the coin.

Merle Davis (Heather Angel) tips off Shayne that a disreputable character named Louis Venter (Gannier in the novel), is somehow associated with the Murdocks. Shayne eventually discloses that Venter (Ralph Byrd) has been extorting money from Mrs. Murdock because he had taken a picture that shows her sending her husband plunging to his death.

Before Lieutenant Breeze (Richard Lane) can arrest Mrs. Murdock for slaying her husband, however, she accidentally chokes to death on a piece of T-bone steak—a rather implausible, if convenient, way of disposing of the villainess. After Shayne has solved the case, he is free to pursue the affections of Merle Davis, with whom he becomes enamored in the course of the film, whereas in the novel Marlowe simply feels sorry for her.

Herbert Leeds, a second feature director, had already helmed the two films in the series immediately preceding *Time to Kill*. This film is generally considered his best work, as well as the strongest of the movies that comprise the Shayne series, possibly because of the superior story line derived from the Chandler novel. In addition, Leeds sought to infuse the movie with some inventive touches of his own, which helped to raise it above the level of a routine programmer.

In the opening scene, Shayne is photographed talking on the phone, with his shoes propped up on his desk in the foreground of the shot. This image so pleased Leeds, Clark quips, that "it is repeated ten minutes later."[24] Clark, who rarely misses the point, fails to perceive in this case the significance of the repetition of this image. In the opening shot the soles of Shayne's shoes are shown in closeup to have holes worn in them. This image of his shabby footwear implies that Shayne is short of funds and in need of a case. When the shot is repeated later, however, his shoes have new soles, indicating that the retainer he has received from Mrs. Murdock has already bettered his financial status.

Young salted Shayne's dialogue in the movie with some sardonic remarks reminiscent of Chandler's dialogue in the book. When the no-account Leslie Murdock comes to see Shayne about the case, the sleuth quips,

"Business is really picking up when the worm comes to the early bird." Marlowe is equally sarcastic to Leslie in the novel. When Leslie appears in his office, Marlowe, who quickly tires of Leslie's pompous aristocratic airs, inquires pointedly, "You here on business or just slumming?" (26)

Shayne saves his best epigram for Leslie's mother. When telephoning Mrs. Murdock, he asks to speak with "the old lioness. Pry her loose from her raw meat and put her on the phone." Marlowe's epithet for Mrs. Murdock in the book is "the old dragon" (17). Possibly Leeds and Young preferred the reference to the lioness chewing on her meat as foreshadowing Mrs. Murdock's choking to death on a steak. Luhr terms the manner of her death "an outrageous *deus-ex-machina*"; he argues that it can only be excused by the fact that the industry's censorship code would not allow a murderer to go unpunished.[25] But Leeds and Young could have satisfied the censor by simply having Lieutenant Breeze nab Mrs. Murdock, so her curious demise cannot be justified even on that score.

Leonard Maltin notes that Leeds surrounded Nolan "with seasoned character actors" such as Ethel Griffes (*The Birds*) and Ralph Byrd, who later starred in the Dick Tracy series of B features. Leeds also provided Nolan with an attractive love interest in the angelic Heather Angel (*Lifeboat*). But the acting honors really belong to Nolan, who portrays the tough private eye in his customarily brisk, cocksure fashion.[26] Nolan later went on to be cast against type as a crooked police lieutenant in another Chandler-based film, *Lady in the Lake* (1947).

Despite Lloyd Nolan's creditable portrayal of Halliday's Shayne, William Nolan (no relation) finds it unforgivable that Chandler's Marlowe has been erased from the film. After granting that *Time to Kill* retained several of Chandler's characters and the novel's fundamental plot line, Nolan continues, "The film was watered-down Chandler; . . . and Philip Marlowe and his mean streets were nowhere in sight. Yet, in the persona of Shayne, at least his ghost was present."[27] By contrast, Maltin argues in favor of the Shayne character that Nolan's Shayne came across as "a self-assured (and down-to-earth) private investigator on the screen" before the vogue for the Philip Marlowe–type of hard-boiled detective flourished on the screen later in the 1940s.[28]

In this context Jesse Green opines that the filming of a major detective novel is not in itself "*prima facie* evidence of a crime." *Time to Kill*, like *The Falcon Takes Over*, represents what Green calls "thrifty, literary borrowings," which are "returned after use."[29] Indeed, the plot of *The High Window* would in fact be reused in another film, as we shall shortly see.

Admittedly, *The High Window*, like *Farewell, My Lovely*, underwent radical surgery when it was reshaped into a formula detective film for a preexisting series. Nonetheless, *The High Window*, like *Farewell, My Lovely*, was subsequently made the basis of a more faithful adaptation of the Chandler original, when the noir cycle began to flourish. Chandler did not invent film noir, says Syamala, but he "rode on the crest of its popularity."[30]

The Brasher Doubloon: The Second Film Version

Since Philip Marlowe had demonstrated his popular appeal in *Murder, My Sweet* and *The Big Sleep*, his name was restored in the 1947 remake of *The High Window*, entitled *The Brasher Doubloon*, which had been Chandler's working title for the novel. Concerning the title change of the novel at the time it was published, Chandler wryly remarked to Hamish Hamilton in his letter of October 6, 1946, that he questioned whether publishers know anything at all about titles. Blanche Knopf, we know, had urged him to change the title of the novel to *The High Window*; but, he wrote, "I see Twentieth-Century Fox has restored the original title."[31] (The novel's title was retained, however, when the movie was released in Britain.)

Chandler complained once again that, as we saw in the case of the remake of *Farewell, My Lovely*, the studio had not been required to pay him an additional fee for refilming *Window* because they still owned the screen rights to the novel. Chandler was not alone in his dissatisfaction over this state of affairs. Ernest Hemingway also was disgruntled about receiving no additional revenue from remakes of his novels, such as *A Farewell to Arms*. He complained, "My hand is virtually palsied from not receiving any moneys" from these remakes.[32]

The director of *The Brasher Doubloon* was a more distinguished filmmaker than the journeyman director of *Time to Kill*. This time around the film was entrusted to John Brahm, who, as Hans Brahm, had directed plays in Berlin before coming to Hollywood in 1937. Brahm hit his stride in Hollywood with two 1944 gaslight melodramas, *The Lodger* and *Hangover Square*, and also with the mood-drenched *Brasher Doubloon*.

Brahm was working in Germany when the movement known as expressionism had a significant impact on both stage and screen. It is not my purpose to dwell in detail on the influence of expressionism on the films of John Brahm or any other directors who emigrated to Hollywood from Germany in the wake of the rise of Hitler, but the following observations are in order.

Expressionism sets itself against naturalism, with its mania for recording reality exactly as it is; instead, the expressionistic artist seeks the symbolic meaning that underlies the facts. Foster Hirsch describes expressionism in the following terms: "German Expressionistic films were set in claustrophobic studio-created environments, where physical reality was distorted." To be precise, expressionism exaggerated surface reality in order to make a symbolic point.[33]

For example, Brahm places Philip Marlowe (George Montgomery) in an elaborate expressionistic setting in the opening sequence of the film, as he approaches the bizarre, Victorian Murdock manor in Pasadena. Huge, gnarled trees, stirred by the howling summer wind, loom large over the imposing fortress. In addition, Peter Sandgren points to the "long-leaved shrubbery that encircles the mansion" and casts forbidding shadows over the whole scene, thereby creating a threatening atmosphere that warns Marlowe of danger to come.[34]

Cinematographer Lloyd Ahern, working in concert with Brahm, made full use in *Brasher Doubloon* of expressionistic lighting, which lends itself so readily to the moody atmosphere of film noir. Thus a sinister atmosphere was created in certain interiors by infusing them with menacing shadows looming on walls and ceilings, which gave a Gothic quality to faces. All in all, the chiaroscuro cinematography, with its night-shrouded streets and alleys, ominous corridors, and dark archways, gave this modestly budgeted feature a rich texture.

Nonetheless, immigrant filmmakers from Germany such as Brahm and Fritz Lang (*The Big Heat*) insisted that they employed expressionism in only a few key scenes in their American thrillers—as Brahm did, for example, in the crucial opening scene of *The Brasher Doubloon*. After all, excessive use of expressionistic techniques in a commercial Hollywood picture would have seemed heavy-handed and pretentious.

Hirsch also notes that directors like Brahm, who began their careers in Europe, became masters of film noir in Hollywood. For their American films often reflected the characteristics of film noir enumerated earlier; for example, a predilection for dark, gloomy settings and for stories that portray the perilous plights of doom-ridden characters. "The best noir directors" were German or Austrian expatriates who shared a worldview "that was shaped by their bitter personal experiences of . . . escaping from a nation that lost its mind." They brought to their American films a taste for "stories about man's uncertain fate, and about psychological obsession and derangement."[35] Brahm's *Brasher Doubloon* is a case in point, as is *Double*

Indemnity, directed by another expatriate from Germany, Billy Wilder. David Thomson singles out *The Brasher Doubloon* in particular as "a very Germanic Chandler adaptation." Mast and Kawin add that noir films like this one "were unmistakably German, from their fatalism to their claustrophobic decor and looming shadows."[36]

Like *Murder, My Sweet* and *The Big Sleep, The Brasher Doubloon* is narrated by Marlowe; this voice-over narration once again serves to capture the authentic flavor of Chandler's first-person narration in the book. As Marlowe approaches the Murdock estate in the opening shots of the film, he comments in a voice-over on the summer winds: "How I hate the summer winds. They come in suddenly off the Mojave Desert, and you can taste the sand for days." Marlowe's woeful remarks about the fierce Santa Ana winds that sear the landscape underscore the bleak setting of this scene, as described above. Brahm charged the opening portion of a "fairly short (seventy-two minute) picture with considerable atmosphere," writes Philip French.[37]

As in the novel, Mrs. Murdock's sun porch is surrounded by almost as many plants as inhabited General Sternwood's hothouse in *The Big Sleep.* The movie's adherence to its literary source is especially obvious during Marlowe's initial conference with Elizabeth Murdock (Florence Bates, in a peerless performance), in which Chandler's dialogue is clearly in evidence. For example, Mrs. Murdock casually denies that she is a wino in a line lifted right from the book (11). She explains self-righteously that she suffers from asthma: "I drink this wine as medicine. That's why I'm not offering you any."

In the course of the interview Mrs. Murdock states that the Brasher Doubloon was stolen from the tray of precious coins in her safe and admits that her son Leslie (Conrad Janis) knows the combination of the safe. Marlowe accepts her retainer and agrees to recover the missing doubloon. So the plot goes into overdrive during this very first sequence.

Screenwriter Dorothy Hannah condensed Chandler's complicated story into a working script. In Hannah's scenario Mrs. Murdock has only one deceased husband, rather than two. So it is Jasper Murdock, not Horace Bright, whom she sends to his death. Hannah further simplified the action by scrapping Leslie's complex scheme to counterfeit the coin; instead, Leslie steals the coin with a view to using the genuine coin, not a replica of it, in the shady deal he has cooked up with Vannier.

A perusal of the screenplay, which is on file at Twentieth Century Fox, shows that George Anson (George Anson Phillips in the book) was to have appeared briefly in the opening sequence at the Murdock domicile, but

George's appearance was not filmed. In the screenplay Marlowe notices "a loudly dressed young man leaving the house" just as he goes in; the chap apparently has some as yet undisclosed link with the Murdock family.[38] Brahm likewise did not shoot a subsequent interchange between Marlowe and this individual, George Anson, who turns out to be a fellow sleuth. In the script at this point George asks Marlowe for protection. He indicates that he has been given the doubloon for safekeeping, and as a result his apartment has been searched. He consequently fears for his life, as long as he is in possession of the precious coin. Marlowe agrees to help him. The purpose of these and other excisions in the screenplay, Pendo explains, was to speed up the shooting schedule "and save production costs."[39]

The only two deletions in the script that leave a hole in the plot, however, are the two appearances of George, just described. In the screenplay Marlowe is made aware that George has some connection with the Murdocks, when he spies George leaving the Murdock estate. Also in the script he has a meeting with George, in which George indicates that the doubloon is in his possession. Consequently, Marlowe readily infers that the precious coin was temporarily given to him by Leslie for safekeeping on that earlier occasion when he observed George emerging from the Murdock mansion, after Leslie had appropriated the doubloon from the safe.

With both of these brief but significant scenes snipped from the screenplay during filming, no explanation is offered in the movie about how George happened to possess the coin. Thus the first reference to George in the finished film occurs when Marlowe eavesdrops on Morningstar as he phones George about the coin, which George quite unaccountably has in his possession. This minor plot flaw does not mar the film significantly. By contrast, we recall, the 1946 film of *The Big Sleep* had more noticeable lapses in narrative continuity as a result of cuts of this kind.

In the movie Marlowe goes to George's rooming house, a dilapidated fire trap in Skid Row. This section of town, Marlowe comments dryly on the sound track, was once a choice place to live in Los Angeles. "Nowadays," he adds, "people live there because they haven't any choice." Marlowe discovers George's corpse on the floor of his claustrophobic quarters. He searches the body and finds a baggage check, which he puts in his pocket. Accordingly, Marlowe proceeds to the railway depot and redeems a small package with the claim check. The parcel contains the doubloon; by contrast, in the novel George personally mails to Marlowe the coin he received from Leslie. Marlowe drives back to see Morningstar about this new development but finds the numismatist lying dead in his grimy, cluttered office.

Marlowe returns to the Murdock mansion, where he informs Mrs. Murdock, Leslie, and Merle Davis (Nancy Guild) that two men who have been directly linked to the Brasher Doubloon, George and Morningstar, have been slain. He then astonishes the trio by producing the doubloon. Leslie confesses that he took the coin to pay off a gambling debt to racketeer Vince Blair (Alex Morny in the novel). For his part, Marlowe emphasizes that he will not relinquish the coin until the murders are cleared up.

Rudolph Vannier (Louis Vannier in the book), a venal weasel, comes to Marlowe's office to bargain with him for the doubloon, which Leslie, his coconspirator, has presumably told Vannier is now in Marlowe's possession. He claims that he has something very valuable to trade for the coin. Marlowe overpowers Vannier (Fritz Kortner) and rifles his wallet, which reveals that Vannier is a freelance newsreel cameraman. The canny private eye deduces that Vannier took some newsreel footage, which can be used for blackmail, and wants to trade it for the doubloon. But the extortionist steadfastly refuses to divulge the contents of the film.

When Marlowe goes back to his digs, he finds Merle waiting for him. Mrs. Murdock has ordered Merle to retrieve the doubloon from Marlowe by whatever means she deems necessary. At first Merle hopes to get Marlowe to relinquish the coin, in return for her answering his questions about her association with the Murdocks. Merle then explains that her phobia about men dates back to the time when she was the secretary of Jasper Murdock, Elizabeth Murdock's ruttish husband. Murdock made a pass at her, and in the course of Merle's struggle with him, her assailant accidentally fell through the open window to the pavement below. Vannier recorded Murdock's deadly fall on film, Merle continues. And Mrs. Murdock has been paying blackmail money to Vannier for some time, in order to keep him from turning the footage over to the police, so that Merle will not be charged with manslaughter.

Merle begs Marlowe to hand over the priceless coin, so that she can give it to Vannier, in return for the incriminating newsreel film. In desperation Merle finally pulls a gun and orders Marlowe to strip, so that she can search his clothes for the doubloon. The detective begins to undress, but tricks her by snatching the gun away from her, before he has divested himself of much of his clothing. The introduction into the film of a strip search, which is not to be found in the novel, indicates Brahm's "commercial concerns," says Sandgren, since such smatterings of piquant sex could increase the film's box office potential.[40] To be specific, the strip search is fraught with sexual innuendo. The scene suggests a penchant for voyeurism on

Merle's part, since Merle's distaste for being touched by men apparently does not prohibit her from wanting to gaze at a male torso in a state of undress. In any case, when he grabs her gun, Marlowe's striptease is short-circuited, in order to satisfy the industry censor.

That same night Marlowe is kidnapped by Vince Blair (Marvin Miller) and is spirited away to the gangster's gambling joint, ironically called the Lucky Club, which is located in a smoky cellar. The mobster threatens Marlowe, in an unsuccessful attempt to scare the meddlesome shamus off the case.

Ignoring Blair's threats, Marlowe meets Merle the next day at Vannier's tatty house, to have a showdown over the newsreel film—only to find the blackmailer's crumpled corpse on the floor. After a thorough search of the junk-filled house, they find the crucial newsreel footage.

Marlowe decides that it is time to have it out with Leslie. He pressures Leslie at gunpoint into confessing to the killings of both George and Morningstar. The paranoid Leslie feared that the two men were going to sell the coin themselves and keep the proceeds. He was, of course, unaware at the time that Marlowe had traced the coin and had it in his possession.

At the film's climax Marlowe orders all of the key figures in the case to congregate in his office. He begins by submitting Leslie's signed confession to Lieutenant Breeze (Roy Roberts). He plans to show Vannier's newsreel film, which clearly shows Elizabeth Murdock—not endeavoring to pull her husband back to safety—but pushing him through the high window to his death.

He explains that Leslie was frantic to recover the precious doubloon so he could give it to Vannier in exchange for the newsreel material. He then planned to turn the newsreel footage over to gambler Vince Blair (Alex Morny in the novel) as his way of settling his gambling debt with the racketeer, because Leslie was aware that Blair planned to utilize the film to blackmail Mrs. Murdock. So Leslie was prepared to betray his own mother by being party to Blair's blackmail scheme.

In the film, therefore, the two principal elements of the plot are primarily tied together by way of Leslie, who was involved in the conspiracy with Vannier to steal the Brasher Doubloon as well as in the plot to blackmail Mrs. Murdock with Vannier's film of her husband's murder.

Mrs. Murdock, who came to Marlowe's office assuming that Marlowe had summoned her to return the Brasher Doubloon to her, is incredulous as she listens to Marlowe's resumé of the whole case. But then Marlowe screens for all present the segment of the newsreel that Vannier fortuitously photographed of her husband's death. Mrs. Murdock goes berserk as she is taken into custody; she hysterically rants about how she avenged herself on her unfaithful spouse, whom, she snarls, "deserved to die." In addition, the old gargoyle blurts out that she liquidated Vannier in order to silence him for good and all.

Chandler assigned the murders of both George and Morningstar to Vannier, whereas in the film Leslie is designated as the killer of both men. In the book Leslie is guilty only of killing Vannier, but since Hannah and Brahm have already burdened Leslie with two other murders in the movie, they shifted the blame for Vannier's death to Leslie's mother. So in the movie it is Mrs. Murdock who is shown to be guilty of slaying Vannier as well as her husband. The box score is that, in the film, mother and son are guilty of all four of the deaths that occur in the story.

As a result, the idle rich, represented by Elizabeth and Leslie Murdock, come off as even more vile in Brahm's movie than they do in Chandler's book. Mrs. Murdock is the quintessential evil older woman, obsessed with control and possessions, who turns up in film noir. She fosters a guilt complex in Merle about Jasper Murdock's death while she herself reaps the benefits of her deceased husband's insurance policy. Besides murdering her husband, she also savagely exterminates Vannier, leaving on his lifeless arm deep scratches, inflicted by her sharp claws. Leslie is a self-centered, spoiled rich boy at heart; he involves himself in a conspiracy to blackmail his own mother and commits two cold-blooded killings besides. In short, Leslie and his mother are selfish and irresponsible parasites who have lost the capacity for real love; they are depravity incarnate.

As in *Time to Kill*, so in *The Brasher Doubloon*, Marlowe takes a shine to Merle Davis, and the film concludes with him personally promising to get her over her phobia about men. As a matter of fact, in nearly all of the movies based on Chandler books we have considered so far, the scriptwriters furnished Marlowe with a love interest that the novelist did not provide for him in any of the books from which these films were derived. Marlowe had a girlfriend in most of these pictures because the front office believed that, in Clark's pungent phrase, the mass audience expected a private eye "to make romantic overtures to any female character within a ten-year age gap."[41]

Nevertheless there are some darker aspects of *The Brasher Doubloon* that place it firmly in noir territory. Thus the forbidding winds that were howling around the Murdock mansion in the opening scene, already described, recur later in the film. When Marlowe and Merle go to Vannier's house, "trees and bushes sway in the wind, creating the effect of ominous shadows incessantly rubbing against the dwelling," Sandgren writes. "The brooding environment" Brahm created for the movie, exemplified in the heavy shadows which crisscross several of the film's settings, link *Brasher Doubloon* "to the noir tradition."[42] Moreover, the movie's faithful reproduction of the underside of Los Angeles, from George's tacky apartment to Blair's murky gambling den, reflects the grim environment of film noir.

The filmmakers did improve on one aspect of the novel when adapting it for the screen. While a single snapshot of Jasper Bright's murder sufficed to serve as evidence of Mrs. Murdock's guilt in the novel, the writer and the director believed that in the film medium it would be more visually impressive to have Jasper Murdock's deadly fall recorded on motion picture film. Furthermore, Marlowe's screening of this film footage for the interested parties provides a stunning climax for *Doubloon*.

In the book Chandler does not deliver either Mrs. Murdock or her son into the hands of the police for the murders they have committed, for reasons already enumerated. The industry censor, however, following the motion picture code, insisted that the film must make it pellucidly clear that crime does not pay. Accordingly, in the film Lieutenant Breeze is on hand to arrest Mrs. Murdock and her son and ultimately arrange a condign punishment for them both.

George Montgomery (*Roxie Hart*) was chosen to don Marlowe's trench coat in *The Brasher Doubloon*, but a number of critics felt that the mantel of Philip Marlowe did not fit him. Montgomery himself said that he was miscast because he was too young for the part; indeed, at thirty he was the youngest of all the actors to enact the role. "In retrospect," he conceded, "I'd like to have played Marlowe when I was a little older."[43] Perhaps Hannah had Montgomery's youthful look in mind when the following lines were inserted into the script. During their first meeting, Mrs. Murdock barks at Marlowe, "To tell the truth, I expected an older man, someone more intelligent-looking." Marlowe snaps back, "I'm wearing a disguise."

In Dorothy Hannah's opinion, Montgomery was "wrong for Marlowe" because "he had all of the charm but none of the toughness of a private eye."[44] Along the same lines, Sandgren affirms that Montgomery was miscast because he lacked "the world-weariness that comes with experience, and the disillusionment that is the natural byproduct of the private eye's profession."[45]

Although Chandler envisioned Marlowe as a rugged shamus, he hazarded more than once that the clean-cut, well-groomed Cary Grant, an Anglo-American like himself, would have made a good Marlowe. Hence

Lid observes that Chandler conceived Marlowe as a "transplanted Englishman with inherently nice manners."[46] Perhaps Montgomery, in portraying Marlowe as a smooth, gallant chap, brought into relief a side of Marlowe not evident in previous screen Marlowes such as Dick Powell, who presented Marlowe as an unshaven, gruff-type of gumshoe.

Chandler pronounced the present movie "definitely bad: poor acting, poor direction, wretched scripting." It should have been the best Marlowe picture of all, he wrote to James Sandoe on March 8, 1947. "I messed up the story" in the novel, "but the story was there. . . . *The High Window,* with all its faults," was a tough, more substantial thriller than the movie derived from it.[47]

Chandler's assessment of *The Brasher Doubloon* was unduly harsh. Although he may not have been entirely satisfied with George Montgomery's portrayal of Marlowe, the film as a whole was not marred by bad acting, as he asserted. Indeed, some of the performances were well above par. Silver and Ward single out the expert performance of Fritz Kortner (*The Razor's Edge*) as the cunning Rudolf Vannier. Kortner was "a veteran actor molded in the Expressionistic cinema of Germany in the 1920s," which had also influenced Brahm. "His depiction of Vannier as one of those weird creatures that populate Chandler's world brings a sense of aberrant vitality" to the movie.[48]

Then, too, Curtis Brown avers that Florence Bates stole the picture in an act of the grandest larceny as an unrepentant old hag who is more evil than the blackmailers with whom she must negotiate. Her performance as Elizabeth Murdock, "the gorgon of a dowager, is worth remembering" precisely because she brought to the role all of the malevolence Chandler had instilled in the character.[49] This is particularly true of her hysterical scene at film's end. This scene has no counterpart in the novel, where Mrs. Murdock is not unmasked as the villainess she really is. But her mad monologue at the end of the picture, when she is arrested, allows Florence Bates to indulge in some bravura acting that makes for a riveting climax for the picture.

Chandler also seems unfair in damning Hannah's "wretched scripting." Silver and Ward concede that Hannah's script does not succeed in carrying over all the complexity of the novel to the film—what Chandler film does? But they compliment Hannah for including in the screenplay the kind of grotesque characters and pithy dialogue which distinguish a vintage film noir from a routine mystery movie.[50]

As for Chandler's charge of "poor direction," one can argue that Brahm skillfully brought to life on screen Chandler's hard-boiled world, with its moody and threatening atmosphere. As it happened, *Doubloon* was made on a stringent budget, and therefore Brahm was forced at times to employ sets built for other movies, which were still standing in the studio. Thus the director commandeered a set that had been constructed for *Forever Amber,* a costume drama, some months earlier, to serve as the Lucky Club in *Doubloon.* Brahm adroitly transformed a bright, cheery seventeenth-century village inn into a dark, dingy twentieth-century urban gambling den by immersing the low-hanging ceilings and brick archways in dense shadows. The dimly lit, murky ambiance of Blair's club once more links the film to the noir tradition.

Brahm's artistry is demonstrated not only in his creating a classic noir environment for the movie but also by the brisk tempo of the action, which keeps the movie from lagging. In summary, Chandler's sweeping denunciation of the film as "definitely bad" seems uncalled for.

Although *The High Window* received a lukewarm critical reception when it was published, it went on to be reappraised more positively later on. By the same token, *The Brasher Doubloon* received a critical drubbing on its initial release, with one critic dubbing it "small change." However, the film has been reassessed more favorably in recent years as a wily morality tale about chicanery and greed, and as an enjoyable, fast-paced private-eye flick in the bargain. Admittedly, the movie does not deserve to be placed in the company of classic noirs like *The Big Sleep,* but then few noirs do. Moreover, Chandler's criticism aside, neither the director nor the cast lapse into autopilot in the course of the film, while Brahm is commendable in allowing a recognizably unglamourous southern California to seep into the fabric of the story line.

6

Dead in the Water

Lady in the Lake

The sky is blue, the sun is shining; and yet you forget that
everywhere there is evil under the sun.
> —Hercule Poirot, private detective,
> in the film *Evil Under the Sun*

This isn't a beach town anymore; it's a sewer.
> —Kevin Dunne, secret agent, in the film *Snake Eyes*

Raymond Chandler, we know, was an inveterate reader of the daily newspapers, which he combed for articles about crimes that might somehow be incorporated into one of his stories. In 1940 he picked up on a front-page story about a Santa Monica doctor named George Dayley who was tried for murdering his wife five years earlier, after he had reported her death as a suicide in 1935.

The newspaper account stated that Dayley had allegedly drugged his wife and carried her out to the garage, "starting the car's engine so that she died from exhaust fumes." When the case was reopened, witnesses testified at the trial that Dayley had bragged about committing the perfect murder. Still, no compelling evidence was produced to convict him, and he was acquitted.[1] Chandler salted the news story away and later worked it into a novella entitled *Bay City Blues,* and still later into his novel *The Lady in the Lake.* Chandler also drew on his personal experience for the same novel. He and his wife Cissy spent several summers at Big Bear Lake in the San Bernadino Mountains, not far from Los Angeles, and he set some of the novel's scenes in this small lakefront summer retreat.

Chandler once again raided his previously published stories in order to glean material for the novel. *The Lady in the Lake,* based on two novellas, *Bay City Blues* (*Dime Detective,* June 1938) and *The Lady in the Lake* (*Dime Detective,* January 1939), was the last novel for which Chandler cannibalized some of his short fiction to provide plot material.[2]

The Lady in the Lake: The Novel

Bay City, the name of the town referred to in the title *Bay City Blues,* is really Chandler's fictional name for Santa Monica. The novella's Dr. Leland Austrian resembles the real-life Santa Monica physician, Dr. George Dayley, in that Austrian's wife is found in the garage dead, apparently from carbon monoxide poisoning. In Chandler's tale Mrs. Austrian is actually put permanently to sleep by Dr. Austrian's nurse Helen Matson, with whom he is having an affair. Austrian bribes the Bay City Police to cover up the crime by declaring Mrs. Austrian's death a suicide, but detective John Dalmas uncovers the truth.

Chandler also drew on his novella *The Lady in the Lake,* which provided the title of the novel. The novella is set at Little Fawn Lake, the fictional name for Big Bear Lake, the resort in the California mountains where Chandler and Cissy summered. Howard Melton, a cosmetics executive, engages Dalmas to find his wife Julia, who has mysteriously disappeared from their cabin at the lake.

Aided by a countrified constable named Tenchfield, the redoubtable Dalmas eventually figures out that Beryl Haines, a flaming bitch with a sordid past history, killed Julia and dumped the lady in the lake because Julia knew too much about Beryl's checkered past. Beryl Haines, of course, is an alluring, manipulative Circe cast in the same mold as the deadly Helen Matson in *Bay City Blues.* The similarities between the two ruthless females enabled Chandler to meld them into a single villainess for *The Lady in the Lake.* Helen Matson and Beryl Haines were thus combined into the character of Mildred Haviland in the novel.

In addition, Howard and Julia Melton from the novella *Lady in the Lake* became Derace and Crystal Kingsley in the novel, and Constable Tenchfield from the same story was transformed into Deputy Sheriff Jim Patton. It goes without saying that John Dalmas, the sleuth in both novelettes, is closely allied to Philip Marlowe in the book that was derived from the two novellas.

It took Chandler nearly four years to produce *The Lady in the Lake,* which he worked on intermittently while he was taken up with other projects. The painstaking task of reworking material from two different stories into the intricate fabric of a novel undoubtedly contributed to the slow development of the book, which has one of the most convoluted plot lines Chandler ever conceived. Consequently, it is not surprising that *The Lady in the Lake* was the last of Chandler's novels in which he cannibalized old material from his short fiction for use in a novel.

The previously mentioned draft letter of July 6, 1951, which cites Chandler's diary, documents that on June 1, 1939, Chandler had begun a novel with the working title *Murder Is a Nuisance*. By June 19 he was on page 191, "and the damned thing is now called *The Golden Anklet*; . . . a gold anklet does figure in the story." The next day Chandler was up to page 203 and was now calling the manuscript *Deep and Dark Waters*. By June 29 he had reached page 337; on the same day a notation in his diary states, "Tragic realization that there is another dead cat under the house. More than three-quarters done and no good."

As noted before, Chandler typed on half-sheets of paper, so he made only half as much progress as the page count would seem to indicate. "Therefore 337 of these pages would make about 55,000 words of rough script," he noted, but this is still a substantial amount of material. Nevertheless, on July 1, "having become disgusted with this project," he abandoned it for the time being, in order to "try something new."[3]

The bulk of his writing for the rest of 1939 and well into 1940 was devoted primarily to *Farewell, My Lovely*, which he finished on April 30. The balance of 1940 was spent mostly on *The Brasher Doubloon*, eventually titled *The High Window*. Chandler worked primarily on that book throughout most of 1941 and finished it on March 1, 1942. He returned at long last to *The Lady in the Lake*. By the spring of that year he was well along with it and concentrated on *Lady in the Lake* for the rest of 1942, and on April 4, 1943, after working on it sporadically for four years, he was able to record, "I finished it."[4]

The action of the novel covers a three-day time span. On the first day cosmetic mogul Derace Kingsley engages Marlowe to find his missing wife Crystal, who he has reason to believe has gone off with Chris Lavery, a high-living gigolo. Marlowe goes to see Lavery, who admits being an intimate friend of Crystal's, but he categorically denies that he and Crystal had any plans to run away together. Marlowe notices in passing that Dr. Albert Almore (Dr. Leland Austrian in *Bay City Blues*), a shady society doctor, is Lavery's neighbor. Marlowe later talks with Adrienne Fromsett, Kingley's executive secretary, and she volunteers the information that Almore allegedly dispenses illegal drugs to his wealthy clients. Although the death of Almore's wife Florence was officially judged a suicide, Adrienne concludes the word on the street is that Almore had a hand in Florence's demise.

Marlowe's next step is to take a trip to Little Fawn Lake, the tourist village near the Sierra Madre Mountains where Crystal Kingsley was last seen. He talks with Bill Chess, a caretaker at the resort and a pathetic alcoholic. Chess informs Marlowe that his wife Muriel abruptly walked out on him after she caught him bedding down with Crystal while he was drunk. It seems that Muriel Chess and Crystal Kingsley disappeared at about the same time. Soon after, the body of a woman boils up to the surface of the lake. The corpse, bloated and disfigured from being underwater for nearly a month, is unrecognizable. The clothes and the necklace she is wearing, however, are easily recognized as belonging to Muriel Chess.

Deputy Sheriff Jim Patton arrests Bill Chess for the murder of his estranged wife. In Chess's cabin Marlowe ferrets out a golden anklet that is mysteriously inscribed "Al to Mildred." Marlowe proceeds to San Bernadino's Prescott Hotel, where Crystal's car has been found in the parking garage. A rather unkempt bellhop confirms that a woman answering Crystal's description was seen quarreling with a man named Chris Lavery in the hotel lobby.

On the second day Marlowe is on the case, he goes back to Los Angeles and makes a bee-line to Chris Lavery's door, to inquire about his crossing paths with Crystal at the Prescott Hotel. In Lavery's expensive domicile he encounters Mrs. Falbrook, Lavery's landlady, who claims that she came to demand the rent. That Lavery is behind in the rent comes as no surprise, since the playboy obviously lives beyond his means. Lavery is apparently nowhere around, she says, so she departs. Shortly afterward Marlowe finds Lavery dead in the shower stall, having been shot while taking a shower.

When the Bay City Police arrive at the crime scene, Marlowe takes the occasion to question them about Lavery's notorious neighbor, Dr. Almore, since Crystal Kingsley, coincidentally, was one of his patients. One of the cops reveals that Florence Almore died of an overdose of morphine—one of the drugs readily available to her dope-dealing husband. The policeman adds that someone on the force managed to have her death officially recorded as a suicide, but rumor has it that Mildred Haviland, Almore's nurse, administered the drugs to Mrs. Almore with the doctor's knowledge and consent.

Kingsley informs Marlowe that Crystal has phoned him, saying that she is desperately in need of some ready cash. Marlowe realizes that the

game is afoot and agrees to deliver the money to her on her husband's behalf at a crummy hotel in Los Angeles. When Marlowe keeps the rendezvous with Crystal, he soon recognizes her as the woman who disguised herself
as Lavery's landlady, Mrs. Falbrook—presumably so that she could escape
from the scene of the crime before Marlowe found Lavery's corpse and accused her of killing him. Marlowe thus refuses to turn over the cash to her
until she discusses these recent events with him.

Marlowe decides to play a game of cat and mouse with her by sharing
his conclusions about his investigation, in order to manipulate her into tip-
ping her hand. He indicates that his findings have led him to believe that
Muriel Chess was known as Mildred Haviland when she was Dr. Almore's
office nurse, at the very time that Florence Almore supposedly committed
suicide.

Marlowe further hazards that when both Muriel and Crystal dropped
out of sight on the same day, he had a hunch that the lady in the lake might
have been erroneously identified as Muriel Chess. To be more precise,
Marlowe is subtly suggesting that the woman he is now conversing with is
none other than Muriel Chess, and that logically means that it was Crystal
Kingsley who was fished out of the lake, not Muriel Chess.

The implication of Marlowe's remarks—that Muriel was involved in
the untimely deaths of both Florence Almore and Crystal Kingsley—is not
lost on Muriel, who reacts by whipping out a pistol. Marlowe comments
mordantly on her action by saying that Muriel is behaving like the villainess
in a cheap detective movie: "I never liked this scene. Murderer produces
gun, points same at detective." But something always happens to prevent
the killer from shooting the super-sleuth, he continues. "The gods don't
like this scene either. They always manage to spoil it."[5] With that, Marlowe
endeavors to wrest the revolver from Muriel's grip, while she flails about
like a predatory jungle beast and claws at him like a ferocious wildcat.

At this moment Marlowe's prediction that the gods will intervene before Muriel can shoot him comes true. For he is knocked cold by a man
wielding a blackjack; he had been hiding behind a window curtain all this
time. When Marlowe comes to, it is Muriel who is dead. He finds her naked
body, which bears enough vicious bruises to indicate that she has been both
strangled and raped. Lieutenant Al Degarmo arrives to investigate the mur-
der-rape, and Marlowe suggests that they interrogate Kingsley about what
he knows concerning Muriel's murder of his wife.

As the third and last day of Marlowe's investigation dawns, he and
Degarmo drive up to Little Fawn Lake to interview Kingsley. Degarmo di-

vulges en route some of what he knows about Florence Almore's demise. He says that Mildred Haviland conspired with Dr. Almore, her lover, to get rid of his wife and to make it look like suicide. When suspicions began to crop up that Florence had been done away with, Mildred decided to sever her relationship with her confederate. In an attempt to bury her past, she fled to Little Fawn Lake, where she married Bill Chess and became Muriel Chess.

Muriel quickly became bored with life in the remote mountain area, however, and contacted Dr. Almore for money to escape from her dull life and even duller husband. Almore did not take kindly to the notion that Muriel obviously planned to extort money from him indefinitely; he sent Lieutenant Degarmo, who just happened to be Mildred Haviland's first husband, on a foray to Little Fawn Lake, with a view to getting Mildred to leave Almore alone.

But Degarmo failed to locate his elusive former spouse, since neither he nor Almore was aware that Mildred Haviland was now known as Muriel Chess. Marlowe had found the golden anklet in the Chesses' cabin engraved "Al to Mildred," and he now understands that the anklet was a pathetic relic of Al and Mildred Degarmo's failed marriage. As a matter of fact, Marlowe had suspected that Mildred Haviland and Muriel Chess were one and the same person ever since he found the anklet with Mildred's name on it among Muriel's effects in the Chess cabin. (One of the working titles of the novel, we recall, was *The Golden Anklet*.)

At this point Chandler has ingeniously interlocked the material he had taken from the two novellas through Mildred Haviland. As Mildred, she is the former wife of Lieutenant Degarmo and the former lover of Dr. Almore, whose wife she conspired with him to murder. As Muriel, she is the estranged wife of Bill Chess and is responsible for the death of Crystal Kingsley, whom Crystal's husband hired Marlowe to find in the first place. The Mildred Haviland material was derived from *Bay City Blues* (where she is called Helen Matson), while the Muriel Chess material was from the novella *Lady in the Lake* (where she is called Beryl Haines).

At all events, Marlowe and Degarmo find Sheriff Patton waiting for them at Kingsley's cabin. Marlowe reveals to the trio that Muriel Chess killed Crystal Kingsley and sank her body in the lake. Muriel was confident that Crystal's body would in due time be identified as Muriel Chess because Muriel saw to it that Crystal was wearing one of Muriel's outfits, as well as her necklace, when it was found dead in the water. The corpse would of course be identified by these false clues because it would inevitably be in an advanced state of decay when it was recovered from the lake.

Muriel faked her own death because she wanted to throw the authorities off her trail, Marlowe further explains. What's more, Muriel rightly assumed that Bill would be blamed for her death because of their recent breakup. Muriel, the quick-change artist, donned Crystal's clothes after the murder and impersonated Crystal in order to shed her identity as Muriel Chess—just as she had earlier discarded her identity as Mildred Haviland—to cover her tracks once more.

But Chris Lavery accidentally encountered her at the Prescott Hotel posing as Crystal, Marlowe continues. Afraid that Lavery would blow her cover, Muriel killed him after they got back to the city. At this point in his presentation, Marlowe plays his trump card. He reasons that when Degarmo got wind of Marlowe's proposed meeting with Crystal in a hotel in downtown L.A., he got to the hotel first and hid behind the window curtains in the hotel room. At the point when Muriel dropped all pretense of being Crystal, Degarmo—still obsessed with his former wife—went into a frenzy.

He blackjacked Marlowe and killed Muriel; he then violated her corpse, hoping to frame Marlowe for a sex crime. Yet the savage fashion in which he gouged his sharp fingernails into her naked flesh after he strangled her, Marlowe avers, implies that he also acted out of revenge. He wanted to avenge himself on the heartless woman who had callously dumped him, after he had covered up Florence Almore's murder for her. At any rate, violating a corpse in such a brutal fashion smacks not only of sexual sadism but also of necrophilia, so clearly Degarmo is deeply disturbed. Degarmo both "loved and hated her," Marlowe concludes. "He was too much of a cop to let her get away with any more murders, but not enough of a cop" to turn her over to the authorities and let justice take its course (261).

With that, Degarmo gives the game away by pulling out a revolver; after a quick exchange of gunfire with Patton, he manages to get away in his car. The self-destructive Degarmo recklessly drives the speeding auto off a cliff and into the canyon below. As Marlowe surveys the scene from above, he sees the wreck of a small coupé, "smashed against the side of a huge granite boulder." A couple of men pull something out of the wreckage, "something that had been a man"—before Mildred Haviland-Muriel Chess had sunk her fangs into him (266).

Speir best sums up this pitch-black study of wickedness when he reflects that the cold reality of a modern metropolis like Bay City has penetrated even the romantic purity of the Little Fawn Lake resort area. The book expands upon the pulp stories on which it is founded "to draw a portrait of evil finding its way even into society's remotest, most idyllic hideaways."[6] Indeed, the image of a corpse floating in the lake, Ralph Willett adds, "represents an incongruity staining nature itself."[7] Evil has escaped the city and reveals itself as the product of avarice and passion, capable of thriving outside the modern urban wilderness that has also been called the asphalt jungle.

Muriel Chess, as she finally came to be known, is the most malignant femme fatale in all of Chandler. As Stephen Hunter puts it, she represents "the sexually voracious and predatory female who uses men to advance her ends, then spits them out and moves on."[8] It is therefore appropriate that she finally takes the name of Chess when she remarries, since Marlowe describes the game of chess on the last page of *The High Window*, Chandler's previous novel, as beautiful, cold, and remorseless—almost creepy in its silent implacability. He could have been describing the villainess of his very next novel, who is named Chess.

Crystal Kingsley turns out to be the lady in the lake of the novel's title, which, in turn, is a literary allusion to Sir Walter Scott's epic narrative poem *The Lady of the Lake*. In the poem, the title character is the lovely heroine named Ellen, who lives a secluded life near a lake. In the novel Crystal is likewise sojourning near a lake in a remote mountain retreat, but Muriel drowns her in that same lake. (No such fate overtakes Scott's heroine.) According to Chandler's austere moral vision, sexual promiscuity carries a heavy penalty, for Crystal Kingsley, Muriel Chess, and Chris Lavery—profligates all—have been eradicated by novel's end.

The Lady in the Lake garnered enough favorable reviews on its initial publication in 1944 to ring up the biggest sales of any Chandler novel to date. Nearly thirty thousand hardcover copies were sold in America and Britain. Some literary critics celebrated *The Lady in the Lake* as a superior whodunit, with a fascinating, highly inventive plot that travels at high speed.

Furthermore, more than one reviewer noted that *Lady* passes itself off as a murder mystery but is actually a picture of a troubled society, since nearly ever character in the book is in some kind of personal trouble. Indeed, the carefully wrought character portrayals with which Chandler enriched the novel bear out this statement. These portraits, which give the novel depth and purpose, range from the irredeemably evil temptress and murderess Muriel Chess to the wretched corrupt cop Al Degarmo, only one of the males she ensnares in her iniquitous schemes. Nicholas Freeling adds that Muriel is the most frightening of Chandler's female killers because she is the most "clearly perceived" and therefore "the most convincing."[9]

The novel's triumph of characterization, though, is the memorable depiction of Marlowe, who is drawn with considerable depth. He is a thoroughly honest man, a saint among sinners. "He is loyal to his clients, hardworking, more interested in justice than in his fee," Lid affirms, and he consistently "sees through sham and hypocrisy."[10]

"The principles of the case are people before they are witnesses, suspects or investigators," Peter Wolfe maintains.[11] Discriminating critics recognized that the novel's literary attributes placed Chandler well above the average authors of detective fiction. As a matter of fact, Chandler planted an in-joke in the novel at the expense of the authors of the mere puzzle-solving detective stories that featured the sort of one-dimensional characters he abhorred. When Marlowe encounters Muriel Chess masquerading as Mrs. Falbrook in Chris Lavery's home, he introduces himself to her as Philo Vance. Vance was the snobbish detective-hero of S.S. Van Dine's mystery stories popular in the 1920s and 1930s, which for Chandler "epitomized the unreality of that tradition" of slick, superficial detective fiction.[12]

In any event, with the publication of *The Lady in the Lake*, it became clear that Chandler's novels were attracting an ever-larger readership. The popularity of his novels was significantly augmented by the release of his first two books in paperback; their combined sales had already reached one and a half million. Chandler's name had certainly become one to conjure with in the field of detective fiction, and so in the summer of 1945 Metro-Goldwyn-Mayer bought the screen rights to *The Lady in the Lake* for thirty-five thousand dollars, a sum more than double the combined fees Chandler had received for the film rights to his previous three books. What's more, the studio asked him to write the screenplay as well because MGM was impressed with the recent success of *Double Indemnity*, which he had coscripted. In addition, the advance buzz in the industry about Chandler's original screenplay for *The Blue Dahlia*, which he finished in the spring of 1945, was that it promised to become a successful picture (and so it did). Paramount still had Chandler under contract, but the studio was willing to lend him to Metro in July 1945, for a thirteen-week period, to write the script for *Lady in the Lake*. (Chandler's other scripts are treated later.)

Lady in the Lake: Chandler's Screenplay

From the start of his stay at MGM Chandler was not content; he found the impersonal atmosphere in the Thalberg Building, the writers' outpost at the studio, much less congenial than the warm, friendly environment he was accustomed to at Paramount. "I once worked at MGM, in that cold storage plant they call the Thalberg Building," he later recalled. The frosty working climate "got to me too quick," as did "the coteries at the writers table in the commissary. I said I would work at home," which was by then his usual practice when writing a screenplay. He was told that Edgar Mannix, the deputy chief of production at Metro, whom he derided as a "potato-brain," had issued orders that no writers could work at home. "I said a man as big as Mannix ought to be allowed the privilege of changing his mind. So I worked at home, and only went over there three or four times" to confer with George Haight, the producer assigned to the picture, whom Chandler conceded was "a nice producer" and "a fine fellow."[13]

Chandler soon found that adapting his own novel to the screen was like reheating last week's stew, as he wrote to James Sandoe in August 1945. "It bores me stiff. The last time I'll ever do a screenplay of a book I wrote myself. Just turning over dry bones." Chandler was so bored that he later wrote Hamish Hamilton on January 9, 1946, that he "practically rewrote the story in order to have something fresh to look at."[14] Since Chandler had labored on the novel off and on for four years before it was published, it was to some extent understandable that he had grown tired of the material and found it stale. "When a man has written a book and rewritten it," he said, "he has had enough of it."[15]

Haight implored Chandler to stick closer to the novel's plot. "Can't we keep some of the book? Isn't it one of your books we bought? Isn't that why you're here?" Haight asked beseechingly in one of their first story conferences. "You keep on writing entirely new scenes." How could he explain to the front office, Haight continued, that a writer who was hired to do the screenplay of his own story "was departing so noticeably from it?" Chandler replied, "I'm sick of it, George. It is so much easier to write the new stuff."

In perusing Chandler's draft of the script, which is preserved in the Roy V. Huggins Private Collection of Chandler's papers, one finds that the opening scene exemplifies the additional episodes that Chandler devised for the script. In this particular incident, which has no parallel in the novel, Marlowe is resisting the efforts of the police to force him to divulge the name of one of his clients. Chandler obviously intended this scene as a prologue, a curtain-raiser that would establish Marlowe's integrity and his loyalty to his clients. In the course of this scene, by the way, a cop is heard describing to a prisoner the horrors of being executed in the gas chamber. This passage of dialogue may well be a veiled reference on Chandler's part to the execution scene in *Double Indemnity* that was deleted from the release prints of that film, as we shall see later.

In point of fact, Chandler diverged from the novel's story line mostly in the early stages of the screenplay. Once he got going, he hewed pretty close to the novel's plot. This shows once again that Chandler was a conscientious studio employee who was committed to fulfilling his employers' expectations of him to the best of his ability.

His conscientious attitude toward his work is precisely why he balked at trying to produce a finished shooting script in thirteen weeks. Chandler subsequently explained his misunderstanding with the studio in this matter in the following terms: "I was under contract to Paramount and was only permitted thirteen weeks' work for another studio." This was not enough time to enable him to do a second, fully revised draft of the screenplay.[16] He expanded on this point to Charles Morton on October 13, 1945. "I assumed in the beginning that a preliminary script would be all they could expect" in thirteen weeks time. "I found out when I began to send it in that they were regarding it as a shooting script." MGM had never had a finished shooting script, ready for filming, in thirteen weeks since the studio was founded, he continued. So Chandler contended that the studio executives were making unreasonable demands on him and would not listen to reason. "That put the heat on me, and I began to get nervous."

As Chandler's deadline approached, he admitted that his first draft of the script was "full of loose ends and tired attitudes, and that . . . they needed a writer with some enthusiasm." After he completed the first draft of the script, therefore, he recommended that some other writer take on the job of revising the screenplay and turn it into something that did not seem like "a dead carnation."[17]

When his contract with MGM had expired, therefore, Chandler declined to have it renewed. Be that as it may, he was unhappy about the prospect of another writer revising his work, even though he had himself suggested that someone else take over the task of writing the script. "These people never play straight with you," he complained to Morton. The studio would inevitably assign another writer to work over the script, and the other writer would expect to receive an official screen credit as coauthor of the script, just for revising Chandler's first draft. Chandler said in conclusion that he was perhaps being unreasonable in begrudging another writer a shared credit on the script. And so he was, since he had asked to be replaced, rather than renew his contract with Metro. As a matter of fact, he conceded that "MGM would have kept me on the script indefinitely, had I wanted to stay."[18]

Chandler remarked to Hamish Hamilton on January 9, 1946, that he had left behind an incomplete draft of the script when he departed from Metro: "I didn't finish it, and it is probably all bitched up by now (or perhaps I bitched it up)."[19] Chandler's statement that he had turned in an unfinished screenplay to the studio has been misconstrued by most commentators on his work, who assume that he meant that there were several scenes that he had not dramatized at the time he quit. But the copy of Chandler's screenplay in the Huggins Collection proves otherwise.

In actual fact, what Chandler submitted to MGM was a complete first draft of the screenplay, which fully dramatizes the scenario, right up to the final fade out. In fact, his first draft runs to 195 pages (though not 220 pages, as Clark mistakenly asserts). Indeed, on the last page of Chandler's draft he describes "a tag scene"—screenwriters' jargon for a brief epilogue—calling for a "clinch" between Marlowe and Adrienne Fromsett, who is Marlowe's love interest in the movie, though not in the book.[20]

What Chandler meant, when he indicated to Hamilton that he had left behind an incomplete script, was that he viewed his version as a preliminary draft that needed some revision; he certainly did not mean that he abandoned the script before he had finished dramatizing all of the plot's action in full. Luhr rightly states that Chandler's draft is actually "something very close to a final shooting script."[21]

The very length of Chandler's draft testifies to the conscientious care with which it was composed. But then the major problem with Chandler's unrevised script was precisely that it had grown to the gargantuan length of nearly two hundred pages, roughly twice the length of the average movie script. Therefore Chandler's script would have resulted in a movie of well over three hours, had it been filmed without cuts. Metro accordingly brought in mystery writer Steve Fisher (*I Wake Up Screaming*) to revise Chandler's draft. Fisher was another *Black Mask* veteran who had taken up screen writing; he had previously collaborated on a script at Warners with William Faulkner, who had coscripted *The Big Sleep*. Fisher's task was first and foremost to condense Chandler's preliminary draft into a script of workable dimensions.

Lady in the Lake: The Film

In general, Fisher utilized Chandler's draft as the basis of his final shooting script. In condensing Chandler's draft, Fisher jettisoned all of the scenes set at Little Fawn Lake, and, along with them, the characters associated exclusively with those scenes, such as Bill Chess and Deputy Sheriff Patton. Nevertheless, the final film retained most of Chandler's deviations from the book's plot—despite the fact that Haight had initially objected to many of Chandler's departures from the novel's story line in his version of the script.

Thus it was Chandler, not Fisher, who decided that Marlowe and Adrienne Fromsett, a minor character in the book, should fall in love in the movie. Chandler was obviously aware that the studio bosses wanted him to shoehorn a little romance into the screenplay, to make the raw, gritty aspects of the tale more palatable to the ticket-buying public, and he was willing to comply with their expectations in that regard. Hence Fisher was following Chandler's lead by having Marlowe romance Adrienne in the film. In general, Fisher retained several of Chandler's scenes and a great deal of his dialogue in his revised script. In the long run Fisher's final shooting script followed the narrative line of Chandler's draft with reasonable fidelity and did not reduce the story to superficial melodrama.

As a gesture of courtesy, Haight asked Fisher personally to deliver his version of the screenplay, which was pared down to 106 pages, to Chandler's home. When Chandler opened the front door, Fisher said cheerfully, "Philip Marlowe, I presume." Chandler was not amused and proved quite disagreeable and cranky during their brief conversation.[22] The fact is, Fisher commented, that Chandler never really reconciled himself to the concept that motion pictures are essentially a collaborative art, and that he needed a collaborator on a screenplay at times as much as any other writer. Chandler just did not see it that way. "If they bring in the Steve Fishers to polish my work," he fumed to Swanson, his Hollywood agent, on August 4, 1946, "why bother with me at all?"[23]

What nettled Chandler the most about the revised screenplay was an alteration that was not Fisher's doing but was dictated by the film's director, Robert Montgomery. The director, who was also set to star as Philip Marlowe, insisted on the use of the subjective camera, whereby almost the entire film was to be shot from Marlowe's point of view. On Montgomery's orders Fisher had recast the script, to tell the story with a first-person camera. (Although Montgomery was making his debut as a director with this film, he had been appearing in important pictures like *Here Comes Mr. Jordan* for over a decade.)

Montgomery's fundamental concept, writes William Phillips, was that the film should be "an experiment in sustained point of view." That is, virtually everything and everyone should be seen through Marlowe's eyes, and as a rule Montgomery would himself be visible as Marlowe only when his image was reflected in a mirror.[24] Fisher remembered that it was apparent after his short visit with Chandler that Chandler vehemently disapproved of the use of the "seeing eye" camera, "because he called the studio the next day to tell them that it wouldn't work."[25]

Chandler was convinced that "the camera eye technique of *Lady in the Lake* is old stuff in Hollywood. Every young writer or director has wanted to try it. 'Let's make the camera a character'; it's been said at every lunch table in Hollywood at one time or another."[26] Although Chandler employed first-person narration in all of his novels, he rarely employed a narrator in any of his screenplays. Still he was prepared to concede that the first-person camera technique could be effective if used sparingly in a film. He had actually written part of a sequence in that manner in his own draft of the script, but he took a very dim view of employing the subjective camera throughout the movie.

Montgomery had for some time been considering the possibility of directing a film in which the subjective camera would serve as the eyes of the main character, long before he took on *Lady in the Lake*. As a matter of fact, the technique had been utilized for an occasional scene in various movies in the past, but it had never before been used throughout a full-length motion picture. MGM was reluctant to approve Montgomery's proposal, so he prepared a reel of test footage, which he screened for Edgar Mannix (not Edward Mannix, as Montgomery referred to him); Mannix "eventually gave me the go-ahead" to use the first-person camera in *Lady in the Lake*.[27]

The main problem with this format, Montgomery recalled, was to get the actors to look directly into the camera lens when they were addressing Marlowe. "I had a basket installed under the camera and sat there," he explained, "so that whoever was speaking to the camera would have someone to address, even if they did have to look above me."[28] Regardless of Chandler's strong reservations about this approach to shooting a movie, Montgomery, in collaboration with Academy Award–winning cinematographer Paul Vogel (*Battleground*), made deft use of the subjective camera throughout the movie.

In essence, the filmgoer is supposedly looking through Marlowe's eyes at the action as it transpires. Accordingly, when Adrienne Fromsett kisses Marlowe seductively, she bends forward with puckered lips and, in a manner of speaking, makes love to the camera. By the same token, when gigolo Chris Lavery angrily socks Marlowe for asking prying questions about his private life, Lavery throws a punch right at the camera. The image sways, goes out of focus, and fades to black, as Marlowe loses consciousness.

By employing the subjective camera, Montgomery thus provided what

Ed Muller terms "a visual corollary to Chandler's first-person narration" in the novel.[30] Moreover, Montgomery effectively evoked the first-person feel of Chandler's novels by accompanying his use of the seeing-eye camera with Marlowe's running commentary, voice-over on the sound track.

In revamping the screenplay according to Montgomery's specifications, Fisher was scrupulous in ensuring that the story was told almost exclusively from the point of view of the camera. But he also included four brief scenes in which Montgomery, as Marlowe, addresses the camera; Marlowe appears in these vignettes in order to explain material, mostly from the Fawn Lake episodes, that had been excised from Chandler's draft.

Marlowe first appears in the film's prologue, sitting behind his desk, as he addresses the audience directly. "My name is Philip Marlowe; occupation: private detective," he begins. Then he offers some foreshadowing of the film's story line by adding, "Somebody says, 'Find that female.' So I find her. And what do I get out of it? Ten bucks a day and expenses."

Marlowe is "inviting us to join in the game of detection," notes J.P. Telotte, and he makes it clear that he is functioning "as the source of all that we see."[31] As such, Marlowe is both a witness and a guide, as he describes and analyzes for the viewer the investigative process whereby he solves a case. "You'll see it just as I saw it," Marlowe promises. "You'll meet the people; you'll find the clues. Maybe you'll solve it quick and maybe you won't." Moreover, the filmgoer will also see the corrupt underside of Los Angeles through Marlowe's critical eye, just as the reader is party to similar observations of Marlowe's in the novel.

As Marlowe begins to narrate what the newspapers have dubbed "the case of the lady in the lake," he mentions that "the whole thing started just three days before Christmas." When Montgomery was later asked the reason Fisher changed the time setting in the film to Christmas, the director answered that the Christmas season made an ironic contrast to a murder case. Actually, Fisher implies for the viewer his motive for the Christmas setting during the opening credits. The credits are printed on Christmas cards, each of which is placed before the camera one at a time by a hand, while a choir carols over the sound track. When the last card is pulled away, a gun is revealed beneath it. "One does not generally associate guns with Christmas," Luhr notes; thus the Yuletide atmosphere is meant as a jarring counterpoint to the sinister events in the story, as Montgomery suggested.[32] The movie follows the novel's three-day time span and so concludes on Christmas Day itself.

Composer David Snell (*Alias Dr. Kildare*) took his cue from the use of

Christmas cards in the opening credits to accompany the credits with Christmas carols. In composing his musical score for the picture, Snell limited the background music solely to that same chorus, singing wordlessly without musical accompaniment. In utilizing only a choir singing a capella for the movie's underscore, Snell complemented the stark black-and-white photography with an equally spare "black-and-white" score. That is to say, the composer limited the score to an unaccompanied choir as a counterpart to the way in which Montgomery had limited his color spectrum. The underscore is by and large very effective, although the intrusion of choral music into a love scene between Adrienne and Marlowe, which takes place in her apartment, makes the filmgoer wonder if she has the Westminster choir tucked away in her linen closet.

Marlowe also states in his opening remarks that he is "tired of being pushed around for nickels and dimes; so I decided to write about murder. It's safer." When Marlowe mentions the going rate for his services as a shamus, it is clear that he has unaccountably taken a severe cut in pay. In this film he is charging ten dollars a day, instead of the twenty-five dollars a day he got, for example, in both the novel and the 1946 film of *The Big Sleep*. It is therefore understandable that he aims to supplement his negligible income as a sleuth by writing for the pulps. Interestingly enough, Marlowe's prospective publisher pays a penny a word, which was the usual rate for *Black Mask* writers when Chandler himself began publishing his stories in its pages.

Fisher is not responsible for putting into the film Marlowe's aspirations to be a writer of pulp fiction, as Silver and Ward assume. It was Chandler who wrote that new facet of Marlowe's role into the movie's scenario. Consequently, this represents yet another of Chandler's alterations of the novel's plot that Fisher transplanted into the final shooting script from Chandler's draft. Making Marlowe a prospective mystery writer involved transforming Derace Kingsby (Kingsley in the book) from a cosmetic manufacturer in the novel to the publisher of pulp fiction in the picture. Thus in the film, when Marlowe submits a story to Kingsby Publications, Adrienne Fromsett (Audrey Totter), Kingsby's chief assistant, takes the occasion to hire him as a private detective.

Montgomery committed himself to shooting each scene in the picture in a single, unbroken take. But he kept the camera perpetually on the go, to keep the film from looking static or stagy. In the course of these extended takes Montgomery cleverly works the camera around the actors, as it unobtrusively glides about the set, so that the pace of the action never falters.

The director thus employs the procedure known as "pre-cutting inside the camera" by closing in at times for a close shot to emphasize a key gesture or to capture a significant facial expression, and then falling back for a medium shot as the action continues. Because Montgomery rarely chose to interrupt these extended takes by the insertion of other shots when the footage was finally cut together, he virtually eliminated the need for any editing in the movie. "We had to learn pages of dialogue," Audrey Totter remembered, "because there was no cutting; every scene was complete in itself."[33]

In the first scene following the prologue Marlowe submits his story to Kingsby Publications, which he characterizes in a voice-over as specialists in gore. In this scene the final shooting script adheres very closely to Chandler's draft, even borrowing much of his dialogue, as Marlowe is interviewed by Adrienne Fromsett.

The extended takes, uninterrupted by cuts to other camera angles, that Montgomery employed throughout the picture enabled an actor to give a sustained reading of a long speech, and thus deliver it more effectively. For example, when Marlowe claims in this scene that his manuscript is "based on an authentic case," Adrienne replies petulantly in a long speech taken from Chandler's draft; she delivers it directly to the camera as Marlowe feeds her cues. She says, in part, "The people who know the facts usually can't write—and the people who can write usually don't know the facts. Authenticity has very little to do with it. If the people who read our magazines knew the facts of life, Mr. Marlowe, they wouldn't be reading our magazines."[34]

In this speech Chandler may have been implicitly justifying the fact that he wrote detective fiction without the inside experience of a Dashiell Hammett, who had been a private investigator before becoming a writer. Chandler, as mentioned, compensated for his lack of personal experience in the realm of crime and detection through research.

Adrienne jump-starts the phlegmatic Marlowe, who is fed up with the private-eye racket, by cleverly offering to accept Marlowe's manuscript, in exchange for his accepting a commission to find Kingsby's missing wife Crystal, whom she suspects has gone off on a toot with a male companion. At first Marlowe is reluctant to accept the case, since he insists that he has sworn off sleuthing, but he finally takes the bait when he sees a chance to get his first story published. Adrienne comments icily, "We have a nasty little motto around here: 'Every man has his price.'"

Marlowe first goes to see the rakish Chris Lavery (Richard Simmons), who he knows was seeing Crystal. Lavery is a Swede who affects the refined manners and the southern drawl of a courtly southern gentleman, a stance that presumably ingratiates him with his female companions. When Marlowe curtly presses him about his involvement with Crystal, however, Lavery's southern hospitality wears thin; he sheds the bogus accent, courtly manners, and brutally smashes Marlowe with his brass knuckles. That leaves Marlowe with a shiner, which he stoically terms an occupational hazard in his profession.

Adrienne later urges Marlowe to carry his investigation to Little Fawn Lake, beyond Lake Arrowhead, where Crystal was last seen. Furthermore, Adrienne informs him that she has heard from a newspaper reporter that Bill Chess, a caretaker at the mountain resort, is accused of drowning his wife Muriel in the lake. But Adrienne suspects that Crystal may have liquidated Muriel, both literally and figuratively, by drowning her, since the two women were known to have had a jealous quarrel over Lavery. Marlowe gets her point, and says, "You think Crystal Kingsby shoved this lady in the lake and took a powder, which is why she's missing."

At this point in the film there is another brief exposition scene, in which Marlowe sits at his desk and addresses the camera directly. In effect, he gives the viewers a progress report, by bringing them up to date about information pivotal to the plot, which he has just uncovered at Little Fawn Lake. He states that he has discovered that Muriel Chess was really Mildred Haveland (Haviland in the novel), and that she had married Bill Chess because she was on the run from the law and needed a new identity. He adds that he personally inspected Muriel's corpse in the local morgue, "but after a month underwater, there wasn't much left of her."

It is now Christmas Eve, and Marlowe returns to Lavery's house, where he meets Lavery's scatterbrained landlady, Mrs. Falbrook. After the woman leaves, there is a wordless scene that depicts in purely visual terms how Marlowe ransacks the house for clues that would link Lavery to Crystal or Muriel. In a single, uninterrupted tracking shot Montgomery's camera glides around the premises, taking in the entire first floor with its panoramic gaze. The camera then climbs the stairs to the second floor and peers into the bathroom, where it focuses on Lavery's naked body, slumped in the corner of the bullet-riddled shower stall.

Montgomery thus displays the virtuosity of the subjective camera in one of the most effective uses of it in the whole movie, as the filmgoer sees exactly what Marlowe sees while the shamus searches the house. Furthermore, Montgomery's long takes, as exemplified here, are every bit as skillfully executed as Alfred Hitchcock's extended takes in *Rope* a year later. But Montgomery concealed his technical craftsmanship by making the camera work seem so effortless that one hardly notices the infinite care with which these prolonged takes were accomplished.

On Christmas night Marlowe goes to Adrienne's apartment to compare notes with her about the case. He is already conversant with the fact that Lieutenant De Garmot (Degarmo in the book), who is investigating Lavery's slaying, had been involved with Muriel Chess when she was still known as Mildred Haveland. Adrienne confides to him that Mildred Haveland once worked as a nurse for a Dr. Almore. Dr. Almore's wife Florence died under suspicious circumstances, and he and his nurse were co-suspects in the case. Adrienne adds that Lieutenant De Garmot (Lloyd Nolan), managed to have Mrs. Almore's death declared a suicide.

Kingsby suddenly appears on the scene, blustering that Crystal has phoned him, demanding money because "she's in awful trouble; the police are after her." He urgently requests that Marlowe convey the cash to her at the scruffy fleabag hotel where she is holed up. Marlowe suspects that his supposed meeting with Crystal may be a trap, engineered by De Garmot, who is well aware that Marlowe has been checking up on him. So he asks Adrienne to send the police to Crystal's hotel, in case he needs backup.

At the film's febrile, gothic climax, Marlowe meets the woman who purports to be Crystal Kingsby and tells her how he interprets the facts of the case. He discusses the facts with her in an icy tone of voice, flatly asserting that she is not Crystal Kingsby at all, but Mildred Haveland, Dr. Almore's erstwhile nurse (Jayne Meadows). Mildred, he explains, only became Muriel Chess after she broke off her sordid relationship with Dr. Almore and married Bill Chess.

In due course, Muriel killed Crystal and "dumped her body in the drink," Marlowe continues. This treacherous harpy assumed Crystal's identity in an attempt to elude De Garmot, who aimed to wreak havoc on her for ditching him.

In addition, she also pretended to be Mrs. Falbrook, when she ran across Marlowe in Lavery's house, after she shot him. Mildred Haveland, Marlowe concludes, had by now collected enough different names to start her own phone book.

Lieutenant De Garmot, who had in fact followed Marlowe to the hotel, intervenes at this juncture, gun in hand. Muriel shouts fiercely to De Garmot, "Kill him!" and Marlowe coolly interjects, "He's going to kill you for double-crossing him." De Garmot endorses Marlowe's shrewd observation when he speaks acridly to Muriel, "You made a sucker out of me; but I still loved you, even after you ran away. But tonight's the end. You made a bad cop out of me. You're a murderess, but you're all though killing. I'm going to leave you dead." De Garmot pulls the trigger and exterminates Muriel, as if he were a hunter felling a predatory jungle beast. Marlowe sardonically remarks, "First you cover up Florence Almore's murder for her, and then you kill her. Petticoat fever."

Adrienne shows up with Captain Kane (Captain Webber in the book), who immediately sizes up the situation. He promptly fires at Lieutenant De Garmot, before De Garmot can turn his revolver on Marlowe; De Garmot falls dead next to Muriel's body. Noticing that they are lying side-by-side in death, Marlowe comments laconically, "De Garmot killed her for a wonderful motive; he was in love with her."

Since the final shooting script eliminated the Little Fawn Lake sequences from Chandler's draft, Lieutenant De Garmot does not meet his doom by driving his car off a cliff near the lake, as he does in the book. Instead, in the film he receives instant justice by being dispatched by Captain Kane immediately after the rubs out Muriel.

When Captain Kane, played by Tom Tully (*The Unseen*), demands a full account of the whole case from Marlowe, the sleuth shrugs off his queries by saying, "I'll write it and see that you get the first copy out of the typewriter." Marlowe is going to become a professional writer after all; he will compose stories based on his personal experiences, and Adrienne will edit them for publication. Following Chandler's script once again, the film concludes according to the typical Hollywood romantic formula, with Marlowe and Adrienne in a clinch—the only time they are seen on the screen together in the same shot in the entire film.

Director-star Montgomery deserves a good deal of credit for creating a topnotch, hard-hitting thriller from Chandler's story. To begin with, he gives an immaculate performance as Marlowe. Montgomery's rude, crude, cynical gumshoe runs counter to the actor's screen image as the polished gentleman he often played in pictures. "At heart," Pendo writes, Montgomery's Marlowe remains Chandler's Marlowe, "carrying on when the chips are down, . . . struggling to see justice done."[35]

Furthermore, Montgomery elicited ensemble playing of a high order from his capable cast. Pendo singles out Jayne Meadows's riveting performance as the virago Muriel Chess. In Muriel's climactic confrontation with Marlowe, her rapid-fire speech and quick, nervous gestures indicate that Muriel is close to hysteria, as she desperately seeks to disavow the horrendous charges that Marlowe lays at her door. In his interview with Jon Tuska several years after he made the movie, Montgomery complimented Jayne Meadows (*David and Bathsheba*) on her fine portrayal of "the landlady." Montgomery had by this time forgotten that Mrs. Falbrook was only one of the incarnations of the chameleon-like villainess whom Meadows played in this "femme noir."[36]

Lloyd Nolan, who played Michael Shayne, the gumshoe based on Philip Marlowe in *Time to Kill*, gives a tight-lipped portrayal of the bitter, broken rogue cop, De Garmot. Audrey Totter (*The Set-Up*) was required, in the role of Adrienne, to start off approaching Marlowe as a starchy magazine editor, but her icy manner gradually melts in to that of a cooing lovebird, and she brought off this transformation splendidly.

One actor listed in the cast credits does not actually appear in the film at all, an in-joke on Montgomery's part. Crystal Kingsby, already dead before the movie begins, is listed in the credits as being played by Ellay Mort, which in phonetic French means "she is dead." (Crystal's name was misspelled as Chrystal in the cast list, but her name is correctly spelled, without the *h*, when it appears in the course of the film on an old telegram that Marlowe comes across.)

While handing out bouquets for the movie, I cannot overlook Steve Fisher, who certainly merits praise for adroitly coping with Chandler's complicated story line. Indeed, intricate plotting of this kind has since become all but a lost art in commercial motion pictures, so one appreciates the inventive and plausible plot twists in *Lady in the Lake*. Nevertheless, Chandler thoroughly detested Fisher's revised screenplay, particularly because he repudiated absolutely the use of the first-person camera technique, which, after all, was Montgomery's idea, not Fisher's.

But Chandler had other gripes, some of which amounted to nitpicking. He whined, for example, that "they even got Marlowe's first name wrong. They spelled it with an extra 'l'—as Phillip—on his office door," and also in the cast credits. So despite the film's critical and commercial success, Chandler convinced himself that it was "a godawful mess!"[37] Montgomery's film had "nothing much to do with the book," he asserted in correspondence. "I didn't like the way it was done and refused to have my name on it" (as coauthor of the screenplay), in spite of the fact that Metro wanted him to share the official screen credit with Fisher.[38]

In refusing to accept an official cowriting credit on the film, Chandler was really cutting off his nose to spite his face. A close comparison of his draft of the screenplay with the finished film demonstrates that, aside from

Fisher's condensing Chandler's script and rearranging the action for the sake of the subjective camera, Fisher's revamped screenplay remains essentially true to Chandler's script. In summary, Fisher's final shooting script not only retains generous portions of Chandler's dialogue, but also preserves whole scenes from Chandler's draft. Hence, Chandler to the contrary, *Lady in the Lake* is fairly faithful to Chandler's script and to his novel. It is also a first-class example of film noir, in the grand tradition of Hawks's *Big Sleep* and Dmytryk's *Murder, My Sweet.*

Louis B. Mayer, the studio boss, initially shared Chandler's strong reservations about the seeing-eye camera technique, and was displeased when he learned that his principal assistant, Edgar Mannix, had authorized its use in the picture. Still, "Mayer was quite happy to accept credit for it after the film was well-received," Montgomery liked to point out.[39] *Lady in the Lake* grossed $4 million on its original release, four times what it cost to make the movie.

The film's box office success was undoubtedly aided by enthusiastic reviews. R.W. Lid went so far as to state in his notice in the *Partisan Review* that *Lady in the Lake* "screens better than it reads." The reason is that Chandler's "conventions admirably suit the movies, where the camera . . . establishes the proper sense of desolation—that miasmic, Dantesque background of California roadways, police stations, and office buildings in which Chandler specializes."[40]

Several more critics found that first-person camera made the movie an unusual thriller and the device was much examined and discussed by the critics as an interesting tour de force. Moreover, some other noir films soon followed Montgomery's lead by using the "I am a camera" technique in selected sequences. Delmar Daves employed the first-person camera for the first third of *Dark Passage,* released eight months after *Lady in the Lake.* In it Humphrey Bogart stars as Vincent Parry, an escaped convict. "The early sequences, which detail his escape from San Quentin, are shot from his point of view. . . . This often makes for queasy, claustrophobic viewing," says *Sight and Sound,* but it also makes for an engrossing movie. "When Parry is in the quack doctor's chair, having plastic surgery to alter his face, we feel as if we're there with him."[41]

Curtis Bernhardt's *Possessed* (1947) contains one extended subjective sequence: The deranged heroine (Joan Crawford) is wheeled into the psychiatric ward of a hospital and is confronted with a series of coldly detached specialists who examine her. All of these encounters are photographed from her point of view.

In his landmark study of narrative techniques in the cinema, J.P. Telotte attests that Montgomery's employment of the roving first-person camera in *Lady in the Lake* has had an enduring influence on commercial cinema, to the extent that Hollywood films continue to utilize this technique "in lengthy though isolated sequences." Hitchcock, for example, used the stalking camera in *Frenzy* (1972); in fact, he reverses the shot in *Lady in the Lake* in which the camera climbs the stairs to the site of a murder, already described.

In *Frenzy*, when a serial killer leads an unsuspecting victim into his flat to kill her, the camera stops at the doorway and does not follow them inside. Instead, it slowly retreats down the shadowy staircase and out into the sunshine of the busy street, as if recoiling from the unspeakable act that is taking place behind curtained windows.

Chandler notwithstanding, Montgomery's skillful use of the subjective point of view in *Lady in the Lake* has been often imitated, never surpassed. There is no doubt, Telotte concludes, that since Montgomery's pioneering implementation of this technique in *Lady*, the use of the first-person camera has been assimilated into the visual vocabulary of the cinema.[42]

7

Decline and Fall

Marlowe

Hooray for Hollywood. . . .
Where any office boy or young mechanic can be a panic
With just a good-looking pan.
Where any shop girl can be a top girl,
If she pleases the tired business man.
—Words and music by Johnny Mercer
and Richard Whiting

Hollywood . . . is the Roman circus, and damned near the end
of civilization.
—Raymond Chandler

Raymond Chandler's novel *The Little Sister* was published in 1949, after he had been working in Hollywood off and on for more than five years. Into *The Little Sister* Chandler poured all of his experiences of serving time in the film colony. By this time Chandler had become thoroughly disenchanted with Hollywood. "He frequently complained to friends about the decadent condition of the film industry," Philip Durham notes, "and this attitude was, of course, to seep into his fiction."[1] Chandler's grim portrait of Los Angeles in the novel sets the stage for his black valentine to the film capital.

Los Angeles is artificial in a literal sense, as filmmaker John Schlesinger (*Midnight Cowboy*) told me in conversation. "The first time I saw a crane planting a full-grown tree in a garden," he said, "I realized that Hollywood is not organic; nothing grows or develops naturally there." Similarly, Tom

Reck notes, "All its features, whether flora, fauna or freeway, have had to be imported because it is built on a desert where nothing grows naturally." Chandler depicts L.A., Reck continues, as "a paradise gone sour," plagued as it is by "smog, pollution, street violence, and hip subcultures." The city's hotels and apartment buildings, in Chandler's eyes, look like leftover film sets that have been uprooted from a studio back lot and transplanted onto residential streets. They are "contemporary equivalents of Dante's *Inferno*, with sinners hiding behind the frosted glass doors." Los Angeles is "the manufacturer of movie sex fantasies," Reck concludes, and "Marlowe is the city's Jeremiah, exposing its fetidness and prophesying its doom."[2]

There is, for example, the decrepit beachfront boarding house where Marlowe goes looking for a missing person in *The Little Sister:* "The block in front of it had a broken paving that had almost gone back to dirt." The house itself had a "shallow, paintless front porch"; the green window shades were "full of cracks"; next to the front door was "a large printed sign, 'No Vacancies,' that . . . had got faded and fly-specked."[3]

Indeed, Chandler's picture of "the underbelly of the city," writes Ralph Willett, evokes slum tenements, waterfront dives, marijuana dens, and other havens for pickpockets, grifters, and drifters.[4] In Reinhard Jud's 1993 documentary for Austrian television on hard-boiled crime novelist James Ellroy (*The Black Dahlia*), Ellroy gives the viewer a Cook's tour of the underside of L.A., which he calls "the city of nightmares." Ellroy, a self-acknowledged disciple of Chandler, points out that the "ugly, dark, violent, suppurating world" pictured in Chandler's stories set in L.A. has not changed essentially over the years. A typical slum dwelling in Los Angeles, now as then, can be a purgatory for the depraved.

Chandler had begun writing about the film colony long before he planned his own Hollywood novel; his first two stories for *Black Mask* focused on Hollywood, a full ten years before he began writing screenplays. The detective in both of these early Hollywood novellas, *Blackmailers Don't Shoot* and *Smart Aleck Kill,* is a precursor of Marlowe called Mallory. Mallory's clients in both of these stories, a has-been movie star in the first, a washed-up director in the second, are both consorting with the mob, one reason that Roger Schatzkin comments that in Chandler's view, "involvement in Hollywood is never far removed from ethical compromise, if not outright illegality."[5] These early stories seem to be a dress rehearsal for *The Little Sister,* which Wessells describes as "perhaps his fullest exploration of the moral bankruptcy of Hollywood." For this "caustic look at the movie business" contains some of Chandler's most sardonic reflections on the movie industry.[6]

The Little Sister

"It has always been fashionable amongst novelists writing about Hollywood to depict producers as boorish illiterates," says writer-director Bryan Forbes (*The L-Shaped Room*), and certainly several of these accounts were founded in fact. Novelists such as Scott Fitzgerald and Nathanael West "carried away scars" from their sojourns in Tinsel Town, continues Forbes, and they used them as the basis of Hollywood novels—Fitzgerald in *The Last Tycoon* and West in *Day of the Locust*. After all, writers "were low men on the totem pole; . . . so it was not surprising that, if and when they escaped the treadmill, they sought to hit back in their fictions."[7] For example, *Day of the Locust,* Timothy Corrigan writes, "paints an extremely bleak picture" of the "desperation and numbing frustrations" that beset the individual struggling to maintain his artistic integrity in the movie industry.[8]

Chandler wrote in 1947 that "the Hollywood novel . . . interests me because it has never been licked." This is because such novels as West's *Day of the Locust* focus too much on Hollywood stereotypes: "a hot-pants actress, an egomaniac director, a snide executive," and so on. "The story that is Hollywood will someday be written," Chandler concluded, but it must rise above stereotypes and clichés "and endeavor to paint an authentic picture of the grandeur and decay, the poignant humanity and icy heartlessness of this . . . colossus, the movie business."[9] Two years later, Chandler managed to get both the grandeur and the decay of the film industry into *The Little Sister* (1949). As Al Clark puts it, in the novel "the film world provides the moneyed backdrop against which Chandler plays off his reproachful recollections of a world in which he was never at ease."[10]

Chandler began writing the novel in 1944, while he was still at Paramount. He worked on it intermittently between film assignments but could not make much headway. In early 1946 he told Hamish Hamilton that he hoped to have completed the as-yet-untitled novel by the following June, "unless I get mad and throw it away." In his letter of October 6, 1946, to Hamilton, he confessed that he had not made much progress on the "new Philip Marlowe story," which was now entitled *The Little Sister*. On March 8, 1947, his letter to James Sandoe indicated that he was working on another Marlowe novel, *The Little Sister,* because "I think the guy is too valuable to let die out." He had to lay aside the manuscript yet again, though, to write the screenplay of *Playback* for Universal, which took nearly a year.

Withal, Chandler completed the first half of the novel, about thirty thousand words, in June 1948. Furthermore, he was able to report to

Hamilton on August 10, 1948, that he would have a rough draft completed shortly. He added, however, that he was not particularly satisfied with his work. "The plot creaks like a broken shutter in the October wind," he moaned, possibly because he had not been able to write with any regularity.[11] In a follow-up letter on August 19, he told Hamilton that he was in the home stretch but writing about all this "Hollywood rubbish" had well nigh exhausted him: "I may be all washed up."[12] Indeed, he described the finished product to H.N. Swanson, his agent, on October 15 as "ill-written and ill-constructed; 75,000 words of nose-thumbing" at Hollywood and its denizens. In writing a Hollywood novel, it seemed that Chandler was biting the hand that fed him, since he had not yet finished working in the movie business for good and all, as we shall see later.

Still Chandler feared that his talent as a novelist had grown rusty during his years in Hollywood. His five years in the salt mines, he believed, had left him with "a typical case of arrested development, and the more I stay away from the picture business, the better I like it." In yet another sideswipe at the movie capital, Chandler wrote to a Mrs. Holton, a staff member at Houghton Mifflin, on March 26, 1949, that he should have included an apology at the front of the novel, in which the author "admits with shame" that there really is "a place called Hollywood and a place called Los Angeles," and that he more accurately should have referred to L.A. as "Smogville."[13]

The Little Sister commences with Marlowe being hired by Orfamay Quest, a prim, prissy girl from Manhattan, Kansas, to locate her brother Orrin, who had left home in a quest for a career as a professional photographer on the West Coast. Marlowe's search for Orrin takes him to a seedy boardinghouse, where he finds Lester Clausen, the room clerk, stabbed to death with an ice pick; but Orrin has checked out.

Marlowe later interrogates George Hicks, a petty crook whom he has reason to believe is linked somehow to Orrin; soon after, Hicks likewise turns up with an ice pick buried in his body. Marlowe later recovers some photographs that had been in Hicks's possession. They show Mavis Weld, a movie star, in the company of Sonny Steelgrave, a mobster, at his gambling casino. The photos, which depict Mavis's sordid association with a gangster, could damage her career. Thus incriminating photographs propel the plot of *The Little Sister,* just as they did the story line of *The Big Sleep* and *The High Window.*

Marlowe has a talk with Mavis, in the company of Dolores Gonzales, Mavis's longtime friend. Dolores claims to be from Mexico but is actually a native of Cleveland, Ohio; she thus exemplifies the typical Hollywood imposter. At any rate, Mavis maintains that she does not need Marlowe's help in coping with her precarious situation.

Marlowe's investigation of the Orrin Quest case points the way to a physician named Vincent Lagardie, who denies knowing Orrin, yet shortly afterward Marlowe stumbles across Orrin in Lagardie's clinic—dead from a bullet wound. In searching Orrin's corpse, Marlowe uncovers an ice pick, and suspects that Orrin was the ice-pick murderer. Marlowe reasons that Orrin had failed to make it as a reputable photographer in Hollywood and thus had taken to blackmailing celebrities with compromising photos as an alternate occupation. Consequently, Marlowe concludes that it was Orrin who snapped the incriminating pictures of Mavis Weld and Steelgrave together, with a view to blackmailing the actress. Moreover, Marlowe deduces that Orrin iced both Clausen and Hicks with an ice pick, to keep them from horning in on his lucrative scheme to extort money from Mavis.

Marlowe moves on to Steelgrave's hideaway to interrogate him, and discovers the racketeer dead from a bullet wound. After another conversation with Mavis, Marlowe figures out that Mavis Weld is really Leila Quest, the half-sister of Orfamay and Orrin Quest, and that her own half-brother was blackmailing her with Orfamay's knowledge and encouragement.

Marlowe subsequently confronts Orfamay and forces her to admit that she followed Orrin to Hollywood because her brother had ceased sending her regularly a cut of his ill-gotten gains as an extortionist. Orrin, assuming that Orfamay was loyal to him, had revealed to his little sister that he was holed up in Dr. Lagardie's clinic to escape from Steelgrave, who was gunning for Orrin, in order to squelch Orrin's extortion plot. But Orfamay took revenge on her big brother for cheating her out of her share of the proceeds from his blackmail business by selling him out to Steelgrave. Thus Orfamay, the pious puritan from the plains, shows herself to be the hypocrite she really is when she gets to Los Angeles. Liahna Babner writes, "She sheds her spectacles (which Marlowe calls 'cheaters'), her scruples, and her virtue, revealing the cunning self-seeker beneath."[14] One wonders at what point her soul turned to poison.

When last heard from, Orfamay is on her way back to Kansas, since she had no prospects of being party to any more furtive money-making schemes in Hollywood. In *The High Window,* David Smith reminds us, "poor little bespectacled Merle Davis can go home to Wichita" for a wholesome life. "But now, in *The Little Sister,* the evil has entered the soul even in Kansas," whence the conniving Orfamay came to Hollywood in search of Orrin.

And she returns to Manhattan, Kansas, just as amoral as ever.[15] While he was mapping out the novel, Chandler had described Orfamay to Hamish Hamilton as an innocent girl from Kansas who might not be as innocent as she looks. That, as they say, is putting it mildly.

By the same token, Chandler described Dolores Gonzales to Hamilton, in his letter of August 19, 1948, as "the nicest whore I ever didn't meet."[16] Like Orfamay, Dolores is not the nice person she at first appears to be. Dolores is really a nymphomaniac who attempts to seduce Marlowe early on, but he is not taken in by her feminine wiles and in due course builds a solid case against her. Dolores, it turns out, is the typical Hollywood failure, who lacks the talent to pursue a successful film career and is jealous of those who do succeed. Hence, while Mavis has become a film star, Dolores has failed to make the grade as a movie actress, since her efforts to masquerade as a sultry Mexican spitfire for the benefit of casting directors have not paid off.

So Dolores has bitterly settled for being a high-class call girl, while still retaining her fake Spanish accent, in order to pose as a seductive Latin siren for her customers. Marlowe eventually figures out that Dolores, in order to wreak vengeance on Mavis for winning the success that has eluded her, seduced Orrin, whom she met through Mavis, into blackmailing his own half-sister. Dolores subsequently killed Orrin herself because she was afraid that he would eventually stick an ice pick in her, just as he had done to Clausen and Hicks, in order to avoid sharing with Dolores the spoils of the blackmailing scheme he had hatched against Mavis. "He was more than a little crazy," Dolores explains to Marlowe when he has a showdown with her, "and in the end he would have killed me" (247). Ironically, Dolores murdered Orrin before Steelgrave got a chance to do so.

To make matters worse, Marlowe's dogged investigation ultimately discloses that Dolores was once married to Dr. Lagardie, whose clinic is actually a front for his clandestine narcotics ring—that explains Lagardie's willingness to harbor Orrin Quest, a drug addict who was one of Lagardie's best customers. Dolores had jilted Lagardie for Steelgrave, who was in collusion with Lagardie in his shady drug operation. Later on Dolores had a fresh reason for resenting Mavis, when Mavis lured Steelgrave away from her. Dolores accordingly decided that if she could not have Steelgrave, neither would Mavis, so she summarily shot Steelgrave.

Before the law can catch up with Dolores, however, Lagardie, her erstwhile husband, intervenes. He has never forgiven Dolores for leaving him for Steelgrave; in a fit of despair, he corners Dolores in Mavis's apartment and stabs her to death. Because she banished him from her bed in favor of another man, Lagardie ends by penetrating her one last time, but with a knife. Marlowe had guessed that Lagardie planned to have it out with Dolores, so he alerted Lieutenant Christy at police headquarters to rush with him to Dolores's rescue.

When Marlowe and the police arrive at the apartment, however, it is already too late. Marlowe finds Lagardie, as if in a trance, holding the dead Dolores "pressed against his heart" (250). Lagardie has not committed suicide in the wake of the murder, as William Marling mistakenly states; he is not dead, but in a daze because he had murdered the woman he loves. Agatha Christie's detective, Miss Marple, says in the telefilm *A Murder Has Been Announced* that nearly everyone assumes that people kill out of hatred, but it may be out of love. That observation is borne out in *The Little Sister,* when Dolores slays Steelgrave because she loves him, only to be murdered by Lagardie because he loves her. Thus Dolores expressed her motive for killing Steelgrave this way: "The man I loved is dead. I killed him. That man I would not share" (247).

In *The Little Sister* both Orrin and Dolores represent a sort of character that is a fixture in Hollywood novels. They are the typical outsiders who live on the fringe of the film industry and yearn to be insiders, but they have never been able to break into the movie business. Consequently, they remain on the outside looking in, and wondering angrily how they were excluded. Mavis, to quote the song "Hooray for Hollywood," was "the shop girl" who became "a top girl." In the case of Orrin and Dolores, these two Hollywood outsiders express their frustration and disillusionment by turning to crime.

The Little Sister tells a nasty tale of how blackmail, greed, and jealousy can rupture friendships (Mavis and Dolores) and family ties (Mavis, Orfamay, and Orrin). Hollywood, comments Peter Wolfe, "divides and degrades." Moreover, Wolfe sees Hollywood as a dream factory that churns out seductive fantasies for its audiences, which "lead people astray, deluding them with false hopes of wealth, glamour, and fame." Hollywood, "America's dream factory," he continues, "peddles false values, rewarding the gaudy and the superficial; and, with its promise of easy money, encourages crime."[17]

Like West's *Day of the Locust* and Fitzgerald's *Last Tycoon,* Chandler's *Little Sister* presents Hollywood, for all its surface glitter, as the dumping ground for failed dreams. Too late the likes of Dolores Gonzales and Orrin Quest learn, to their great cost, that the only place that dreams are guaranteed to come true in Tinsel Town is on the silver screen—in the films manufactured by the Hollywood dream factory.

In reflecting on the Hollywood rat race, Marlowe muses about Mavis

Weld, "Wonderful what Hollywood will do to a nobody. It will make a radiant glamour queen out of a drab little wench, who ought to be ironing a truck driver's shirts" back in Kansas. Hollywood has turned a smalltown girl like Mavis into an "international courtesan . . . so blasé and decadent" that her idea of a good time is to consort with the local hoodlums. "And so, by remote control, it might even take a small town prig like Orrin Quest and make an ice pick murderer out of him in a matter of months," in the dogged pursuit of the Almighty Dollar (158). Marlowe observes that dealing with the various Hollywood types he encounters in the course of his investigation makes him feel as if he were himself a character in a cheesy low-budget movie.

I have examined Chandler's depiction of Hollywood in the novel in some detail to give the lie to the assertion made by Durham and other Chandler scholars that *Sister* does not qualify as a Hollywood novel like *Day of the Locust* or *The Last Tycoon*. On the contrary, the book's analysis of the movie colony as an emblem of moral degradation is unremitting; it extends from the moguls in the front offices at the top of the heap down to the losers and nobodies at the bottom of the barrel.

One of the representations of Hollywood in the novel is Jules Oppenheimer, who heads the studio that employs Mavis Weld. Chandler indicated in his letter to Mrs. Holton that "the people and events in this book are not entirely fictional."[18] Thus Oppenheimer was modeled on Y. Frank Freeman, the arrogant and high-handed Paramount chief executive during Chandler's years at Paramount. (The standing joke about this mogul around the lot was for someone to ask, "Why Frank Freeman?") Marlowe chances to meet Oppenheimer during a visit to the studio, and Chandler utilizes Freeman's predilection for dogs as the source for a satirical vignette. Oppenheimer's fondness for his three boxers extends to allowing them to urinate on the corner of his desk. "Drives my secretary crazy," he says airily. "Gets into the carpets, they say" (124). This episode epitomizes Chandler's picture of Hollywood as a world capital of vulgarity. "The motion picture business is the only business in the world in which you can make all the mistakes there are and still make money," Oppenheimer opines to Marlowe. Oppenheimer is confident that the public will buy whatever Hollywood sells them, no matter how inferior the product (125).

During his foray onto the studio lot Marlowe also talks with Sheridan Ballou, Mavis's agent, about protecting her from the extortionists who are plaguing her. Chandler later penned an acerbic article about high-powered Hollywood agents, in which he described the typical agent as "a sharp shooter with few scruples" with a heart "as big as an olive pit."[19] Sheridan Ballou certainly fits this description. After getting past Ballou's secretary, who has "a voice that could have been used as paint remover," Marlowe has an audience with the great man himself (107).

The self-inflated Ballou strides up and down the carpet, swinging a Malacca cane, an echo of Chandler's association with Billy Wilder. Wilder's habit of brandishing such a cane during script conferences, we shall see, annoyed Chandler very much. In a not-so-subtle side swipe at Wilder, Marlowe says to Ballou, "It could only happen in Hollywood. . . . That an apparently sane man could walk up and down inside the house with a monkey stick in his hand" (117). When Ballou's assistant warns Marlowe more than once that he cannot address the boss in such a disrespectful manner, Marlowe responds sarcastically, "I forgot to bring my prayerbook. This is the first time I knew God worked on commission" (113). Despite Marlowe's insolent tone, Ballou engages him to foil Mavis's blackmailers; and Marlowe eventually does just that, thereby saving Mavis's career.

Chandler had a habit, we know, of visiting actual locations around Los Angeles that figured in his novels and screenplays, in order to gather material that would lend an authentic flavor to the bleak world he was portraying. He had paid a visit to police headquarters in Los Angeles to do background research for the sequence in *The Blue Dahlia* screenplay in which the police question the suspects in a sensational murder case. Chandler employed the same notes that he had taken on that occasion to provide a true-to-life atmosphere for the scenes in *Sister* in which Philip Marlowe compares notes with Lt. Christy French in French's office about the blackmail case.

In his "Notes on Homicide Bureau," dated January 25, 1945, now in the Helga Greene Private Collection of Chandler's Files, he writes: the captain in charge of the Homicide Bureau "has a flat-top business desk and . . . a hard, wooden swivel chair." Across from his desk is "one straight wooden chair without arms." At another desk sits a secretary with "faded orange-colored hair, . . . making out reports of investigations."[20]

In the novel Marlowe describes "the flat desk" at which Lieutenant French sits in a "swivel chair." In addition, "a woman with orange-colored hair was typing out a report on a typewriter stand beside the desk. . . . I sat down across from him in a straight oak chair without arms" (167, 216). Such was Chandler's attention to authentic detail.

The novel sold seventeen thousand copies in its first hardcover edition in the United States and twenty-seven thousand copies in England, indicating once more that Chandler was more popular in Britain than in his native America. But the French edition, published in the *Série Noire* series (from which the term *film noir* was derived), sold forty-two thousand copies, demonstrating that he was more popular still in France. American reviews of the novel were decidedly mixed. One reviewer termed Chandler a talented hack—which is precisely what Chandler had called George Marshall, the director of *The Blue Dahlia*. Still Chandler could take comfort in the fact that although some American critics thought the book fell below his usual standard, that also meant that the standard Chandler had set for himself in his previous fiction was very high indeed. A few undiscerning American reviewers thought Chandler's scathing exposé of the dirty side of the picture business had degenerated into a sour indictment of the human race.

The notices in the British press were by and large more positive, and English novelist Evelyn Waugh (who had published his own Hollywood novel, *The Loved One,* the year before) even called Chandler "the best writer in America."[21] In a similar vein, novelist-playwright J.B. Priestly placed Chandler's book in the larger context of American fiction. Priestly found that Chandler's Hollywood novel was an exciting, if depressing, picture of Southern California, and that Chandler had rendered his dyspeptic portrait of the movie colony "much more adroitly" than Scott Fitzgerald and Nathanael West, who had also fictionalized in novels their experiences as indentured servants in the studios, had managed to do. He concluded, "It was care for the human race, not his hatred of it, that inspired the vision he presented."[22]

"Chandler's sun-bleached landscape, for all its Hollywood glitter," writes R.W. Lid, "is in part a fallen paradise, a Garden of Eden after the serpent has done his work." The Hollywood of *The Little Sister* is a sink of vice, moral duplicity, and deception, Lid continues. It is a demiparadise populated with grifters, imposters, and hoodlums, and by "lone women on the make or on the downhill, ... people with better days behind them."[23] It is deeply ironic, therefore, that director Paul Bogart (*Torch Song Trilogy*) was able to film Chandler's cynical novel about Hollywood as the land of unfulfilled ambitions and mislaid dreams on the home territory of the very industry that the novel lampoons.

Marlowe: The Film

Chandler himself did not hold out much hope that the screen rights of *The Little Sister* would be purchased by a movie company. As he wrote to Hamish Hamilton on January 11, 1950, "The book is not too admiring of Hollywood," and the studios are "tired of the private dick stories," which had been run to death by a series of inferior detective flicks.[24] By the late 1960s, however, there was a resurgence of interest in the private-eye picture. This revival encompassed, for example, two popular films featuring Frank Sinatra as a gumshoe named Tony Rome: *Tony Rome* (1967) and *The Lady in Cement* (1968). The second film borrowed from *Lady in the Lake*, to the extent that the title character turns up dead in the water.

And so it was that twenty-two years after *The Brasher Doubloon* and *Lady in the Lake* were released in 1947, Metro-Goldwyn-Mayer, which had produced the latter picture, decided to film *The Little Sister* with Paul Bogart at the helm. Academy Award–winning screenwriter Sterling Silliphant (*In the Heat of the Night*) was brought in to do the screen adaptation. Silliphant had met Chandler when Silliphant lived in San Diego, not far from Chandler's home in suburban La Jolla. He admired Chandler's work and wanted to capture the mood of the novel in his script. The world of Raymond Chandler, Silliphant, explained, is one in which the private eye inevitably finds corpses, tangles with low-lifes, and gets roughed up as he hacks his way around Los Angeles. "I put myself on Chandler's stage," Silliphant continued, and "moved along in his footsteps."[25]

The front office at Metro decided to transpose the story's time frame to contemporary Los Angeles. Hence, before beginning the script, Silliphant recalled, he personally scouted locations for the film all over L.A., "finding places that I felt would remind one of the forties," yet had survived into the 1960s. For instance, Silliphant "capitalized on the seedy splendor of the old Hotel Alvarado," and had it stand in for the dilapidated flophouse where the petty criminal George Hicks is ice-picked. Moreover, the old Broadbury Building, which possessed a faded, deteriorated look, seemed just right for Marlowe's office and had actually been used in some forties noir films.

Paul Bogart also wanted to be true to Chandler; thus he wanted to preserve the disenchantment that pervades the novel. "I tried to do what the book told me," he stated, because he saw the director as the instrument of the author. So Bogart wanted Marlowe to appear "tired and threadbare," as in the novel, and he agreed with Silliphant that Marlowe's office should look slightly shoddy. Furthermore, "I had to stop people from cleaning his car every time we were going to do a shot."[26] This situation suggests how Billy Wilder, wishing to establish that the character of Phyllis in *Double Indemnity* was not much of a housekeeper, had to restrain his crew from dusting the set of her living room.

Silliphant updated Chandler's *Little Sister* only in minor ways as he composed the script for the film, entitled *Marlowe* (1969). For example, he made Mavis Wald (Weld in the book) the star of a television sitcom, rather than a movie star, because by the 1960s television had supplanted motion pictures as the dominant medium of mass entertainment. He finished the first draft of the screenplay by the end of June 1967, and it was submitted to Geoffrey Shurlock, who had succeeded Joseph Breen as the industry censor. On July 24 the censor responded that his chief complaint about the screenplay had to do "with various degrees of undress." For example, "Mavis's costume, as described in scene 140, should not be such as to draw vulgar attention to her semi-nudity."[27]

Silliphant's final draft of the script, which is on file at MGM, is dated May 15, 1968, but it includes additional revisions dated from May 27 through July 2, 1968. The final version of scene 140, which is dated July 2 in the final shooting script, indicates that when Marlowe questions Mavis in her apartment, she "wears a hostess gown and little else."[28] Still Marlowe makes no reference in the dialogue to her scanty attire, in keeping with the censor's warning that attention should not be drawn to Mavis's provocative apparel.

Nevertheless, despite the censor's strictures on costuming, the fact remains that the freedom of the screen, as already noted, had progressed by the 1960s well beyond what had been the order of the day when film noir flourished in the 1940s and 1950s. Consequently, "by the late 1960s," William Luhr states, "the reigning structure of censorship" did not prevent the presentation of material considered morally unacceptable in the earlier period. By this time films "could explicitly show material that previously could only be hinted at."[29]

The opening credits of *Marlowe* offer a case in point. During the credits a torrid love scene takes place beside a swimming pool. A young woman emerges from the pool and kisses her lover passionately. Because of the swimming context, they are both nearly naked, attired as they are in brief swim suits. As the pair kiss and caress each other, the screen divides in half. On the left side of the split screen the couple are locked in an embrace, while on the right side a young man is shown hiding in the bushes nearby, photographing them as they make love.

By the end of the credit sequence, then, the plot has been set in motion. The young woman, we subsequently discover, is television star Mavis Wald (Gayle Hunnicutt), the man is her mobster lover, Sonny Steelgrave (H.M. Wynant), and the photographer is none other than Mavis's own brother Orrin Quest (Roger Newman). Orrin is not only a blackmailer but a voyeur, since he seems to enjoy watching the love making he is photographing. His perverse behavior is all the more reprehensible in retrospect, because it involves his own sister (not his half-sister, as in the book).

Asked about the heavy petting in which the couple indulge during this sequence, Bogart shrugged, "It *was* 1969," adding that the actress's exposure in this scene and scene 140, mentioned before, "was relatively temperate" and only "mildly" erotic by the standards of the period when the film was produced.[30]

When Orfamay Quest (Sharon Farrell) shows up in the office of Philip Marlowe (James Garner), his slightly shabby office testifies that he is an honest private eye, and is therefore broke much of the time. She commissions Marlowe to locate her brother Orrin, who has disappeared. Marlowe goes to the ramshackle Hotel Alvarado, where he intends to interrogate Grant Hicks (George Hicks in the novel), whom he had questioned earlier about his connection with Orrin. Hicks is played by Jackie Coogan, best remembered for the title role in Chaplin's classic film *The Kid* (1918). Since *Marlowe* is set in contemporary Hollywood, perhaps the presence of an actor who dates back to the old Hollywood of silent pictures would be recognized by the cognoscenti as a reference to Hollywood's venerable past.

In any case Marlowe finds Hicks dead this time around. It seems that Orrin rubbed out Hicks, who had attempted to muscle in on his scheme to blackmail Mavis Wald. Marlowe next goes to Mavis's apartment for an interview and meets both Mavis and her close friend Dolores Gonzales (Rita Moreno). Rita Moreno was actually born in Puerto Rico, so in the film Dolores is really Hispanic. Hence Dolores is not a pseudo-Latino as she is in the novel, but the genuine article; in the film she is a fiery Latin temptress who works in a strip club. As it happens, both she and Mavis prove uncooperative when Marlowe endeavors to question them, so he gives up for the moment and departs.

Steelgrave, who has gotten wind of Marlowe's visit to Mavis, is waiting for him with three of his goons when Marlowe comes out of the swanky apartment building. Marlowe is brutally beaten by Steelgrave's heavies in an attempt to warn him off the case. Silliphant wanted this scene to be deadly and savage, but he stated that Bogart, who claimed to have a strong distaste for depicting graphic violence on screen, undercut the brutality of this and other violent scenes when he shot them. As a result, Silliphant believed that some of the film's vigor and power were eroded.

Bogart conceded that he wanted to tone down the violence in the film, since mayhem was usually depicted with a minimum of blood and guts in the noir films of the 1940s and 1950s. "There is very little violence in the film," he pointed out. "The one time Marlowe is beaten up, you see it mainly through the car windows," from Steelgrave's point of view, as he watches from inside the car. The fact that the movie avoids the direct depiction of violence adds to the "old fashioned Forties feeling I wanted to convey."[31] Bogart emphasized the film *Marlowe* is not characterized by an excess of violence, as he noted about Marlowe's beating, or of sex, as indicated in his observations about the credit sequence.

A careful examination of the final shooting script makes it clear that some of the nifty lines one hears spoken from the screen are not in the final draft. Thus in the course of the pummeling that Marlowe endures from Steelgrave's thugs, he blurts out to one of them a memorable bit of dialogue: "Does your mother know what you do for a living?" As this dandy payoff line does not appear in the final screenplay, it must have been improvised during the rehearsal of the scene before the cameras turned.[32]

Marlowe returns to his office, only to be met by yet another of Steelgrave's henchman, Winslow Wong (martial arts actor Bruce Lee). When Marlowe rejects Wong's offer of hush money to keep mum about what he has uncovered about Mavis, Wong systematically demolishes Marlowe's office with a few kung fu moves in reprisal.

Wong then cavalierly dons his dark glasses as he goes out into the sunlight. The brilliant sunshine brings into relief how brightly lit several of the exterior scenes are. Since *Marlowe* was the first Marlowe film to be shot in color, Bogart decided to replace the ominously dark atmosphere of the earlier films of the Forties with some grim scenes of violence shot in broad daylight. Both the beating of Marlowe and the trashing of his office take place on the same sunny day.

These scenes imply that, in a savage world, evil is just as likely to strike in the daytime as at night, under cover of darkness. Hence, although *Marlowe* is suffused with noir-like sadism and double-dealing, it is photographed by Academy Award-winning cinematographer William H. Daniels (*The Naked City*) in band box colors. The glossy brightness of the movie's color, comments Charles Gregory, "only re-emphasizes the harshness of the Southern California landscape."[33]

Undeterred by threats and bribes, Marlowe makes a junket to the television studio where Mavis films her show in order to confer with Mr. Crowell (Sheridan Ballou in the novel), Mavis's high-powered agent. Silliphant describes Crowell in the script as sitting behind "a desk Napoleon might have owned if he hadn't blown Waterloo."[34] Crowell (William Daniels, not to be confused with cinematographer William H. Daniels) gives Marlowe a tour of the studio, and they wind up in a television control room, briefly watching on a television monitor a noisy dance number from a crass variety show that Crowell is involved with. But Marlowe's eyes stray to another monitor, on which he can view, according to the script, "an old MGM movie on the early show."[35] Marlowe then has an interchange with Crowell, which is not in the screenplay and presumably was invented by the director and the actors on the set.

The old MGM movie Marlowe is watching (which Silliphant does not specify in the screenplay) is the 1932 Greta Garbo starrer *Grand Hotel*. Watching Garbo emote, Marlowe muses wistfully, "She was great, wasn't she?" Pointing to the other monitor, Crowell barks irritably, "The show we are doing is over there!"

"The updating of Chandler's Hollywood setting to television works well," says Kim Newman; and Mr. Crowell, the nervy television agent who has to explain to Marlowe, among other things, what a sitcom is, is a "perfectly Chandleresque figure."[36] Crowell is a satirical portrait à la Chandler of a typical television executive, who simply cannot comprehend how Marlowe could prefer a classic film to the latest television pap. (Chandler's low opinion of television executives, gained from his negotiations about a Marlowe television series, will be mentioned later.) At all events, the clip from a vintage Garbo movie, as well as the presence of old time movie star Jackie Coogan in the cast, may be taken as references to the glory days of old Hollywood, now long gone.

In addition, Marlowe's preference for a golden oldie like *Grand Hotel* over a trashy, banal contemporary television show is also significant because it implies that Marlowe is old fashioned. As Edward Gallafent observes, Marlowe's adherence to the old fashioned values of the past "is constantly being reinforced in the film," for the movie exposes "the central characters, apart from Marlowe, as more or less representative of the worthlessness of contemporary society."[37] Finally, the insertion of the clip from *Grand Hotel* is an implicit homage to cinematographer William H. Daniels, who was renowned for photographing Garbo's best movies, *Grand Hotel* among them.

In a later scene Crowell engages Marlowe to protect his invaluable client from the blackmailers. As Crowell puts it, Mavis's public must never know that she has been "shacking up with public enemy number one." In this scene Bogart and Silliphant make use of Chandler's dialogue, as they do elsewhere in the picture. For example, Crowell frankly tells Marlowe in the film that he respects him as a private investigator with some integrity, in these words from the book: "One of these days I'm going to make the mistake a man in my spot dreads above all other mistakes. I'm going to find myself doing business with a man I can trust, and I'm going to be just too damned smart to trust him" (121).

Still later Marlowe reports Steelgrave's slaying to Lieutenant French (Carroll O'Connor); it is not the first corpse that Marlowe has stumbled on in the course of his investigation. Lieutenant French, who does not share Crowell's positive attitude of Marlowe, takes this occasion to tell him so. In his opinion, Marlowe is a bungling gumshoe, a cheap keyhole peeper, whose meddling in police affairs has done more harm than good. French's lengthy, bitter diatribe against Marlowe is taken almost verbatim from the novel. I reproduce here some of the passage from the book, in order to give its flavor, indicating by brackets lines that Silliphant cut in the script:

> It's like this with us, baby. We're coppers and everybody hates our guts. And if we didn't have enough trouble, we have to have you. [As if we didn't get pushed around enough by the guys in the corner offices, the City Hall gang. . . . As if we didn't have to handle one hundred and fourteen homicides last year out of three rooms that don't have enough chairs for the whole duty squad to sit down in at once.] We spend our lives turning over dirty underwear and sniffing rotten teeth. We go up dark stairways to get a punk with a skinful of hop and sometimes we don't get all the way up. . . . But that ain't enough to make us entirely happy. We've got to have you. (novel, 211–12; cf. screenplay, 115)

After French finishes his denunciation of Marlowe, the latter admits to the tired cop that a policeman's lot is not a happy one, but, he adds, neither is the lot of a hapless shamus. He expands on this remark later in the picture. Recalling the savage going over he got from Steelgrave's thugs and the demolition of his office by Winslow Wong, Marlowe reflects that he has been beaten and "generally snookered. I ache all over. My office qualifies for urban renewal. I'd say that's an average day" for a private eye.

As in the novel, Marlowe has come to realize by this time that what his current case amounts to, in essence, is that he was hired by a bitch to find scum. That is, the wily Orfamay Quest sent him to find her no-account brother Orrin, solely in order to cash in on Orrin's plot to blackmail their own sister.

Marlowe meets with both Orfamay and Mavis at his house; when Mavis grasps the fact that her little sister was bent on exploiting her for financial gain, she furiously slaps Orfamay across the face, and they engage in a free-for-all. Marlowe breaks up the family brawl, then he warns Orfamay that he will turn her over to the police, unless she goes back to Manhattan, Kansas, and stays there. She exits, weeping and whining about how badly her older brother and sister have treated her; thus she behaves to the last like the helpless little girl that she has always pretended to be. Marlowe, for good measure, burns the compromising photos of Mavis and Steelgrave, in order to foil in advance any further attempts on the part of Orfamay or anyone else to extort money from Mavis, who is now his client.

Next Marlowe proceeds to the strip club where Dolores does her lewd act; he watches her perform, while he sits in the wings close to the stage. Marlowe tells Dolores, as she dances by, the way he has finally sorted things out: Dolores spurned her husband, Dr. Lagardie, and took up with Steelgrave; she subsequently shot Steelgrave when he jilted her for Mavis. Dolores dances close to the place where Marlowe is sitting, just out of sight of the audience, and confesses killing Steelgrave out of sexual jealousy: "I couldn't share him," she says, "not even with Mavis." She likewise admits her abiding professional jealousy of Mavis's success as a film star: "Why should Mavis get all the goodies?"

In transferring Marlowe's showdown with Dolores from Mavis's apartment in the book to the gaudy strip club, says Kim Newman, Bogart cannily allows the tramp Dolores to be revealed as the culprit "during a marvelously raucous jazz strip routine."[38] Furthermore, her exposure as the villainess is implicitly linked with her stripping off her costume during her nightclub act, as Marlowe exposes the bare facts about what she has done and why.

At this point Dr. Lagardie, who has followed Marlowe to the club, comes in the stage door with blood in his eye. From the wings he shoots Dolores dead, right in the middle of her act, then turns the gun on himself. The stunned Marlowe phones the police. Lagardie's fingernails scrape against the wall as he sinks slowly to the floor, symbolizing his life ebbing away.

In the book Lagardie does not commit suicide after he murders Dolores. Nor does he kill himself in the script, which follows the novel on this point; instead, the screenplay describes the doctor as gazing at Dolores's corpse "while his eyes are filled with tears."[39] Bogart's departure from both book and the script by having Lagardie take his own life allows us to call into question Bogart's contention that he wished to minimize the violence in the film. After all, he supplies two bloody deaths at the finale, where Chandler and Silliphant provided only one.

Not a few Chandler scholars agree that James Garner (*The Great Escape*) makes an acceptable Marlowe on screen; his breezy, flippant style recalls Dick Powell's "appealing chipper-whatever-the-odds attitude," says Curtis Brown.[40] The Nash-Ross *Motion Picture Guide* erroneously asserts that Garner's performance lacks the cynical edge that Alan Ladd brought to the role; Ladd, we shall see, starred as Johnny Morrison in Chandler's *Blue Dahlia* but never played Philip Marlowe.[41] Indeed, Garner enacts the role of Marlowe pretty much as Chandler conceived the character, as a knight errant maintaining his code of honor in a deceitful and corrupt world. Silliphant averred that Chandler's Marlowe was relevant to contemporary society. Chandler envisioned Marlowe as a "shabby knight with all kinds of chinks in his armor," said Silliphant. Nevertheless, his knightly ideals seem even more noble in today's society than in the 1940s, he continued. "I do not agree with the critics who say that Marlowe's attitudes do not fit with contemporary society. I say, rather, that contemporary society's attitudes do not fit with Marlowe's attitudes, but Marlowe's are more enduring." And that is all the more reason why Silliphant endeavored in his script to "preserve the purity of the original character."[42]

Putting it another way, Paul Bogart's 1969 film is reasonably loyal to Chandler's 1949 novel, to the extent that the movie adaptation shows that Chandler's hero has survived from the 1940s into the 1960s, with his strength of character intact. Moreover, *Marlowe* "retains the flavor of the earlier Marlowe films," according to Charles Gregory, the movie's strongest champion. Thus Bogart and Silliphant drew of the noir tradition in their careful selection of period locations. "Marlowe's old office building, with its rococo iron work and wood interiors," Gregory comments, suggests a faded glamour that reminds us of "the dying inner city." So does the disreputable Hotel Alvarado, where Orrin Quest and other low lifes hang out.

In addition Bogart foregrounds characters who harken back to the conventions of film noir, in which the previous Marlowe films are steeped, such as the femme fatale. Like the book, *Marlowe* provides not one but two such evil females. Dolores, the alluring showgirl who seems to have a soft heart, finally emerges as a deadly siren with a heart of steel. The Oscar-winning actress Rita Moreno (*West Side Story*) gives a powerful performance as the tough, soiled Dolores. Sharon Farrell (*The Reivers*) ably plays the puritanical little sister from the farm belt, who turns out to be a calloused, cold-blooded predator. Gregory says that, taken together, Dolores and Orfamay suggest a greater breadth of corruption in the movie "than a single femme fatale would project." They both have the tang of genuine noir. In brief, the film demonstrates that it is possible to delineate an intricate mystery plot without marginalizing the complex characters involved.

The body count at film's end is significant: Orrin exterminates two grifters; Dolores, in turn, slays Orrin as well as Steelgrave; and Lagardie, in turn, murders Dolores and then kills himself. It is evident that in film noir death is the regular solution to problems. Bogart's assured direction, Silliphant's literate script, and Garner's polished performance as Marlowe "all gain in confidence and richness because they are working within a real tradition," Gregory concludes. "*Marlowe* doesn't add to the noir tradition, but rather maintains it in a worthy manner."[43] I have highlighted Gregory's enthusiastic assessment of the film to counteract the lukewarm critical reception that greeted the movie when it opened. Gregory makes it clear that *Marlowe* is a film of impressive scale and craft. Along with *The Brasher Doubloon,* it is one of the most underrated Marlowe movies up to this time.

Garner recreated the role of Philip Marlowe under the name of shamus Jim Rockford in the television series *The Rockford Files.* The series, which had a successful run from 1974 to 1980, was produced by Roy Huggins, a Chandler aficionado who assembled the Huggins Private Collection of Chandler's Papers. Rockford's affinity with Marlowe is clear from the series pilot, in which Rockford recalls Marlowe in several ways: Like Marlowe, Rockford is an honest gumshoe who operates out of a crummy office; he extends his help even to impecunious clients who cannot afford his fee; and he is a prickly thorn in the side of the police department. Moreover, the pilot episode, entitled "Backlash of the Hunter" (1974), is reminiscent of *Farewell, My Lovely,* in that Rockford must deal with a wealthy ex-chorine who is being blackmailed by a wiley confidence man who knows about her sordid past (think of Helen Grayle and Jules Amthor).

In addition, a special feature-length segment of the series, "Lions, Tigers, Monkeys and Dogs" (1979), which co-stars Lauren Bacall (*The Big Sleep*) has Rockford pitted against just the kind of femme fatale who is a staple of Chandler's fiction, from Helen Grayle to Eileen Wade—a wicked lady who is prepared to liquidate anyone who is able to unmask her shady past.

In another entry in the series, "The Kirkoff Case" (1974), Garner repeats a line from the movie *Marlowe;* he inquires of a thug in the television episode, just as he did in the theatrical film, "Does your mother know what you do for a living?" (All of the episodes mentioned above are available on video cassette, so the reader may judge for himself or herself the striking parallels between Marlowe and Rockford.)

Garner was reunited with Rita Moreno in a 1978 episode of the series in which she won an Emmy for her role as a trollop with the proverbial heart of gold. Moreno appeared again in the same part opposite Marlowe's Chandleresque private eye in the 1999 television feature film of *The Rockford Files.*

At all events, *The Little Sister* has not lost its appeal. In 1997 Simon and Schuster released a version of the book as a graphic novel. That is, the story is told with drawings, comic-book-style. Marilyn Stasio praised this version of Chandler's novel, entitled *Raymond Chandler's Philip Marlowe: The Little Sister,* for the dialogue, "respectfully extracted by Michael Lark from Chandler's bitter, twisted" novel, and for Lark's "boldly executed illustrations." As in the novel itself, lies spill from the lips of alluring women, and Marlowe is pictured brooding behind the blinds of his dingy office, while the city outside is bathed in a sinister darkness.[44]

Perhaps Nicholas Freeling was unwittingly predicting the illustrated version of *The Little Sister* when he described Dolores Gonzales in the novel as a lady with a "phony Spanish accent and phonier emotions," like a character drawn for a comic strip.[45] Anyway, if the graphic novel of *The Little Sister* sends its readers to Chandler's book and/or the film on video, so much the better.

Raymond Chandler and director Billy Wilder at work on *Double Indemnity*. Despite their fierce creative differences, they turned out a superior screenplay. (UCLA Raymond Chandler Collection)

(Above) Femme fatale Phyllis Dietrichson (Barbara Stanwyck) eavesdrops on Walter Neff (*left,* Fred MacMurray) and Barton Keyes (Edward G. Robinson) in *Double Indemnity.* (Museum of Modern Art/Film Stills Archive) *(Below)* Walter Neff (*left,* Fred MacMurray) and Barton Keyes (Edward G. Robinson) in the alternate ending of *Double Indemnity,* which replaced the original ending. (Museum of Modern Art)

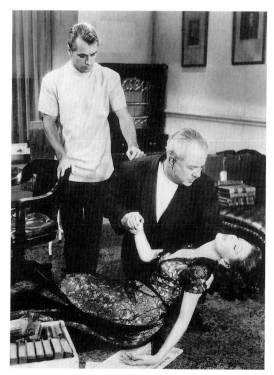

(Above) Left to right: Jasper Goodwin (Norman Lloyd), Dr. Charles Evans (Herbert Marshall), and David Fielding (Joel McRae) compare notes in *The Unseen,* a thriller that Chandler cowrote. (Museum of Modern Art) *(Right)* Dr. Merek Vance (*standing,* Alan Ladd) and Dr. Weeks (Cecil Kellaway) tend to their patient, Emily Blair (Loretta Young) in a tear jerker for which Chandler supplied some lively dialogue. (Museum of Modern Art)

(Above) Johnny Morrison (Alan Ladd) and Joyce Harwood (Veronica Lake) are apprehensive in *The Blue Dahlia,* the only original screenplay of Chandler's to reach the screen. (Museum of Modern Art) *(Below)* The carousel scene from *Strangers on a Train* as filmed, with Bruno Antony (Robert Walker) and Guy Haines (Farley Granger, *dark blazer*) locked in a death struggle. (Museum of Modern Art)

Alfred Hitchcock and Robert Walker take a breather while shooting the climatic merry-go-round sequence in *Strangers on a Train,* the last screenplay Chandler cowrote. (Museum of Modern Art)

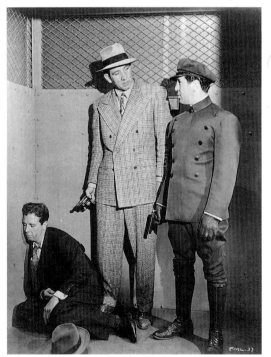

(Above) George Sanders (*right*) as the sleuth and Allen Jenkens as his sidekick in *The Falcon Takes Over*, loosely based on Chandler's *Farewell, My Lovely.* (Museum of Modern Art)

(Left) The unconscious detective Philip Marlowe (Dick Powell), hoodlum Moose Malloy (*center,* Mike Mazurki), and Moose's henchman in *Murder, My Sweet,* a faithful rendition of *Farewell, My Lovely.* (Museum of Modern Art)

(Above) The perfidious Jules Amthor (*left*, Otto Krueger) and Moose Malloy (Mike Mazurki) have a showdown with Marlowe (Dick Powell) in *Murder, My Sweet.* (Museum of Modern Art) *(Below)* Robert Mitchum (*left*) plays Philip Marlowe and Jack O'Halloran plays Moose Malloy in the third film version of *Farewell, My Lovely,* filmed with the novel's title. (Museum of Modern Art)

Gangster Eddie Mars (John Ridgely) stands in the background as his mobsters search Philip Marlowe (Humphrey Bogart) in *The Big Sleep*. (Museum of Modern Art)

Lauren Bacall, as Vivien Rutledge, and Humphrey Bogart, as Marlowe, in *The Big Sleep.* Bogart is considered the best of all of the actors who played Marlowe. (Museum of Modern Art)

(*Above*) Robert Mitchum plays Marlowe and Sarah Miles plays Vivian in the remake of *The Big Sleep*. (Museum of Modern Art) (*Below*) Merle Davis (*seated*,
Heather Sears) listens as the private eye (Lloyd Nolan) examines evidence with a
cop (Richard Lane) in *Time to Kill*, freely adapted from *The High Window*. (Museum of Modern Art)

(Above) Nancy Guild plays Merle Davis and George Montgomery plays private detective Marlowe in the faithful adaptation of *The High Window* entitled *The Brasher Doubloon.* (Museum of Modern Art) *(Below)* Mrs. Murdock (Florence Bates) misleads Marlowe (George Montgomery) in *The Brasher Doubloon.* (Museum of Modern Art)

Because the camera photographs the action of *Lady in the Lake* from the point of view of Philip Marlowe (Robert Montgomery), he is usually seen only when his image is reflected in a mirror, as here, with Adrienne Fromsett (Audrey Totter). (Museum of Modern Art)

(*Above*) Marlowe (Robert Montgomery) and Adrienne Fromsett (Audrey Trotter) in the final scene of *Lady in the Lake,* the only time they are seen on the screen together in the same shot in the entire film. (Museum of Modern Art) (*Below*) Marlowe (James Garner) is open for business in *Marlowe,* based on *The Little Sister.* (Museum of Modern Art)

Marlowe (James Garner) is attacked by an irate client, Orfamay Quest (Sharon Farrell), in *Marlowe*. (Museum of Modern Art)

(*Above*) Novelist Roger Wade (*seated,* Sterling Hayden) and his wife Eileen (Nina van Pallandt) lie to Philip Marlowe (Elliott Gould) in *The Long Goodbye.* Chandler fans complained that the film made some unforgivable departures from the novel. (Museum of Modern Art) (*Below*) Marlowe (*center,* Elliott Gould) confronts the sinister Dr. Verringer (*right,* Henry Gibson) in *The Long Goodbye.* (Museum of Modern Art)

James Caan plays Marlowe in *Poodle Springs*, based on Chandler's last, unfinished novel, which was completed by Robert B. Parker. (Museum of Modern Art)

8

Modern Times

The Long Goodbye

Los Angeles is the city of grime, crime, and slime.
> —Catherine Tango, a cabaret performer,
> in the film *Tango and Cash*

Let's watch the world go to hell, one soul at a time.
> —Ferris, a secret agent, in the film *Crossworlds*

Raymond Chandler was determined to make *The Long Goodbye* his major effort as a novelist. It is not only one hundred pages longer than any of his previous books but also filled with all sorts of reflections about the world in which Marlowe lives and works. These comments on modern society, says Frank MacShane, "are a natural part of the story and are not obtrusive"; what's more, they enrich the narrative.[1]

Chandler devoted himself to the book in earnest, once he had severed his Hollywood connection in 1947, in the wake of his unpleasant collaboration with Hitchcock on *Strangers on a Train*. The working title of the novel was *Summer in Idle Valley;* Idle Valley was Chandler's name for the exclusive suburb of Los Angeles inhabited by the very rich characters in the book. On May 14, 1952, he sent the first draft of ninety-two thousand words to Bernice Baumgarten, an associate of his literary agent, Carl Brandt. Chandler emphasized to her that his intention was to make the book a serious novel first and foremost, and only secondarily a mystery story. Chandler explained that, as he matured as a novelist, he became increasingly more concerned about both character development and moral dilemmas, "rather than who cracked who on the head." He was not interested in turning out "comic books" like his fellow crime writer Mickey Spillane (*Kiss Me Deadly*). Chandler did not even care whether he solution to the mystery was fairly obvious, but, he said, "I cared about the people, about this strange, corrupt world in which we live." Most of all, he cared about Marlowe "and how any man who tried to be honest looks in the end either sentimental or plain foolish."[2]

Baumgarten replied on May 22 that she and Brandt both agreed that Chandler had made Marlowe too much of a virtuous white knight, even Christ-like. Chandler was troubled, not to say resentful, about this critique of the novel. He responded to Baumgarten on May 25 that he was aware that he had softened the character of Marlowe somewhat, he had done so deliberately because he was convinced that Marlowe was becoming too hard-boiled. But he decidedly did not believe that Marlowe had become Christ-like. Chandler stated that although he planned to revise the manuscript, he had no intention of making Marlowe less heroic than he had presented him in the first draft.

Chandler pictured Marlowe as pursuing his career as a PI in a savage, materialistic world in which individuals chisel each other to get ahead. By contrast, he presents Marlowe as espousing a chivalric code of honor that is considered obsolete by the cynical types he encounters, who sneer at him for being "plain foolish." In addition, Marlowe, in carrying on his crusade against crime, never racks up a decisive victory over the forces of evil; to that extent he remains something of a failure. Nevertheless, although Marlowe sees himself ultimately as a loser, he always goes down swinging, and there is something to admire in that.

After all, Chandler had always envisioned Marlowe as a noble figure. A detective like Marlowe, Chandler had affirmed more than once, must be "a man of honor. . . . He must be the best man in his world."[3] "I know that, whatever errors of emphasis or plot" the manuscript contains, he concluded in his letter to Baumgarten, "it is fundamentally all right."[4] Disgruntled with Baumgarten's criticism of the manuscript, he terminated his association with the Brandt agency not long after.

Chandler spent the summer vacationing abroad; in the fall he began working diligently on the second draft of the novel, which he was determined would be the most ambitious of the Marlowe books. Chandler completed the second draft in June 1953 and shipped copies off to both his American and British publishers. Hamish Hamilton, Chandler's English publisher, and Roger Machell, his editor at the London press, thought the working title of the book *Summer in Idle Valley,* somewhat anemic. Chandler then came up with *The Long Goodbye,* which has more resonance.

Although Chandler had ceased to cannibalize his short fiction for his novels as a regular practice, he did use in *The Long Goodbye* a small bit of material from *The Curtain,* the same novella he had cannibalized extensively for *The Big Sleep.* E.M. Beekman points out that a comparison of the opening of *The Curtain* with the opening of *The Long Goodbye* illustrates "Chandler's method of skillfully amplifying a brief sentence" into an elaborate and vivid description.[5] *The Curtain* begins: "The first time I ever saw Larry Batzel he was drunk outside Sardi's in a secondhand Rolls-Royce."[6] The very first sentence of the novelette is transformed into an entire paragraph in the novel, with Larry Batzel now called Terry Lennox: "The first time I laid eyes on Terry Lennox he was drunk in a Rolls-Royce Silver Wraith outside the terrace of the Dancers. . . . You could tell by his eyes that he was plastered to the hairline, but otherwise he looked like any other nice young man in a dinner jacket who had been spending too much money in a joint that exists for that purpose."[7]

Marlowe takes charge of Terry, and he decides to shepherd him to his own place and "sober him enough to tell me where he lives" (5). Marlowe's behavior on this occasion proves that he will dutifully aid people whom no one else is inclined to help. After Marlowe saves Terry from a trip to the drunk tank, they become friends and drinking buddies.

Marlowe's rescue of Larry at the Dancers is only the beginning of Larry's dependence on him. Terry arrives on Marlowe's doorstep one morning at 5:00 A.M., his face hidden under a fedora so that he will not be recognized by any of the neighbors. He asks Marlowe to drive him to Tijuana, a town on the Mexican border. Terry hints that his wealthy wife Sylvia has been murdered, and that he is unjustly accused of the crime on the basis of purely circumstantial evidence. Abiding by the principle that a friend in need is a friend indeed, Marlowe stands by Terry in this crisis and agrees to Terry's request. He even insists that Terry tell him nothing specific about his escape plans, so that he will be unable to give the police any information about Terry's whereabouts. But Marlowe spends three days in the jug just the same, for refusing to cooperate with the police investigation of Terry's disappearance right after Sylvia's murder.

Later on Marlowe receives word that Terry has killed himself in Otatoclán, a Mexican village, and left behind a suicide note confessing that he murdered Sylvia. Marlowe believes that Terry is dead, but he suspects that the so-called suicide note is a forgery and loyally refuses to believe that

Terry murdered Sylvia. Nevertheless, the police consider the case officially closed. Marlowe receives a farewell letter from Terry, written before his suicide, along with a five-thousand-dollar bill.

At this point in the novel Chandler breaks off the Terry Lennox plot and introduces a second story line. Eileen Wade engages Marlowe to find her missing husband Roger, a hack writer, author of best-selling escapist fiction, and an alcoholic. In creating Roger Wade, Chandler was possibly cribbing from his own life, since he was both a novelist and a heavy drinker.

Marlowe resourcefully tracks down Roger at a disreputable private sanatorium, where he has gone to dry out. The shady clinic is run by Dr. Verringer, who unethically dispenses illegal drugs to his patients. Chandler thus gives us yet another quack medico, cast in the same mold as the physicians in *Farewell, My Lovely, The Lady in the Lake,* and *The Little Sister.* In any case, Marlowe insists on taking Roger home, over Dr. Verringer's vociferous objections.

In checking up on Roger Wade, Marlowe ferrets out some unpleasant facts about him, among them that Roger was having an affair with Sylvia Lennox, Terry's deceased wife. This fact provides a link between the Terry Lennox case, which he still refuses to accept as closed, and the Roger Wade case. Before Marlowe can carry his investigations much further, though, Roger is found in his study dead from a gunshot wound, which may or may not have been self-inflicted. According to the investigating officer, Lt. Bernie Ohls, Roger perhaps shot himself in drunken despair because he had been suffering from writer's block for some time. Bernie Ohls, by the way, is the friendly cop who first appeared in *The Big Sleep.*

After Roger dies in questionable circumstances, Marlowe focuses his attention on digging up what he can about Eileen. He soon discovers that Eileen was married to Terry, when he was known as Paul Marston, but she had lost contact with him after he was captured by the Nazis and interned in a prisoner-of-war camp during World War II. Eileen's erstwhile husband, Paul Marston, was presumed to have died in captivity, and in due course she met and married Roger Wade.

Later on, however, Paul Marston, now known as Terry Lennox, turned up quite unexpectedly in Los Angeles, where he wooed and won Sylvia Potter, an heiress. Then, in one of those rather extraordinary coincidences that crop up in Chandler's fiction, the Lennoxes move into the same neighborhood where the Wades live. However, neither Eileen nor Terry ever acknowledged publicly their past relationship. Chandler melds the Terry-Sylvia plot line with the Eileen-Roger plot line through Terry: he is not only still legally married to Eileen (since they were never divorced) but also the putative husband of the murdered Sylvia (who never knew that Terry was a bigamist). Marlowe advises Eileen that he has deduced that it is she, not Terry, who killed Sylvia; her motive was sexual jealousy, since she still loved Terry passionately. She also wiped out Roger and arranged his death to look like suicide, because he had guessed that she had savagely slaughtered Sylvia, and he was too much of an unstable drunk to be relied upon to keep her guilty secret.

Eileen soon after pens a suicide note, confessing to both the murder of Sylvia and of her husband, and then takes a fatal overdose of drugs. The intrepid Marlowe surreptitiously gets hold of a copy of Eileen's confession and leaks it to the press, in an effort to clear the name of his dead friend Terry. When the sensational scandal hits the local papers, the denizens of Idle Valley feel that, although it is not yet high summer, things are heating up in all directions.

Marlowe receives a visit in his office form a Señor Cisco Maioranos, who says that he knew Terry. But Marlowe sees past his visitor's disguise and realizes that the man is actually Terry Lennox, whose features have been altered by plastic surgery. Terry had faked his own suicide in order to bail himself out of the trouble caused by Sylvia's death; he was, after all, the prime suspect in the case. Terry, with his enduring talent for self-deception, is unrepentant; he cannot see that he has any reason to reproach himself for his actions. As he sees it, he may have abandoned Eileen to marry an heiress, but that freed her to marry a rich writer, after Terry's own disappearance. Furthermore, he could not have foreseen that Eileen would eventually rub out both his wife and her husband, with a view to being ultimately reunited with him. Marlowe, however, is totally disillusioned with his conniving former friend and tells him so; he even returns the five-thousand-dollar bill Terry had mailed to him from Mexico. Moreover, Marlowe refuses to renew his friendship with Terry, and they part for good at novel's end.

In retrospect, we see that Eileen Wade is a bona fide femme fatale, in the tradition of other Chandler villainesses, such as Helen Grayle and Muriel Chess. Such a creature, writes William Phillips, is "an attractive, young, worldly woman who is . . . evasive, dangerous, perhaps even lethal, especially to the men who succumb to her wiles and charms"—for example, her putative husband, Roger, whom she married on the rebound after losing Terry and finally shot.[8]

Chandler believed enough in *The Long Goodbye* to refine the manuscript with diligence. As a matter of fact, the passages he rewrote encompass

250 half-sheets of typescript. The typescript of the novel in the Chandler Collection at the UCLA Library shows, for instance, his careful reworking of the book's penultimate paragraph. The original version of the paragraph reads: Terry "turned away and went out. I watched the door close and listened to his steps going away. After a little while, I couldn't hear them, but I kept listening."[9]

The final version reads: "He turned and walked across the floor and out. I watched the door close. I listened to his steps going away down the imitation marble corridor. After a while they got faint, then they got silent. I kept on listening anyway. What for? Did I want him to stop suddenly and turn and come back and talk me out of the way I felt? Well, he didn't. That was the last I saw of him" (379). The final version of the paragraph reveals more clearly Marlowe's emotional state. He deeply regrets the irrevocable loss of a friendship he had once cherished. "In general," MacShane correctly comments, "Chandler's revisions make the episodes more dramatic and give them deeper texture, so that the reader is brought more fully into the minds and feelings of his characters."[10]

Gershon Legman, we know, contended that Marlowe's friendships with attractive young men like Terry in this novel or "Red" in *Farewell, My Lovely* prove that Marlowe is, like his namesake Christopher Marlowe, the Elizabethan playwright (*Doctor Faustus*), "clearly homosexual."[11] Indeed, Chandler reported receiving a "nasty" letter from Gershon Legman in which Legman asserted quite gratuitously that Chandler himself was a "homosexualist."[12]

On the contrary, Chandler had been quite a womanizer in his younger days. As a rule, he did not socialize with the homosexual set in Los Angeles; screenwriter Christopher Isherwood (*The Loved One*) was virtually his only homosexual friend. Then, too, Hiney cites Chandler's critical observations about homosexuals: "I do think that homosexuals, . . . however artistic and full of taste they may be, always lack any deep emotional feeling. Their physical bravery was proved in the war, but they are still essentially the dilettante type."

What's more, Hiney points out that Legman seemed totally unaware that, from the days when the hard-boiled detective stories first emerged in the pages of *Black Mask,* the conventional hero-protagonists "were invariably bachelors" like Marlowe, who usually got along best with other men. Consequently, Chandler's novels, Hiney emphasizes, should never be analyzed outside "the context of their *Black Mask* roots," if they are to be properly understood.[13]

In the particular case of Marlowe's friendship with Terry Lennox, Beekman points out that "Marlowe finds himself enticed into a bond of friendship" with Terry because of the warmth and compassion he often feels toward someone in trouble.[14] "Terry Lennox made me plenty of trouble," Marlowe reflects after their first meeting. "But after all that's my line of work" (6). Marlowe continues to befriend Terry after that first encounter, because genuine friendship demands such loyalty. As a result, Marlowe drives Terry to Tijuana, with no questions asked, as a simple gesture of friendship. And he refuses to disclose to the police the place where he took Terry because "no man likes to betray a friend" (48).

Marlowe's relationship with Terry does not turn sour until Terry resurfaces as Cisco Maioranos. Peter Wolfe opines that chameleonlike characters who operate under a variety of names in Chandler's fiction, like Muriel Chess and Terry Lennox, lack a "stable selfhood." Like Muriel Chess, Terry had acquired enough different names to start his own phone book, to paraphrase Marlowe in the film of *Lady in the Lake*. Whenever the going gets tough for Terry, he manufactures another identity for himself, so that his multiple identities have finally robbed him of "a firm foothold" in life, according to Wolfe.[15] Even Eileen Wade, in her suicide note, expressed pity for Terry because he had become "the empty shell" of the man she had once known as Paul Marston (328–29).

Terry's final pseudonym is Maioranos (*mayor años*, "better years" in Spanish). Terry had certainly seen better days (and years) before he went into self-imposed exile south of the border and pretended to be dead. As he explained to Marlowe, he pretended to commit suicide to get the police to stop looking for him, because he feared that he would be railroaded into the gas chamber for Sylvia's murder. "Look, I couldn't help what I did," he whines. "I didn't want anyone to get hurt. I wouldn't have had a chance up here" (376). Marlowe is not impressed with Terry's lame excuses; in the last analysis, he rejects Terry because Terry is a crass opportunist, who slyly manipulated Marlowe for his own purposes. He simply does not meet Marlowe's moral standards of honest and decent behavior. Marlowe tells Terry that his personal standards have "no relation to any kind of ethics or scruples" (377).

By novel's end, Marlowe is painfully aware that "the loyalty he bestowed on Terry Lennox" seems mere "folly," says Robert Merrill.[16] Going a step further, one could say that Marlowe's mourning period for his "deceased" friend Terry—Marlowe's long goodbye—has been nothing more than the pointless act of a dupe and a chump.

Therefore it comes as no surprise that, when Terry pleads with Marlowe to renew their friendship during their last encounter, his efforts are fruitless. To Terry's remark that "we were pretty good friends," Marlowe replies laconically, "That was two other fellows" (376–77). Indeed, Terry does not even have the same identity that he had when Marlowe knew him. Moreover, under his real name, Paul Marston, he and Philip Marlowe were symbolically linked by sharing the same initials. But Paul Marston and Terry Lennox have both been replaced by Cisco Morianos, with whom Marlowe senses no kinship whatever. Marlowe pounds the last nail into the coffin of their relationship by stating flatly, "It was nice while it lasted. So long, amigo. I won't say goodbye. I said it to you when it meant something" (378).

The novel takes its title from a French proverb—"To say goodbye is to die a little"—which Marlowe quotes toward the end of the novel (365). When Marlowe renounces his "deep personal attachment" to Terry, Wolfe notes, he is left "feeling bruised and alone."[17] He has, in fact, died a little. *The Long Goodbye* charts the fading friendship between Marlowe and Terry, which finally dies when Marlowe discovers that Terry is unworthy of the personal investment that he made in him.

If there is a homosexual relationship in *The Long Goodbye*, it is between Dr. Verringer and Earl Wild, the musclebound young caretaker of Verringer's rest home. Earl's gaudy silk shorts and skin-tight pants smack of the male hustler. Dr. Verringer is obviously smitten with Earl, despite the lad's wild temper tantrums, and he is subservient in ministering abjectly to Earl's whims. Verringer is emotionally dependent on his relationship with a younger male in a way that Marlowe is not. The doctor maintains his relationship with Earl, regardless of how the selfish young man manipulates him. By contrast, Marlowe jettisons his friendship with Terry once he sees how Terry has taken advantage of his good will.

Perhaps to give the lie to Legman's speculations about Marlowe's sexual orientation, Chandler manufactures in the novel a brief affair for him with Linda Loring, the sister of Terry's dead wife Sylvia. At the end of the book she proposes to marry Marlowe, after she divorces her husband, Dr. Loring. But Marlowe is not buying. He maintains that their brief encounter could never be transformed into a lasting marriage. Although their relationship shuts down at this point, Linda will reappear in Chandler's later fiction, as we shall see.

Hamish Hamilton scheduled *The Long Goodbye* for publication in Britain in the autumn of 1953, while Houghton Mifflin issued the novel in the United States the following spring. One index of Chandler's preference for the book is that he continued to tinker with the text in the period between its publication in England and in America. These revisions, Robert Miller states, "do not alter the plot or overall tone of the novel." They are, rather, "polishings" designed to improve the text with a more felicitous word or phrase, or to correct minor inaccuracies. For example, one character's hair had inexplicably changed from blonde to brown in the course of the novel. These alterations "show the work of an attentive author," says Miller, "and are improvements over the original, no matter how slight some of them may be."[18]

For example, in the first British printing of the book Terry Lennox says of Harlan Potter, father of Sylvia Lennox and Linda Loring, "Both his daughters are tramps." Yet in the first American edition and in all subsequent printings in America and Britain, Terry says instead, "Sylvia is a tramp" (24). This change was most probably dictated, Miller surmises, "to complement the more sympathetic picture that Chandler provides of Linda Loring later in the novel," when she falls in love with Marlowe. Miller concludes, "Such meticulousness and concern for his text again justifies an impression of Chandler as a craftsman."[19]

When *The Long Goodbye* was finally published, the text was 125,000 words, making it one of the longest detective novels ever written in English. Indeed, it is Chandler's largest canvas, for the book not only deals with a mystery to be solved but also qualifies, in its carefully observed study of the major characters, as a serious novel of considerable literary worth. It is in fact a grueling dissection of the moral bankruptcy of contemporary society, as represented by the wealthy denizens of Idle Valley, epitomized by Eileen and Roger Wade, Sylvia and Terry Lennox.

In Chandler's view these people have every resource modern civilization can offer, yet they are worse off then their grandparents when it comes to coping with life. More specifically, the novel is about conspiracy and betrayal between human beings, in spite of their declared loyalties. Unquestionably the novel is enriched by Chandler's sage observations about the moral deterioration of modern life.

A number of reviews, from the *London Times* to the *New York Times*, extolled Chandler's latest novel as a masterpiece, which far exceeded the confines of mere escapist detective fiction by frankly depicting the noble and honest protagonist lost in an unfriendly universe. As a matter of fact, some reviewers were convinced that Chandler had finally raised hard-boiled fiction to the lofty realms of literature. Moreover, more than one critic felt that Chandler had at last achieved the stature of Ernest Hemingway, whom

Chandler had much admired from his earliest days as a writer. Van Dover cites the rave review in the *New Statesman and Nation,* in which Marlowe is pictured as "crusading along the California coast against venal cops, ugly gangsters, and self-indulgent women. . . . He is a very remarkable creation, the redeemer of all our modern sins." Marlowe is a kind man in an unkind world. In addition, "the rhythm of Chandler's prose is superb, and the intensity he packs into his pages makes every other thriller writer look utterly silly and superficial."[20]

In short, Hammett took murder out of the rose garden and dropped in into the alley, but Chandler had now taken murder out of the alley and dropped it into the parlor. For Eileen's tragic relationships with both Terry and Roger make *The Long Goodbye* domestic tragedy, a melancholy meditation on life and loss among the idle rich. Eileen in particular represents a member of high society who has fallen to a very low estate. Chandler was gratified by the reception of the novel, but the frosting on the cake was that he was awarded an Edgar (after Edgar Allan Poe) by the Mystery Writers of America for *The Long Goodbye* as the best mystery novel of the year.

A television adaptation of *The Long Goodbye* was broadcast on CBS on October 7, 1954, with Dick Powell reprising the role of Philip Marlowe, which he had first played in *Murder, My Sweet.* This hour-long live telecast was marred by an actor playing a murdered man who thought the scene was over and walked off the set in full view of the television audience.

It was nearly another two decades before United Artists (UA) announced, on May 13, 1972, that a film version was at long last to be produced. The expectations of the novel's fans were aroused by the fact that the picture would be made by a major American director, Robert Altman (*M*A*S*H*). Whether or not the resulting film would justify such high hopes was another matter.

The Long Goodbye: The Film

Producer Elliott Kastner (*Farewell, My Lovely*) had been interested off and on in launching a movie adaptation of *The Long Goodbye* ever since he first acquired the screen rights to the novel in 1965. By 1968 screenwriter Sterling Silliphant (*Marlowe*) had done a script, but the project failed to get off the ground because, among other reasons, Howard Hawks, who had by then retired from directing, would not take it on. By 1972 Kastner was seriously pursuing the project once more, and he had initially settled upon filmmaker Brian Hutton (*Where Eagles Dare*) to direct. He decided against using

Silliphant's script, instead commissioning Leigh Brackett, who had cowritten the script for *The Big Sleep,* to compose a fresh screenplay to be set, like *Marlowe,* in contemporary Los Angeles. Brackett completed the first draft of the screenplay before Hutton bowed out to make an Elizabeth Taylor vehicle.

Brackett recalled that she found adapting *The Long Goodbye* for filming was more difficult than adapting *The Big Sleep,* because *The Long Goodbye* was "an enormous book, the longest one Chandler ever wrote. It's tremendously involuted and convoluted. If you did it the way he wrote it, you would have a five-hour film."[21] Creating a screenplay of a reasonable length would entail substantial cuts in the story line. Furthermore, she recalled that the action of *The Big Sleep* was brisk, a swift succession of scenes. By contrast, *The Long Goodbye* moved along at a slower pace, developing in meticulous detail two plot lines, the Terry Lennox story and the Eileen Wade story. As a result, "the complicated progression of the overlapping stories" slowed down the action. "What a reader will hold still for and even savor and enjoy on the printed page is one thing," Brackett explained. Transferring this same material to a visual medium is quite another matter; moviegoers begin to squirm if a film proceeds at too leisurely a pace.

Brackett's screenplay sought to streamline the plot by eliminating a number of minor characters. "There were some characters I felt we could lose," said Brackett. Mostly "the corrupt and sinful Idle Valley types": Sylvia Lennox, who winds up dead shortly after the novel starts; her sister Linda, who makes a play for Marlowe in the novel; and Earl, Dr. Verringer's kept poodle. The remaining characters were "all we had room for." In this way the narrative was "greatly simplified."

Although Brackett emphasized that she attempted to preserve "the flavor" of the Chandler original, she could not accept Chandler's solution to the mystery. "Eileen Wade's confession and death come through, at least to me," as implausible. This was a plot premise that in her view simply did not work, because it savored too much of old fashioned melodrama. "I didn't believe it for a moment." So she decided in discussions with Hutton and producers Kastner and Jerry Bick that the only way out was to make Terry Lennox "a clear-cut villain." Accordingly, in the film it is Terry, not Eileen, who kills his wife Sylvia, whom Brackett described as a "gorgeous, oversexed" nymphomaniac. Then Robert Altman replaced Brian Hutton as director, Brackett concluded, "and things began to fall into place."[22] Altman held a week of story conferences with Brackett in which they made some revisions in her draft of the screenplay, which we shall examine shortly.

As *The Long Goodbye* (1973) gets underway, Philip Marlowe (Elliott Gould) acknowledges that the private-eye business is not as lucrative as it used to be. In fact, he drives a rickety old 1948 Lincoln Continental (with the license plate PVT EYE) and gets paid fifty dollars a day, plus expenses— half the rate Marlowe charged in the film *Marlowe* five years earlier. John Houseman once asked Chandler why Marlowe always seems to demand less than the going rate for his services throughout the novels. "Why does he work for such a pittance?" Chandler wrote to Houseman. The answer to that, he replied, is that it is tough to be both honest and financially success- ful in a rotten world.[23]

When Marlowe's friend Terry Lennox (Jim Boutan, a former baseball star) comes to visit him, Terry's sports car and expensive clothes indicate that he is more affluent than Marlowe, since he has married Sylvia, an heir- ess. Terry asks Marlowe to drive him to the airport in Tijuana; on Marlowe's return to Los Angeles, however, he is interrogated by the police in the wake of Sylvia's savage murder. The police, however, soon receive word that Terry has confessed to Sylvia's murder and has taken his own life in Otatoclán, Mexico. At the request of Eileen Wade (Nina Van Pallandt), Marlowe then searches for her husband Roger.

Marlowe traces Roger Wade (Sterling Hayden) to a sanatorium pre- sided over by the epicene Dr. Verringer, an unscrupulous leech (Henry Gibson). Roger is virtually a prisoner at the clinic, and Marlowe rescues him and restores him to his wife. Marlowe inquires if Roger and Eileen knew Terry and Sylvia Lennox, since the Lennoxes' home is located nearby, but the couple claim that they were not acquainted with the Lennoxes. Yet Marlowe later discovers that Eileen was romantically involved with Terry (though not married to him, as in the novel). He further learns that Roger had likewise had a liaison with Sylvia. So much for the veracity of the Wades.

Marty Augustine (Mendy Menendez in the book), a gambler and drug dealer, tells Marlowe that Terry absconded with $355,000 of Augustine's money when he fled to Mexico—money Terry was supposed to deliver to Augustine's Mexican drug supplier. Augustine (played by film director Mark Rydell) knows that Marlowe was the last person to see Terry before Terry's flight, and demands that Marlowe retrieve the missing cash. Marlowe in- sists that he was not in cahoots with Terry just because he gave Terry a lift to the Mexican border, and denies knowing anything about the money. In the novel Terry did not abscond with the gangster's money when he went south of the border, so in the film Terry is already revealed to be a more devious character than he was in the book. In making Terry a clear-cut villain in the film, Brackett presents Terry early on as a bagman for a racketeer. Thus Brackett shows Terry to be part of the Southern California bogus elite, whose livelihood depends in part on their covert dealings with the underworld.

Marlowe subsequently uncovers a connection between Roger Wade and Marty Augustine, in that Roger owes Augustine $10,000 for a gambling debt. Roger, a burned-out, broken, alcoholic writer, eventually kills himself in drunken despair by walking into the ocean near the Wades' beachfront home. In a letter to Stephen Pendo, dated February 27, 1975, Brackett confirmed that she included in her first draft of the script "a scene between Roger Wade and Marlowe in which they discuss suicide, which led up to Roger's demise."[24] In the scene as written, Roger, referring to Terry's supposed suicide, inquires if Marlowe ever thought of killing himself. The screenplay indicates that Roger is fondling one of the pistols in his gun collection while he muses that suicide puts an end to all of one's troubles: "It's beautiful, Marlowe; sweet, silken, swift. How's that for words? I live by words, and when they run away from me, I die."[25]

Here Brackett clearly suggests that one of Roger's principal reasons for contemplating suicide is the intolerable depression he endures because he cannot overcome his writer's block. This scene was therefore designed to foreshadow Roger's eventual self-destruction, but Altman instructed Brackett to scrap the scene when she revised the script. As a result, the viewer is reduced to guessing that Roger's abiding depression over feeling that he is all washed up as a professional writer is a key motive for his taking his own life, although this is never articulated in the film as it is in Brackett's first draft of the screenplay.

As the action continues, Marlowe is questioned by Augustine in the hoodlum's apartment about the drug money that Terry stole from him, when suddenly the missing loot is inexplicably returned. Marlowe spies Eileen leaving Augustine's apartment building shortly afterwards, and he correctly assumes that Eileen returned the money, calling her his "fairy godmother" for saving him from the wrath of Marty Augustine.

Brackett told Pendo that she had written into the final shooting script a scene in which Eileen received from Terry, whom she knew was still alive, "a message and the suitcase containing the money, which she was to return to the gangster, in order to get Terry off the hook." She continued, "This scene was shot, this scene was in the rough cut. But this scene had, unaccountably, vanished from the print I saw in the theater."[26] Consequently the filmgoer must wait until Marlowe meets up with Terry at film's end to discover that Terry had been in contact with Eileen for some time and that she was following his instructions in returning the drug money to Augustine. Altman never indicated to any interviewer why he scuttled the scene at the eleventh hour.

The fact remains that it was a tactical error to remove both this scene and the one in which Roger and Marlowe discuss suicide from the finished film. As Pendo observes, these scenes would have "helped to clarify some of the characters' actions and rectify the plotting weaknesses." As a matter of fact, Brackett confessed that she was "thoroughly confused" by the film, the first time she saw it.[27]

In any case, Marlowe, who has been incredulous about Terry's supposed suicide all along, goes to Otatoclán to investigate the circumstances of Terry's purported death. He bribes the local officials with a "donation to charity" to admit that Terry is still among the living. In fact, Marlowe finds Terry basking in a hammock in the fountained courtyard outside his luxurious home on the outskirts of the village.

Marlowe squeezes out of Terry his confession that he did slaughter Sylvia. Terry explains that Sylvia had found out that he had been carrying on a clandestine affair with Eileen, and she already knew that he was a courier for Augustine and regularly carried over the border illegally Augustine's payments to his supplier in Mexico. Since both Sylvia and Terry had a peripatetic sex life, Terry continues, their marriage was by this time on the rocks. So Sylvia decided that a convenient way to shed her unwanted husband was to turn him in to the authorities as a racketeer, and threatened to do just that. Terry was just as anxious to divest himself of his undesired wife, and so he had no qualms about disposing of her by beating her to death. Marlowe interjects, "I saw the photographs: you bashed her face in." He is appalled that his friend could be capable of such cruelty.

After the vicious slaying Terry split for Mexico and appropriated for himself the satchel full of money, which he was supposed to pass on to Augustine's supplier. Terry admits that he employed Eileen—who at this point is still in regular contact with him—as a go-between in returning Augustine's drug money to him, since Terry was painfully aware that otherwise Augustine would never give up searching for him to wreak vengeance on him for the robbery.

Terry shows absolutely no compunction over the crimes he has just confessed to Marlowe, or for his cruel manipulation of his erstwhile friend. "You used me," says Marlowe, glowering at Terry; for Terry had assured Marlowe that he was innocent of Sylvia's death in order to get his old chum to help him escape to Mexico. Terry responds with a shrug, "What are friends for?" He adds with studied indifference, "What the hell; nobody cares." Marlowe replies with barely suppressed anger, "Nobody cares but me." Terry counters, in a voice dripping with condescension, that he has come out of the whole affair a winner, whereas Marlowe is a born loser. "You'll never learn," he concludes.

Terry freely admits to Marlowe all of his offenses because he is confident that, since he is living in exile with a new identity, he is beyond the long arm of the law. Moreover, Terry is not afraid that Marlowe will blow the whistle on him. Brackett comments, in an aside in the screenplay at this point: "He isn't afraid of Marlowe. He doesn't worry about good old square Philip."[28] In addition, Eileen is about to join him, so that Terry and Roger's widow can live happily ever after on Roger's money. In summary, Terry, who has been involved in tearing relationships and friendships apart, now stands revealed as the soulless, gutless human being that he really is—a much more disgraceful individual than he is in the book.

In summing up the changes she made in the novel's plot up to this point in the screenplay, Brackett noted that she had made Roger a suicide in the film and made Terry Sylvia's killer in the movie, whereas Eileen murdered both Roger and Sylvia in the novel. Accordingly, Brackett had "relieved Eileen of all crimes except adultery," and Terry was now patently the number one villain of the piece. Brackett was convinced that the accumulated alterations she had wrought in Chandler's story line called for a different ending from the one the novelist had invented. For one thing, she found Marlowe's final parting with Terry in the book "unsatisfactory and unresolved." In having Marlowe sever his relationship with Terry, Chandler, she assumed, was probably implying that "most human relationships are unsatisfactory and unresolved." But she believed that this conclusion to the story just did not work.

Brackett reasoned that, since Terry was now the culprit, it seemed that the only possible conclusion was "for the cruelly diddled Marlowe to blow Terry's guts out, partly to keep Terry from getting away with it all, partly out of sheer human rage." Brackett conceded that this was "something the old Marlowe would never have done."[29]

But she thought this resolution of the plot was honest and right, not only because the enraged Marlowe feels a keen sense of betrayal but also because he is a "totally honest man in a dishonest world, which has reared up and kicked him in the face."[30] Marlowe views Terry's cold-blooded crimes as symptoms of a morally bankrupt society in which "nobody cares," as Terry puts it, and in which corruption and betrayal are the order of the day.

Brackett reflected, "I met Chandler only once; I know he wanted Marlowe to be depicted as an honest man and somebody who was his own man."[31] She was sure, therefore, that it was right and proper that Marlowe should take the law into his own hands and "execute" Terry. So, with Altman's approval, she opted to stage the brutal outcome of Marlowe's last meeting with Terry in the final shooting script exactly as she had concocted it in the draft script.

Early in the film Marlowe's cat ran away and he never got it back, though he made inquiries about it intermittently during the movie. Hence, when he draws a bead on Terry in their final encounter, he agrees with Terry that he is a born loser, just as Terry said, and he adds sardonically, "I even lost my cat." Then Marlowe pulls the trigger and literally liquidates Terry, whose body falls into the fountain in the courtyard.

More than one critic objected vociferously to the film's ending, which was unquestionably a major departure from the book. Brackett remembered that the tone of outrage in some of the notices suggested that, by doing violence to Chandler's ending, she and Altman were tampering with Sacred Scripture. Her own reaction was that no sacrilege had been committed; she admired Chandler's work, but nevertheless expressed her doubts that even Chandler regarded his work as Holy Writ.

After Marlowe exterminates Terry, he saunters down the tree-lined road outside Terry's secret haven. Eileen drives toward him in a jeep, on her way to join her lover, whom she will, of course, find floating face-down in his courtyard fountain. Marlowe passes right by her, impassively declining to acknowledge her presence, while Eileen, in turn, continues on her way to Terry's hideaway. This shot recalls the ending of Carol Reed's *Third Man* (1949), in which an estranged couple pass by each other in stoic silence, never to meet again.

Altman added to this final sequence the following brief wordless coda, which is not in Brackett's first draft of the script: As Marlowe continues down the shady lane, he begins to play his harmonica and to dance exuberantly. He encounters an elderly woman in the road and twirls the old lady around in an impromptu dance step; he then kicks up his heels and recedes into the distance.

Altman emphasized repeatedly in interviews that Marlowe's slaying of Terry was morally justified, and so he shows Marlowe behaving cheerfully at the final fadeout, thereby implying that Marlowe does not regret what he has done. David O'Brien likewise sees Marlowe as visiting a condign punishment on Terry: "The law can't touch him (he is legally dead), so it is up to Marlowe to see justice done and execute the guilty man," who is, after all, a brutal murderer and a racketeer. "Marlowe will face no legal retribution for his act (a man cannot be killed twice)." Furthermore, Eileen is also punished for her complicity in his crime as an accessory-after-the-fact to murder. She has lost everything she strived for: Her Mexican paradise with Terry Lennox, her adulterous love, now will never be.[32]

Brackett's original draft of the script, dated March 2, 1972, is available at the Wisconsin Center for Film and Theater Research in Madison. A detailed comparison of Brackett's draft script with the finished film indicates that Brackett added some new material to the final shooting script at Altman's behest. Altman confirmed that he had asked Brackett to add "a situation or two" to the screenplay; still he maintained that "the finished film was pretty much like" Brackett's first script: "There were no great changes."[33]

Moreover, Altman, whom I talked with at the New York Film Festival, said that, like Howard Hawks, he made a practice of occasionally changing during a rehearsal any dialogue that no longer fit the flow of the shooting as it had been progressing. It was not a question of the actors merely ad-libbing; rather, they improvised some dialogue, in tandem with the director and the writer, to fit the action of the scene better.

Actually, Altman stated after the film was finished, just a couple of scenes were improvised, such as the one in which Marlowe and Roger "were drinking together" early in the film. He denied unequivocally the rumor that circulated in some quarters that much of the dialogue was made up on the set.[34]

In her letter to Pendo, Brackett mentions an episode involving Marty Augustine and "the gangster's girlfriend," which was originally "not in the script," and was added to the final shooting script at Altman's suggestion.[35] In this scene, Augustine is certain that Marlowe knows where Terry has hidden the gangster's suitcase full of drug money. He therefore attempts to intimidate Marlowe into revealing this information, which in fact he does not possess. Without any warning, Augustine suddenly explodes into an outburst of gratuitous violence. He aims a Coke bottle at his young mistress's face, which is fit for a magazine cover, then smashes the bottle in her face, wilfully disfiguring her. His apparent purpose is to threaten Marlowe by impressing him with the fact that he means business. "That's someone I love," he barks. "You I don't even like."

As a matter of fact, this incident was appended to the final shooting script at the last minute, since it is dated June 21, 1972, a week after principal photography had commenced. David O'Brien is virtually alone in insisting that this is one of the best amendments that Altman instructed Brackett to write into the final shooting script. O'Brien says that this episode demonstrates how Augustine's insecurity about his status as an important mob boss "manifests itself in misdirected brutality."[36] Augustine, it appears, is a prime example of the cesspool of human depravity that the movie depicts.

Still, audiences were bewildered by this outrageous, random violence. Asked about this scene, Altman responded, "That was a calculated device; the Coke bottle sequence brought violence into the film." It was designed to remind the audience that "in spite of Marlowe, there is a real world out there; and it is a violent world." It was the same with Roger Wade's suicide, Altman continued; he wanted to portray it on screen, rather than only have Marlowe discover the body after Roger had drowned, because that "made the suicide real."[37]

In shooting the suicide scene, Altman positioned Marlowe and Eileen on opposite sides of the wide screen, as they stand in front of a picture window that overlooks the seashore. There is an empty space between them, so the filmgoer can see past Marlowe and Eileen and glimpse Roger through the window, as he wades into the Pacific Ocean and is engulfed in the waves.

This scene is an example of canny filmmaking on Altman's part. In general, when a director gives the viewer information that the characters lack, he can build up suspense throughout the entire scene. So here the viewer knows that Roger intends to drown himself and wants to blurt out a warning to Marlowe and Eileen so they will go and save him, but they do not notice Roger splashing around in the ocean until it is too late to rescue him.

Although Altman modified Brackett's draft script in various ways, he endorsed her ending for the picture, whereby Marlowe eliminates Terry without any remorse. Altman even asserted that he would not have directed the picture if it had had a different ending: "I liked the idea of Marlowe killing his best friend." Altman went on to explain that Marlowe's worst mistake was depending on the friendship of a low-life like Terry. By the time Marlowe tracked down Terry, Marlowe was world-weary and close to the end of his tether. He saw himself as a loser betrayed by his only friend; so, in Altman's mind, Marlowe had to murder Terry.[38]

After Marlowe shoots Terry, he skips lightly down the road and disappears into the distance. As he does so, Altman tunes in a vocal rendition of "Hooray for Hollywood" on the sound track—the same tune that played during the film's opening credits. The song is from the 1937 musical *Holly-wood Hotel,* which starred Dick Powell, well before he himself played Marlowe. Altman added the song at the end of the film he said, because he "wanted to say to the audience, 'It's just a movie, folks.'"[40] O'Brien believes that the song has an ironic function at film's end: "There is nothing to cheer about in the Hollywood Altman has just shown us. All references to the movie industry—present throughout the film but fairly peripheral—look back to the Golden Age."[41]

Many of the allusions to movies of the past that crop up in *The Long Goodbye* are to noir films of the 1940s, the Golden Age to which O'Brien refers. There is, for example, the allusion to *The Third Man* at the end of the picture, already cited. In addition, the security guard at the Malibu Colony where the Wades and the Lennoxes live does impersonations, as of Barbara Stanwyck in *Double Indemnity:* "I don't understand why I don't understand, Walter." He also does an impression of Cary Grant, who was, we recall, Chandler's first choice to play Marlowe. Moreover, Marlowe makes reference to other movie private eyes, as when he calls a terrier that trots by his car "Asta," which was the name of the pet belonging to Nick Charles, Dashiell Hammett's sleuth in the *Thin Man* series of movies.

What's more, when Augustine grills Marlowe about the missing drug money, he orders Marlowe to submit to a strip search, which recalls Merle Davis commanding Marlowe to undress at gunpoint in *The Brasher Doubloon.* One of Augustine's goons mutters that tough guy actor George Raft (*Johnny Angel*) "never had to take his clothes off" for a search. As in *Brasher Doubloon,* Marlowe's strip search is halted before it goes very far, in this instance because Augustine gets the word that the money has been returned. The most movielike snatch of dialogue in the whole film comes directly from the novel (38). When the police interrogate Marlowe about Terry's disappearance, Marlowe, referring to detective flicks, quips, "This is where I say, 'What's this all about?' and you say, 'We ask the questions.'"

Altman contended that these glib references to 1940s noir were satiri-cal thrusts aimed at the film colony, not at Chandler's private eye. "I think that the satire in the film was pointed more at films" than it was at Chan-dler, Altman noted.[42] "Hollywood itself is never far away from the movie's mind," writes Donald Lyons. "The Malibu Colony, a real-life locus of in-dustry glamour types, is where the film's corrupt dwell," in this case the Wades and the Lennoxes.[43] Furthermore, Marlowe lives in the Broadview Terrace Apartments, in the very heart of Hollywood.

The Long Goodbye "isn't just Altman's private eye movie—it's his Hollywood movie, set in the mixed-up world of movie-influenced life that is Los Angeles," Pauline Kael opines. "It's a reverie on old movies. . . . Altman's references to old movies don't stick out—they're just part of the texture."[44] Gerard Plecki adds, "Those allusions indicate the cinematic past from which the director draws. They also complement his indictment of the easy morality and insubstantial values of Hollywood," which were also on display in *Marlowe*.[45]

Altman told Jon Tuska that he instructed the cast and crew to read *Raymond Chandler Speaking*, a collection of Chandler's essays and letters about his work as a novelist and screenwriter, because he wanted Chandler to influence the film. Indeed, both Altman and Brackett contended that they stuck very closely to Chandler's concept of Marlowe as a gumshoe who holds on tenaciously to a rigorous code of honor and fair play.

Chandler himself characterized Marlowe as a "loser," Brackett pointed out, at least in a society where money alone is the measure of success. But Marlowe is "a man who is pure in heart, who is decent and honorable and cannot be bought—he is incorruptible," Brackett continued. In fact, Brackett bought Chandler's description of Marlowe as a modern-day knight: "Here is the knight in shining armor with a shabby trench coat and snap-brim felt hat. I think he is a universal folk hero who does not change through the ages," except that he carries a gun rather than a sword. "I think the concept was damn good, a very moral concept."[46]

Chandler did characterize Marlowe as a loser; he said that Marlowe, as he had drawn him in *The Long Goodbye*, would indeed look plain foolish in the corrupt modern world that we live in. Certainly Marlowe is thought of as a chump, who is out of touch with the times, by several of the characters he encounters in both the book and the film. In brief, says O'Brien, the film, like the novel before it, is "a study of a moral and decent man cast adrift in the selfish, self-obsessed society where lives can be thrown away without a backward glance, and any notions of friendship or loyalty are meaningless."[47]

Altman attracted first-rate talent to work on the movie, starting with screenwriter Brackett; in addition, there was Academy Award–winning composer John Williams (*Star Wars*) and Oscar-winning cinematographer Vilmos Zsigmond (*Close Encounters of the Third Kind*). Altman collaborated very closely with Zsigmond in particular throughout the production period, which commenced on June 15, 1972, and concluded on August 24. Altman, who favored location filming over relying on studio sets, shot the entire film in and around Los Angeles. The Wades' ocean front residence in the Malibu Colony, used in Roger's suicide scene, described above, was really Altman's own home. Marlowe's apartment was in the old stucco apartment building called Broadview Terrace, just back of the Hollywood Bowl, which Chandler had written into *Farewell, My Lovely* as the home of Jules Amthor. The Mexican sequences were shot in the villages of Tepoztlan and Chiconcuac in Mexico. In short, not one frame of the movie was shot on a Hollywood sound stage. Altman and Zsigmond selected locations that had "that gritty Los Angeles reality which Chandler knew so well," writes Edward Lipnick.[48]

Similarly, Peter Lev says that Altman successfully emulates Chandler by being the same sort of acute observer of Los Angeles that Chandler was. Thus Altman follows Chandler's example by portraying unsentimentally this "demi-paradise," from "the unhappy enclaves of the rich" to the gaudy lairs of pretentious gangsters.[49] To give sun-baked Los Angeles the grim, unbecoming look Altman wanted, Zsigmond immersed the film in pastel shades, thereby eliminating bright colors from the look of the film as much as possible.

To accomplish this he evolved a complicated process of desaturating the film's color when the footage was processed in the technicolor laboratory during postproduction, so that the picture is actually muted technicolor. This enabled Zsigmond to give the movie a diffused, sun-bleached look that fit the drab, gloomy atmosphere required by the story. Indeed, the cold blue shadows cast over the interiors and the murky night exteriors give the picture a tone as ominous as the grays and blacks of the classic noir films of the 1940s and 1950s. Zsigmond was deservedly named the best cinematographer of the year by the National Society of Film Critics for *The Long Goodbye*.

To test audience reaction to the film, Altman agreed to be present at a prerelease screening at a weekend film conference in Tarrytown, New York. Film critic Judith Crist, who presided over the conference, suggested to Altman that "since his was the sixth Raymond Chandler screen adaptation, we'd show the five earlier ones," from *Murder, My Sweet* through *Marlowe*. "Unwittingly, we so hooked the audience" on the earlier films, that by the time *The Long Goodbye* was screened, "the audience hated not only the film, but Altman and me. We very simply—and innocently—cut our own throats."[50]

The fundamental objection to the film voiced by the conference audience, which included film professionals such as director Joseph Mankiewicz (*All About Eve*) and several film critics, was that Elliott Gould's performance as Marlowe was no match for the likes of Bogart and Powell, whom they had seen essay the role in the course of the conference. Asked later if she thought Elliott Gould (*M*A*S*H*) was miscast in the role, Leigh Brackett responded, "I thought he did a beautiful job," except that he was not hard-boiled enough. "His face is gentle, his eyes are kind, and he doesn't have that touch of cruelty" one associates with a shamus like Bogart—until the very end when he wastes Terry Lennox. When the film was released on videotape in England, *Sight and Sound* endorsed Gould's Marlowe: "Gould here isn't far removed from the character in the novels—he wears the right clothes and drives a Lincoln Intercontinental."[51]

The Long Goodbye was initially released in March, 1973, in just a few major cities, such as Los Angeles and Chicago. From the outset the movie caught a lot of flack for betraying Chandler's book. For one thing, Altman's film is the only Marlowe movie that does not carry over from the source novel the femme fatale, a key figure throughout Chandler's fiction; Eileen Wade is not the multiple murderess in the film that she is in the book.

For another thing, Altman's picture is the only Marlowe film in which Marlowe is responsible for a homicide that is not in its literary source. In addition, Marlowe's homicide in the present film cannot be justified as self-defense, as was the case with Marlowe's icing Canino in the book and both films of *The Big Sleep*. So some reviewers felt that, when Marlowe kills Terry, he ceases to be Chandler's heroic private eye and becomes a man no better than the rest of us. Consequently, Curtis Brown observes, *The Long Goodbye* "did not enjoy the success many feel its bold conception deserved."[52]

The critical response to the movie by and large bordered on open hostility. One of the early reviews even asserted that *The Long Goodbye* would stand for years to come as the nadir of filmmaking; the bar for what constituted poor moviemaking had just been lowered another notch. Another notice hazarded that the actors gave poor performances because they seemed to be acting under protest.

Needless to say, the box office receipts were extremely disappointing; as a result, United Artists abruptly canceled the New York opening, and the movie was temporarily withdrawn from further distribution. There were rumors that the picture would be drastically cut or even shelved, but the front office made no such panicky decisions, as they already had $1.7 million invested in the film, big money in those days.

After some marketing research, UA executives decided that the original advertising campaign for the movie had misled the public into assuming that the picture was a traditional private-eye movie, complete with a happy ending in which the gumshoe goes off with his girlfriend on his arm at the final fadeout. By contrast, *The Long Goodbye* was the first Marlowe movie in which the scenario did not supply the detective with a love inter-est—and the brutal ending was anything but happy. To paraphrase Billy Wilder, the audience came into the theater expecting a cocktail and instead Altman served them a shot of vinegar.

The revised ad campaign, redesigned to prepare the public for Altman's more unsettling, pessimistic take on the detective genre, featured a carica-ture of Marlowe and described him with mordant wit as "a hard-bitten, cynical private eye doing battle with a mean mobster who disfigures help-less women."[53]

When *The Long Goodbye* was relaunched in October 1973, the fresh ad campaign gave the movie a new lease on life when it opened in New York, and the picture gained some champions among the critics. More than one reviewer saw the film as a serious, unique work, not a routine detective flick. Leading the pack was *New Yorker* critic Pauline Kael; noting that the picture had closed out of town seven months earlier, she called *The Long Goodbye* "probably the best American movie ever made that almost didn't open in New York." Kael went on to endorse Gould's Marlowe, contending that Gould gives a wooly, strikingly original performance as Chandler's scruffy, "wryly forlorn knight.... He's the gallant fool in a corrupt world"— which, we remember, is precisely what Chandler himself called Marlowe. "He's the only one who *cares*. That's his true innocence," and it keeps the film "from being harsh or scabrous."

As for Marlowe's startling act of violence, which provides the devas-tating conclusion for this noir film, Kael continued, "It isn't from Chandler; and its logic is probably too brutally sound for Bogart-lovers to stomach." She concluded, "The corrupt milieu wins," but that should come as no sur-prise to readers of the novel: "The good-guys-finish-last conception was implicit in Chandler's L.A. all along."[54]

Still other critics who reviewed the movie at this time singled out film director Mark Rydell (*On Golden Pond*) for his weird, on-the-edge por-trayal of the horrifying, sadistic Marty Augustine, adding that the tension he brings to his scenes is jolting. Sterling Hayden, who is associated with vintage noir films like Stanley Kubrick's *The Killing*, found more favor for his enthrallingly hammy depiction of the self-destructive novelist Roger Wade than he did the first time around. The hulking Hayden, bearded like Ernest Hemingway, was clearly meant to evoke the macho author of tough-guy novels like *To Have and Have Not*, who had in fact committed suicide, just as Roger does in the film (if not in the book). What's more, the film eventually turned up on the *New York Times* list of the ten best films of the year. Nevertheless, *The Long Goodbye* was still not well-received in the rest of the country, either by reviewers or ticket buyers.

To their credit, UA executives made an unusual effort to give the picture a second chance. Be that as it may, Altman denounced the front office in an interview in the *New York Times,* in which he alleged that the studio had mishandled the original promotional campaign. "Before, they tried to sell it as though it was a detective story," that is, a conventional mystery movie, along the lines of the Burt Reynolds vehicle *Shamus,* which opened around the same time. Altman further indicated that he had to convince UA to junk that approach and try another one. David Picker, who was president of UA at the time, was incensed by the interview. "When he went to the press and s—— all over us," Picker recalled, "and took credit for getting us to do something that we had volunteered to do, I was totally offended by it."[56]

Leonard Matlin notes that when *The Long Goodbye* was initially shown on television, television executives, aware of the outcry raised by movie critics against Marlowe's killing of Terry, excised the shot of Marlowe blowing Terry away. This deletion left Marlowe turning his back and walking away from Terry, who was presumably still very much alive. It goes without saying that Altman disowned this television version of the movie, and the original version of the movie is now the only one shown on television or anywhere else.[57]

Over the years critical response to *The Long Goodbye* has become more benign, when the film has resurfaced on television and on video cassette. "Killer Marlowe was a scandal in 1973," says Donald Lyons. "Today he seems . . . a moral agent," endeavoring to reestablish morality in modern times, in a society that appears to ignore it. Altman may have satirized the conventions of the Hollywood crime film, "but the private eye's quest . . . for a pure and friendly heart is finally not mocked."[58]

Not a few critics have reassessed *The Long Goodbye* as a sophisticated detective yarn. Thus Parrish and Pitts cite approvingly Roger Ebert as saying, "Gould has enough of the paranoid in his acting style to really put over Altman's view of the private eye."[59] In the last analysis, the wholesale dismissal of the movie when it first opened was unquestionably preemptory and unwarranted, since there is much to be said for the film, given the top-flight collaborators Altman assembled to work with him on the picture.

Furthermore, Altman cannot be faulted just because he created the darkest of all the Marlowe films, since it is derived from the most pessimistic of Chandler's novels. Altman's Southern California is not as far removed from Chandler's as some critics contend. Dr. Verringer operates his odious private clinic, where he dispenses illegal drugs to wealthy clients, in a respectable suburb of Pasadena in both book and movie. "Much of the commentary on the chaos and soullessness of Southern California is perfectly in keeping with the original novel," James Naremore maintains; "and despite the fact that it creates a new ending," the movie "preserves Chandler's basic plot."[60] Still, there is no getting around the fact that, as Dave Kerr notes, a film like *The Long Goodbye* is harsh even by Altman's standards. Indeed, it exemplifies how Altman was losing some of "the grace and lyricism that once balanced his misanthropic vision" in earlier movies such as *McCabe and Mrs. Miller.*[61]

It is worth noting that in two later movies there are allusions, amounting to homages of sorts, to *The Long Goodbye*. In the similarly titled *The Long Kiss Goodnight* (1996), a private eye (Samuel L. Jackson) is shown in a motel room watching *The Long Goodbye* on television; it is a film that, as a gumshoe, the Jackson character admires. In *Star Trek: First Contact* (1996), Captain Picard (Patrick Stewart) shoots a couple of vile aliens and then says that his act of violence reminds him of a sleuth in a detective story entitled *The Big Goodbye,* which suggests both *The Long Goodbye* and *The Big Sleep.* And so it seems that Philip Marlowe, as portrayed in Altman's film, has walked straight into cinema mythology, on the strength of a line of dialogue about a lost cat and a shot of a man disappearing down a country lane playing the harmonica.

Altman's final word on the film was, "The people who were disappointed with *The Long Goodbye* were disappointed, not with my handling of Raymond Chandler, but because Humphrey Bogart wasn't in it." Hence they decried Elliott Gould's performance as Marlowe because "they were using as their model Humphrey Bogart in *The Big Sleep,*" which did not seem fair either to Gould or the film.[62]

Leigh Brackett always insisted that she did right by Chandler in her screenplay for *The Long Goodbye.* "I'm an old Chandler fan from way back," she wrote. "He was a powerful influence on my work. . . . I think he might have liked Altman's version of *The Long Goodbye.*"[63] Given the opprobrium that Chandler heaped upon perfectly respectable films like *The Brasher Doubloon* and *Lady in the Lake,* Brackett's hope that Chandler would have endorsed Altman's *Long Goodbye* borders on wishful thinking.

In Part Two we shall examine Chandler's own work as a screenwriter in order to ascertain how successful he was in composing scripts based on the work of other authors.

Part Two

Exiled in Babylon

Chandler's Screenplays

9

Lured

Double Indemnity

Many gentlemen make the mistake of trusting the lady of the
moment.
—Mr. Mauribus, a police officer,
in the film *Singapore*

Hell does not always look like hell; even on a good day it can
look a lot like L.A.
—Dr. Eugene Sanders, in the film *Playing God*

In Chandler's essay "Writers in Hollywood," which he wrote after he finished work on *Double Indemnity,* he commented, "The creative writer who
makes literature cannot survive the clichés of a long series of" script conferences. Moreover, Chandler, a morose, touchy man, preferred to work alone;
he detested the collaborative effort endemic to writing a screenplay. In addition, Chandler had a low opinion of screenwriting. "There is no art of the
screenplay," he asserted in the same essay.[1] Screenwriting, as far as Chandler was concerned, was "a loathsome job," consisting of "beating the hell
out of the poor, tired lines and scenes until they lost all meaning."[2]

Chandler went so far as to satirize Hollywood's concept of a rewarding motion picture as "a vehicle for some glamorpuss with two expressions
and eighteen changes of costume, or for some male idol of the muddled
millions with a permanent hangover, six worn-out acting tricks, the build
of a lifeguard, and the mentality of a chicken strangler."[3]

Nevertheless, Chandler was prepared to return to Hollywood whenever his ailing finances required a transfusion. As a matter of fact, Chandler found it necessary to continue writing for the movies even after he began to acquire a reputation as an important novelist, since his book and magazine earnings were never large. He thus continued to seek employment in Hollywood—in spite of the fact that he felt that the screenwriter was viewed as a second-class citizen in the film colony.

Pauline Kael affirms that in Hollywood the writer sees himself as "an underling whose work is trashed; or at best he's a respected collaborator without final control over how his work is used." And so he can develop an antipathy toward the studio bosses and the producers—all of those people he feels have "no right to make decisions about his work" but do so just the same.[4]

Writer-director Preston Sturges (*The Miracle of Morgan Creek*), a contemporary of Chandler's at Paramount, recalled in acrid terms that it was not uncommon for a platoon of screenwriters to work on the same script. "Writers worked in teams, like piano movers," he recalled.[5] This was a system Chandler deplored.

Chandler's abiding dislike of Tinsel Town has led some commentators on his life and work to surmise quite gratuitously that he carried out his studio assignments hastily and carelessly, just to take the money and run. Yet there is a great deal of evidence that Chandler did try conscientiously to give the studios that hired him an honest week's work in return for his wages. In fact, the quality of the scenarios to which he applied his creative energies attests to the seriousness with which he viewed his obligations to his employers. John Houseman, a producer at Paramount during Chandler's tenure there, vouched in print for Chandler's seriousness more than once in later years.

Be that as it may, Chandler still resented the script conferences that screenwriter-director Billy Wilder imposed on him when they collaborated on the script for *Double Indemnity*, Chandler's first studio assignment. James M. Cain's novella *Double Indemnity* was first considered for filming by the major studios in 1935, shortly after it was serialized in *Liberty* magazine. This lurid tale describes how a femme fatale named Phyllis lures Walter, an insurance salesman, into a conspiracy to murder her husband for his insurance money—a conspiracy that becomes a recipe for their destruction. Metro-Goldwyn-Mayer inquired of Joseph Ignatius Breen, the industry censor, if Cain's novelette was suitable for filming. Breen shot back a letter to Metro executive Louis B. Mayer, dated October 10, 1935, in which he asserted, "The story deals improperly with an illicit and adulterous sex relationship. The general low tone and sordid flavor of this story make it . . . thoroughly unacceptable for screen production."[6] Breen's letter scared off not only MGM, but every other studio in town from considering *Double Indemnity* as a viable film project.

Tom Hiney wryly comments in his biography of Chandler that the industry censor, who had also discouraged the studios from optioning other hard-boiled novels for filming, "held hard-boiled crime fiction to be everything" he was protecting the American public from.[7] Cain remembers his agent showing him a copy of Breen's report: "It started off, 'UNDER NO CIRCUMSTANCES,' and ended up, 'NO WAY, SHAPE, OR FORM.' My agent asked me if I wanted to hear what was in between, and I told him I could guess."

Eight years later, when *Double Indemnity* was published in book form, "my new agent, H.N. Swanson, sent it again to eight studios," Cain recalled. Joseph Sistrom, a producer at Paramount, passed it on to Wilder, who snapped it up and immediately, "took it home and read it."[8] And the rest, as they say, is history.

Double Indemnity

On September 21, 1943, Paramount sent Breen a screen treatment (detailed synopsis) of *Double Indemnity,* which Wilder had prepared in conjunction with his longtime collaborator, Charles Brackett. The censor felt that the revised story line, which they had composed according to his specifications, had overcome in large measure his original objections to the subject. Breen added that, after all, "adultery is no longer quite as objectionable" as it once had been in motion pictures.[9]

Nonetheless, Brackett found this sort of hard-boiled story too grisly for his taste and refused to collaborate with Wilder on the screenplay. Wilder had hoped to engage Cain himself to help him adapt his novella for film, but Cain was then under contract to Twentieth Century Fox and could not accept a writing assignment at another studio. As both Cain and Chandler were considered eminent crime novelists, Wilder turned to Chandler to compose the screenplay.

Wilder had read two of Chandler's novels, *The Big Sleep* and *The High Window,* and was impressed with Chandler's lively narrative style and pungent, slangy dialogue. As a rule, Wilder welcomed the opportunity to collaborate with another screenwriter on the scripts for his films. "The remarkable thing, human nature being what it is," Wilder later wrote, "is that so many fine films have resulted from this struggle (or collaboration, call it what you will) between writer and director."[10]

For his part, Chandler had serious reservations about working for the movies. Indeed, he had confided to George Harmon Coxe, another *Black Mask* alumnus, in his letter of April 9, 1939, "Personally, I think Hollywood is poison to any writer, the graveyard of talent. I have always thought so."[11] Withal, Chandler was most willing to work with a writer-director who had already made an important wartime thriller, *Five Graves to Cairo* (1943). Consequently, Chandler accepted Wilder's offer to draft the script for *Double Indemnity*, despite the fact that he had no previous experience in screenwriting.

When Wilder scheduled his first meeting with Chandler in his office on the fourth floor of the Writers Building at Paramount, on May 12, 1943, he expected the author of *The Big Sleep* to be a tough-looking former private eye like Dashiell Hammett. Instead, Wilder recalled, he beheld a fifty-five-year-old gentleman wearing a frayed tweed jacket that made him look like a somewhat eccentric British schoolteacher. Chandler also had a sickly complexion, which to Wilder betokened that Chandler was a heavy drinker.

Chandler informed Wilder, "This is already Tuesday; I cannot promise you the script until next Monday." Chandler was obviously laboring under the misconception that he was expected to write the screenplay on his own and in record time. Wilder responded that the studio was prepared to offer Chandler $750 a week for writing the script in collaboration with Wilder himself. To the mystery writer, accustomed to paltry payments from pulp publishers, this seemed a handsome sum. Still, Wilder warned Chandler, "You don't know how scripts are written."[12]

Not heeding Wilder's warning, the neophyte screenwriter showed up at his next meeting with the director toting sixty-five pages of script, while Wilder had turned out three pages of the opening scene. For the most part, Richard Schickel records, "Chandler had typed up Cain's dialogue in the best imitation he could manage of screenplay form," adding camera directions like "camera dollies in for a close-up."[13] Wilder took one look at Chandler's batch of script pages, tossed them back at him, and barked, "This is crap, Mr. Chandler." He further suggested that Chandler use the manuscript for a doorstop. "You don't know a damn thing about writing for the screen," Wilder reiterated. "But I'll teach you.[14]

Wilder went on to explain that Cain had written the novella in a hurried, slapdash fashion when he needed money, as Cain was the first to admit.[15] As a result, the story's narrative structure and character development needed shoring up. He concluded by advising Chandler to forget about inserting camera directions into the script, since that was the director's business. "Just let's write characters and situations."

Chandler resented having to collaborate with this brash, opinionated filmmaker on a daily basis. He grew more testy and disagreeable as time went on. As a matter of fact, the pair had numerous petty squabbles while they were engaged in coauthoring the script.

Admittedly, Wilder was a volatile, excitable man who had his share of eccentricities; and they bothered Chandler. After all, Chandler had never before been forced to write in the same room with another person. Wilder paced back and forth while they discussed the screenplay, often brandishing a Malacca cane, which he sometimes would rudely wave in Chandler's face as he emphasized a point. Chandler saw this as the height of incivility.

For his part, Wilder had some grievances of his own. He later testified that Chandler smoked a pipe, from which emanated clouds of noxious smoke, and then insisted that the office windows remain tightly shut because he was convinced that the Los Angeles smog was hazardous to his health. One day, in exasperation, Wilder snapped, "Ray, would you raise the window just this once?"[17]

Finally, four weeks into coauthoring the script, Chandler (who was an inveterate collector of injustices, real or imagined) declined to report for work one morning. Instead, he issued a written ultimatum to Wilder. It was a letter of complaint, the director recalled, in which Chandler maintained that he was fed up with Wilder's rudeness. The letter, which is preserved among Chandler's papers in the Research Library at UCLA, insists that Mr. Wilder "is at no time to swish under Mr. Chandler's nose or to point in his direction the thin, leather-handled Malacca cane which Mr. Wilder is in the habit of waving around while they work. Mr. Wilder is not to give Mr. Chandler orders of an arbitrary nature, such as 'Ray, will you open that window?'"[18]

Wilder and Chandler made a truce, although Wilder reminded him that "for God's sake, Ray, we don't have court manners around here." But he apologized just the same, simply because he still admired Chandler's writing ability and very much wanted him to continue collaborating on the script. Wilder had learned what screenwriter Matthew Robbins (*Sugarland Express*) called a "script conference axiom: there is no relation between affability and talent."[19] Nevertheless, for a tyro screenwriter to exact an apology from an influential film director was deemed something of an achievement at the writers' table in the Paramount commissary. The rancor that characterized their relationship, however, did not interfere with Chandler's successful collaboration with Wilder on the script.

Chandler conscientiously did fieldwork while working on the screenplay by visiting various locations that figured in the film, taking copious notes all the while. For example, he hung around Jerry's Market on Melrose Avenue in preparation for writing a scene in which Phyllis Dietrichson pushes "a shopping cart up and down the aisles of a supermarket, wearing dark glasses and planning the murder of her husband with Walter Neff over canned goods."[20]

Chandler and Wilder had initially planned to borrow as much of Cain's tough, spare dialogue from the novelette as possible. By this time, however, Chandler had realized that the novella's dialogue needed reworking for the screen. Wilder disagreed, Cain remembered, "and he was annoyed that Chandler wasn't putting more of it in the script." To settle the matter, Wilder enlisted a couple of contract players to read passages of Cain's original dialogue from the book. "To Wilder's astonishment, he found out it *wouldn't* play," said Cain.[21] After the actors read a scene straight from the book, Chandler pointed out to Wilder that the dialogue sounded like "a bad high school play. The dialogue oversaid everything and, when spoken, sounded quite colorless and tame."[22]

As Chandler later told Cain in a consultation Cain had with Chandler and Wilder, "Jim, that dialogue of yours is for the *eye*," not for the *ear*. "I tried to explain it to Billy."[23] Chandler continued, telling Cain that his clipped dialogue seemed fine when one read it from the printed page, but it had no sting and even sounded flat when it was spoken aloud. In a follow-up letter to Cain on March 20, 1944, Chandler added that the book's dialogue, particularly the exchanges between Phyllis and Walter, had to be "sharpened and pointed" for the screen.[24] Cain graciously replied that he fully understood why Chandler and Wilder had not used more of his "deathless dialogue" in the picture.[25]

The upshot was that the film's taut, cynical dialogue owes more to Chandler and Wilder than it does to Cain. "We improved it quite a bit," Wilder said later. He also indicated that he was impressed with the way Chandler could "get the flavor of California" into his flip and mordant writing, in both his scripts and his novels. "It's very peculiar that the only person who caught the California atmosphere in prose was an Englishman—Chandler."[26] Wilder was obviously unaware that, although Chandler was educated in England, he was actually born in Chicago and lived most of his life in the United States.

Joseph Sistrom, among others, also thought that Chandler was British, so Wilder was not the only Hollywoodite to associate Chandler's tweed jacket and pipe with an English gentleman—a misconception that Chandler never made any effort to correct because he liked being considered a sophisticated Englishman. More recently, film historian Michael Wood referred to both Chandler and the British-born director Alfred Hitchcock as "foreigners," great European exiles who worked in Hollywood. So the misconception that Chandler was a British author who migrated to California in later life persists.[27]

Double Indemnity deals with the great American pastime of cheating an insurance company, and it does so with deadly seriousness. According to Wilder, Cain based his novella on the notorious Snyder-Gray case, which had fascinated Wilder as well.[28] Indeed, John McCarty writes that Cain's novelette offers striking parallels to "the real-life murder case of Ruth Snyder and Judd Gray, who conspired to kill Snyder's husband for $100,000 in insurance money" in Queen's Village, New York, in 1927. "Unlike Cain's fictional couple, however, Snyder and Gray were caught and sent to the electric chair."

Pete Hamill writes that Ruth Snyder achieved tabloid immortality when she became the first woman in New York to be executed. Moreover, a photojournalist smuggled a camera into the execution chamber at Sing Sing on January 12, 1928, and snapped a picture of Snyder just as the juice was turned on. The next day the (in)famous photograph appeared on the front page of the *New York Daily News*. Certainly the photo would have drawn Cain's attention to the trial, if he had not been following it already. Damon Runyan described Snyder in his coverage of the case at the time as a frosty-looking blonde; and that is precisely how Wilder pictures her counterpart, Phyllis Dietrichson, in the film.[29]

The title of the film refers to the double insurance benefit paid out in the event of accidental death. Phyllis Dietrichson (Barbara Stanwyck) seduces Walter Neff (Fred MacMurray), an insurance agent, into helping her murder her husband (Tom Powers), making it look like an accident so they can cash in his insurance policy. Phyllis is confident that Walter can aid her in defrauding the insurance company successfully, since he is employed by the same firm that has insured her husband.

Walter's willingness to buy into Phyllis's sordid money-making scheme brings clearly into prominence a theme that often surfaces in Wilder's films. As Wilder himself formulated that theme, "People will do anything for money; except some people, who will do *almost* anything for money."[30] This is Wilder's satirical comment on the erosion of values in our modern acquisitive society. Without a doubt, Walter is just as willing as Phyllis to do anything for money, not excluding homicide. "In *Double Indemnity*," writes Stephen Farber, "love has become indistinguishable from greed."[31] Walter and Phyllis feign love for each other, when in fact their relationship is fundamentally grounded in their mutual desire to collect the death money.

Although Chandler and Wilder had to revise Cain's dialogue when they incorporated it into the screenplay, at times they were able to employ a passage of dialogue from the novella just as Cain originally wrote it. For example, in the book Walter admits that he had considered bilking the insurance company that employed him long before he met Phyllis, and Chandler and Wilder reproduced this passage virtually intact in the film.

Walter begins by explaining how he had become an expert in heading off policyholders who try to defraud the company. He continues: "You're like the guy behind the roulette wheel, watching the customers to make sure they don't crook the house. And then one night you get to thinking how you could crook the house yourself and do it smart, because you've got the wheel right smack under your hands. You know every notch in it by heart. And you figure all you need is a plant out front, a shill to put down the bet. Suddenly the doorbell rings, and the whole set-up is right there in the room with you."[32]

Referring to this passage, as it appears in both book and film, J.P. Telotte says, "It is Walter's understanding of the insurance industry and how its policies operate that leads him to give free rein to his desires and to believe that his murder and insurance collection scheme could be perfect."[33]

Principal photography commenced on September 27, 1943. Wilder aimed to give an uncompromising picture of the decadence of the underside of American life, as represented by the back streets of Los Angeles, where the film is set. Consequently, he shot a number of scenes on location in and around the city. It is a drab world, devoid of beauty and decency.

The grey atmosphere reflects the bleak lives of the characters, who live in rundown neighborhoods that have seen better days. Thus Walter occupies a chintzy bachelor flat, while Phyllis lives with a husband who is nearly twice her age in a crumbling stucco bungalow. (The house used in the film is located at 6301 Quebec Street in the Hollywood Hills.) As Wilder mentions in the foreword to this book, Phyllis is a poor housekeeper, which is an index of her indifference to her husband.

Barry Norman notes that Wilder saw to it that Barbara Stanwyck was made up to look slightly tarnished, complete with a garish blond wig and a gaudy ankle bracelet, in order to suggest the cheap, metallic look of "the archetypal, desirable slut."[34] In other words, Wilder wanted Phyllis to look as tawdry as her home. It is ironic, then, that when Neff meets Phyllis for the first time, she is draped in the white bath towel she had donned for sunbathing. Phyllis's white apparel suggests purity in color only, for, as the story unfolds, she will display her true colors.

The opening credits of the film show the silhouette of a man hobbling toward the camera on crutches; his shadow grows progressively larger until it fills the screen. This menacing image prefigures how Walter Neff will temporarily impersonate Phyllis's crippled husband after Walter has murdered him.

The film proper opens with a stunning sequence: A speeding car careens down a dark street late at night; a stoplight in the foreground of the shot changes from go to stop, but the auto runs the light. "This is, of course, a visual symbol for everything we are about to learn about the car's occupant, Walter Neff," says Richard Schickel. Walter "has run all the stoplights in his relationship with Phyllis Dietrichson."[35] Putting it another way, Walter has ignored all the warning signs that foretold that he would be wrecked by his dangerous liaison with Phyllis.

Nursing a gunshot wound in his shoulder, Walter lurches into the building that houses the offices of the Pacific All-Risk Insurance Company, where he is employed. He settles down at his desk, inserts a cylinder into the dictaphone, and begins to dictate a memo to Barton Keyes (Edward G. Robinson), chief claims investigator for the insurance company. The memo takes the form of a confession, which Walter narrates, voice-over on the sound track, while the story of his deadly alliance with Phyllis is portrayed in flashback. Walter's caustic voice-over narration thus provides a running commentary on the events unfolding on the screen.

Since Walter is dictating an office memorandum, he supplies some vital statistics, starting with the date, July 16, 1938. He identifies himself as "Walter Neff, insurance agent, thirty-five years old, unmarried." He glances down at the bullet wound in his shoulder and adds, "No visible scars, until a little while ago, that is." Then, with a line lifted from a later scene in the book (80), Walter observes stoically that he killed Dietrichson: "I killed him for money and a woman. I didn't get the money and I didn't get the woman." It is remarks such as this that Walter makes in the course of the movie that lend the film a fatalistic atmosphere, for the viewer knows that Walter is doomed from the start.

With that, Walter begins to tell his tale, voice-over on the sound track.

Wilder reminds the viewer during the film that Walter is relating his own story by periodically returning to Walter sitting before the dictaphone, and each time Wilder does so, the bloodstain on Walter's suit coat gets gradually larger. As Walter starts to narrate his story, he begins with lines once more taken over directly from the novella (3). He says, "It all began last May. I remembered this policy renewal on Los Feliz Boulevard, so I drove over there," to the home of H.S. Dietrichson.

Chandler and Wilder concocted some salty innuendo-strewn interchanges for Walter and Phyllis not found in Cain's novelette. A striking example occurs during their first encounter. Walter gets fresh with Phyllis after eyeing her provocatively draped in a beach towel. Phyllis responds in a playful, coy fashion that demonstrates that she is Walter's match when it comes to naughty innuendo: "There's a speed limit in this state, Mr. Neff."

"Suppose you get down off your motorcycle and give me a ticket," Walter replies. "Suppose I let you off with a warning this time," Phyllis answers with a smirk. This passage of dialogue, involving a speeding ticket, of course, reminds the viewer of Walter's reckless driving in the film's opening scene.

At any rate, the banter continues; as Walter prepares to leave, he inquires suggestively if Phyllis will be home when he returns to see her husband. "I wonder what you mean," Phyllis says. Walter retorts, "I wonder if you wonder." As a matter of fact, when Walter returns for another visit, Phyllis is home but she has made sure that her husband is not. Phyllis broaches to Walter the possibility of his drawing up a double indemnity accident policy for her husband. In due course, this leads to their planning Dietrichson's death for the insurance money.

Walter's better judgment tells him not to get involved with a femme fatale like Phyllis, writes Frank Krutnik, and Walter's "voice-over commentary provides a suggestively phallic metaphor for the danger and excitement" of the enterprise.[36] "I knew I had hold of a red-hot poker," Walter muses, "and the time to drop it was before it burned my hand off." Walter ignores his misgivings, however, and goes along with Phyllis's plot. In short, although Walter is capable of recognizing evil when he sees it, he still succumbs to it.

A central metaphor in the Chandler-Wilder script, according to William Luhr, is that of a trolley car, on which one must ride till the end of the line. When Walter agrees to help Phyllis liquidate her husband, he says that their plan "has got to be perfect, straight down the line." Walter immediately comments in a voice-over, "The machinery had started to move, and nothing could stop it." As Walter prepares to kill Dietrichson later that same night, he reflects on the sound track that Fate "had thrown the switch. The gears had meshed." The trolley "had started to move, and nothing could stop it."

After the murder Keyes parallels Walter's "straight down the line" perception. Keyes suspects Phyllis of having engineered her husband's death with the help of an as-yet-unknown accessory to her plot. "They've committed a murder," he says, "and that's not like taking a trolley ride together, where each one can get off at a different stop. They've got to ride all the way to the end of the line. And it's a one-way trip, and the last stop is the cemetery." Dave Kehr comments that in the film Keyes becomes an "almost supernatural agent of justice . . . who systematically tracks, traps, and punishes the guilty." He emerges as a "pure moral force."[37]

The scene in which Walter murders Phyllis's husband provides a dramatic high point in Walter's narrative. Dietrichson is determined to take a train trip, despite the fact that he has a broken leg and must walk with crutches. As Phyllis drives him to the train station, Walter crouches unseen in the back seat of the car. When Walter suddenly pounces on Dietrichson and chokes him to death, the camera moves in on a closeup of Phyllis, who stares unflinchingly at the road ahead. Wilder later explained that he allowed the audience to imagine the murder, while it takes place off camera, "because what the audience does not see can sometimes be more frightening than what they do see."

Because Dietrichson is slain when he has a broken leg, Walter impersonates him by boarding the train on crutches—thereby recalling the image of the dark figure on crutches in the opening credits. Walter must make it appear that the crippled man was killed as the result of an accidental fall from the train. He accordingly rides the train for a few miles and then jumps off, crutches and all, at the prearranged spot where Phyllis is waiting for him with her husband's corpse still in the car. Walter dumps the body, along with the crutches, on the railroad track, so that it will appear that Dietrichson accidentally fell from the moving train. In this way, Walter and Phyllis hope to collect the double indemnity accident policy.

At this point Wilder introduced a moment of suspense into this scene that was not in the script. When he had finished shooting the segment of the sequence in which Walter and Phyllis make their getaway, after depositing the corpse on the tracks, Wilder interrupted filming for lunch. "I'm on my way to get into my car; I had a lunch date," he remembered. "And my car wouldn't start. And suddenly I said, 'I'm going to do it again . . . differently!'"[38]

This time around, Wilder added the following bit of action: Phyllis attempts to start the car, but the motor stalls because the battery is low. Phyllis and Walter stare at each other in panic. Then Walter desperately reaches over to the dashboard, turns the key in the ignition and guns the motor until the sputtering engine turns over and races. Then they speed away from the crime scene. Wilder thus made the sequence more suspenseful.

It certainly looks as if their plan has worked, and Fate is on their side. But Keyes proves to be an obstacle to the success of their plot, as he continues to suspect that Dietrichson was murdered by Phyllis and an unidentified accomplice. Hence Walter and Phyllis fear that Keyes may eventually finger Walter himself as Phyllis's partner in crime if he happens to see them together.

In one scene Phyllis is about to knock on the door of Walter's apartment when she hears Walter talking with Keyes inside. As the door opens and Keyes comes out, Phyllis quickly hides behind the half-open door, so that Keyes will not be aware of her presence. Fred MacMurray told me that Wilder "tampered with realism" in that scene by having the door open *outward* into the hall, so that Phyllis could conveniently disappear behind it as Keyes leaves—despite the fact that doors normally open inward. Be that as it may, this particular scene provides another suspenseful highlight in the film, as Cain himself noted: "I wish I had thought of something like that."[39]

Later on Walter's relationship with Phyllis completely unravels when he discovers the real reason she has been using him to help her obtain the payoff from the insurance company. She actually plans to double-cross Walter by taking the money and running off—not with him, but with still another man. Walter forces a showdown with Phyllis in her stifling, shuttered living room. "Tangerine" is being crooned somewhere in the night, "probably from a neighboring radio" (as the final draft of the script has it), and the romantic ballad wafts into Phyllis's living room.[40] The love song is an ironic comment on the romantic illusions Walter had nurtured earlier about the faithless Phyllis.

Walter tells Phyllis about Keyes's theory that two people who commit murder are trapped on a trolley car and their only way out is death. He then ruefully informs Phyllis that he is not going to ride the streetcar to the end of the line; rather, he plans to get off the trolley "right at this corner." With that, the pair shoot it out. Phyllis grievously wounds Walter and is about to fire again when she experiences a split second of remorse. She admits that she is "rotten to the heart." Then she looks into his eyes and begs Walter to embrace her. She hesitates to fire the second shot, which will finish him off, and instead professes her need for him. As Bernard Dick describes Phyllis,

"We see what Neff sees—a face that, for an instant, loses its rodent-like sharpness and becomes almost human. But it is only for an instant.[41] Walter, convinced of her deep duplicity, has trusted her for the last time. "I'm sorry, Baby; I'm not buying," he mutters. "Goodbye, Baby." Walter embraces her, then he fires two shots and kills her on the spot. Thus Walter's final embrace of Phyllis ends when he ejaculates bullets into her; it is the logical consummation of their sordid liaison. Walter, though gravely wounded, still has enough life in him to make it to his office and record his confession for Keyes.

After viewing *Double Indemnity,* Cain remarked that it was "the only picture I ever saw made from my books that had things in it I wished I had thought of; Wilder's ending was much better than my ending."[42] It is easy to agree with Cain on that point. The novelette ends with Walter and Phyllis fleeing to Mexico on board a steamer. But they have reason to believe that they have been recognized aboard ship, and so Phyllis, who has by now sunk completely into madness, convinces Walter to join her in a suicide pact in jumping overboard. Phyllis, a grotesque figure dressed in a blood-red shroud, with her face painted a deathly white, materializes like a ghostly apparition in Walter's cabin in order to summon him to his doom. To cite Macbeth, they have supped full with horrors and are prepared to die. The mass audience, Bernard Dick quite rightly judges, "would not understand anything quite so operatic."[43] But they would understand the two erstwhile conspirators having a falling out and shooting each other, which is the way the film portrays their doom.

Keyes, in describing his job as a claims investigator for Walter earlier in the movie, defines his role as "a doctor, a bloodhound, a cop, a judge, a jury, and a father-confessor, all in one." Certainly Keyes is Walter's father-confessor, since it is to Keyes that Walter confesses his crimes on the dictaphone. In fact, the father-son relationship between Walter and Keyes is evident throughout the film. Indeed, Wilder confirmed in conversation that Walter's nonsexual male relationship with Keyes is contrasted in the movie with his sexual involvement with Phyllis. Moreover, Cain added, "there's a hint" of the filial relationship of Walter to Keyes in the book, "but it was extended in the movie."[44]

Brian Gallagher notes that in the novella "the only hint of anything more than a business relationship between Keyes and Walter comes in this rather flat exchange," after Walter confesses to Dietrichson's murder.[45] Keyes says, "I'm sorry. I've kind of liked you." Walter answers, "I know, same here" (104).

By contrast, in the film Walter makes his confession via the dictaphone to Keyes, his father-confessor, in recognition of the bond that exists between them. As Walter finishes dictating his memo to Keyes, he looks up and sees Keyes, who has been summoned by the night porter; he has been standing in the doorway, unobserved, for some time. Walter tells Keyes that he could not identify Dietrichson's murderer "because the guy you were looking for was too close. He was right across the desk from you." Keyes replies laconically, "Closer than that, Walter." Walter responds wryly, "I love you too." Despite his offhand, almost mocking tone of voice, the remark nonetheless reflects the deep affection and respect he nurtures for Keyes.

In essence, Walter expressed something to Keyes that he could never have said to Phyllis.

Indeed, the notion of love surfaces more than once in the easy banter in which Walter and Keyes indulge at times. For the bond of mutual respect and trust shared by Walter and Keyes, says Telotte, "sharply contrasts with the skewed relationship of desire that links Walter and Phyllis; they ultimately seem to lack any respect or trust for each other. In fact, they never describe their mutual attraction as 'love.'"[46] Actually, there is something touching about the manner in which Walter cleanses his soul by confessing his sins to Keyes and finds comfort in the presence of his surrogate father as he lies dying.

Walter's strength is ebbing away, but he still manages to put a cigarette in his mouth, and Keyes lights it for him. By doing so, Keyes is performing for Walter the ritual gesture of friendship that Walter had often performed for him. Throughout the film Walter lit Keyes's cigar for him, as an implicit gesture of filial feeling for his father figure. Now Keyes, with a veiled display of affection, returns the favor, as they await the police.

Some critics have inferred a hint of homosexuality in the relationship of Walter and Keyes, but such a reading of a Wilder movie misconstrues the value the director places on male companionship in a number of his films. In the present instance, Walter has never experienced a significant relationship in his life. Consequently, he experiences in his friendship with Keyes a meaningful platonic relationship that is fulfilling for him—and for Keyes—on a deep emotional level that has nothing to do with sex.

Tony Thomas, in his otherwise admirable book on the films of the 1940s, erroneously asserts that "the story ends with Walter in the gas chamber."[47] In point of fact, writes William Marling, Wilder actually filmed Walter "dying in the gas chamber at Folsom Prison, a set that cost Paramount $150,000 and took five days of shooting." (Perhaps Wilder had the Snyder-Gray execution in mind when he developed the execution scene with Chandler.) Nevertheless, after Wilder viewed the completed sequence, almost eighteen minutes of footage, he felt uneasy about it.[48] He found the execution scene unduly gruesome and too harsh for the mass audience to digest, so he decided to end the film with Walter lying grievously wounded in the company of his fatherly friend.

In point of fact, the execution scene was shot before the scene portraying the last meeting between Walter and Keyes. Once that final, intimate exchange between Walter and Keyes was in the can, Wilder began to wonder if the execution scene was not superfluous. What's more, without the execution scene to follow it, the viewer easily infers that Walter will soon die of his fatal wound. Thus, when Walter begs Keyes to give him time to make it across the border to Mexico, Keyes replies, "You'll never make the elevator." Walter nevertheless staggers toward the exit, only to collapse helplessly in the doorway, where he lies at death's door. Presumably, one assumes, he will die in Keyes's arms, perhaps even before the police arrive.

The final version of the screenplay omits not only the execution scene but also an additional line of dialogue spoken by Walter to Keyes just after Walter says, "I love you too"—which is actually the last line in the final script and in the film as released. At this point in the original draft, Walter makes a final request of Keyes: "At the end of the trolley line, just as I get off, you be there to say goodbye, will you, Keyes?"[49] This line was originally meant to serve as a transition to the execution scene, for, as James Naremore remarks, the initial version of the script "went on to show Keyes at the penitentiary, honoring his friend's wishes."[50] Walter's reference to the trolley car hearkens back to Keyes's earlier observation to Walter that Phyllis and her partner in crime were trapped on a trolley car that would carry them to their doom. With or without the execution scene, Keyes's ominous prediction remains true.

Richard Schickel assumes that the ending of the released version of the film constitutes "new material" that Wilder and Chandler devised as a substitute for the execution sequence. A comparison of the original version of the screenplay (dated September 25, 1943) with the final version of the script, both of which are preserved at the Library of the Motion Picture Academy, shows his assumption to be false, however. The final script is shorter than the original screenplay simply because it omits the death chamber sequence and ends the film with the final encounter of Walter and Keyes in the insurance office. In any case, the gas chamber sequence seems to be an anticlimax to the story. By contrast, the ending of the movie as it stands is much more powerful and moving, and could not be bettered.

As Wilder told the young director Cameron Crowe (*Jerry Maguire*) in Crowe's 1999 book, *Conversations with Wilder,* "I didn't need" the gas chamber scene. "I knew it when I was filming the next-to-last scene. The story was between the two guys. I knew it, even though I had already filmed the gas chamber scene.... What the hell do we need to see him die for? Right? So we just took out the scene in the gas chamber."[51]

Schickel sees the darkened office in which Walter dictates his confession as representing "the darkness that has closed more and more tightly around him ever since his first meeting with Phyllis."[52] That shadowy, sinister atmosphere implies that *Double Indemnity* is an example of film noir. In fact, *Double Indemnity,* as a dark pitiless meditation on the primal passion of greed, ranks as one of the summits of film noir.

Principal photography was completed on November 24, 1943, less than two month after it began. Fred MacMurray was pleased with the way the picture had turned out, he said in conversation. He had initially hesitated to accept the role of Walter Neff, because he normally played "happy-go-lucky good guys" and feared that Wilder's wish to cast him against type as a cad and a scoundrel would ruin his screen image. But Wilder wanted MacMurray to play Walter Neff precisely because Walter's charming manner and affable grin belie the lust and larceny inside him; and MacMurray's surface charm made his performance all the more chilling as a result. Similarly, Barbara Stanwyck initially hesitated to accept the role of Phyllis Dietrichson, since she temporarily balked at playing a woman so thoroughly malicious and unscrupulous. (Indeed, MacMurray and Stanwyck had been previously paired in a 1940 romantic comedy written by Preston Sturges, *Remember the Night.*)

One might hazard that, because Wilder changed Phyllis's last name from Nirdlinger to Dietrichson and had Stanwyck wear an icy blond wig throughout the movie, Phyllis was meant to suggest the cold-blooded villainesses played by Marlene Dietrich in pictures such as *Blonde Venus.* Be that as it may, Barbara Stanwyck's portrayal of Phyllis won her a place in film history as the quintessential femme fatale. Phyllis, William Phillips affirms, is the "attractive, dangerous woman" who totally outmatches the eager, gullible males she manipulates. "She is a femme who in more than one sense is fatale."[53]

Wilder remembers that after a sneak preview of the picture in a theater in Westwood Village, Cain waited for him in the lobby and told him that he much admired the film. Critics hailed the movie as a thriller deftly served up by master chefs, with a superior script and inspired direction, topped off by Miklós Rózsa's stark, angular, throbbing musical score.

Chandler was much less amiable than Cain. His parting shot at Wilder came in his essay "Writers in Hollywood," in which he observed, "The first picture I worked on was nominated for an Academy Award (if that means anything), but I was not even invited to the press review held right in the studio."[54] Chandler rather ungraciously neglected to mention in the essay that he had been kept on salary during the eight-week shooting period and that no changes were made in the screenplay without his approval—a very rare accommodation to a screenwriter in those days. Wilder was understandably offended by Chandler's statement. "We didn't invite him to the preview? How could we?" Wilder retorted. "He was under the table drunk at Lucy's," a bistro near Paramount, frequented by Chandler and other studio employees.[55]

A Paramount press release about Chandler, cited by Al Clark, blithely asserted that "Chandler rarely touches alcohol at any time, and never while working. When at work, Chandler stimulates himself continually and exclusively with tea." It is true that Chandler had officially sworn off liquor by the time he went to work at Paramount, Clark comments, but Chandler was a closet alcoholic who kept a pint bottle of bourbon stashed in his briefcase, and he would sneak a nip in his office or elsewhere during the working day, whenever he thought no one was looking. "Chandler responded all too easily to the climate of genial dipsomania" that prevailed among many of the writers, and regularly drank with them at the end of the day at Lucy's.[56]

Frank MacShane adds that the drinking led Chandler to womanizing. Married to a woman nearly twenty years his senior, Chandler found that the young secretaries and starlets employed at the studio reminded him of his lost youth. He therefore had a roving eye as he moved about the studio lot. Chandler's liaisons never lasted very long, though, MacShane concludes, because his wife and his home "remained the center of his life."[57]

Admittedly, Chandler's relationship with Wilder turned sour while they were coscripting *Double Indemnity.* Nevertheless, in fairness to Chandler, it must be stated that it was Wilder who got things off to a bad start by literally throwing Chandler's first draft of the script in his face. In addition, Wilder had stormy relationships with other screenwriters besides Chandler. For the record, Charles Brackett, with whom Wilder coscripted *Sunset Boulevard* and other movies, had an especially contentious professional relationship with Wilder. Furthermore, Harry Kurnitz, who cowrote with Wilder the screenplay of *Witness for the Prosecution,* was another veteran of the Wilder wars. He quipped, "Let's face it, ... Billy Wilder at work is actually two people—Mr. Hyde and Mr. Hyde."[58]

That is certainly how Wilder appeared to Chandler. Years later, in a letter to a British publisher, Hamish Hamilton, dated November 10, 1950, Chandler wrote that his collaboration with Wilder was "an agonizing experience and has probably shortened my life; but I learned from it as much about screenwriting as I am capable of learning, which is not very much."[59] Referring to this letter, Wilder noted, "Chandler later said that he had a miserable time with me because I was a son-of-a-bitch. However, he also said that all he knew about pictures was what he had learned from me." Chandler would be the first to admit that he could be grumpy and grouchy, Wilder went on. "When I did see him, he would kind of growl." Wilder then added, much to Chandler's credit, that he preferred working with a "rather acid man" like Chandler to the kind of novelist who sees Hollywood solely as a source of easy money and never takes screenwriting seriously. Not so Chandler. "Give me a collaborator like Chandler any day." Asked by Cameron Crowe why he had upgraded his opinion of Chandler over the years, Wilder replied, "The anger gets washed [away]. You forget it. I certainly forgive Mr. Chandler."[60]

After all is said and done, the screenplay for *Double Indemnity* proved once and for all that Chandler could tackle a job on order and for hire and do it well, thereby vindicating the confidence that Wilder had placed in him. In actual fact, Chandler was very pleased with the way the picture had turned out. With the perspective that comes with distance, Chandler said a decade later that *Double Indemnity* "was the favorite film of all he had been associated with" and described Wilder as "an odd little director with a touch of genius."[61]

Furthermore, it is worth noting that the American Film Institute honored the best one hundred American films made during the first century of cinema with a television special aired on June 16, 1998. Numbered among the films, which were chosen by a panel of film professionals and critics, was *Double Indemnity*.

It was after the release of *Double Indemnity* that Chandler published "Writers in Hollywood" in the *Atlantic Monthly*. He wrote to Charles Morton, the magazine's managing editor on December 12, 1945, that "my blast at Hollywood was received here in frozen silence." He then quoted Charles Brackett, Wilder's longtime collaborator, as saying in reply to the essay, "Chandler's books are not good enough, nor his pictures bad enough, to justify that article." Chandler countered, "I would reply to Mr. Brackett that if my books had been worse, I should not have been invited to Hollywood; and if they had been better, I should not have come."[62]

10

No Way to Treat a Lady

The Blue Dahlia and Other Screenplays

Somewhere along the line the world has lost all of its standards
and all its taste.
> —Mrs. Gerald Hayden, a matriarch,
> in *Where Love Is Gone*

The bottom is loaded with nice people; only cream and
bastards rise.
> —Lew Harper, private investigator,
> in the film *Harper*

Sometime after Chandler finished with *Double Indemnity,* John Houseman asked him to collaborate on Houseman's first assignment as a producer at Paramount. It was the film version of *Her Heart in Her Throat* by Ethel White, the author of the novel on which Alfred Hitchcock had based his 1938 film *The Lady Vanishes.* Filmmaker Lewis Allen (*The Uninvited*) was assigned to direct.

The Unseen

An early draft of the screenplay, dated July 6, 1943, was written by Ken Englund. His script, as well as the subsequent drafts of the screenplay, are in the Paramount Collection of the Library of the Motion Picture Academy.

Englund's preliminary screenplay was put into the hands of Hagar Wilde, whom Houseman remembered as a "witty, neurotic" author. She completed a draft, in consultation with Houseman, on April 24, 1944.[1] The story centers on Elizabeth Howard (played by Gail Russell), a young governess who journeys to a genteel rural town. An embittered young widower (Joel McCrea) has engaged her to take care of his two small children, Barnaby and Ellen. Fielding's gloomy house is falling into disrepair, and Joseph Goodwin (Norman Lloyd), a friend of David's, urges him to sell the old place.

Elizabeth soon becomes aware of sinister, weird happenings in the cellar of the deserted, boarded-up house next door. A prowler has more than once been glimpsed by a passerby through the windows of the spooky, shuttered mansion in the night. To make matters worse, Elizabeth learns that the corpse of Alberta, a maid employed by David, has been found near the Fielding home, and Davis is a possible suspect in the murder case. Some other suspicious characters who people the story are Marian Tygarth (Isobel Elsom), the middle-aged woman who owns the mysterious, portentous domicile next door to David's home and plans to reopen it, and the enigmatic Dr. Charles Evans (Herbert Marshall), who seems to know more about the secrets of the old Tygarth mansion than he is prepared to reveal.

Hagar Wilde failed to provide a solution to the mystery for the film version of the novel that was any more plausible than the one in the novel. When Wilde took sick, William Dozier, who supervised the Story Department at Paramount, suggested that Houseman invite Raymond Chandler to come on board and finish the job. Chandler accepted Houseman's offer of one thousand dollars a week to polish Wilde's script draft, a substantial salary raise over what he had made on *Double Indemnity.* He set to work on the script for the next seven weeks. Chandler and Houseman eventually opted to finger Dr. Evans as the villain of the piece.

At the movie's climax David follows Marian Tygarth into the murky, forbidding basement of her neighboring house, where she has a secret meeting with Evans, while David himself remains unobserved as he eavesdrops. David learns that twelve years earlier Marian was scheduled to move to Europe with her husband, Commodore Tygarth. But the night before their departure she conspired to have Evans, her lover, murder the Commodore and bury his body in the cellar. Marian took off for Europe the next day, after giving out the story that her husband was accompanying her. She had promised to share her husband's wealth with Evans, but she took along the Commodore's fortune when she departed and left Evans, her dupe, behind.

When Evans got word that Marian had recently returned to America and planned to reopen the old, dark house, he took to sneaking into the mansion and searching the basement for any telltale signs that the Commodore's corpse was buried in the cellar, so that Tygarth's murder would never come to light. It was Evans, then, who murdered David's maid, Alberta, because she had actually seen him emerging onto the street from the cellar of the Tygarth residence while it was still boarded up.

In the wake of Marian's discussion of these past events with Evans, Marian realizes that Evans plans to avenge himself on her for double-crossing him. She abruptly pulls a gun, in order to shoot him before he has a chance to kill her, but Evans is quicker on the trigger than Marian, and he shoots her dead, while he escapes unwounded. David sends for Police Detective Sullivan (Tom Tully) post haste. Then he confronts Evans about his guilt, and Sullivan arrives in time to take the murderer away.

Given the significant contribution Chandler made to the final shooting script of *The Unseen,* it comes as no surprise that the ending he worked out with Houseman is reminiscent of the conclusion of *Double Indemnity.* Like Phyllis Dietrichson, Marian Tygarth manipulated her lover into murdering her husband for his money, all the while planning to leave him in the lurch. Like Walter Neff, Evans wreaks vengeance on his ex-lover for double-crossing him. Therefore I cannot agree with Tom Hiney that "Chandler's touch is invisible" in the film.[2] For it is Chandler, in tandem with Houseman, who devised the film's riveting conclusion.

Furthermore, Houseman had asked Chandler to toughen Wilde's rather bland dialogue, and Chandler complied by peppering the dialogue with some of his own sardonic wit. Thus David, who is often exasperated with his mischievous children, at one point spies them staring at him through the bannister bars on the stairs and snaps, "That's where they belong: behind bars."

The usually precise Philip Durham mistakenly asserts that *The Unseen* was "directed by John Houseman," instead of by Lewis Allen.[3] Allen himself remembered Chandler as a rather down-to-earth chap who would not stand for any nonsense from a producer. "Look, John," Chandler would say, when Houseman attempted to take his blue pencil to the script and alter some of Chandler's lines, "I'm the fucking writer."[4] Norman Lloyd, who played Jasper Goodwin, was not so positively impressed with Chandler. "The one time I met Chandler was in Houseman's office," he recalled. "We went across the street and had a cup of coffee. He was a rather irascible sort of *itchy* guy, but interesting, of course."[5]

Houseman believed that the "surprisingly favorable reviews we received" on the movie's release were due in some degree to Chandler, who had helped to provide a solid and well-constructed script for this taut, gripping thriller.[6] Even the hard-to-please James Agee thought the film was done with "intelligence and sophistication."[7] Moreover, more than one critic made a point of mentioning Chandler's association with the picture. Such observations clearly indicated Chandler's increasing visibility as a Hollywood screenwriter.

And Now Tomorrow

Chandler was involved in two vehicles for Alan Ladd during his time at Paramount. The first was *And Now Tomorrow* (1944), made just before *The Unseen*. Ladd had received an honorable discharge from the U.S. Army in November 1943, and Chandler was assigned to polish the dialogue of the script for the picture that marked his return to the screen. *And Now Tomorrow* was a gauzy tearjerker that Frank Partos had adapted from the Rachel Fields best-seller. This kind of story was not Chandler's cup of tea, but he gave the script his best shot.

Like *The Unseen, And Now Tomorrow* takes place in a sleepy village. Dr. Merek Vance (Alan Ladd), a young doctor who grew up there on the wrong side of the tracks, returns to the community from Pittsburgh at the invitation of Dr. Weeks (Cecil Kellaway), a local general practitioner. The Blairs, the first family of the town, own the local mill. The aristocratic, spoiled Emily Blair (Loretta Young) has lost her hearing as a result of an attack of meningitis and has accordingly postponed indefinitely her marriage to Jeff Stoddard (Barry Sullivan).

As luck would have it, Merek is experimenting with a new ear serum, which he hopes will restore the hearing of his deaf patients. After Emily collapses in his office during a preliminary examination, Merek asks her if she would like to be the first patient to try the new serum; she accepts the invitation. The operation is an unqualified success. "The ex-proletarian doctor restores her hearing and, presumably, dissolves her snobbery," as James Agee puts it,[8] for Merek and Emily plan to begin life anew in Pittsburgh.

In contrast to *The Unseen, And Now Tomorrow* shows few signs of Chandler's stamp on it, beyond some scattered lines of tough, witty dialogue. For example, in the copy of the shooting script in the Chandler Collection at the UCLA Research Library, dated December 3, 1943, we find Merek flippantly addressing the counterman at a coffee bar: "Coffee. Hot, strong, and made this year." Paul Jensen observes that Chandler's "presence" can be felt in this line because it is lifted from Chandler's 1939 novel *The Big Sleep*.[10]

Barry Sullivan, who played Jeff Stoddard, recalls seeing Chandler on the set, "behaving very much like an observer; and I only got to know him because we'd go across the street at lunchtime and have a couple of snorts at Lucy's," the same café where Chandler hung out while he was working on *Double Indemnity*. At the time Sullivan never thought of Chandler as anyone special: "When you know somebody in the present, you never think they will eventually be legends."[11]

Some reviewers judged *And Now Tomorrow* to be low-wattage melodrama, a maudlin soap opera aimed at the washboard weepers in the mass audience; one even said that it is the kind of picture that you go to optimistically and come away from misty optically. Others, while conceding that it was a three-handkerchief movie, contended that director Irving Pichel (*The Pied Piper*), aided by a competent cast, had wrung a good deal of honest emotion from this sentimental yarn about a poor little rich girl disabled by a serious disease. In any event, the picture did a brisk business at the box office, mostly because Alan Ladd was one of the biggest superstars of the period. Be that as it may, the fact remains that the three films with which Chandler had been associated thus far had all been box office favorites.

Years later Chandler recalled that William Dozier "had some confidence in me, because I had (unwillingly) rescued" some turkeys for him. Chandler no doubt had both *And Now Tomorrow* and *The Unseen* in mind, since both films benefited from his script doctoring. "I don't regard myself in any way as a really good screenwriter," he added, but "I am a good dialogue writer."[12] Nonetheless, Chandler was by this time growing tired of script doctoring. Making a movie, he told a friend, is like executing an oil painting "in Macy's basement with the janitor mixing your colors."[13] This was his way of saying that he disliked merely touching up scripts that were mainly the work of other writers. He longed for the day when he could write an original screenplay that was all his own. Little did he know that that day was at hand.

The Blue Dahlia

Like William Dozier, John Houseman also had confidence in Chandler. He indicates this in his account of how Chandler came to author an original screenplay for *The Blue Dahlia*, which he recalls in his introduction to the published screenplay. Early in 1945 the front office at Paramount realized that Alan Ladd would be returning to the army within three months. At a meeting of the studio's producers, Henry Ginsberg, the head of production, urged those present to propose a vehicle for Ladd that could be rushed into production and shot before Ladd reentered the service. Two days later, while Chandler was lunching with Houseman at Lucy's, Chandler mentioned that he had reached a dead end on the novel he was writing and was toying with the idea of turning the story into a screenplay instead. Houseman asked if he could read the uncompleted novel, and Chandler agreed.

They went to Chandler's home, where Houseman read the manuscript, entitled *The Blue Dahlia*, which amounted to 120 pages. Houseman enthusiastically took the typescript back to the studio, and in another two days Paramount had purchased the screen rights to *The Blue Dahlia* for twenty-five thousand dollars. The film was to be produced by Houseman, under Joseph Sistrom's supervision as executive producer. Chandler's title was adopted by the tabloid press reporting a real Hollywood murder case, the slaying of a call girl they nicknamed "the Black Dahlia." But the only connection the actual case had with Chandler's scenario was the title.

Chandler forthwith prepared a detailed treatment of the film's main plot, including some sample dialogue passages. He submitted this scenario to the studio on January 18, 1945. Chandler said at the time that he had managed to compose the ninety-page treatment in less than two weeks: "It was an experiment; and for a guy subject from early childhood to plot-constipation, it was rather a revelation. Some of the stuff is good, some very much not."[14]

Spenser Selby errs in saying that *The Blue Dahlia* is "Chandler's only original screenplay," since *Playback* was also an original screenplay. He is right, however, in stating that *Dahlia* "emphasizes the major noir theme of a war veteran's difficult, disillusioning return to the states.[15] The treatment, which is in the Paramount Collection of the Library of the Motion Picture Academy, begins with three returning navy veterans. Each has been accorded an early discharge "because of wounds or stress" they suffered in combat.[16] Johnny Morrison (Alan Ladd) is mustered out of the navy with his buddies George Copeland (Hugh Beaumont) and Buzz Wanchek (William Bendix), and they return home to Los Angeles. Buzz in particular had been severely wounded in battle when a shell fragment struck his head. Buzz and George are bachelors and decide to share an apartment. But Johnny goes home to his wife Helen, only to discover that she has been living it up with her wealthy, decadent friends. She now resides in a bungalow at the posh Cavendish

Court Hotel, courtesy of her gangster boyfriend Eddie Harwood (Howard Da Silva). "Counterpointing the sacrifices and heroism" of Johnny and his comrades, Nicholas Christopher writes, is "the obvious self-indulgence" of Johnny's unfaithful wife Helen (Doris Dowling) and her lover, who is the owner of a Sunset Strip nightclub called the Blue Dahlia. A film like *The Blue Dahlia*, Christopher concludes, draws a sharp contrast between those who took their licks at the front and "those who stayed home, living high off the hog." Helen's crowd is "not just soft, but rotten."[17]

On the night of Johnny's return, Helen is murdered—that, as the saying goes, is no way to treat a lady. The police, once they hear about Johnny's disastrous "homecoming," immediately single out Johnny as the prime suspect. Johnny tries to solve the case in order to vindicate himself. That same night, he by chance meets Joyce Harwood (Veronica Lake), the estranged wife of Eddie Harwood. Joyce feels a certain kinship with Johnny, since her husband cheated on her with Helen, who in turn was two-timing Johnny with Eddie. Joyce therefore agrees to help Johnny find his wife's killer, so that he can clear himself. As the story unfolds in Chandler's treatment, he depicts the underbelly of Los Angeles, with its racketeers and shady ladies, in an incisive manner that parallels his fiction.

The treatment concludes with Buzz being revealed as the unwitting slayer of Johnny's wife. Buzz, it seems, has a steel plate in his skull, the result of his war injury, and the plate causes him severe headaches and memory lapses. When the case is wrapped up, it becomes evident that Buzz, Johnny's loyal sidekick, deeply resented Helen's shoddy treatment of Johnny. Hence, when Helen made some disparaging remarks about Johnny in his presence, he became enraged and murdered her. Buzz then suffered a blackout, which totally blotted out his memory of the deed. In the end, when Johnny reluctantly decides to have Buzz institutionalized, he mutters wistfully, "I hope he never remembers it."[18]

After the studio approved the treatment, Chandler set to work on a full-scale screenplay; he delivered the first half of the script within three weeks, averaging about five pages a day. This was not a miraculous feat, since Chandler had already mapped out all of the action in the treatment and employed much of the dialogue from the unfinished novel in the screenplay. After the first seventy-five pages of the shooting script had been mimeographed, the front office decreed that principal photography would commence in three weeks in order to finish shooting the picture before Ladd went back to war.

Veteran filmmaker George Marshall (*Destry Rides Again*), an efficient

journeyman director, was set to direct the picture, and shooting got underway on schedule. Filming moved along at a brisk pace; indeed, Marshall
was two days ahead of schedule by the third week of production. By the
fourth week Marshall was rapidly gaining on Chandler. The director had
shot the bulk of the pages that Chandler had already supplied and would
soon run out of material if Chandler did not work faster.

"Ray's problem with the script," said Houseman, "was a simple one;
he had no ending."[19] Houseman seems to imply that Chandler's progress
on the second half of the screenplay was impeded because he was suffering
from writer's block. In actual fact, Chandler had devised a perfect ending
for the film, as outlined in the treatment, whereby Buzz was identified as
the murderer. But that ending was rejected out of hand as unacceptable for
the script.

The facts behind this turn of events were these: Since World War II
was still being waged, the studio submitted the screenplay to the Department of the Navy. Chandler was advised that the navy censor absolutely
refused to approve the script's closing episodes because the culprit turned
out to be a mentally disturbed navy veteran, and that would prove harmful
to the service's image—during wartime no less.

So Chandler's solution to the mystery was jettisoned; as a result, he
became discouraged and experienced great difficulty in coming up with a
solution to the crime that was as good as the original one. To be precise, he
had to decide which of the other suspects he could plausibly pin the murder on. Among the possibilities were Eddie Harwood, who knew that Helen
was not above trying to blackmail him by threatening to reveal to the police
a dark secret from his past of which she was aware. Then there was Dad
Newell (Will Wright), the disreputable house detective at the Cavendish
Court Hotel where Helen lived, who exploited his position as a house detective to cover up the crooked activities in which he was involved on the
sly. This devious house dick was certainly capable of murder.

Meanwhile the camera continued to eat up the pages of the shooting
script, and still Chandler had not provided an alternate solution for the
mystery that he personally found satisfying. Finally, Henry Ginsberg warned
Chandler that the studio would suffer a serious financial setback if the remaining pages of the screenplay were not delivered on schedule and offered
Chandler a five-thousand-dollar bonus if he met the deadline. Chandler
was so incensed by Ginsberg's proposal that he went straight to Houseman
and threatened to resign from the picture.

To Chandler, Houseman later explained, the proffered bonus was nothing short of a bribe. "To be offered a large sum of money for the completion of an assignment . . . which he had every intention of fulfilling" was, according to Chandler's ethical standards, an insult. Furthermore, Chandler, like Houseman, had been educated in England, and he had always proudly maintained that he and Houseman were the only two studio employees who were graduates of English public schools—and as such they shared a common code of honor unknown to their colleagues at Paramount. Moreover, Chandler pointed out to Houseman that Ginsberg had made his proposal "behind your back, John." Chandler was therefore convinced that "he had been invited to betray a friend and fellow public school man" by being invited to make a private deal with the studio chief.[20]

At this juncture Marshall sent word to Houseman from the set that he had only a few pages of script left to shoot, including some scenes that could not be shot until Chandler had settled upon the identity of the murderer. When Houseman accordingly reminded Chandler that Ladd was scheduled to return to active service within ten days, Chandler withdrew his threat of resigning.

The next day Chandler made the following proposal to Houseman. Chandler declared that he was unwilling and unable to attempt to finish the screenplay sober. But, because "alcohol gave him energy and self-assurance he could achieve in no other way," he was willing and able to complete the script drunk. Chandler then presented to the startled Houseman a sheet of yellow, lined paper (the same kind as that on which he had composed his list of complaints against Billy Wilder while they were coscripting *Double Indemnity*).

The list of requirements outlined on the page included two limousines, "to stand by day and night outside the house with drivers available for . . . taking script pages to and from the studio." In addition, "six secretaries—in three relays of two—to be available at all times for dictation and typing."[21] Houseman conferred with Joseph Sistrom, who said that he would tell the front office that Chandler was suffering from a virus and had to work at home. Sistrom would then requisition the limos and secretaries according to Chandler's specifications. Norman Lloyd, who knew both Chandler and Houseman at Paramount, believed that Chandler offered to take such extraordinary measures to finish the script because "there was between Houseman and Chandler this *tie*" (the "old school tie" was, of course, the bond between them). "I don't think Chandler would have done it . . . if he didn't have great respect for John."[22]

In David Thomas's 1988 television documentary, *Raymond Chandler:*

Murder He Wrote, John Houseman recalls visiting Chandler at home while he was finishing off the screenplay: "He worked fairly fast; he did three or four pages a day. What's more, he corrected his own work. He was absolutely lucid, as far as the script was concerned." Chandler's finished pages would be ferried by limo to Paramount, where they would be promptly mimeographed. Finally, a lad would bicycle them to the set and deliver the pages, still wet from the mimeo machine, directly into the hands of George Marshall.

The finished shooting script was dated March 15, 1945, and shooting was completed with six days to spare, so that Ladd was ready to return to the service in good time. At all events, Ladd was never reinducted into the army, according to film historian Ed Muller, who cites Beverly Linet's definitive biography of Ladd. It was near the end of the war and the government was easing up on recalling married men over thirty with children; Ladd qualified on all of these scores. "He hung around his ranch in Hidden Valley while his wife, Sue Carol, negotiated a new deal with Paramount."[23] Surprisingly, Houseman never mentioned this ironic twist to the tale of Chandler's harried rush to finish *The Blue Dahlia* while fueled by bourbon. Yet as a Paramount producer, Houseman must have known that Ladd did not have to reenlist.

Although there is something melodramatic about Chandler going on a week-long bender to finish the script, the fact remains that he had indulged in serious drinking during his entire time at Paramount. He began drinking alone in his office while he was collaborating with Wilder on *Double Indemnity*, as already mentioned. As we know, Barry Sullivan recalled drinking with him at lunchtime at Lucy's while Chandler was working on *And Now Tomorrow*. In addition, as also recorded above, Chandler was in the habit of boozing regularly at Lucy's at the end of the day with various colleagues from the studio throughout his Paramount stint. To go further, Hiney reports that Chandler was having trouble keeping up the pace of writing the screenplay of *Dahlia* as fast as Marshall was shooting it— not just because the navy had scotched his original ending, but because he had been drinking heavily for some time. In fact, he took to showing up at the studio some days in no condition to work because he was nursing a hangover.

Houseman was apparently aware of Chandler's drinking after hours, but not that Chandler had been drinking during the working day, both at lunchtime and in his office. Consequently, when Chandler requested Houseman's permission to finish the screenplay while drunk, he was really getting Houseman to sanction officially something that Chandler had been doing on the sly all along: drinking on the job. "*The Blue Dahlia* was certainly written under the extreme influence of alcohol," from beginning to end, Hiney bluntly concludes.[24] Accordingly, Chandler's offer to complete the script drunk was not just a question of his wish to accommodate Houseman, as Houseman and Lloyd maintained. Chandler's imbibing heavily while finishing the *Dahlia* screenplay was really just a salient example of his increasing dependence on alcohol.

Chandler was pleased with several of the scenes in his script. In a letter to Dale Warren on November 7, 1951, he explained that a script writer must avoid being too wordy when composing screen dialogue. "The best scenes I ever wrote were practically monosyllabic," he continued. The best short scene he ever wrote was in *The Blue Dahlia,* when Buzz meets Helen Morrison by chance in the bar of the Cavendish Court Hotel where she lives. Both Buzz and Helen are unaware of each other's identities at this point. In an ultimately futile effort to pick him up, Helen buys Buzz a drink and patiently listens to his aimless chatter. Chandler notes that Helen says, "Uh huh" three times, "with three different intonations; and that's all there is to it."[25]

There are some departures from Chandler's screenplay, which are discernible when one compares the final shooting script, which is in the Raymond Chandler Collection of the UCLA Research Library, with the finished film. One such alteration is when Johnny is kidnapped by Leo (Don Costello), Eddie Harwood's partner in crime. Leo has learned that Johnny had found out that Eddie's surname is really Bauer, and that, as Bauer, Eddie is wanted for murder by the New Jersey state police. So Leo takes Johnny to Eddie's hideout, a deserted ranch, where he and one of Eddie's henchmen plan to give Johnny a brutal beating as a way of terrorizing him into keeping his mouth shut about Eddie's guilty secret.

While shooting this scene, in which Johnny grapples with Leo and his cohort, actor Don Costello accidentally broke a toe. Marshall informed Houseman of this accident but assured him that the scene in the script could be modified so that Costello could play the rest of the scene while lying on the floor, after Johnny decks Leo in the brawl. "Chandler was not available for this chore because he was at home completing the screenplay," Matthew Bruccoli explains, so Marshall had to revise this portion of the script himself.[26] Marshall, who was known to improvise new material on the set while directing a picture, had no difficulty altering Chandler's screenplay to make allowances for Costello's injured foot. A comparison of the scene as Marshall emended it with the same scene in the shooting script demonstrates that the director departed from the scene as originally written only when necessary, to accommodate Costello's injury.[27]

In the scene as filmed, the skirmish ends with both thugs knocked cold and lying unconscious on the floor. Then Eddie shows up; Johnny addresses him pointedly as "Mr. Bauer" and threatens to turn Eddie over to the authorities, once Johnny has made good his escape from Eddie's hideout. At this point Leo revives and pulls out his revolver. Johnny commences wrestling with Leo on the floor (since Costello could not stand on his feet). Leo's gun goes off during the scuffle; the stray bullet misses Johnny and hits Eddie instead. Moreover, in the course of his struggle with Leo, Johnny manages to turn the revolver on Leo himself and pull the trigger, with the result that the scene ends with both Leo and Eddie dead, while the other hoodlum remains unconscious. Johnny then makes his getaway.

Since the navy would not permit Buzz to be guilty of Helen's murder, as Chandler had intended, Chandler dutifully supplied an alternate killer. Dad Newell, the corrupt house detective, was chosen as the culprit, quips Bruce Crowther, because "he hadn't seen loyal service in the war." Crowther adds that Dad "didn't see enough service in the movie to be a convincing fall guy."[28]

On the contrary, Dad appears often through the course of the movie. He is shown creeping around the hotel, sneaking behind window curtains, lurking behind bushes on the grounds, and peeping into windows. In this fashion, Dad has been able to gather enough information about some of the guests to blackmail them. As a matter of fact, "Dad," who is nobody's "father figure," manages to extort hush money from nearly everyone who is suspected of Helen's murder. So he is not quite the marginal character that Crowther contends he is.

Houseman notes that Chandler had to plant some lines earlier in the film that would lead up to the final revelation that Dad was the killer. There is, for example, the scene in which Captain Hendrickson (Tom Powers, who played H.S. Dietrichson in *Double Indemnity*) first interrogates Dad. Hendrickson foreshadows the later revelation of Dad's guilt by ruefully suggesting to him that "plenty of genial old parties like you commit murders."

Chandler gave Dad a speech at the climax of the movie in which Dad explains why he rubbed out Helen. Dad had attempted to blackmail Helen in exchange for not revealing to her husband, after Johnny came marching home, that she had been cheating on him all the time he was gone. Helen contemptuously dismissed Dad as a mere amateur extortionist and refused to pay up. Moreover, there was a good chance that Helen might blow the whistle on Dad's extortion racket. In a towering rage, Dad shot Helen dead. Helen thought he was just a cheap blackmailer, he explains to Hendrickson. "Found out differently, didn't she?" Dad goes on to express his savage resentment for those who consider themselves his social betters, epitomized by Helen herself, who laughed him to scorn. "Maybe I could get tired of being pushed around by cops and hotel managers and ritzy dames in bungalows," he fumes. "Maybe I could cost a little something just for once—even if I do end up on a slab!" Dad jerks out a gun, but Hendrickson shoots first and kills him.

Chandler's revised ending for the film reflects some compassion for Dad, as when Hendrickson muses after Dad is dead, "I must be getting old; I'm kind of sorry for the old devil at that." Dad was, after all, a "bitter old man, an ex-cop living on meager wages from a thankless job," Gay Brewer comments. Hence Hendrickson expresses his compassion for Dad as a luckless criminal, "compelled by fear, anger, and dissatisfaction" toward his own inevitable doom.[29]

Nonetheless, some commentators on the film echo Bruce Crowther's complaint that Chandler should not have pinned Helen's death on a minor character like Dad Newell, yet the fact remains that murderers in film noir not infrequently turn out to be peripheral characters. For example, in Fritz Lang's *Blue Gardenia* (1953; the title of which recalls *The Blue Dahlia*), an old flame of a hoodlum materializes at film's end to confess to murdering him because he had jilted her. The guilty party, in fact, appeared only briefly in one early scene of the picture. Similarly, in Nicholas Ray's *In a Lonely Place* (1950), the murderer of a dead girl is revealed to be her fiancé, who admits his crime at the denouement, after having been absent from the bulk of the film; moreover, no solid motive whatever is advanced for the killing. By contrast, Dad Newell surely played a meaty enough role in *Dahlia* to make a plausible villain, for he is visible throughout the movie, snooping around and spying on the principals.

The Blue Dahlia concludes with an epilogue that differs markedly from the ending Chandler wrote for the final shooting script. In the screenplay Johnny is with Joyce in front of the Blue Dahlia nightclub. They bid each other a fond farewell, as they mutually agree to go their separate ways. Joyce gets into her car and drives off, while Johnny is joined by his two navy chums, Buzz and George. They watch the club's neon sign go dark for the last time, since the night club is being shuttered for good in the wake of Eddie Harwood's demise. Then George says, "Did somebody say something about a drink of bourbon?" and the three comrades head for the nearest bar.[30] (The reference to bourbon is interesting, given the fact that Chandler was drinking heavily when he wrote this scene.)

The film, on the other hand, concludes with Johnny saying goodbye to Buzz and George before going off with Joyce, Eddie's widow, who is standing nearby. Johnny reminds Joyce that he had said earlier, "Every guy has seen you somewhere before, but the trick was to find you." With that, Johnny is united with Joyce at the fade out, instead of ending up in the company of his two buddies, as the screenplay would have it.

Chandler was irritated that Marshall brought Johnny and Joyce together at the finale, since he wanted the film to end as it began: with the three veterans reaffirming their friendship, which has sustained them through the war and through the recent crisis over the murder of Johnny's wife. In this manner the story would have come full circle. (*Double Indemnity*, we remember, ended with an affirmation of friendship.)

Chandler was not the only screenwriter who resented this sort of tampering with their work. Wendell Mayes (*Anatomy of a Murder*) stated in a 1997 interview, "One of the things that drives a screenwriter absolutely crazy with many producers and directors is that they won't call the writer" when they need an additional line of dialogue; they simply handle the situation themselves, without consulting the author of the script. "It isn't done quite so much anymore," Mayes concluded; but it was more common in Chandler's time.[31]

Chandler wrote to James Sandoe, a specialist in crime fiction, in May 1946 about how both the navy and the studio had tampered with his screenplay for this movie. "*The Blue Dahlia* would have been a much better show if the Navy Department hadn't butted into it."[32] Expanding on his remarks about the navy in a later letter to Sandoe dated June 17, 1946, Chandler observed, "What the Navy Department did to the story was a little thing like making me change the murderer and hence make a routine whodunit out of a fairly original idea." In his preliminary scenario, Chandler recalled, Buzz killed Johnny's wife in a fit of rage "and then blanked out and forgot all about it." Buzz remembered enough to make it clear to Johnny who the murderer was "but never realized it himself."[33]

After all is said and done, Mike Phillips maintains, Chandler's substituting Dad Newell for Buzz Wanchek as the killer "makes little difference to the overall impact" of the movie. "Chandler's script was Oscar-nominated, and it's a witty, grim noir" just as it stands.[34]

One year after the release of *The Blue Dahlia*, Edward Dmytryk (*Mur-*

der, My Sweet) directed *Crossfire* (1947), in which a neurotic anti-Semitic war veteran kills a Jew. In this instance, Naremore notes, the armed services did not object to having a returning veteran portrayed as a mentally disturbed killer, because World War II was over, and depicting members of the armed forces as uniformly noble heroes was no longer the order of the day.[35]

As for Chandler's dissatisfaction with the studio's altering the script for *Dahlia,* he stated in still another letter to Sandoe on October 2, 1947, "It is ludicrous to suggest that any writer in Hollywood, however obstreperous, has a 'free hand' with a script; he may have a free hand with the first draft," as Chandler certainly did in this case, but "what happens on the set is beyond his control." Chandler said that he threatened more than once to walk off the picture while it was still in production "unless they stopped the director putting in fresh dialogue out of his own head." Chandler conceded, however, that since Don Costello "actually did break his toe," Marshall was compelled to improvise some dialogue to accommodate the situation.[36]

George Marshall sought to set the record straight some years later by asserting that Chandler had not threatened at any time to walk off the picture just because Marshall had revised some of his dialogue: "He was in no shape to walk anywhere—certainly not from the studio, because he wasn't there; and certainly not from home," because John Houseman was "locking him in the closet to try and get the script finished."[37] Marshall added that he supported unequivocally Chandler's protests about having to change the solution of the mystery at the behest of the navy.

In a more benign tone Marshall wrote to Matthew Bruccoli on December 16, 1974, that he was so impressed with Chandler's original scenario that he remarked at the time that "in all the years I had been making films I had finally found a story which was so beautifully written" that he could shoot it just as it was. "Why would I want to rewrite something which I had thought so perfect at the beginning?" The only part of the script Marshall admitted that he revised was the scene in which Costello was injured.[38] Marshall apparently forgot that he altered the final scene of the film, so that Johnny and Joyce are apparently going to live happily ever after, a fact that Clark documents.[39]

Peter Wolfe wrongly assumes that the film ends the way the script does, with Johnny leaving Joyce behind in favor of going off to drink with his friends. Wolfe even speaks of the "male comradeship evoked by the film's final shot"—when the film's final shot is actually of Johnny's friends departing and leaving him with Joyce.[40]

Chandler was particularly chagrined that Marshall had tampered with his screenplay because he simply did not regard Marshall as a competent filmmaker. In a letter to Hamish Hamilton, dated January 9, 1946, Chandler described Marshall as a "stale old hack who had been directing for thirty years without ever achieving any real distinction."[41] Film historians are kinder to Marshall than Chandler was; he is usually described respectfully as an old maestro, a pioneer who had begun directing features in 1919. By the time he made *The Blue Dahlia*, Marshall had built a solid reputation in the industry as an able director, if not a genius. What's more, David Thomson singles out *Dahlia* as one of Marshall's best films, "an excellent . . . romantic thriller."[42]

Chandler himself got numerous compliments on his screenplay, but one well-meant observation about the script, made by someone at Paramount, bothered him no end. "I love the homosexual angle," this party said, referring to the relationship of Buzz and George, who lived in the same apartment. Chandler replied curtly, "They shared the same apartment and ate meals together. That makes them homosexuals, does it?"[43] Since some critics of *Double Indemnity* had mistakenly assumed that the friendship of Walter and Keyes was really homosexual, Chandler wanted to discourage the same misunderstanding from cropping up all over again with respect to Buzz and George in *Dahlia*.

In spite of all of Chandler's complaints about the making of *Dahlia*, the picture grossed $2,750,000 on its initial release—big bucks in those days. Moreover, Chandler received his second Academy Award nomination, plus an Edgar Award from the Mystery Writers of America for his screenplay. In addition, the film was referred to in several reviews as a Raymond Chandler movie. A number of critics enthusiastically lauded Chandler's craftsmanship as a writer. James Agee, for example, termed *Dahlia* "convincing and entertaining. . . . I hope there will be more films of the quality of *The Blue Dahlia*," because it is "about as good a movie as can be expected from the big factories."[44]

The Blue Dahlia went on to achieve the status of a classic noir. Indeed, the Blue Dahlia, a legendary nightclub in Chicago, was named after the movie, and flourished on North Avenue until the 1960s. Moreover, Alan Barbour, in reassessing the movie in 1997, lavished praise on Chandler's "tough, gritty story, . . . a mystery that will have you guessing right up to the very end. The sensational cast," headed by Ladd, Lake, and Bendix, "the stylish photography by Lionel Lindon, plus a fine score by Victor Young (*Around the World in 80 Days*) add to the quality of this release" on video-cassette.[45]

Even Chandler was prepared to judge the film positively in later years. Only a year before his death in 1959 he wrote to Houseman, "Do you remember *The Blue Dahlia*? Not tops, of course; but I found the script in my storeroom the other day and began to read it; and I thought it rather good. Of course, I was never a good screenwriter and always knew it." But he had often declared that he was consoled by the fact that in *Dahlia* he had composed a good original screenplay, which he had written "from the ground up," and good original screenplays, he believed, "were almost as rare in Hollywood as virgins."[46]

The Innocent Mrs. Duff

Chandler was by this time fed up with Hollywood and sick of screenwriting, so his efforts to negotiate a new contract with Paramount in the early winter of 1946 were at best half-hearted. In the meantime, he simply ceased to report for work, so the studio brass finally lost patience with him and placed him on temporary suspension in January 1946. In a letter dated January 12, he insisted to Alfred Knopf, his publisher, that he could not convince anyone on the Paramount lot that his dissatisfaction with the studio had nothing to do with the salary increase he had been offered. "What I want is something quite different: a freedom from datelines and unnatural pressures" and a right to work with those few individuals in Hollywood whose goal is "to make the best pictures possible within the limitations of a popular art, and not merely repeat the old and vulgar formulae."[47]

When *The Blue Dahlia* opened in New York in May 1946, and reviewers applauded Chandler's screenplay, Paramount finally relented and decided to make peace with their delinquent employee. They recommended to him a number of novels that he might adapt for the screen, but he eventually settled on a book of his own choosing, *The Innocent Mr. Duff* by Elizabeth Holding. "For my money, she's the top suspense writer of them all," he stated. "Her characters are wonderful."[48]

Holding's novel tells the story of Jacob Duff, who is a morose and emotionally disturbed alcoholic. Duff slyly draws his chauffeur into a plot to murder a man whom he suspects of having an affair with his wife. Mrs. Duff is innocent, yet her husband refuses to believe that his suspicious are groundless. At any rate, after the murder is committed, the chauffeur informs the police of what has transpired. Duff, who has manifested a self-destructive streak from the outset, decides to commit suicide, since he finds the prospect of going to prison, where he would be deprived of alcohol, unendurable. (Perhaps Chandler was drawn to this story because he implicitly saw a parallel between Duff's alcoholism and his own.)

The studio assigned another writer to collaborate with Chandler on the screenplay for a ten-week period, but Chandler did not get along with his fellow writer, nor with the producer supervising the project. When the agreed term of his contract expired, Chandler declined to renew it, so the project was shelved indefinitely, and Chandler left Paramount for good. He took with him, of course, the eighteen thousand dollars he had earned for his work on the aborted script. Under the circumstances, the studio was not sorry to see him go. In endeavoring to justify his conduct to his Hollywood agent, H.N. Swanson, Chandler explained that he simply did not work well under supervision.

If Paramount had had the good sense to allow him to write a rough draft of the script of *Mrs. Duff*, "without the interference of a producer" who was eager "to dominate a project to his own advantage, they would have got something in a comparatively short time," Chandler declared. It would not have been perfect, he continued, but it would have been a scenario with probably several scenes blocked out that could have been used in the final script. In brief, he concluded, the front office is convinced that they can get the best "from me, and at the same time control every move I make and every idea I have. It just can't be done."[49]

With that, Chandler left Hollywood behind and moved to La Jolla, a suburb of San Diego, to a home that overlooked the ocean, where he lived the remainder of his life. Chandler took leave of the film colony officially by writing an essay entitled "A Qualified Farewell" in 1947, which was in fact published only posthumously. Recalling his days at Paramount, Chandler remembered a producer at the studio who advised Chandler's agent that Chandler was just not cut out to be a "sole screenwriter," that is, a writer who can "all by himself produce a clean and wholesome shooting script which, as it stands, will satisfy all concerned."[50] On this point, Bruccoli comments wryly that when Chandler "was in a position to write *The Blue Dahlia* alone, he had to anesthetize himself" with bourbon to get the job done.[51]

"The qualifications for permanent success in Hollywood, which I lack," Chandler continued, "are a tremendous enthusiasm for the work in hand, coupled with an almost complete indifference to the use which will be made of it."[52] He was referring, of course, to the fact that filmmaking is a collaborative art, and that, once the script is finished, it falls into the hands of the director. And it is the director, as George Marshall put it, who "must be able to translate the words as written in the script into a visually entertaining" work of art. Chandler never accepted the fact that it was the director—and not the writer—who is, in Marshall's words, "the guiding force" behind the making of a motion picture.[53]

Bruccoli expresses surprise that Chandler found it difficult to collaborate comfortably with the professionals with whom he worked, since he was associated with some of the best in the business—from directors like Billy Wilder and George Marshall to top stars like Barbara Stanwyck and Alan Ladd.

Unlike Chandler, novelist William Faulkner (*Sanctuary*), who co-wrote the screen version of Chandler's *The Big Sleep,* was an obliging collaborator. If a writer is to survive in the movie business, Faulkner contended, he must realize that "a moving picture is by its nature a collaboration; and any collaboration is compromise, because that is what the word means—to give and take."[54]

By contrast, Chandler found that filmmaking frequently involved more compromises than he was prepared to make, as is obvious from his battle royal with Billy Wilder over the *Double Indemnity* script. On the other hand, Chandler at times demonstrated his willingness to compromise. He dutifully manufactured an alternate culprit for *Dahlia,* for example, instead of quitting the picture when the navy meddled with the script.

Chandler endeavored, according to his lights, to adjust to the demands of living and working in the movie capital as best he could. The fact remains that he collaborated, as writer or script doctor, on four hits in a row while he was at Paramount, from *Double Indemnity* to *The Blue Dahlia,* inclusive. And he was prepared to go back to Hollywood in the years to come, whenever his diminished finances required it. Well might Chandler "qualify" his farewell to the film industry, since he was far from finished with Hollywood. Nor was Hollywood through with him.

11

Dance with the Devil

Strangers on a Train and *Playback*

If you shake hands with a maniac, you may have sold your soul to the devil.

—Raymond Chandler

When you dance with the devil, the devil don't change; the devil changes you.

—Max California, a vice lord, in the film *8mm*

If Raymond Chandler had not yet given up on Hollywood, the movie colony had not yet given up on him. In 1950 Alfred Hitchcock (*Spellbound*) commissioned Chandler to write the screenplay for his film of Patricia Highsmith's novel *Strangers on a Train*. Prior to hiring Chandler, Hitchcock had prepared a treatment of the scenario with Whitfield Cook (*Stage Fright*). He then extended an invitation to Chandler to compose a full-fledged screenplay based on the treatment.

Strangers on a Train

Hitchcock chose Chandler because he was interested in working with this eminent crime novelist and screenwriter. Chandler, in turn, accepted Hitchcock's invitation "partly because I thought I might like Hitch," whom he judged to be one of the few intelligent filmmakers in Hollywood, "and partly because one gets tired of saying no; and someday I might want to say yes and not get asked."[1]

Chandler was also interested in Highsmith's book because the novel clearly indicates that Highsmith believed that "there was evil in everyone," that it was a part of human nature, as Nora Saye has noted.[2] "I'm very concerned," Highsmith herself stated, with the way that good and evil exist in everyone "to a greater or lesser degree."[3] Chandler, like Highsmith, was very much preoccupied with bringing to light the dark corners of the human psyche, and so he agreed to draft the script for the movie.

Indeed, many a reader has come away from a Chandler work with some sobering thoughts about human nature as Chandler viewed it—that good and evil can bundle together, like sly lovers, in the same personality; that people are not always what they seem, and hence one is never sure who can be trusted. Chandler's bleak vision of contemporary society depicts modern man gradually being corrupted by living in a violent, materialistic world in which one individual exploits another in the mass effort to survive. Consequently, as indicated in the discussion of Chandler's moral vision earlier, every Chandler work reflects the provocative worldview of the artist who created it.

In July 1950, Chandler signed a contract with Warner Brothers, the producer of the film, to write the script, in return for a salary of twenty-five hundred dollars a week. Preferring to work alone, Chandler resented the preliminary script conferences that Hitchcock imposed on him before he was allowed to get to work on his own and was not mollified even when Hitchcock agreed to come to his home in La Jolla, California, for the sessions. One day, while watching Hitchcock get out of the studio limousine in front of his house, the disgruntled writer mumbled testily to his secretary, "Look at that fat bastard trying to get out of his car," adding that he cared not if the director overheard him. Hitchcock probably did, since that was the director's last trip to La Jolla.[4]

Chandler later grumbled that he detested these "god-awful jabber sessions, which seem to be an inevitable although painful part of the picture business."[5] For his part, Hitchcock was none too happy with Chandler's interaction with him during their story conferences. Hitchcock recalled that he would say to Chandler, "Why not do it this way?" and Chandler would snap back, "Well, if you can puzzle it out, what do you need me for?"[6]

Chandler followed his literary source very closely in the early scenes of the screenplay. *Strangers on a Train* begins with a railway journey, in the course of which Bruno Antony (Robert Walker), a wealthy homosexual, ingratiates himself with Guy Haines (Farley Granger), a handsome tennis champion. The slightly effeminate, effete Bruno has all the earmarks of a textbook case in abnormal psychology, for he combines a deep-seated, implacable hatred of his tyrannical father with a curious attachment to his eccentric mother. As the two lunch together on the train, it is evident that Guy, who is unhappily married to a conniving, promiscuous spouse, is fascinated by this fey, coyly ingratiating creature. So much so that from the start there is an unacknowledged homosexual undertone to their relationship. Screenwriter Arthur Laurents (*Rope*) said, "Farley Granger told me once that it was Robert Walker's idea to play Bruno Antony as a homosexual."[7] On the contrary, it should be obvious from foregoing remarks about Bruno's background and behavior that his approach to Guy, as a rather blatant homosexual courting a latent one, is embedded in the supple screenplay and not something Walker, as brilliant as he is in the part, superimposed on the characterization on his own.

Before they part company at journey's end, Bruno attempts to manipulate Guy into agreeing to exchange a murder with him, with Guy killing Bruno's father and Bruno doing away with Guy's wife Miriam. Since neither has an ostensible motive for committing the other's crime, they would both, according to Bruno, successfully elude detection.

The script's dialogue at this point is very close to that of the novel, in which Bruno says, "We meet on a train, see, and nobody knows we know each other." He continues, "We murder for each other, see? I kill your wife and you kill my father."[8] In Chandler's description of the principal characters, which appears at the beginning of the final version of the script, he says of Bruno, "In the moments when his candor becomes shrewd calculation, it is all the more frightening because of his disarming charm and cultured exterior."[9] In fact, Bruno's proposal appeals to Guy more than he is prepared to admit even to himself. Consequently, Jane Sloan observes, Guy does not decisively reject it. Instead, "Guy humors him" by saying that Bruno's theory is "O.K."[10]

Taking Guy's hedging for tacit approval, the deranged Bruno soon dispatches Miriam and demands forthwith that Guy keep his part of the bargain; Guy agrees to do so, just to put Bruno off. The manner in which Bruno plays on the baser instincts of the fundamentally good-natured Guy signifies the duality that lies at the heart of human nature—a recurring theme in Highsmith's fiction. Putting it another way, Guy is dancing with the devil and does not even know it.

Patricia Highsmith subsequently said that adapting *Strangers on a Train* for film "gave Chandler fits."[11] Actually, it was Hitchcock, not Highsmith, who gave Chandler fits. Chandler complained that he found conferring with Hitchcock on the screenplay frustrating precisely because Hitchcock was not as troubled as he was by questions of narrative logic and character motivation.

To his chagrin, Chandler discovered that Hitchcock seemed less pre-occupied with the fundamental plausibility of the story than with creating a series of striking visual scenes. On August 17, 1950, he wrote to Ray Stark, his Hollywood agent, "Hitchcock seems to be a very considerate and polite man, but he is full of little suggestions and ideas, which have a cramping effect on a writer's initiative. . . . He is always ready to sacrifice dramatic logic (in so far as it exists) for the sake of a camera effect." This is very hard on the screenwriter "because the writer not only has to make sense out of the foolish plot if he can; but he has to do it in such a way that any sort of camera shot that comes into Hitchcock's mind can be incorporated into it."[12] It was as if Hitchcock simply directed the picture in his head, with little concern for the sorts of questions about narrative logic and character development that troubled Chandler.

As a result, "you find yourself trying to rationalize the shots he wants to make, rather than the story," Chandler told Hamish Hamilton in his letter of September 4. To Chandler this explained why some of Hitchcock's pictures "lose their grip on logic and turn into wild chases. Well, it's not the worst way to make a picture."[13] As far as Chandler was concerned, it was also not the best way.

Referring to Hitchcock in a letter to a studio executive, Chandler re-marked dyspeptically that he preferred to deal with a director "who realizes that what is said and how it is said is more important than shooting it up-side down through a glass of champagne."[14] Little did Chandler know that there was a shot something like that Hitchcock's 1928 film *Champagne*! (A girl tangoing in a ballroom is photographed through the bottom of a cham-pagne glass.) In the course of my appearance in Michael Epstein's 1999 television documentary, *Hitchcock, Selznick and the End of Hollywood*, I com-mented that David Selznick, who produced Hitchcock films such as *Rebecca*, criticized Hitchcock in exactly the same terms as Chandler.

Chandler was particularly worried about the scene in which Guy ten-tatively promises to take the life of Bruno's father. Guy must convince a reasonable percentage of the audience, Chandler recorded in his notes, that "a nice young man might in certain circumstances murder a total stranger just to appease a lunatic." Otherwise the viewers would not be sufficiently involved in the subsequent development of the plot. "The premise is that if you shake hands with a maniac, you may have sold your soul to the devil." He concluded with some exasperation, "Or am I still crazy?"[15]

In the book Guy does in fact carry through his promise to murder Bruno's father, but Chandler contended that, given Guy's status as the likeable hero of the movie, the film audience would not be prepared to believe that he is capable of committing a homicide. So, in consultation with Hitchcock, Chandler made a substantial change in the scenario at this point. Guy merely pretends that he plans to kill Bruno's father. Explaining that he simply wants to get the whole affair over with once and for all, Guy informs Bruno that he has decided to do what Bruno wants that very night. Guy actually intends to warn Mr. Anthony about his son's desire to have him slain. With noir inevitability, Guy's plan goes hideously wrong. Bruno rightly suspects Guy's actual reason for showing up at the Antony mansion and heads him off before he can see Mr. Antony. Bruno also serves notice to Guy in a threatening tone that he does not take kindly to being double-crossed.

Although Chandler was making headway on the screenplay, he did not find the task entirely rewarding. "I'm still slaving away for Warner Brothers on this Hitchcock thing," he wrote to Bernice Baumgarten, who worked for his New York literary agent. "Some days I think it is fun, and other days I think it is damn foolishness."[16]

Chandler was not alone in criticizing Hitchcock for being more interested in riveting his audience's attention with a number of visually exciting scenes than he was in knitting together the overall continuity of the story. John Gielgud, who starred in Hitchcock's *Secret Agent* (1936), recalled that Hitchcock was inclined to start out "with various locations that had caught his fancy" and then concentrate on getting his characters from a situation set in one of these scenic locations to another as quickly as possible, "with a minimum concern for probability."[17] Since *Strangers on a Train* is set in and around Washington, D.C., Hitchcock decreed that certain scenes take place at various landmarks in the nation's capital—picturesque sites that in themselves have precious little to do with the story. Robert Corber comments, "In shot after shot, the dome of the Capitol building appears in the background brilliantly lit up." When Guy visits the Jefferson Memorial, for example, he unexpectedly encounters Bruno there.[18]

In Hitchcock's defense, Paul Jensen has written that Chandler's approach to script writing was in open conflict with Hitchcock's concept of how a screenplay should be devised; it was inevitable that they would clash. In essence, Hitchcock tended to sidestep the demands of dramatic logic, which were uppermost in Chandler's mind, in favor of creating what Chandler termed visually striking scenes. As Hitchcock remarked in conversation, "I am not so much interested in the stories that I tell, as in the means I use to tell them."[19] On one occasion, when he was asked by a journalist what happened to the criminal who hid in the baggage car of a train in *The Lady Vanishes* (1938), Hitchcock retorted that so far as he knew the chap was still there. He simply did not think that that particular loose end of the plot was all that important in wrapping up the story as a whole.

Specifically, Hitchcock believed that the fast-paced plot of a thriller like *Strangers on a Train* was not meant to be analyzed too closely. The moviegoer should be so caught up in a suspense melodrama that he buys the story completely, warts and all, while he is seeing it, and detects faulty plot contrivances only while reflecting on the film as he raids the icebox before going to bed. So long as the film absorbed the viewer's attention the whole time he was watching it, Hitchcock was not personally concerned about any flaws in the machinery of the picture's plot that might come to light only with the application of what he aptly tagged "icebox logic." Pauline Kael has written that part of the fun of seeing a Hitchcock suspenser was that it "distracted you from the loopholes, so that, afterwards you could enjoy thinking over how you'd been tricked and teased."[20] In other words, Chandler was inclined to care more about "ice box logic" than, all things considered, Hitchcock himself did.

To be precise, Chandler found that a Hitchcock film was strewn with eye-catching, slick little set pieces, which, though engaging for the moment, in the long run contributed little to the overall fabric of the film as a whole. As a result, Chandler maintained that Hitchcock managed merely to amuse his audience, when his artistry could have been more effectively employed in genuinely involving them with the characters and their perilous predicaments.

An example of one of Hitchcock's clever little set pieces is the opening sequence of *Strangers on a Train*: A taxi drives up to a railway station and discharges a passenger. We see only the feet of a man wearing flashy two-toned shoes getting out. Then a second taxi pulls up and unloads another traveller: we see a pair of plain brown Oxfords emerging from the cab. The ostentatious saddle shoes that belong to Bruno indicate that he is a fancy dresser and perhaps a frivolous type. By contrast, the modest dark wing tip shoes Guy is wearing suggest that he is a conservative dresser and probably a more sensible individual.

Both men approach the train from opposite directions, and once the train leaves the depot, there is a shot of intersecting railroad tracks, as the train proceeds along its route. The crisscrossing rails foreshadow how the lives of these two individuals will likewise converge. Soon after, the shoes of Guy and Bruno accidentally touch as they cross their legs in the parlor car. They take the occasion to strike up a casual conversation, which will in fact lead Guy into a dangerous relationship with Bruno that Guy could not have foreseen.

On the one hand, Hitchcock was proud of the painstaking care with which he had shot and edited this sequence. "It's a fascinating design," he commented. "One could examine it for hours." On the other hand, novel-ist-screenwriter Graham Greene was not impressed with the kind of facile visual displays with which Hitchcock punctuated his movies. Indeed, he shared Chandler's dislike for what Greene termed Hitchcock's gimmicky, pretentious cinematic technique. As a storyteller, Hitchcock was, in Greene's opinion, "appallingly careless: he has cared more for an ingenious melo-dramatic situation than the construction and continuity of his story."[21]

One of the tense scenes to which Jensen refers is that in which Bruno follows Miriam, Guy's estranged wife, and her two escorts to a carnival.[22] They all take a ride on the carousel and sing along with the calliope as it plays "The Band Played On." Then Bruno lures Miriam away from her boy-friends to a secluded corner of the amusement park and strangles her.

The murder is ironically accompanied by the distant music of the merry-go-round's calliope as it grinds out its cheery rendering of "The Band Played On." Horrified, we watch the murder as it is reflected in Miriam's glasses, which have fallen to the grass during her struggle with Bruno, a shot incidentally, that John Frankenheimer copied in his 1961 film *The Young Savages*. Photographed in this grotesquely distorted fashion, the strangling looks as if it were being viewed in a fun-house mirror, another reminder of the grimly incongruous carnival setting of the crime.

At this point the viewer might even recall the lyrics of "The Band Played On," heard only a few moments earlier, which take on an ironic tinge in retrospect: "But his brain was so loaded it nearly exploded" (a ref-erence to Bruno, the psycho), "The poor girl would shake with alarm" (a reference to Miriam, his victim). It is interesting to find that the final shoot-ing script, dated October 18, 1950, which is on file at Warner Brothers, merely indicates that "Miriam and her boy friends begin to sing along with the song being played on the calliope."[23] Hitchcock himself purposely supplied "The Band Played On," presumably because of its implicit relevance to Miriam's murder.

Given the fact that Guy subconsciously wanted to kill Miriam himself, he has in effect done so through the mediation of Bruno as his proxy; to that extent Bruno embodies the underside of Guy's own personality, which underlines Highsmith's statement that the good and evil forces warring within Guy reflect the duality of human nature itself. In *Strangers on a Train* we have a perfect example of a basically decent person who is morally stained by capitulating in some degree to a wicked influence on his life.

That Guy has become, however inadvertently, allied with the perverse force for evil that Bruno represents is concretized in the scene in which the two men stand on opposite sides of a wrought iron fence as Bruno informs Guy that he has taken Miriam's life. When a squad car appears across the street, Guy instinctively joins Bruno on the same side of the barrier and thus implicitly acknowledges his share of the guilt for Miriam's demise. Moreover, the image of Guy's troubled face barred by the sinister shadows of the gate grill signals his imprisonment by Bruno in an unholy alliance from which he is for now unable to extricate himself.

This dark tale of obsession and murder clearly belongs to the realm of film noir. The milieu of noir is essentially one of shadows and is exemplified in the scene just described. For the shadows that fall across Guy's figure imply the morbid, murky world in which he is imprisoned with Bruno.

In Highsmith's novel, as mentioned, Guy actually murders Bruno's father in order to stop Bruno from ceaselessly tormenting him to do it. Guy is then wracked by guilt and eventually surrenders to the private detective who has been investigating Miriam's death. Bruno, meanwhile, gets drunk during a party on a yacht, accidentally falls overboard, and drowns. It is clear, therefore, that Chandler kept Highsmith's plot intact up to and including Miriam's murder. But when Chandler had Guy draw the line at slaying Mr. Antony, Chandler parted company with the book in a substantial way and took the story in another direction.

Hitchcock confirmed that in the screenplay Guy is painfully aware that Miriam's death has freed him of the two-timing wife he despised. Consequently, Guy strives to bring Bruno to justice in the film in order to expiate his own subconscious guilt for Miriam's slaying, since "Guy felt like murdering her himself."

Guy is given the chance to redeem himself by pursuing Bruno back to the scene of Miriam's murder, in one of those "wild chases" that Chandler deplored in Hitchcock's work, and forcing Bruno to confess the truth about her death. As they wrestle each other aboard the carousel, the mechanism suddenly goes berserk, changing what is normally a harmless source of innocent pleasure into a whirling instrument of terror. The carousel thus serves as still another reflection of Hitchcock's dark vision of our chaotic, topsy-turvy planet. As the runaway merry-go-round continues to twirl at top speed, its rendition of "The Band Played On" is also accelerated to a dizzying tempo, and mingles macabrely with the screams of the hysterical riders trapped on board. A mechanic at last manages to bring it to a halt, but it stops so suddenly that the riders go sailing off in all directions as the machinery collapses into a heap of smoldering wreckage, bringing this sequence to a spectacular climax.

Bruno dies in the debris, unrepentant to the last. His irredeemably perverse personality distinguishes him, even in death, not so much as the Dr. Jekyll and Mr. Hyde type he has sometimes been called, but solely as Mr. Hyde, since he does not seem to have a good side to his personality.

Bruno expires on the same merry-go-round on which he rode with Miriam just before he killed her, bringing the film full circle. Chandler looked on the end of the ordeal of writing the screenplay for the movie with relief, once he had mailed the final pages to the studio on September 26, 1950. He wrote to Ray Stark the next day that he took pride in the fact that once he began composing the actual screenplay on his own, he had completed the task in five weeks and right on schedule. "Not bad for a rather plodding sort of worker like myself," he added. He confessed that "some of the scenes are far too wordy, partly because, as Woodrow Wilson once said, 'I didn't have time to write it shorter.' . . . It must be rather unusual in Hollywood for a writer to do an entire screenplay without a single discussion" with the director while he is writing it.[24] That last remark implied that Chandler was nettled by the way Hitchcock had treated him. More precisely, Chandler was offended that, after their preliminary script conferences, Hitchcock never contacted him again. In fact, he subsequently informed Finlay McDermid, head of the Story Department, on November 2 that Hitchcock never offered him a single word of criticism or appreciation about the pages of the script he regularly submitted to the director by mail. Perhaps, Chandler suggested to McDermid, Hitchcock thought it more prudent in the long run to leave him alone and not interfere. Chandler insisted that he had followed faithfully the story line that he, in tandem with Hitchcock, had hammered out during their story conferences. Still, he went on, there are always points that a writer needs to discuss with the director: "There are always places where a writer goes wrong, not being himself a master of the camera. There are always difficult little points which require the meeting of minds, the accommodation of points of view. I had none of this. . . . I find it almost incomparably rude."[25]

It seems, in retrospect, that Chandler was at a loss to decide to what extent he wanted Hitchcock's collaboration on the screenplay. At the outset Chandler complained that Hitchcock's consultations with him interfered with his efforts to work out the story line. When Hitchcock ceased contacting him, once he began writing the screenplay, he felt neglected. In any case, Chandler's ire at Hitchcock was further increased when he learned that Hitchcock had asked screenwriter Ben Hecht (*Notorious*) to revise Chandler's script. As it happened, Hecht was otherwise engaged, but he lent Czenzi Ormonde, his assistant, to Hitchcock to do the job. "When Hitchcock told me Raymond Chandler had worked on it," Ormonde remembered, "I wondered what I was doing there, being a great fan of Mr. Chandler's."[26] With an assist from Hitchcock himself and from Ben Hecht, Ormonde sharpened the dialogue—which Chandler himself had admitted was "too wordy"—and tightened the narrative structure of the script.

Some of Ormonde's emendations to the screenplay are not very impressive. For example, in Chandler's draft of the screenplay, which is in his private files, Guy says, after a quarrel with Miriam, "I felt like breaking her cute little neck."[27] In the film he says, "I'd like to break her foul, useless little neck." Guy, who is given to understatement, would be more likely to express himself in the sardonic words that Chandler gave him, rather than in the bald, brutal language Ormonde supplied.

Chandler received a copy of the final shooting script in December and reacted negatively, as might have been expected. He believed that Hitchcock had jettisoned too much of what he had written, and debated whether he should accept the shared screen credit with Ormonde that the studio offered him.

In an acerbic letter to Hitchcock, which he wrote on December 6 but wisely never mailed, he conceded that "there are minor changes in the construction or plot . . . which don't bother me at all." But other alterations made in his draft script irritated him a good deal. There is, for example, the fact that Guy comes under police surveillance because he is the prime suspect in the investigation of his wife's murder. "The ease with which he evades the watch" in order to pursue Bruno himself and prove that Bruno killed Miriam reduces this episode "to absurdity." Chandler was convinced that the final shooting script was marred by other improbable incidents as well. "I think that the fact you may get away with" a certain amount of implausibility in a film "doesn't prove you right," he declared. Chandler ended by posing for Hitchcock one overriding question. If Hitchcock wanted the sort of mediocre script that this one had turned out to be, Chandler asked, why did the director go to the trouble and expense of hiring a writer of his caliber in the first place?[28]

In the end Chandler opted to accept a shared screen credit for *Strangers on a Train,* because he had not had a screen credit since *The Blue Dahlia* and decided that he should take the credit as offered. It must be recorded that Warner Brothers granted Chandler a writing credit on the film over Hitchcock's strenuous objections. "Hitchcock had argued with the front office because he wanted me to have the sole credit on the picture," said Ormonde; while the studio executives insisted that "Raymond Chandler have his name on the picture and that it should come first," since Chandler's name would add some additional distinction to the movie, particularly among mystery buffs. Ormonde concluded that she declined to wage a "self-aggrandizing" battle with the studio over the matter and so let the shared credit stand.[29]

As a matter of fact, John Russell Taylor, Hitchcock's authorized biographer, with whom I compared notes on the film, believes that the studio's decision to acknowledge Chandler's contribution to the picture was entirely appropriate. Taylor confirms that "there are very Chandlerish elements in the film as made."[30] For example, once Chandler had opted to have Guy decide against killing Bruno's father, the film's plot line develops along lines similar to that of Chandler's original screenplay for *The Blue Dahlia,* in which the hero is also suspected of slaying his estranged wife.

Chandler's final word on the subject of *Strangers on a Train* was recorded in a letter to his literary agent Carl Brandt on December 11, 1950. "The fallacy of this operation was my being involved in it at all, because it is obvious to me now . . . that a Hitchcock picture must be all Hitchcock," he said. Chandler's draft of the script "was far better than what they finished with. It just had too much Chandler and not enough Hitchcock." Putting it a little differently, Larry Gross writes that everything done by Hitchcock's talented and literary collaborators" came out of endless conversation and intrusion by Hitchcock, with the result that "all the different, talented writers who worked with him ended up writing films that look . . . and sound like Hitchcock films."[31]

Admittedly, Chandler's creative association with Hitchcock was just as acrimonious as his collaboration with Billy Wilder had been. But just as Chandler was not the only screenwriter to run afoul of Wilder, so too he was not the only screenwriter to register complaints about Hitchcock. Leading the pack is John Michael Hayes (*Rear Window*), whose comments about working with Hitchcock echoed those of Chandler.

Hayes scripted four pictures for Hitchcock between 1954 and 1956; by the time the fourth, *The Man Who Knew Too Much,* was released in 1956, critics began to focus on Hayes as Hitchcock's regular collaborator. "I was being linked with him," said Hayes. "When you show up in the same sentence—Alfred Hitchcock and John Michael Hayes—that was more than he could bear." Hitchcock did not wish to be known as the comaster of suspense.

Thus the initially harmonious working relationship of Hitchcock and Hayes ultimately turned sour. Hitchcock liked to minimize the contribution of writers to his films, Hayes noted, yet he had "some big writers on his films": Robert E. Sherwood (*Rebecca*), Thornton Wilder (*Shadow of a Doubt*), as well as Raymond Chandler. "Hitchcock," Hayes concluded, "was so unkind about giving credit." That statement is certainly borne out by Hitchcock's concerted effort to deny Chandler a writing credit on *Strangers on a Train.* Be that as it may, Frank Rich indicates that Chandler "got more credit for what was on-screen than did the obscure author of the novel that was its source."[32]

It would seem that one reason Hitchcock attempted to deny Chandler a screen credit on the movie, then, was that Hitchcock did not wish critics to identify the picture as a Hitchcock-Chandler film any more than he wanted *The Man Who Knew Too Much* to be known as a Hitchcock-Hayes film. Screenwriter Ernest Lehman (*West Side Story*) told me that, although he spent several months working on the script for Hitchcock's *North by Northwest,* "somehow the picture turned out the way *he* wanted it to. He always got his own way, and I have never figured out how he did it." Neither could Raymond Chandler, who grudgingly admitted that in the last analysis *Strangers on a Train* was clearly a Hitchcock picture, not a Chandler picture. (By contrast, *The Blue Dahlia* is often referred to as a Raymond Chandler movie rather than a George Marshall movie.)

In 1992 an alternate version of *Strangers on a Train* was unearthed in the vaults at Warners. It turned out to be the version that Hitchcock prepared for release in Great Britain. The British cut of the film differs noticeably from the American version in two scenes in particular.

First, Hitchcock restored to the British version some dialogue he had excised from the American prints. These lines occur in the scene in which Guy and Bruno first meet aboard the train and point up Bruno's homosexuality in a rather overt fashion. For example, some of the additional lines of dialogue bring into relief Bruno's stereotypical hatred of women, epitomized by his utter contempt for Miriam, who has been unfaithful to Guy. "Let's not talk about it any more," Guy responds stoically. But Bruno is not to be dissuaded: "Women like that can sure make a lot of trouble for a man." Bruno then brings up the subject of revenge by expressing his theory that "everybody is a potential murderer. Now, didn't you ever feel that you wanted to kill somebody? Say, one of those useless fellows that Miriam was playing around with?" Guy brushes aside Bruno's question, but Bruno persists in following this line of thought by unveiling his plan that he could liquidate Miriam and Guy could reciprocate by disposing of Bruno's father.

Bill Desowitz declares that the complete Bruno-Guy dialogue contained in the British cut of the movie amplifies Bruno's homosexual attitudes by foregrounding his hatred for the opposite sex and his corresponding preference for the members of his own sex. The result, says Desowitz, is that "the complete Bruno-Guy sequence is richer and more outlandish than the U.S. compression; it enlivens the exchange between Bruno and Guy" and makes Bruno appear "more evil, more seductive."

In short, it appears that Hitchcock deleted this passage of dialogue, amounting to two minutes of screen time, from the American release prints because of their strong homosexual content, which he assumed the industry film censor would disapprove of. Hitchcock was aware that, at the time that he made *Strangers on a Train,* Joseph Breen, the censor, maintained that homosexuality was too strong a subject for American motion pictures. He was backed up by the censorship code, which stated flatly that any reference to "sex perversion" was forbidden. As Thomas Doherty comments, Breen was committed to keeping homosexuals in "the celluloid closet."[33]

By contrast, the British Board of Censors (BBOC) permitted a rather forthright treatment of the subject in films released in England. Accordingly, Hitchcock toned down to some degree the homosexual implications of the scene in question in the American version of the movie but allowed the scene to stand just as he shot it in the British prints, with the endorsement of the BBOC.

The other slight alteration that Hitchcock made for British release involves the film's tag (epilogue). In it Guy and Ann (Ruth Roman), his fiancée, run into an Anglican minister on a train. When the minister attempts to engage Guy in conversation, Guy prompts Ann to scurry away with him from the minister, since Guy is not prepared to have an interchange with another stranger on a train. Hitchcock snipped from the British prints this short scene, which he referred to as the "minister tag" in his production notes, now preserved in the Warner Brothers Collection at the University of Southern California Library. His motive was apparently that

British filmgoers might have seen the minister tag as a joke at the expense of the Anglican clergy.

Accordingly, the British version of *Strangers* concludes with Guy's phone call to Ann, informing her that Bruno has finally been identified as Miriam's murderer. This scene is, of course, the penultimate scene in the American version, immediately preceding the short epilogue involving the minister.

Interestingly enough, Chandler mentions in the never-mailed letter to Hitchcock that he had the minister tag in his notes: "But I didn't put it in my script." He believed that since the movie told a fairly dark story, it should be kept pretty grim right up to the end, "and that you couldn't end it with a joke."[34] So it appears that Chandler got his own back, to the extent that Hitchcock wound up removing the minister tag at least from the British prints of the film—an epilogue that Chandler thought was superfluous to begin with, and had omitted entirely from his script draft.

In any event, the minister tag was really an afterthought on Hitchcock's part, since the addition of this scene to the screenplay was the very last revision made in the script. The scene is dated December 16, 1950, in the final shooting script, while all of the previous last-minute additions to the screenplay were added a few days earlier.[35] (Additional pages of revisions that are inserted into a shooting script are customarily dated, in order to indicate that they supersede earlier versions of the same material.)

With or without the minister tag, the film ends with the happy prospect of Guy marrying Ann. "Guy's pleasant future of marriage to Ann," MaryKay Mahoney wryly notes, "has been provided for him courtesy of Bruno, who removed Miriam, the only obstacle to Guy's happiness."[36] That final irony is surely one that is savored by the savvy filmgoer. For Guy not only benefited from the crime but also subconsciously wanted Miriam dead.

It is a pity that, although both Chandler and Hitchcock specialized in the thriller genre, their artistic views were in many ways so incompatible.[37] Hitchcock was, like Chandler, dissatisfied with the end product of their unpleasant collaboration. For his part, Hitchcock did not find some of the performances compelling; he particularly thought that Farley Granger and Ruth Roman lacked conviction. But then that was not necessarily the fault of the actors. After all, as Robert Harris and Michael Lasky observe in their book on Hitchcock, the film's dialogue, as revised by Czenzi Ormonde, was merely adequate in some scenes. Hence they declare, "The dialogue was not as strong as it could have been and the characters were consequently not as defined as they might have been."[38]

Be that as it may, Hitchcock still regretted that the studio had imposed Granger and Roman on him, when he would have preferred other actors. He joked that Walt Disney, as a cartoon maker, had "the best casting: if he doesn't like an actor, he just tears him up!"[39]

Withal, the film was a phenomenal critical and popular success when it premiered in July 1951, with reviewers toasting the film as a topnotch thriller. One critic even mentioned how subtly the film appeals to the outlaw lurking in all of us. After seeing the film, Chandler stated flatly that he could not figure out why the movie caught on. As a matter of fact, some reviewers echoed Chandler's ongoing complaints that Hitchcock had been careless about narrative logic and character motivation. More than one critic called the plot implausible, while Manny Farber went much further when he called *Strangers on a Train* "fun to watch, if you check your intelligence at the box office." Farber contended that Hitchcock cleverly masked the movie's implausibilities "with a honey-smooth patina of sophistication . . . and general glitter"—a remark that is in complete harmony with Chandler's criticism of the film.[40]

Withal, Patricia Highsmith stated in *Plotting and Writing Suspense Fiction* that she considered *Strangers on a Train* "one of the best of the films" made from her novels. In fact, when she was asked before her death in 1995 which of the movies from her work she preferred, she had not changed her mind. "Walker in *Strangers on a Train*," she replied. "He got it." When one considers that other films derived from her work were directed by such distinguished European directors as René Clement (*Purple Noon*) and Wim Wenders (*The American Friend*), that is a substantial bit of praise. In addition, *Strangers on a Train* can be favorably compared to Anthony Minghella's 1999 remake of *Purple Noon* under the novel's title, *The Talented Mr. Ripley*, in which Matt Damon plays a sly homosexual psychopath reminiscent of Bruno Antony. In fact, the *New Yorker* affirms that "the prototype of Ripley was Bruno in *Strangers on a Train*, immortalized by Robert Walker in Hitchcock's film."[41] In sum, *Strangers on a Train* is still the Highsmith movie to beat.

Playback: The Screenplay

There remains one other Chandler screenplay to consider, one which unfortunately went unproduced. Like the Hitchcock film, it begins with the meeting of two strangers on a train. Chandler eventually turned the script into a novel, when there was no longer any hope that it would be filmed. The occasion of the *Playback* screenplay was an offer that Universal-International Pictures (UI) extended to Chandler in March 1947, after his association with Paramount had been terminated.

Both Joseph Sistrom, who had produced *Double Indemnity* at Paramount, and William Dozier, who had been head of the Story Department at the same studio, were now executives at UI. They were enthusiastic about commissioning Chandler to write an original script for UI, because Chandler had earned screenwriting credits at Paramount for four films, all of which went on to be notable commercial successes, while *Double Indemnity* and *Blue Dahlia* were both nominated for Oscars.

The arrangement that Dozier and Sistrom worked out with Chandler's Hollywood agent, H.N. Swanson, was "one of the most unusual deals ever made in Hollywood, or so I'm told," Chandler stated at the time. He submitted to the studio a five-page outline of an original screenplay, which UI immediately accepted. He in turn agreed to develop this short scenario into a full-fledged script at a salary of four thousand dollars a week. The studio would retain the exclusive right to make a picture from his script, with Joseph Sistrom assigned to be the producer. The most unusual facet of this groundbreaking contract, Chandler continued, was that the studio agreed "to buy the motion picture rights to something I write in my own way, and without any supervision."[42] That meant that Chandler was free to work at home at his own pace, without punching a time clock at the studio. Chandler was committed to delivering the screenplay by the end of August.

Chandler chipped away at the screenplay slowly, with the same sort of care he lavished on his novels. He completed the first draft of the screenplay on September 30 and set about revising it. He was at pains to tighten the narrative structure and sharpen the dialogue. Chandler said at the time that he found the process of polishing a screenplay to be "a delicate art, and about as fascinating as scraping teeth." He added that, given the amount of time he was spending on the project, anyone would have thought that he was building a pyramid.[43] In fact, the final version of the script is a carefully crafted piece of work.

Nevertheless, by the time Chandler submitted the script to UI on March 24, 1948, the studio was experiencing financial difficulties and retrenchment was the order of the day. Moreover, as Chandler explained later on, the studio informed him that shooting extensively on location in Vancouver, British Columbia, where the bulk of the story took place, was risky because of the "uncertain weather," which might cause expensive delays while filming outdoors.[44] In addition, William Nolan affirms that studio officials were disappointed with *Playback* because "the script lacked a dynamic hero," since "the mild-mannered Canadian detective" did not have the makings of a compelling hero.[45] Accordingly, the studio reluctantly decided to shelve the project indefinitely and absorb Chandler's salary of $140,000 as a corporate tax write-off. The final draft of the script was discovered in the Universal Studios archive nearly forty years later and was duly published in 1985.

As mentioned, Chandler set the film principally in Vancouver, on the Canadian-American border. The heroine, Betty Mayfield, is fleeing to Vancouver in the wake of a scandalous East Coast trial in which she was acquitted of murdering her husband, who died under suspicious circumstances. Aboard a train bound for Canada, Betty meets Larry Mitchell, a handsome ladies' man; they encounter each other as two strangers on a train. Their first interchange is a typical example of the brittle dialogue that characterizes the screenplay. When Mitchell inquires how far Betty is going, she answers, "How far does this train go?" He tells her, "Vancouver, B.C.," and she replies laconically, "I'm going to Vancouver."[46] Her remark indicates that, at this juncture, Betty is more preoccupied with what she is running away from than where she is going.

While both of them are staying at the Royal Hotel in Vancouver, Betty learns that Larry is an unsavory character with mob affiliations. In due course Larry turns up dead on the balcony of Betty's hotel suite. When she is once again falsely accused of murder, the situation seems a "playback" of the unjust murder charge leveled at her after her husband's demise.

Jeff Killaine, a Canadian police detective, is assigned to the Mitchell slaying. Jeff's investigations prove that a racketeer named Clark Brandon murdered Larry Mitchell when Mitchell had a falling out with his mob. So Brandon had tried to frame Betty for what was actually a gangland killing. Although in the end Betty is exonerated, the world Chandler depicts in his screenplay remains "bleak, cold, and largely hopeless," comments Gay Brewer. For it is a world marred by hatred, betrayal, and death.[47]

Chandler took some solace in the large sum of money he received for the script, even though the movie was never produced. Furthermore, some years after he had written it, he salvaged the script by utilizing it as the basis of his last novel, also entitled *Playback*.

Playback: The Novel

Since UI had acquired only the screen rights to *Playback*, there was no reason why Chandler could not turn the script into a novel. He began working on the novelization of the screenplay in 1953.

As we saw in examining Chandler's novels and the films made from them in the first part of this study, all of the novels are narrated in the first person by Chandler's detective-hero, Philip Marlowe, who is the controlling voice of each novel as well as its protagonist. The problem that Chandler immediately encountered in attempting to transform his screenplay into a Marlowe novel was that Marlowe's counterpart in the script, Jeff Killaine, is not the central character of the screenplay, and he does not narrate the story. In fact, Killaine does not make his first appearance in the script until page twenty-eight. The main character of the screenplay is, of course, Betty Mayfield. Hence the plot of the screenplay revolves around the basic situation in which she "has narrowly escaped taking the rap for a murder she didn't commit and then going a long way off to hide under a different name," as Chandler explained to Swanson on January 5, 1953. Then she finds herself in a situation "similar to the original catastrophe" and is once again accused of murder.[48]

Crime novelist Robert Parker states in his introduction to the published screenplay that Chandler was obliged "to wrestle his *Playback* story into the Marlowe narrative frame" so that the novel could be told from Marlowe's first-person point of view. "Everything that happens must happen before Marlowe's eyes." As a result, Chandler had to exclude from the novel some interesting scenes in the script simply because Marlowe was not present when they transpired. Such events, continues Parker, "are no longer available to us, because they are not available to Marlowe."[49]

Consequently, Chandler had to scuttle the screenplay's opening scene, in which Betty and Mitchell first meet on the train, and with it, the intriguing interplay between the pair, as Betty cagily endeavors to keep a total stranger from getting fresh with her.

Another alteration that Chandler had to make in the screenplay in transforming it into a Marlowe novel was to transplant the action to the baroque southern California world that is Marlowe's stamping ground. He patterned Esmeralda, the town where much of the action transpires, after La Jolla, a coastal town in greater San Diego, where he himself resided at the time he wrote the book.

The novel begins with Betty arriving in southern California from the East, after she was acquitted of liquidating her husband. So the novel, like the screenplay, is concerned with Betty Mayfield's efforts to escape from her past. Philip Marlowe, of course, substitutes for the script's Jeff Killaine as the detective who figures in the story. It is Marlowe who sets out to prove Betty innocent of murdering Larry Mitchell, after he is found dead in her hotel suite. Marlowe eventually unmasks Clark Brandon as Mitchell's killer, as Killaine does in the script.

Chandler completed about half of the novel as planned during 1953, then lost interest in it and put it aside in favor of working on other projects. He did not return to the novel until 1957, when he resolved to finish the manuscript by the end of the year. He was able to meet his self-imposed deadline "by getting up at 6 A.M. and working ten hours straight with no food but coffee and Scotch," he wrote to Paul Brooks at Houghton Mifflin, his publisher, on December 28, 1957. "I think it will stand up."[50] This is the same regime Chandler imposed on himself in order to finish the screenplay of *The Blue Dahlia* some ten years earlier. Given the fact that he was now nearly seventy, it is surprising that he was able to endure such a debilitating regimen, but he survived.

The extensive overhauling of the original story line of the screenplay, which was necessary in order to integrate Philip Marlowe into the plot of the novel, brings into relief the fact that the book is not the mere "patched-up film script" that Durham calls it.[51]

Playback is the only Chandler novel in which the author plays a small cameo role. Perhaps he was inspired to include a self-portrait-in-miniature in the book by the example of Alfred Hitchcock, who did a walk-on in most of his films. (In *Strangers on a Train,* for example, Hitchcock is seen getting on a train just as Farley Granger gets off.) In *Playback* Chandler appears as Henry Clarendon IV, an elderly gentleman who resides at the Casa del Poniente, the same hotel where Betty is staying; Marlowe interrogates Clarendon about Betty at one point. Clarendon resembles his creator in some subtle ways. Thus Clarendon walks with a cane, just as Chandler did in later life. In addition, Clarendon wears white gloves indoors, as did Chandler, who suffered from an unsightly skin malady on his hands. Hence, when Marlowe offers to shake hands with him, Clarendon begs off. "I never shake hands," he explains. "My hands are ugly and painful. I wear gloves for that reason."[52]

While discussing the afterlife with Marlowe, Clarendon reflects, "I don't think I should really enjoy a heaven in which I shared lodgings with . . . a Hollywood producer."[53] In the light of Chandler's unhappy experiences as a screenwriter, Clarendon's remark surely expresses a sentiment with which Chandler could agree.

When the novel appeared critics were well-nigh unanimous in reluctantly acknowledging that, while *Playback* was a workmanlike piece of writing, Chandler had passed his peak as a novelist. Try as he might, he could not recapture the verve that characterized his previous novels. Chandler was at long last running out of steam. The novel, says Robert B. Parker, is the product of age and hard work rather than of the facility of a youthful talent. "In the failing of his powers," Parker reflects, "we are made to realize how vigorous they once were."[54] As Chandler himself put it, while referring to aging authors like himself, who continued to write in the twilight of their careers, "The champ may have lost his stuff. . . . But when he can no longer throw his hard high one," he throws one last pitch from the heart. "He doesn't walk off the mound and weep."[55] *Playback* was Chandler's last pitch.

Chandler as Screenwriter

Looking back on Chandler's Hollywood years, one finds that the two films nominated for Oscars, *Double Indemnity* and *The Blue Dahlia,* deserve to rank as screen classics, while another film, *Strangers on a Train,* is not far behind. Not a bad record for a writer who some years after he had coscripted *Double Indemnity* stated that he had learned from Billy Wilder "as much about screenwriting as I am capable of learning, which is not very much."[56]

Chandler had mixed feelings about working in Hollywood. He wrote to Alfred Knopf on January 12, 1946, "Please do not think I despise Hollywood, because I don't." The best proof of that statement, he continued, was that he would have been willing to work again for every producer he had been associated with up to that time, from Joseph Sistrom to John Houseman, "and every one of them, in spite of my tantrums, would be glad to have me."[57]

Still, Chandler had some serious reservations about functioning as a writer within the studio system, which he rehearsed for Hamish Hamilton in a letter written on November 19, 1950. Chandler recalled that, like almost every writer who goes to Hollywood, "I was convinced in the beginning that there must be some discoverable method of working in pictures" that would not totally stultify whatever creative talent he might happen to possess. Like others before him, though, he inevitably discovered that this was a dream: "It's nobody's fault, it's part of the structure of the industry. Too many people have too much to say about a writer's work. It ceases to be his own."[58]

On this point an upcoming Hollywood screenwriter says, "I don't feel the position of writers in Hollywood has changed much over the years," since Chandler's time. "We know no script is going to start shooting without some changes being made, but there's this idea in the studios that everybody should be allowed to contribute to the process, that the script should please everybody."[59]

Putting it another way, Chandler said that he gave up screen writing because "I am a writer, and there comes a time when that which I write has to belong to me, has to be written alone and in silence, with no one looking over my shoulder, no one telling me a better way to write it. It doesn't have to be great writing, it doesn't even have to be terribly good. It just has to be mine."[60]

Elsewhere Chandler summed up his whole experience of working in the studio salt mines in a much more caustic tone: "The overall picture," he said in the letter to Knopf, already cited, "is of a degraded community whose idealism even is largely fake. The pretentiousness, the bogus enthusiasm, the constant drinking and drabbing, the incessant squabbling over money"— it all smacks of a comic opera. "Only you suddenly know that this is not funny; this is the Roman circus, and damn near the end of civilization."[61]

Chandler once described the making of a film as an endless contention of tawdry egos, almost none of whom are capable of anything more creative than self-promotion and credit-stealing. Hence it was not surprising that there were those in Hollywood who breathed a sign of relief when Raymond Chandler rode out of town. Still, whatever Chandler's gripes about the studio system, he worked conscientiously at the craft of screenwriting while he was employed by the studios. When adapting another author's work for film, Chandler endeavored to be true to the thematic intent of his source, as when in the screenplay of *Double Indemnity* he and Wilder stuck as close to James M. Cain's grim, gritty tale of lust and violence as the censor would allow.

Television, like the film medium, has turned to Chandler's work for material; and so it would be worthwhile to survey the television productions of Chandler's work in order to ascertain whether the big screen or the little screen has been more felicitous in presenting his work for the mass audience. Let us take a brief look, then, at Chandler and the television tube.

12

The Stag at Eve

Poodle Springs and Other Telefilms

The stag at eve had drunk his fill.
> —Sir Walter Scott, *The Lake of the Lake*

Forget your personal tragedy. We are all bitched from the start.
. . . You're not a tragic character. Neither am I. All we are is
writers and what we should do is write. Just call them the way
you see them and the hell with it.
> —Ernest Hemingway to another writer

Philip Marlowe actually debuted on radio long before he appeared on television. After the success of *Murder, My Sweet* and *The Big Sleep* on film, NBC radio executives decided to cash in on Marlowe's popularity with the mass audience by launching a half-hour radio series, *The Adventures of Philip Marlowe,* as a summer replacement for *The Bob Hope Show* in the summer of 1947. Academy Award–winner Van Heflin (*Johnny Eager*) played the lead.

In September 1948, Marlowe returned to the airwaves on CBS in *The Adventures of Philip Marlowe,* starring Gerald Mohr, a minor film star (*Detective Story*). The series ran through the spring of 1950 and returned briefly from July to October 1951, for a total of more than a hundred episodes. Initially Chandler had considered asking for script approval for the Marlowe radio series, but ultimately he decided to have no connection with the scripting of the programs. He contented himself with the weekly royalties he received for the use of his character, while professing himself "moderately pleased" with Gerald Mohr's portrayal of Marlowe.[1]

Inevitably Raymond Chandler's private eye surfaced on the television screen. There was, for example, the television adaptation of *The Long Goodbye*, broadcast on CBS on October 7, 1954, with Dick Powell reprising his role as Philip Marlowe from *Murder, My Sweet*. As mentioned before, there was general agreement at the time that the telecast did not qualify as a satisfactory treatment of Chandler's novel. Still, the possibility of a Philip Marlowe television series eventually surfaced.

Philip Marlowe, Detective: The First Television Series

Chandler had for a long time shied away from authorizing a Marlowe television series, explaining, "To me, television is just one more facet of the considerable segment of our civilization which never had any standard but the soft buck."[2] He referred to television producers as lunatics, the kind of "sub-human hucksters" who made low-budget films in Hollywood and controlled radio. "The writing, I suppose, is no worse than it was in lots of radio shows," he added, but it was definitely substandard by any other criterion. "If you have spent fifteen years building up a character, a fairly complicated character, you can't deliver him to the sort of people who do these shows. . . . I simply can't afford to have the character murdered by a bunch of yucks."[3]

Withal, when television producers Mark Goodson and Bill Todman approached him about a Marlowe series in late 1958, Chandler felt that he had held out long enough and finally relented. After all, the emolument he would regularly receive for the use of his character was too substantial to pass up. The producers settled upon Philip Carey, a movie star of the second magnitude (*Mr. Roberts*) to play the title role in *Philip Marlowe, Detective*.

Carey remembered that Chandler wanted the series set in the 1940s, the time frame of all of the Marlowe feature films that had been produced up to that time. But the producers countered that the Marlowe movies were set in the 1940s because they were *made* in the 1940s and held out for a contemporary setting for the series. Chandler was subsequently vindicated when the series was later criticized by television critics for not sticking to the forties time frame of the Marlowe films.

Before the series was premiered, Carey had a conference with Chandler, during which Chandler "asked me what I thought of some of the people who played Marlowe in films. . . . He wasn't very coherent, but he liked the way I looked." Chandler agreed to help promote the series by appearing on some television talk shows with Carey; these rare public appearances by the reclusive Chandler testified to his overall willingness to help the series succeed. Carey looked back on Chandler in the last year of the novelist's life as "rather crusty, and not a very nice man to be around"—a comment often made by those who crossed Chandler's path in Hollywood through the years. As with the radio series, Chandler did not wish to supervise the television scripts; "but as long as he felt some involvement," he was content, Carey concluded.[4] Chandler was no doubt pleased that each segment included a statement in the opening credits that the series was "created by Raymond Chandler."

Goodson and Todman sold the series to ABC, and the first segment was broadcast on October 6, 1959, shortly after Chandler's death the previous March, so he did not live to see any of the telecasts. In all, twenty-six episodes were filmed (British film critic Philip French sets the number at thirteen because only half of the segments were actually shown in Britain). The episodes were essentially original teleplays that relied very little on any of Chandler's fiction for source material.

One of the last entries to be aired was "Murder Is a Grave Affair" (March 8, 1960), written by Gene Wang (not Gene Wong as Clark calls him). Wang was a regular contributor to the series. It is noteworthy that "Murder Is a Grave Affair" has a Hollywood setting, since, as mentioned before, Chandler's first two novellas, *Blackmailers Don't Shoot* and *Smart-Alec Kill,* plus one of his novels, *The Little Sister,* all have a Hollywood background. As the telefilm gets underway, filmmaker Larry Gilbert (Gene Nelson) has seduced starlet Lydia Mitchell and then welshed on his promise to put her in his next picture. Lydia is devastated when Larry callously discards her. Soon after, Lydia is found dead in her walk-up apartment; she has been asphyxiated by fumes from her gas heater.

Lydia's distraught father enlists Marlowe to prove that Larry murdered Lydia to keep her from causing a scandal. When Marlowe accompanies Lt. Mannie Harris (William Schallert) to Larry's home for an interrogation, they find Larry dead of a gunshot wound. Lieutenant Harris immediately assumes that Larry got the guilts over his treatment of Lydia and took his own life. "This is not suicide, but murder," Marlowe counters. "Larry was a southpaw; yet the gun is in his right hand."

Marlowe turns his attention to Larry's widow, Marian Gilbert, who openly cheated on her husband because he was two-timing her. In one of the few interchanges in the telefilm that smacks of Chandler's tart dialogue, Marian admits to Marlowe that she is a golddigger and married Larry for his money. "You don't approve of me, Mr. Marlowe," she observes. "Don't' let it worry you," he retorts. "I don't approve of myself."

Marlowe learns that the medical examiner has ruled that Lydia Mitchell's death was accidental, so Larry neither murdered Lydia nor killed himself in remorse for slaying her. The question remains as to who wiped out Larry.

At first Marlowe assumes that Marian did not kill Larry because she of all people would have known that her husband was left-handed and would not have made the mistake of placing the gun in his right hand. Marlowe does a complete about-face, however, and makes a shrewd guess that Marian deliberately put the gun in Larry's right hand after she shot him, precisely because she knew that the police would assume that she would not have made such an error. Then Marlowe trips her up in her prefabricated alibi for the night of the murder and accuses Marian of eradicating Larry, not only to get even with him for his infidelity but also to cash in his lucrative insurance policy. Her first mistake, of course, was admitting to Marlowe that she was a fortune hunter in the first place.

Marian Gilbert provides a link with Chandler's fiction, to the extent that she is the sort of deadly femme fatale who reappears throughout the Chandler canon, starting with the murderess in Chandler's first Hollywood story, *Smart-Alec Kill*. Like all of the others, Marian is a smart, privileged individual who in the end turns out to be all rotten inside. In particular she evokes Mrs. Murdoch in *The High Window*, who also murdered her unfaithful husband for the death money provided by his insurance.

This segment of *Philip Marlowe, Detective* was released on videocassette in 1998 as part of a boxed set entitled *TV from Radio*, a collection of episodes from television series that began their creative life on radio; as such, it is the only episode of the Marlowe series available for viewing. By all accounts "Murder Is a Grave Affair" is representative of the undistinguished character of the series as a whole. To be fair, journeyman director Paul Stewart did a competent job of directing his cast, some of whom deserve honorable mention. Gene Nelson (*Oklahoma!*), the best-known actor in the lineup, guest-starred as Larry Gilbert and turned in a worthy performance as a garden-variety Hollywood cad, and the reliable character actor William Schallert (*In the Heat of the Night*) lent good support as the flinty Lieutenant Harris.

On the other hand, Philip Carey was no more than adequate as Marlowe. In an attempt to make Carey look more hard-boiled, the producers decreed that he have a scar on his cheek, a scar worn by no other actor playing Marlowe before or since. Still, he came across as a rather bland and well-to-do private investigator, with a smart apartment overlooking the harbor at Newport Beach, where he kept a cabin cruiser to help in his adventures. "The affluence did not sit well on Chandler's down-at-the-heels" gumshoe, notes Philip French. Certainly Carey was "indistinguishable from the other homogenized private operatives" who were distilling their cases into half-hour episodes on the tube in those days.[5]

What's more, to judge by the individual segments from the other private-eye series in the *TV from Radio* set, from *Ellery Queen* (Lee Bowman) to *Richard Diamond* (David Janssens), *Philip Marlowe, Detective* was definitely on a par with the rest. The show received a somewhat less than enthusiastic reaction from both television reviewers and viewers, and it was canceled at the end of its first and only season. Moreover, the fact that only half of the episodes were broadcast in Britain by BBC-TV in the spring of 1960 indicates that the series found even less favor in England than in America. But there was another Marlowe series to come.

Philip Marlowe, Private Eye: The Second Television Series

Marlowe fared better in the 1983 television series, *Philip Marlowe, Private Eye* than he did in the earlier *Philip Marlowe, Detective* series. *Philip Marlowe, Private Eye*, which comprised five one-hour episodes, was made in Britain and broadcast on cable in the United States, from April 16 to May 14, 1983. The series starred Powers Boothe (*Tombstone*) as a gritty, blue collar Philip Marlowe, much closer to the Chandler original than Philip Carey's well-heeled Marlowe. The British series was narrated by Stacey Keach, who did not play Marlowe, as Clark asserts. By contrast, Carey narrated the earlier American series in the person of Marlowe, thereby following the lead of the Marlowe movies of the 1940s by having Marlowe's first-person narration punctuate each segment.

Philip Marlowe, Private Eye consisted of television adaptations of five of Chandler's novellas: *Smart-Alec Kill* (*Black Mask,* July 1934), *Finger Man* (*Black Mask,* October 1934), *Nevada Gas* (*Black Mask,* June 1935), and *The King in Yellow* (*Dime Detective,* March 1938), plus the late short story "The Pencil," which was published posthumously in various journals in 1959. Since Chandler did not introduce Philip Marlowe as his detective-hero until his first novel, *The Big Sleep,* the detective-protagonists who figured in the four early stories dramatized for the series were all precursors of Marlowe, but the private investigator in each case was renamed Philip Marlowe in the teleplays, to provide continuity for the series.

The telefilms in the series were recently released on video and are now available for screening. The most prominent filmmaker to direct a segment of the series was Bryan Forbes, who directed "The King in Yellow." As both a screenwriter and a director, Forbes admired Chandler's essays about the writer in Hollywood and is cited in the epigraph of this book as affirming that Chandler's articles on the subject would be "required reading" for those who work in the industry. "I won't say I knew Ray," Forbes has told me in correspondence, "but I met him on several occasions in London toward the end of his life." Roger Machell, Chandler's editor for the novelist's London publisher, was an old friend of Forbes, and Forbes attended many a luncheon in Machell's flat, held in Chandler's honor, whenever Chandler visited England in his last years. The guests would include such notables as novelist Truman Capote and playwright S.N. Behrman. Forbes remembers that Chandler was "heavily into the juice" but was nevertheless "a great raconteur," and Forbes enjoyed Chandler's company.

"'The King in Yellow' was one of five episodes done in a co-production effort between a British TV company and an American TV company," Forbes recalled. "I shot my episode at Twickenham Studios in England and finished off" with some location work in Los Angeles.[6] The plot centers on the murder of jazz trombonist King Leopardi. As the story unfolds it becomes clear that he was killed by two brothers. They wished to avenge the suicide of their beloved sister, who had taken her own life after being used and abused by Leopardi. The brothers eventually have a falling out, and one of them murders the other. The survivor, in turn, commits suicide, thus ending his life as his sister had ended hers, so the case has come full circle.

Martin Pitts writes that *Philip Marlowe, Private Eye* was applauded because the episodes were set in the same period as Chandler's original stories, in contrast to the earlier Marlowe series, which was roundly criticized for updating the stories to the period in which the series was telecast. In the present instance, Pitts agrees that "the old L.A. atmosphere" was conveyed very well indeed in the telefilms.[7] For his part, Forbes heartily endorsed the producers' decision to place each of the teleplays in the period setting.

"Because Chandler was such an individual writer and chose to set his Marlowe stories in a particular period," Forbes explains, "updating them always seemed to me to water them down for no particular good reason. The actual locations which we used and which, at the time, still existed in reasonable condition (they had not been bulldozed and replaced by high-rise apartments) gave the films an authenticity."[8]

I shall move on to other Chandler-related television productions that are accessible for viewing. There is, for example, a biographical television film about Chandler, *Raymond Chandler: Murder He Wrote.*

Raymond Chandler: Murder He Wrote

Because of Chandler's eminence as a crime novelist, he seemed a logical subject for a television documentary about his life. Furthermore, given Chandler's especially strong reputation in England, it is not surprising that the telefilm was originally produced for British television and later shown here. The hour-long documentary was originally broadcast by London Weekend Television in 1988 and was telecast in 1994 on the Arts and Entertainment network cable series *Biography*. The title, *Raymond Chandler: Murder He Wrote*, is a reference to the television series about a female shamus, *Murder She Wrote* (1984–96).

Raymond Chandler: Murder He Wrote, a superbly crafted, thoughtful documentary directed by David Thomas, features interviews with a wide variety of people who knew Chandler personally, such as John Houseman; authorities on his life and work, such as Frank MacShane; plus Robert Mitchum, who played Marlowe in two Chandler films. In addition, film actor Robert Stephens (*The Private Life of Sherlock Holmes*) appears on screen reenacting key events from Chandler's life, while his voice is heard, voice-over on the sound track, impersonating Chandler as he comments on the action, usually by way of passages lifted from Chandler's letters and essays.

While studiously emphasizing his achievements, the telefilm pulls no punches about the unpleasant aspects of Chandler's life. After all, dark threads run through Chandler's last years, from chronic alcoholism to mental instability and suicide attempts. Neil Morgan, editor of *The San Diego Tribune*, knew Chandler when Chandler lived in La Jolla, a suburb of San Diego.

Morgan recalls in the telefilm the suicide attempt Chandler made after Cissy's death on December 12, 1954, following a prolonged illness. "Chandler drank very heavily after her death," Morgan remembers. At 3:30 P.M. on February 22, 1955, two months after Cissy's demise, Chandler tried to shoot himself in his own bathroom shower, while in a drunken stupor. Because he was intoxicated, the shots went wild. "He fired one shot that went through the bathroom ceiling," Morgan continues. On this point, Bryan Forbes, a close friend of Chandler's London editor Roger Machell, has told me that "it was Roger Machell whom Ray rang from La Jolla when he attempted to shoot himself in the shower; and it was Roger who alerted the La Jolla police to a possible tragedy" by phoning them from London.[9]

In the documentary Morgan, who was a young newspaperman at the time, goes on to say that, when the police arrived at Chandler's home, "they had no alternative but to haul him away" to the alcoholic ward of the County Hospital. "I read it in the paper the next morning; I went by the hospital to see the superintendent, who was startled to learn that he had Mr. Chandler behind bars" in the alcoholic ward. Morgan accompanied the superintendent to see Chandler. "The superintendent said to him, 'Would you like to get out of here?' A very abashed Raymond Chandler said, 'I would like that very much, sir.' No bravado, no bitterness; he was like a wet puppy." Morgan took Chandler to a private sanatorium, where he spent six days drying out. Nevertheless, Chandler was hospitalized several more times before his death for alcoholic-related maladies. As a matter of fact, his final illness should be diagnosed as bronchial pneumonia exacerbated by alcoholism.

Raymond Chandler: Murder He Wrote goes on to document the last years of his life. "After Cissy's death," the narrator notes, Chandler returned to England, "where, to his surprise, he was taken seriously by the London literary establishment" as a prominent American novelist, not just a mystery writer. As a matter of fact, after Chandler spent a long sojourn in England in 1955, the British authorities claimed him officially as a British subject exclusively. They pointed out that he was still a British citizen through his mother, who was born in England. Chandler, of course, contended that he was an American citizen through his father, who was born in America, as was Chandler himself. Chandler, we remember, had identified himself as a British subject as well as an American citizen at various times throughout his life. Indeed, he never did anything to correct the widely held assumption in Hollywood while he was working there that he was an expatriate Brit.

Nevertheless, when the question of his dual citizenship had first arisen in 1948, the Southern District Court of California had ruled that "at all times since his birth" Chandler had been "a citizen of the United States."[10] Finally, in 1955, to avoid further skirmishes with the British government that might cost him his American citizenship, Chandler settled once and for all for being recognized solely as an American citizen.

On the question of Chandler's citizenship, it is worth noting that one reason J. Edgar Hoover had the FBI investigate Charlie Chaplin's loyalty to the United States in the early 1950s was because Chaplin maintained his

British citizenship while living in America. That was during the tense cold war years, the period that spawned the House Committee on Unamerican Activities' witch hunt for Communists and other disloyal citizens. In Chandler's case, the FBI has assured me that there is no record that Chandler's loyalty to America was ever questioned because he had at times pledged allegiance to Great Britain as well as to the United States.[11]

The Chandler television documentary concludes by presenting the circumstances surrounding his death. "The final years of his life were not fertile ones for Chandler," the telefilm's narrator states. Nonetheless, Chandler was always more stable when he was writing, so it is good that he attempted another novel, *Playback,* in his twilight years, the narrator continues. But *Playback* "was a shadow of its predecessors," as we know from the treatment of the novel in an earlier chapter of this study. "Towards the very end Chandler embarked on a new Marlowe novel, *The Poodle Springs Story,* in which Marlowe was to get married," the narrators adds, "but Chandler never finished it." Morgan comments, "Marlowe did all of the things that Chandler wished he could do. . . . Marlowe was a lady killer; and so in that last fragmentary book Chandler had Marlowe getting married." Chandler had considered getting remarried after Cissy's death, Morgan notes, but he never did take another wife.

"Raymond Chandler died in La Jolla on March 26, 1959," at the age of seventy, the narrator intones. He was buried beside Cissy in Mount Hope Cemetery in San Diego. Rev. Donald Glazebrook conducted a simple Episcopal ceremony at graveside. Morgan recalls that "only a handful were at the funeral"—seventeen by actual count. "It was a very tragic affair, attended by his solicitors, some functionaries, and very few friends." Also present was a representative of the Mystery Writers of America, which had elected Chandler their president shortly before his death. "It was a massive irony," Morgan explains, "that he was buried in Mount Hope Cemetery, which is where the city of San Diego buries its indigents." Chandler left an estate of sixty thousand dollars, big money in those days, so he was hardly destitute at the time of his demise, but he had left no funeral instructions, and he was accordingly given a rather austere interment in Mount Hope, "where the police cases go," Morgan concludes.

Since Chandler's life ended in so pathetic a fashion, *Raymond Chandler: Murder He Wrote* concludes with a reaffirmation of Chandler's status as a major American novelist. Peter Graves, the host of the *Biography* series, which aired the documentary in 1994, comments, "The happy ending proved just as elusive for Raymond Chandler as it did for his alter-ego, Philip

Marlowe. But today, many years after his death, Raymond Chandler is considered what he always wanted to be: one of the true greats of American writing."

In the acceptance speech Chandler delivered to the Mystery Writers of America, he speculated about his stature as a writer: "I am sure you realize I take this honor as a token of a long career.... Most of my life has been spent in trying to make something out of the mystery story—perhaps a little more than it was intended to be—but I am not at all sure I have succeeded."[12]

A number of obituaries that appeared in the wake of his death left no doubt about Chandler's contribution to the art of fiction. The *London Times* declared on March 27, 1959, "His name will certainly go down among the dozen or so mystery writers who, working the common vein of crime fiction, mined the gold of literature."[13] Nearly four decades after his death, Chandler was back in the spotlight when a telefilm of his last, unfinished novel was premiered on television.

Poodle Springs

Although no adaptations of Chandler's fiction have come out of Hollywood in recent years, television has turned to his work as a source of telefilms, notably the *Philip Marlowe, Private Eye* series. In addition, there is the made-for-television movie *Poodle Springs* (1998), derived from *The Poodle Springs Story*, which Chandler had abandoned in 1959. The title of Chandler's last effort brings into relief an interesting fact about the titles of his novels. Perhaps by coincidence, the titles Chandler gave to each of his novels turned out to be in alphabetical order: *The Big Sleep; Farewell, My Lovely; The High Window; The Lady in the Lake; The Little Sister; The Long Goodbye; Playback;* and *The Poodle Springs Story.*

At the very end of Chandler's last completed novel, *Playback* (1958), Marlowe receives a transatlantic phone call from Linda Loring, a wealthy socialite, who is in Paris. Her sudden intervention in the story is totally unexpected, since Linda, although a character in Chandler's previous novel, *The Long Goodbye,* plays no part in the action of *Playback* until this brief epilogue to the story. The reappearance of Linda Loring demonstrates Chandler's penchant for summoning characters he had employed before in his fiction to take part in later works. He similarly reprised police lieutenant Bernie Ohls, who first appeared in *The Big Sleep,* in *The Long Goodbye.* Chandler believed that these characters belonged to him and he could reenlist them in his work whenever he had need of them.

Marlowe and Linda had had a brief tryst toward the end of Chandler's previous novel, *The Long Goodbye*. Now she proposes marriage to him over the transatlantic wire, and he accepts, provided that she will allow him to pay her plane fare back to California. He insists on paying for Linda's plane ticket, Wolfe opines, "because he wants to declare at the outset his financial independence" from Linda. Yet Wolfe wonders, "How can Marlowe hope to live harmoniously with a near-stranger he hasn't seen for a year-and-a-half?"[14] Well might he ask. Indeed, Linda's high-toned, cloying manner throughout *The Long Goodbye* suggests a second-rate version of Tallulah Bankhead. Her supercilious airs and her patronizing overuse of the term "darling" when addressing just about everyone reinforces this image.

Chandler further explored the possibility of Marlowe's taking a wife in *The Poodle Springs Story*. He maintained that Maurice Guinness, a cousin of Helga Greene, his business manager, had encouraged him to marry off Marlowe to Linda Loring in his upcoming novel. He wrote to Guinness on February 10, 1958, "I plan my next Marlowe story with a background of Palm Springs," where he had on occasion vacationed. "'Poodle Springs,' I call it, because every third elegant creature you see has at least one poodle."[15] Chandler was also egged on to marry off Marlowe by Ian Fleming, who had by then written his first James Bond novel, *Casino Royale*, which Chandler had professed liking very much.

Ward and Silver note that in the opening four chapters of the novel, which are all that Chandler completed, Mr. and Mrs. Philip Marlowe return from "a quickie Mexican marriage to take up residence in a deluxe desert home. Marlowe plans to open a branch office in Poodle Springs, but promptly discovers that both the town law and the local mob think this is a bad idea."[16]

Chandler had written to a correspondent on December 12, 1957, that the struggle between Marlowe and Linda as to whether he is willing to live her extravagant kind of life or continue with his own modest life-style would constitute an interesting subplot for a detective novel: "Either she will give in, or the marriage will bust up. I don't know. But I do know that nobody is going to keep Marlowe from his shabby office and his unremunerative practice." Chandler added that Linda will most probably want to redecorate his office, but she will not get to first base with him on that proposition.[17]

To another correspondent, Chandler wrote on October 16, 1958, that Marlowe will abhor the rather chi-chi house in Poodle Springs that he and Linda move into after the wedding. "He will detest the bunch of freeloaders" he meets at the swanky parties that Linda hosts. She for her part will never comprehend why he is determined to stick to a dangerous and poorly paid profession.[18]

Linda Loring's posh house in Poodle Springs was modeled on the home of Jessie Baumgardner, a wealthy acquaintance of Chandler's. Clive James quips that "the Hammond organ-cum-cocktail bar in the honeymoon house" would be disturbing to a man of simple tastes like Marlowe. In fact, James is convinced that the marriage of Marlowe to Linda, "the classiest of Chandler's dames, the richest bitch of all," was doomed from the start.[19] Chandler finally gave up on the novel and toyed with the idea of converting it into a short story.

Academy Award–winning British screenwriter Tom Stoppard (*Shakespeare in Love*), who wrote the script for the television adaptation of *The Poodle Springs Story,* indicates why Chandler abandoned the novel. He points to a letter Chandler wrote to Guinness on February 21, 1959, in which Chandler states simply, "I think I may have picked the wrong girl."[20] It is surprising that Stoppard did not cite the lines immediately following in the same letter, in which Chandler goes on to say, "As a matter of fact, a fellow of Marlowe's type shouldn't get married, because he is a lonely man, a poor man, a dangerous man, and yet a sympathetic man, and somehow none of this goes with marriage. I think he will always have a fairly shabby office, a lonely house, a number of affairs, but no permanent connection. . . . But somehow I think he would not have it otherwise."[21]

Chandler affirmed this view more bluntly in "Casual Notes on the Mystery Novel," a 1949 essay: "A really good detective never gets married."[22] Little wonder that Chandler could not paint himself out of the corner that he had painted himself into when he allowed Marlowe to marry in *The Poodle Springs Story,* and finally despaired of ever finishing it.

Nonetheless, *The Poodle Springs Story* was eventually finished, though not by Raymond Chandler, nearly three decades after Chandler jettisoned the project. At the behest of the Chandler estate, crime novelist Robert B. Parker took on the task of finishing the novel in the fall of 1988, by adding several more chapters to Chandler's original four. Although Jon Breen believes that Parker is "not quite the addition to the Hammett-Chandler . . . pantheon he seemed at first," he has built himself a firm reputation as a major crime writer.[23] Furthermore, Stoppard believes that Parker did a creditable job in finishing the book, entitled simply *Poodle Springs,* because Parker, who had already featured Philip Marlowe in one of his own novels, *Perchance to Dream,* a sequel to *The Big Sleep,* "is good at Chandler and knows the game."[24]

The critics largely agreed with Stoppard's opinion of the novel, when *Poodle Springs* was published in the fall of 1989. "It is impossible to think of any other writer in the world better qualified for the task," crime novelist Ed McBain wrote in the *New York Times,* since Parker is himself the creator of several "literate, witty and tremendously readable" detective novels. Parker fashioned from Chandler's beginnings "a rattling good mystery."[25]

Parker provides "a nifty plot and vintage dialogue," said R.Z. Leonard in *Time;* but, he added, "Chandler's sentences are usually punchier than Parker's."[26] For example, Chandler writes of the honeymoon house in one of his chapters in *Poodle Springs* in these vivid terms: "It was a very handsome house, except that it stank decorator. The front wall was plate glass with butterflies imprisoned in it. . . . The floor of the hall was carpeted with blue vinyl with a geometric design in gold."[27]

Parker provides a description later in the book of Marlowe's office, which is the scruffy sort of place that Marlowe could afford on his personal income. Parker, however, writes in a rather pedestrian manner that is a cut below Chandler's knack for description: "I found an office, finally, as close to a dump as Poodle Springs gets, south of Ramon Drive, upstairs over a filling station. It was the usual fake adobe. . . . One room with a sink in the corner and a cheap deal desk left over from the previous tenant, a guy who maybe sold insurance and maybe other stuff" (24).

On the credit side, Parker very convincingly allows the marriage of Linda and Marlowe, who stubbornly resists becoming Linda's poodle, to turn sour. Parker rounds the story off with Linda planning to divorce Marlowe because he insists on sticking to his profession, one that Linda denigrates as grubby and unprofitable, and as leaving little room for her in his life. Yet at novel's end, Linda refuses to renounce her relationship with Marlowe entirely. "We can end the marriage, but we cannot end the love," she explains. "Probably we can't live together. But why must that mean we can't be lovers?" Marlowe replies tentatively, "Well, it makes sense to me" (289).

Poodle Springs, as finished by Robert Parker, proved a best-seller, and the book served as the basis for the 1998 teleplay, scripted by Tom Stoppard. As Stoppard explains, "My main idea for *Poodle Springs* the movie was to move the action forward to 1963, and likewise to advance Marlowe's age, making him middle-aged, over the hill, a quaint survivor of the 'wrong decade,' the only private eye who still wore a hat," and a dated fedora at that.[28] Admittedly Marlowe did not age significantly from one Chandler novel to the next, but he did grow perceptibly older in the later Marlowe films, when he was portrayed by the aging Robert Mitchum in *Farewell, My Lovely* and *The Big Sleep*. To that extent Stoppard had a precedent from the later Marlowe movies, if not from the Chandler novels, for making Marlowe middle-aged.

Filmmaker Bob Rafelson (*Five Easy Pieces*) seemed to be the right choice to direct the telefilm, since he had already filmed James M. Cain's *The Postman Always Rings Twice* (1981). Rafelson's faithful remake of the watered-down 1946 version of the Cain novel restored the earthy, tawdry sensuality that makes Cain's characters so intriguing. Rafelson is not one to dissect one of his films for an interviewer. Indeed, when I talked with him, I asked him what a particular scene was about, and he replied laconically, "it was about ten minutes."

He was more responsive when queried about his first foray into film noir with *The Postman Always Rings Twice*. "I have never considered myself a fan of film noir," he answered. Rather, he saw the Cain novel as a character piece about some low, corrupt people. Rafelson's remark is in harmony with Rodney Farnsworth's observation that Rafelson means "to explore the darker sides of the characters."[29] Small wonder, then, that Rafelson was drawn to film Cain's *Postman Always Rings Twice* and, more recently, the Chandler-Parker *Poodle Springs,* since both books are populated with low, corrupt characters. Michael Barson sees Chandler as congenial to the director because Rafelson's work reflects "the tender treatment of individuality," and Philip Marlowe is nothing if not a quirky individual who always goes his own way. Besides, Marlowe is typical of the kind of Rafelson hero who is "touched and perplexed by people."[30]

One actor who has worked with Rafelson recalls, "Bob is a very cerebral director. He had a lot going on in his head. On the set he was remote, aloof. He was result-oriented. . . . Bob told you where he wanted you to get to; he didn't care so much how you got there."[31] Rafelson certainly got good results from James Caan (*The Godfather*). Caan was elected to be the eighth incarnation of Philip Marlowe in a feature-length film (excluding the two Marlowe television series), following such illustrious predecessors as Dick Powell, Humphrey Bogart, and Robert Montgomery. Caan believes that he has a kinship with Marlowe. "The older I get, I'm more like Marlowe," he said while shooting the television film in the fall of 1997. "You find it easier just to shake your head" when things go wrong in life.[32]

Poodle Springs premiered on cable television on July 25, 1998. The telefilm, as described by Avis Weathersbee, "drags Marlowe and his code of ethics ('I can't be bought or pushed') grudgingly into the 1960s and a world of car phones, smack and S and M."[33] Aside from updating the story by fifteen years and moving Marlowe into middle-age, Stoppard's teleplay for the most part sticks closely to the Chandler story, as amplified by Parker. Thus the opening sequence is derived directly from the Chandler chapters; Marlowe has just married a young heiress, Laura Parker (the book's Linda Loring, played by Dina Meyer). Her father, P.J. Parker (Joe Don Baker), a rich power broker, has acquired a fancy house for the newlyweds as a wedding gift; it is located in Poodle Springs, California, a wealthy desert town on the Nevada border. But Marlowe soon finds out that even a desert paradise can have more than its share of crime and corruption.

Throughout the Chandler novels Marlowe consistently refuses to take divorce cases, because he is not interested in wasting his time popping flashbulbs in dirty hotels. True to his established policy, Marlowe refuses a divorce case offered to him over the phone by a prospective client. But when another shamus, Paul Krause, phones Marlowe, apparently from his car phone, to seek his help on a dangerous case, that is another matter. Krause says he called Marlowe because he knows him by reputation. As Marlowe converses with Krause, he hears shots fired over the phone, and the line promptly goes dead. Marlowe immediately goes to the crime scene, since Krause had told him that he was parked at the pier in San Pedro. He arrives before the police and seizes the opportunity of searching the corpse; he appropriates a private notebook he has found in the victim's coat pocket.

Marlowe proceeds to the office of Larry Victor (David Keith), a professional photographer, about whom Krause has made a recent notation in his notebook. Larry coolly asserts that Paul Krause is unknown to him and claims to have been with his wife at the time of Krause's murder. Marlowe mistrusts Victor and keeps him under surveillance, soon learning that this charming scoundrel is only a so-so photographer; in fact, his photography business is a mere front for his pornography racket. Marlowe also discovers that a stripper named Lola Faithful, a former employee of Larry's, wants to blackmail him into buying back from her a pornographic picture that she stole from his office. Marlowe also learns that Larry has a young wife named Angel.

At this point Rafelson dramatizes a scene taken over from the very last chapter Chandler wrote for the book. Manny Lipschultz, proprietor of a nighterie called the Agony Club, dispatches two of his goons to persuade Marlowe to come and see him posthaste. Not one to be intimidated by a couple of half-baked hoodlums, Marlowe cavalierly brushes them aside, saying that he will pay a call to their boss when he gets around to it. From this point onward, of course, the telefilm draws on the additional chapters of the novel supplied by Parker.

Lipschultz, who maintains an illegal gambling operation at his night-club, engages Marlowe to locate one Charles Nichols, who has skipped town, leaving Lipschultz with a $100,000 marker. Nichols happens to be married to Miriam "Muffy" McNichols (Julia Campbell), a rather plain Jane who is the daughter of Clayton Blackstone (Brian Cox). Blackstone is a criminal plutocrat who is the brains behind Lipschultz's shady club. Marlowe is aghast to discover later on that Charles Nichols is also Larry Victor.

When Lola Faithful is killed, Marlowe informs Larry of her death. Larry explains that Lola tried to blackmail him with an obscene photograph, de-picting Muffy in an attitude of bondage, shackled to a post in a provocative pose. Muffy, the kinky rich girl who is being blackmailed for posing willingly for porno pictures, clearly recalls Carmen Sternwood in *The Big Sleep*. More-over, Larry's being married to two different women while maintaining two different identities evokes Terry Lennox in *The Long Goodbye*. It appears that Stoppard, following Parker's lead, is making references to Chandler's fiction, which would certainly not be missed by Chandler's avid fans.

At any rate, Larry admits unabashedly being a bigamist when Marlowe interrogates him, but he firmly denies knowing anything about Lola's mur-der and strenuously maintains that he has not welshed on a $100,000 marker held by Lipschultz. Marlowe then interviews Muffy's father, who divulges that he had Lipschultz engage Marlowe to track down Charles Nichols on the pretext of making Nichols pay his gambling debt. Blackstone's real rea-son for having Marlowe trace Nichols, a motive that he wanted to conceal from Muffy, was that he feared Nichols was unfaithful to her. Blackstone also admits paying Nichols a monthly allowance of $2,000 to stay married to Muffy, who remains devoted to Nichols, despite the fact that her way-ward husband has neglected her so shamelessly.

The intrepid Marlowe also discovers that Paul Krause was seen hang-ing around the Pasada, a bordello masquerading as a motel. He is startled when he encounters Larry's other wife working there as a hooker, in order to support her drug habit. When Marlowe inquires if the girl, who is ironi-cally named Angel, knows that Larry has another wife, Angel answers him defiantly, "That poodle-bitch is worth $2,000 a month to Larry and me." Marlowe strong-arms Angel into confessing that Paul Krause had stumbled on the information that Muffy's husband had a second wife who was work-ing at the Pasada Motel, and demanded hush money from Larry and Angel. Marlowe guesses the rest.

"So you made a date with Krause somewhere far away from the Pasada Motel," says Marlowe. As this juncture Rafelson inserts a flashback, in which we see Krause driving up to a pier in San Pedro, where Angel sits waiting for him in her car. Without a word Angel aims a pistol through her car window and fires, killing Krause instantly. Marlowe continues, voice-over on the sound track, "You went home and gave Larry the gun; and he tried to give you an alibi. He thought of another private eye Krause might have called from his car phone." Larry is shown phoning Marlowe and impersonating Krause, whom Marlowe had never spoken to before. During the course of the call Larry reenacts Krause's murder by shooting the gun into a pillow. Marlowe had subsequently designated the time of the slaying as the time at which he received the spurious phone call from Larry. By that time, of course, Angel was at home with him. Accordingly, Larry's alibi, given to Marlowe earlier, that he was at home with his wife when Krause was shot, now rings totally false.

Marlowe turns Angel over to the police. They, in turn, inform him that Larry has driven his car into the Pacific Ocean, off Pacific Coast Highway, and drowned—though the body has yet to be recovered. Then Manny Lipschultz turns up dead, and Marlowe decides it is time for a showdown with Muffy and her father, the two suspects involved in the case who are still alive. Marlowe shows them the pornographic photo of Muffy that Lola employed in her endeavor to extort money from Larry and Muffy. Muffy, who is visibly shaken, suddenly speaks up. "Lola Faithful was mean to me," she whines, like the maladjusted creature she is. "And Manny Lipschultz was mean to me too; he said Charles gambled and didn't pay." Marlowe adroitly goads her into confessing to both murders.

When her father breaks the news of her husband's suicide, Muffy, who has been emotionally disturbed for some time, goes totally berserk. "You were all mean to me," she shouts hysterically, as she produces a revolver. "You killed my darling, all of you!" She shoots her father and turns her gun toward Marlowe just as Blackstone's bodyguard returns her fire, killing her instantly. Actually Marlowe pities Muffy, as he looks upon her corpse. To him she was the poor little rich girl, the bird in the gilded cage, spoiled by her overprotective father. For Muffy, love proved to be a self-inflicted wound that never healed; she would never accept the death of the man she called, with her last words, "my darling."

Marlowe reports the double shooting to the police. As for Larry's supposed suicide, Marlowe thinks it was a ruse perpetrated by Larry, presumably to avoid being charged with bigamy and complicity in Krause's death.

Larry, he says sardonically, is "probably in Mexico, growing a beard." Shades of Terry Lennox pretending to be Señor Maioranos at the close of *The Long Goodbye!* In the conclusion provided by Parker for the novel, Larry takes off for parts unknown, and there is therefore no question of his pretending to take his own life. By contrast, Rafelson and Stoppard prefer to leave his fate ambiguous.

The morning following the catastrophe at the Blackstone mansion, Laura shows up in Marlowe's office, asking for a job; she adds, "I'll do it for love." Rafelson then photographs the couple's embrace through the window of Marlowe's office door, on which the words "Philip Marlowe, Private Investigator" are stenciled. Superimposing Marlowe's name and occupation on the couple as they kiss implies that Marlowe's work and their marriage are compatible.

This ending is at odds with the conclusion of the novel. Parker, as we know, offers no such reassurance in the last pages of the book, where Marlowe's wife plans to divorce him, but still meet him for the occasional tryst. Furthermore, Chandler himself became convinced, during the period in which he worked on the novel, that the marriage would not work. His final word on the subject was expressed in a letter to Maurice Guinness, dated February 21, 1959, a month before Chandler's death. Chandler felt that Guinness's idea that Marlowe should marry was "quite out of character. I see him always in a lonely street, in lonely rooms, puzzled but never quite defeated."[34] At all events, the suggestion at the final fadeout of the television movie that Marlowe and Laura will live happily ever after is the only departure from the Chandler-Parker novel worth noting.

"*Poodle Springs* doesn't exactly live up to its predecessors," Avis Weathersbee writes, "but it's an interesting footnote" to the Marlowe movies.[35] Actually, the telefilm has some merit; Rafelson has made a technically accomplished movie. His direction is crisp and efficient, if not inspired, and he manages to keep the story moving along with nary a sag in the action. Furthermore, he skillfully handles his capable cast, headed by the distinguished British actor Brian Cox (*Nicholas and Alexandra*) as Blackstone. In addition, David Keith (*An Officer and a Gentleman*) merits special mention for his restraint as the sly, slick Larry Victor, and Joe Don Baker (*Walking Tall*) is all oily ingratiation as P.J. Parker, Laura's father.

Caan's fine-tuned depiction of Marlowe is the most underrated performance of his long career. Giving Caan his due, Will Joyner rightly praises Caan's portrayal by observing that Marlowe comes across as more than a mere "transom peeper." When Marlowe deals with the assortment of losers and low-lifes he encounters in the course of the teleplay, Caan "knows how to communicate the deep levels of wise, tough sympathy that have defined Marlowe" from his first film appearances.[36]

Marlowe, as Caan depicts him, has no illusions left about the fabled glamour of a gumshoe's life. The quotation from fellow shamus Lew Harper, cited above—"The bottom is loaded with nice people; only cream and bastards rise"—could have been uttered by Marlowe. Marlowe does not have what it takes to be the former, and he certainly will not settle for being the latter. Marlowe is a decent, good-natured private eye, who will continue to sympathize with the lonely and the flawed. Neither cream nor bastard, he will never rise.

Weathersbee concludes that the telemovie "serves as a reminder of how powerful and enduring the genre pioneered by Chandler still is, and why the American private eye remains one of the most resilient images in books and films."[37] Truer words were never spoken.

Endless Night

Chandler is one of the immortals. He wrote thrillers, but very special thrillers. Classics. He is the best of them all.
                                                    —Bryan Forbes

The private eye novel as first spawned by Raymond Chandler has produced a trillion imitators.
                                                    —James Ellroy

The heyday of film noir ended in the late 1950s, when it ceased to flourish as a separate trend in American cinema. But film noir still survives in the tough, cynical crime movies of today. "Once a seedy pulp genre and the mainstay of the B movie, the crime film long ago went mainstream," says *Sight and Sound,* and "movies with guns, garrotting and greed . . . now dominate the output of Hollywood."[1]

What's more, many detective movies made since the days of classic noir qualify as neo-noir, because they have the bench marks of the noir films of yesteryear. Stephen Holden states that the noir formula demands that filmmakers create movies with strong story lines, "with hard-boiled dialogue and multifaceted, often duplicitous characters. Noir may be formula, but it is one with room for compelling flesh-and-blood characters." So neo-noir films continue to be turned out in Hollywood, and, as Richard Jameson puts it, "film noir is still possible, and has no apologies to make to anybody."[2]

Chandler's name is inextricably linked with neo-noir. Indeed, the later Marlowe films, *Marlowe* and *The Long Goodbye,* paved the way for the trend of neo-noirs that followed those two movies. So Chandler's influence on the detective film and on neo-noir remains strong. One indication of this fact is that over the years significant references to the Chandler films, meant as a tribute to Chandler and his legendary sleuth, have appeared in a variety of detective movies and telefilms not based directly on his work.

The Chandler Legacy

British filmmaker Mike Hodges notes that he offered homage to Chandler in *Get Carter* (1970) by beginning the film with the hard-boiled protagonist, "Jack Carter (Michael Caine), reading *Farewell, My Lovely*" on the train which is taking him to the north of England to investigate his brother's murder.[3] This suggests how the movie reverberates with echoes of Chandler. Indeed, Jack's hunt for the killer leads him into the precincts of a gang of hoodlums involved in the same kind of pornography racket which figured in *The Big Sleep* and *The Little Sister*.

At times a director has segued from a discreet quotation of a Chandler movie into a neo-noir movie. They did so in order implicitly to acknowledge that their film "drew strength from the honorable cinematic tradition" of the noir detective film. There is, for example, Buzz Kulik's 1977 movie *Shamus,* a recasting of Chandler in 1970s New York, which contains two scenes patently inspired by Hawks's version of *The Big Sleep,* the most renowned of the Marlowe movies.

In the first instance the private eye played by Burt Reynolds is hired by a millionaire to retrieve some stolen jewels. When the shamus is ushered into his client's refrigerated office, he must don an overcoat to withstand the chilly atmosphere in which this eccentric individual lives. "The scene exists primarily as a one-to-one inversion of Marlowe's interview with General Sternwood in the steaming conservatory" in Hawks's *Big Sleep*.[4] In addition, the scene in which the private eye in *Shamus* beds down with the clerk in a bookstore after hours duplicates a similar scene in *The Big Sleep*.

The commentator in David Thomas's documentary *Raymond Chandler: Murder He Wrote* affirms that Chandler's wisecracking, cynical hard-boiled detective, Philip Marlowe, is "the most imitated private detective in film and literary history." Crime novelist James Ellroy, in the previously mentioned A&E documentary on Chandler, declares his debt to Chandler, affirming that "the private eye novel as first spawned by Raymond Chandler has produced a trillion imitators." Ellroy himself freely admits to imitating Chandler's "complex, well-layered plots." He adds that, like Chandler, he avoids "tidy conclusions, in which justice triumphs unequivocally; after all, the battle against crime goes on."

Furthermore, since the 1940s nearly every noir film about a private detective "has appropriated something from Raymond Chandler in one way or another," states Al Clark.[5] Thus Jack Gittes (Jack Nicholson), the L.A. gumshoe in Roman Polanski's *Chinatown* (1974) is a conscientious, resourceful sleuth cast in the same mold as Philip Marlowe. Moreover, Evelyn Mulwray (Faye Dunaway), the double-dealing dame who slyly manipulates Gittes, is a femme fatale straight out of Chandler. She is, writes Jim Shepherd, "all cool control, sexual independence, and transparent deception."[6]

Naremore declares that "neo-noirs are produced by Hollywood with increasing regularity. Consider such big-budget television productions" as *The Singing Detective;* noir, he concludes, is never going to go away.[7] The homage to Chandler in *The Singing Detective* (1986), a six-part BBC television miniseries scripted by Dennis Potter, is as obvious as it was in *Shamus*. The central character is even named Philip Marlow (without the final *e*); he writes mysteries featuring a private eye likewise named Philip Marlow. Marlow the novelist (Michael Gambon) is composing a Marlow thriller, episodes of which are portrayed in the course of the miniseries. The telefilm is entitled *The Singing Detective* because the sleuth (also played by Gambon) sometimes sings with a dance band as a cover for his activities as a gumshoe.

Marlow the writer portrays Marlow the detective in these episodes from the author's novel-in-progress. He accordingly appears in these scenes decked out in a trench coat and fedora very much like Chandler's own celebrated shamus. The thriller that Marlowe the novelist is constructing is set in 1945 in order to approximate the time frame of the Chandler books. "The unruffled figure of the detective moves into danger and darkness," as Marlow is drawn into an intrigue concerning two prostitutes suspected of being foreign agents. It is a threatening world of conniving trollops, dead-end hoods, and conspiracy very much in tune with Chandler's fiction.[8]

Moreover, the dialogue, which at times possesses the cadences of Chandler's prose, is punctuated with allusions to Chandler's private eye. Thus one of his avid readers inquires of author Philip Marlow how he came to write that "down these mean streets" brand of mystery. This is, of course, an allusion to Chandler's essay, "The Simple Art of Murder," quoted before, in which Chandler says that the detective who goes down these mean streets must be a good man who is not himself mean. The miniseries was enormously successful on both sides of the Atlantic and continues to be available on videocassette.

The films described above, which allude to Chandler and his work, are "not engaged in demolishing or parodying the genre," Jim Shepherd reminds us, but in revivifying it and keeping it alive.[9] Indeed, the vitality of neo-noir continues to be demonstrated by a number of later crime dramas with implicit tie-ins with Chandler. For example, Curtis Hanson's *L.A. Confidential* (1997), adapted from the James Ellroy novel, was consciously planned as a neo-noir.

In the film the protagonist must cope with a desperate group of "lying, duplicitous, and murderous antagonists," just the sort of gangland characters indigenous to Chandler territory.[10] In fact, Pauline Kael has written that the characters in a film like *L.A. Confidential* "talk as if they'd been boning up on Chandler novels."[11] *L.A. Confidential* has been hailed as the best example of neo-noir in the 1990s.

The movie pays homage to Chandler by presenting various parallels to his novels and films. To begin with, the picture is set in the early 1950s, well within the period in which Chandler's novels take place. Both "the dense, labyrinthine plot and the sharp, knowing dialogue" recall Chandler's work, as *TV Guide* notes.[12] The hero, Ed Exley (Guy Pearce), is an idealistic police detective; he shares Marlowe's abiding sense of justice, as reflected in his determination to fight police corruption, which was certainly one of Marlowe's aims as well.

Another link with Chandler in *L.A. Confidential* is the femme fatale, in this movie a call girl named Lynn Bracken (Kim Basinger, in an Oscar-winning performance). Bracken is made up to look like Veronica Lake; what's more, in one scene she is looking at a movie with a client that features Lake and Alan Ladd, costars of *The Blue Dahlia*. In addition, a homosexual involved in a blackmail plot is found murdered; one of the cops terms his slaying just another "Hollywood homo-cide," recalling the killing of Arthur Geiger, the homosexual blackmailer in *The Big Sleep*.[13] Finally, a deceased character is said to have faced "the Big Adios," which implicitly combines the titles of *The Big Sleep* and *The Long Goodbye*.

The title of *Goodbye Lover* (1999), directed by Roland Joffé (*The Mission*), recalls *The Long Goodbye*, but actually it is a reworking of *Double Indemnity*. Sandra (Patricia Arquette), a cool blonde who immediately brings Barbara Stanwyck's Phyllis to mind, conspires with Jake (Dermot Mulroney), who is modeled on Fred MacMurray's Walter, to murder the heavily insured Ben (Don Johnson). In *Double Indemnity*, we remember, both Phyllis and Walter, her accomplice, are claimed by the grim reaper. The present film, however, carries *Double Indemnity* one step further by having Sandra, the femme fatale, survive to inherit an $8 million insurance payoff after Jake perishes. *Goodbye Lover* is a salient reminder that noir films continue to surface in mainstream cinema, with no end in sight.

Foster Hirsch, author of *Detours and Lost Highways: A Map of Neo-Noir*, has told the *New York Times* that "audiences remain intrigued by neo-noir for essentially the same reasons they always were. There is the appeal of a story about characters who are thrown into a kind of nightmare scenario." There is a timeless attraction to characters who are dogged by cruel circumstances and fate.[14]

The title of Daniel Pyne's film *Where's Marlowe?* (1999) is an obvious reference to Chandler's shamus. The movie is about a down-at-the-heels L.A. private dick named Joe Boone (Miguel Ferrer). At one point a photographer takes a voyeuristic peak through his lens at an afternoon tryst, thereby recalling the opening of *Marlowe*. Given the hapless Boone's failure to solve his latest case, the movie's title seems to ask, "Where is Philip Marlowe, now that we need him?" Given the slapdash way the plot is handled in the movie, one is likewise tempted to ask, "Where is Raymond Chandler, now that we need him?"

Curtis Hanson, who directed *L.A. Confidential* and received an Academy Award for coscripting the movie, says in praise of film noir that "movies which take us to the dark side can be among the richest emotionally and thematically. That's what makes us want to see them again and again, long after the plot no longer keeps us guessing." Putting it another way, Raymond Chandler noted in a letter to Helga Greene, dated September 20, 1957, "The test of a writer is whether you want to read him again years after he should by the rules be dated."[15] The continued interest in Chandler's fiction certainly gives testimony to the fact that he has passed this test.

"Chandler took the crude, unpolished, hard-boiled murder mystery and cut, shaped, and polished it until it became a glittering work of art," Baker and Nietzel have pointed out.[16] By the same token, Terry Teachout writes that "Chandler's smoky, side-of-the-mouth prose remains as tartly satisfying as ever."[17] In short, as a novelist, Chandler sustained a level of quality unequaled by any other writer of hard-boiled detective fiction. And that is precisely why Alastair Cooke correctly prophesied as early as 1949 that Chandler would be "remembered when lots of what we now regard as our literary giants are buried in the school books."[18]

L'Envoi

Several endorsements of Chandler have been martialed in the foregoing paragraphs, underscoring the fact that Chandler's achievement as an American novelist is generally recognized in this day and age. Consequently, Robert Parker attests to the fact that Chandler is at last receiving "the kind of consideration he deserves (and sought, unrequited, until his death in 1959 at the age of seventy)."[19] Charles Smith adds, "Thanks largely to Philip Marlowe, the private eye has become a staple" of American fiction and film.[20]

What's more, many of the films of Chandler's fiction have proved to be rewarding cinematic experiences, and some represent excellent examples of the art of adapting a fictional work to the screen. Significantly, Paul Scrabo and Bill Duelly's 1997 television documentary, *Spies, Sleuths, and Private Eyes: Classic Detectives in the Cinema,* singles out Chandler as a crime novelist whose work has strongly influenced the detective film.

Adapting a novel for film requires great skill, for the filmmaker must endeavor "to recreate the literary source in filmic terms, keeping as close to the spirit of the original as possible."[21] Preserving the spirit of Chandler's fiction on film with taste and discrimination calls for gifted screenwriters and directors, and the Chandler films have attracted some of the best: from scriptwriters such as William Faulkner and Leigh Brackett to directors such as Howard Hawks and Robert Altman. Furthermore, Chandler himself labored on screenplays for renowned filmmakers like Billy Wilder and Alfred Hitchcock.

In retrospect, the films derived from Chandler's screenplays and the movies based on his fiction make it abundantly clear that, despite Chandler's complaints about how the studios mistreated him and his work, his creative association with Hollywood yielded some first-class films. It is obvious from Chandler's essays and letters that his relationship with the movie industry "ultimately turned sour," but that "in no way diminishes the profound influence Chandler has had, on film as on American literature."[22] Moreover, the best of these films—*Double Indemnity, The Big Sleep,* and *Murder, My Sweet*—deserve to rank as screen classics, and some others, such as *The Blue Dahlia, The Lady in the Lake,* and *Strangers on a Train,* are not far behind.

In addition, the Library of Congress has selected two of the films that Chandler was associated with to be preserved in the permanent collection of American motion pictures in the national Film Registry at the Library, as culturally, historically, and aesthetically important. They are *Double Indemnity* (chosen in 1992) and Hawks's *Big Sleep* (chosen in 1997).

In addition, the American Film Institute has placed *Double Indemnity* among the one hundred best American films made during the first one hundred years of cinema. What's more, the AFI honored the fifty best actors and actresses of the first century of cinema with a television special aired on June 15, 1999. Humphrey Bogart was chosen by fifteen hundred filmmakers and critics as the top actor, and *The Big Sleep* was singled out as one of his best films. Indeed, more than one critic covering the event referred to the sad-eyed, trench-coated Bogart as the embodiment of film noir in movies like *The Big Sleep*. Lauren Bacall, his costar in that film, ranked twentieth among the actresses enshrined by the AFI, and *The Big Sleep* was likewise mentioned as one of her finest films. These tributes bring into relief how Chandler has enriched the motion picture medium with some classic films.

Graham Greene once summed up for me in conversation his attitude toward the way his work had been treated by the motion picture medium in these terms: "Some of the films have been good, and one finds them a rewarding experience. As for those that have been disappointments, I can only say that, in the long run, the smile will be on the author's face. For the book has the longer life."

On the contrary, in Chandler's case, a number of the films drawn from his work remain accessible for viewing on television and on videocassette. They continue to be seen, just as his novels continue to be read. Moreover, I think it is a safe bet that the best of the Chandler films, with Hawks's *The Big Sleep* and *Double Indemnity* leading the list, will last as long as anything he has written. Indeed, the best of these motion pictures are an enduring tribute to his achievement as a writer.

James Ellroy says that Chandler's dark sensibility suits our own time just as well as it fit his own: Chandler's books, "even though they are set in the 1940s and 1950s, reflect . . . the dark times" in which we live. "I think the things going on then are going on now."

That Chandler's work is still timely is demonstrated by the fact that a second television biography of Chandler, made by Dean Mitchell, was aired on the Arts and Entertainment cable network in 2000. Mitchell's telefilm touched upon some elements in Chandler's life and work in more detail than David Thomas's earlier television documentary about Chandler, highlighting Chandler's screen-writing career, particularly his collaboration with Billy Wilder on *Double Indemnity,* and Chandler's depiction of the city as the citadel of sin, as represented especially by Los Angeles. Among the commentators on Chandler's life and work in Mitchell's documentary are Chandler biographer Tom Hiney, crime novelist Robert B. Parker, who completed Chandler's *Poodle Springs,* and Chandler scholars Alain Silver, Elizabeth Ward, and the present writer.

Despite Chandler's success, he always felt that he was an outsider from childhood onward. He was, for example, expelled from the oil industry (however justly) and was constantly at odds with the Hollywood establishment while employed by the studios. In fact, his novels add up to a plea to accept the outsider, epitomized by Marlowe, who is a dyed-in-the-wool loner.

In discussing Chandler's moral vision throughout this book, I noted that Marlowe lives by a traditional code of honor that sets him apart from the sort of venal and depraved individuals he has to cope with in pursing his investigations. Maintaining his sense of values in a decadent society that flouts them certainly qualifies Marlowe to be labeled as an outsider in the modern world.

Chandler's personal vision was deeply religious; he maintained that, in everything that can be called a work of art, there must be a quality of redemption. It is precisely by Marlowe's striving to live up to his ideals in a fallen world that Chandler's sleuth-knight redeems himself. Novelist William Nolan (*Logan's Run*) perhaps said it best when he wrote that Philip Marlowe, "the lone detective in the rumpled trenchcoat, still prowls his mean streets . . . in pursuit of personal justice," both on page and screen.[23] Kim Newman places Marlowe "among the most memorable, convincing, and influential" detectives in fiction, "at least as important as Sherlock Holmes" or Agatha Christie's Hercule Poirot. What's more, she concludes, "all subsequent private eyes owe much to him"[24]

Thanks to the genius of Raymond Chandler, Philip Marlowe is immortal.

Notes

Any direct quotations in this book that are undocumented are derived from the author's personal interviews with the subjects; direct references to their personal correspondence with the author are documented.

Prologue: Trouble in Paradise

1. Gene Phillips, *Graham Greene: The Films of His Fiction* (New York: Columbia Univ. Teachers College Press, 1974), 14.

2. David Parkinson, ed., *The Graham Greene Film Reader* (New York: Applause Theater Books, 1995), 443.

3. Raymond Chandler, "Writers in Hollywood," in Raymond Chandler, *Later Novels and Other Writings*, ed. Frank MacShane (New York: Library of America, 1995), 995.

4. Parkinson, *Graham Greene Film Reader*, 445.

5. Jane Young, *D.H. Lawrence and Film* (New York: Peter Lang, 1999), 3. See also Barbara Lupack, "On Adapting the American Novel," in *Take Two: Adapting the American Novel to Film*, ed. Barbara Lupack (Bowling Green, Ohio: Bowling Green State Univ. Press, 1994), 4.

6. Vladimir Nabokov, "Foreword," *Lolita: A Screenplay* (New York: McGraw-Hill, 1979), xiii.

7. Alfred Hitchcock, "Film Production," in *Hitchcock on Hitchcock: Selected Writings and Interviews*, ed. Sidney Gottlieb (Los Angeles: Univ. of California Press, 1995), 212.

8. Timothy Corrigan, "Point of View," in *Film and Literature*, ed. Timothy Corrigan (Upper Saddle River: Prentice-Hall, 1999), 82.

9. Avrom Fleischman, *Narrated Films: Storytelling Situations in Cinema History* (Baltimore: Johns Hopkins Univ. Press, 1992), 12, 78–79.

10. Bruce McFarlane, *Novel to Film: An Introduction to the Theory of Adaptation* (New York: Oxford Univ. Press, 1996), 16.

11. J.P. Telotte, *Voices in the Dark: The Narrative Patterns of Film Noir* (Chicago: Univ. of Illinois Press, 1989), 16.

12. Corrigan, *Film and Literature*, 20. See also James Griffith, *Adaptations as Imitations: Films from Novels* (Newark: Univ. of Delaware Press, 1997), 53.

13. Raymond Chandler, "The Simple Art of Murder: An Essay," in *The Simple Art of Murder*, by Raymond Chandler (New York: Vintage, 1988), 18.

14. Paul Skenazy, "Behind the Territory Ahead," in *Los Angeles in Fiction: A Collection of Essays*, ed. David Fine, rev. ed. (Albuquerque: Univ. of New Mexico, 1995),

123. See also Ralf Norrman, *Wholeness Restored: Symmetry in the Writings of Raymond Chandler and Other Novelists* (New York: Peter Lang, 1998), 125.

15. Chandler, "Simple Art of Murder," 18.

16. John Cawelti, *Adventure, Mystery, and Romance: Formula Stories as Art* (Chicago: Univ. of Chicago Press, 1976), 151, 177; John Cawelti, "Generic Transformation in Recent American Films," in *Film Genre Reader Two,* ed. Barry Keith Grant (Austin: Univ. of Texas Press, 1995), 229.

17. William Nolan, "Marlowe's Mean Streets: The Cinematic World of Raymond Chandler," in *The Big Book of Noir,* ed. Ed Gorman, Lee Server, and Martin Greenberg (New York: Carroll and Graf, 1998), 29.

18. Robert Baker and Michael Nietzel, *Private Eyes: One Hundred and One Knights: A Survey of American Detective Fiction* (Bowling Green, Ohio: Bowling Green State Univ. Press, 1985), 36.

19. Pico Iyer, "Private Eye, Public Conscience," *Time,* December 12, 1988, 98.

20. Fredric Jameson, "The Synoptic Chandler," in *Shades of Noir: A Reader,* ed. Joan Copjec (New York: Verso, 1996), 98.

21. Gene Phillips, *Hemingway and Film* (New York: Ungar, 1980), 15.

22. Jerry Wald, "Screen Adaptation," *Films in Review* 5 (1954): 62.

23. Lawrence O'Toole, "Now Read the Movie," *Film Comment* 18, no. 6 (November–December 1982): 37.

1. Introduction: Dead of Night

1. Erich Homberger, "The Man of Letters," in *The World of Raymond Chandler,* ed. Miriam Gross (New York: A and W, 1978), 9. See also Richard Martin, *Mean Streets and Raging Bulls: The Legacy of Film Noir* (Metuchen, N.J.: Scarecrow Press, 1999), 2.

2. Roger Schatzkin, "Doubled Indemnity: Raymond Chandler, Popular Fiction, and Film" (Ph.D. diss., Rutgers University, 1984), 113.

3. For Chandler's criticism of the classic English mystery story, see Raymond Chandler, introduction to *Trouble Is My Business: Philip Marlowe Stories,* Collected Edition (1950; reprint, New York: Vintage, 1992), viii; Chandler, "Simple Art of Murder," 11.

4. Jerry Speir, *Raymond Chandler* (New York: Ungar, 1981), 10. See also Phil Hardy, "Agatha Christie," in *The BFI Companion to Crime,* ed. Phil Hardy (Los Angeles: Univ. of California Press, 1997), 82–83.

5. Raymond Chandler, "The Tropical Romance," in *Chandler Before Marlowe: The Early Prose and Poetry,* ed. Matthew Bruccoli (Columbia, S.C.: Univ. of South Carolina Press, 1973), 69.

6. Stephen Hunter, "Kill Me Again: The Rise of Nouveau Noir," in Gorman, Server, and Greenberg, *Big Book of Noir,* 144; Donald Phelps, "Cinima Gris," *Film Comment* 36, no. 1 (Jan.-Feb. 2000), 64.

7. J.K. Van Dover, "Chandler and the Reviewers," in *The Critical Response to Raymond Chandler,* ed. J.K. Van Dover (Westport, Conn.: Greenwood Press, 1995), 20. Van Dover errs in calling hard-boiled fiction a genre on page 4 of the same book, but correctly labels it a subgenre of detective fiction on page 20.

8. Marilyn Yaquinto, *Pump 'Em Full of Lead: Gangsters on Film* (New York: Twayne, 1998), 75.

9. Bill Prozini and Jack Adrian, introduction to *Hard-boiled: An Anthology of American Crime Stories*, ed. Bill Prozini and Jack Adrian (New York: Oxford Univ. Press, 1995), 8.

10. Donald E. Westlake, introduction to *Murderous Schemes: An Anthology of Classic Detective Stories*, ed. Donald E. Westlake (New York: Oxford Univ. Press, 1996), 5.

11. Clifford May, "The Private Eye in Fact and Fiction," *Atlantic Monthly* 236, no. 2 (August 1975): 30.

12. Raymond Chandler to Cleve Adams, September 4, 1948, *Selected Letters of Raymond Chandler*, ed. Frank MacShane (New York: Columbia Univ. Press, 1981), 54.

13. Chandler, "Simple Art of Murder," 14–15.

14. Matthew Bruccoli, "Raymond Chandler and Hollywood," in Raymond Chandler, *The Blue Dahlia: A Screenplay*, ed. Matthew Bruccoli (Carbondale: Southern Illinois Univ. Press, 1976), 129–30. See also Charles Smith, "Quickness of Fancy: Raymond Chandler's Philip Marlowe" (Ph.D. diss., University of Kentucky–Lexington, 1997), 73–94. Smith indicates why Chandler, more so than Hammett, should be regarded as an artist.

15. *Selected Letters of Raymond Chandler*, 54.

16. Edmund Wilson, "The Boys in the Back Room," in *Classics and Commercials: A Literary Chronicle of the Forties*, by Edmund Wilson (New York: Noonday Press, 1967), 21.

17. *Selected Letters of Raymond Chandler*, 23. For a more positive assessment of Cain, see Ed Muller, *Dark City: The Lost World of Film Noir* (New York: St. Martin's Press, 1998), 56–60.

18. Wilson, "Boys in the Back Room," 19–20. On Hemingway's influence on hard-boiled fiction, see also Carlos Clarens, *Crime Movies: A History of the Gangster Genre*, rev. ed. (New York: Da Capo, 1997), 196–98; Tom Stoppard, "Stalking Raymond Chandler's Spirit," *New York Times*, July 19, 1998, sec. 2, pp. 1, 29.

19. Tom Hiney, *Raymond Chandler: A Biography* (New York: Atlantic Monthly Press, 1997), 74.

20. Edmund Wilson, "Who Cares Who Killed Roger Ackroyd?" in Wilson, *Classics and Commercials*, 262–63.

21. Jameson, "Synoptic Chandler," 33.

22. W. Somerset Maugham, "The Decline and Fall of the Detective Story," in *The Vagrant Mood: Six Essays*, by Somerset Maugham (Garden City, N.Y.: Doubleday, 1953), 129.

23. W.H. Auden, "The Guilty Vicarage: Notes on the Detective Story by an Addict," in *The Dyer's Hand and Other Essays*, by W.H. Auden (New York: Random House, 1962), 151.

24. R.W.B. Lewis, "The Long Goodbye," *New York Times Book Review*, June 22, 1997, 12. See also Robert B. Parker, "Crime/Mystery: Raymond Chandler," *New York Times Book Review*, October 8, 1995, 2.

25. David Smith, "The Public Eye of Raymond Chandler," *Journal of American*

Studies 14, no. 3 (December 1980): 432.

26. Dudley Andrew, "Adaptation," in Corrigan, *Film and Literature,* 270.

27. James Monaco, ed., *Encyclopedia of Films* (New York: Putnam, 1990), 107.

28. David Lehman, *The Perfect Murder: A Study in Detection* (New York: Macmillan, 1984), 136.

29. See Robert Polito, "Note on the Text," in *Crime Novels: American Noir of the 1930s–1950s,* Literary Classics series (New York: Library of America, 1997), 1:983. See also Walter Kim, "Pulp Fiction," *New York Times Book Review,* November 30, 1997, 24–25.

30. Andrew Sarris, *"You Ain't Hear Nothing' Yet": The American Talking Film, 1927–49* (New York: Oxford Univ. Press, 1998), 108; "Blood Read Type: Hard-boiled Fiction," *Sight and Sound,* n.s., 9, no. 9 (September 1999): 4. See also Phil Hardy, "Crime Movies," in *The Oxford History of World Cinema,* ed., Geoffrey Nowell-Smith (New York: Oxford Univ. Press, 1998), 309.

31. Paul Schrader, "Notes on Film Noir," in *Film Noir Reader,* ed. Alain Silver and James Ursini (New York: Limelight, 1998), 53.

32. Nino Frank, "The Crime Adventure Story: A New Kind of Detective Film," trans. Barton Palmer, in *Perspectives on Film Noir,* ed. Barton Palmer (New York: Twayne, 1994), 8.

33. "Editor's Foreword," in Gorman, Server, and Greenberg, *Big Book of Noir,* ix. See also Etienne Borgus, *"Série Noire,"* in Gorman, Server, and Greenberg, *Big Book of Noir,* 237–44.

34. Timothy Corrigan, "Pens and Pulp," in Corrigan, *Film and Literature,* 42–43.

35. Martin, *Mean Streets and Raging Bulls,* 2.

36. Vincent Lo Butto, *Stanley Kubrick: A Biography* (New York: Penguin, 1997), 92.

37. Christopher Orr, "Genre Theory in the Context of Noir Film," *Film Criticism* 22, no. 1 (Fall 1997): 24. See also Stanley Orr, "Postmodernism and Noir," *Literature/Film Quarterly* 27, no. 1 (Winter 1999): 66.

38. Stephen Holden, "Neo-Noir," *New York Times,* March 8, 1998, sec. 2, p. 15. See also Norman Rosenberg, "Law Noir," in *Legal Realism: Movies as Legal Texts,* ed. John Denvir (Chicago: Univ. of Illinois Press, 1996), 280–84.

39. William Phillips, *Film: An Introduction* (New York: St. Martin's Press, 1999), 251.

40. Sarris, *"You Ain't Heard Nothin' Yet,"* 109. See also Ronald Davis, *Celluloid Mirrors: Hollywood Since 1945* (New York: Harcourt, Brace, 1997), 28–29.

41. Vivian Sobchack, "Lounge Time: Postwar Crises and Film Noir," in *Refiguring American Film Genres,* ed. Nick Browne (Los Angeles: Univ. of California Press, 1998), 156.

42. Penelope Houston, *Contemporary Cinema* (Baltimore: Penguin, 1969), 66.

43. David Everitt, "The New Noir: Still Deadly," *New York Times,* Jan. 23, 2000, sec. 2: 28–29.

44. Monaco, *Encyclopedia of Film,* 107.

45. Schrader, "Notes on Film Noir," 56.

2. Paint It Black

1. Richard Schickel, *Double Indemnity* (London: British Film Institute, 1993), 32.

2. Hiney, *Raymond Chandler,* 4.

3. Speir, *Raymond Chandler,* 3.

4. Chandler to Hamish Hamilton, November 10, 1950, in Chandler, "Selected Letters," 1040.

5. Moffat, "On the Fourth Floor," 47.

6. Speir, *Raymond Chandler,* 9.

7. Al Clark, *Raymond Chandler in Hollywood,* rev. ed. (Los Angeles: Silman-James, 1996), 3.

8. Speir, *Raymond Chandler,* 10.

9. Brenda Wineapple, "Grinding It Out: Hack Writers," *New York Times Book Review,* January 18, 1998, 15.

10. Frank MacShane, "Chronology," in Raymond Chandler, *Stories and Early Novels,* ed. Frank MacShane, Literary Classics series (New York: Library of America, 1995), 1184.

11. Smith, "Quickness of Fancy," 77.

12. Baker and Nietzel, *Private Eyes,* 41.

13. Jon Tuska, *In Manors and Alleys: A Casebook of the American Detective Film* (Westport, Conn.: Greenwood Press, 1988), 362–63.

14. Chandler, "Selected Letters," 1041.

15. Frank MacShane, *Life of Raymond Chandler* (New York: Dutton, 1976), 67.

16. J.K. Van Dover, introduction to Van Dover, *Critical Response to Raymond Chandler,* 8.

17. Norrman, *Wholeness Restored,* 124.

18. R.W. Lid, "Philip Marlowe Speaking," in Van Dover, *Critical Response to Raymond Chandler,* 55.

19. MacShane, *Life of Raymond Chandler,* 69.

20. Durham, *Down These Mean Streets,* 37.

3. The Lady Is a Tramp

1. Hiney, *Raymond Chandler,* 64, 90; John Cloud, "L.A. Confidential, for Real," *Time,* September 17, 1999, 44.

2. Marling, *American Roman Noir,* 228.

3. Raymond Chandler, "Plan of Work," in Chandler, *Raymond Chandler Speaking,* 207.

4. Durham, *Down These Mean Streets,* 41.

5. Raymond Chandler, "Try the Girl," in Raymond Chandler, *Killer in the Rain,* ed. Philip Durham (Boston: Houghton Mifflin, 1964), 137. Cf. Raymond Chandler, *Farewell, My Lovely,* Collected Edition (1940; reprint, New York: Vintage, 1992), 30. Subsequent page references to the text of the novel refer to this edition and will appear in parentheses after each citation from it.

6. Cawelti, *Adventure, Mystery, and Romance,* 177.

7. This draft of a letter to an unnamed correspondent, as reproduced in Chan-

dler, *Raymond Chandler Speaking* on 243–47, is undated. Frank MacShane, who has a condensed version of this letter in *Selected Letters of Raymond Chandler* (on 281), supplies the date: July 6, 1951.

8. Raymond Chandler, draft letter, in Chandler, *Raymond Chandler Speaking,* 244–45.

9. Chandler, draft letter, 244.

10. Speir, *Raymond Chandler,* 36.

11. Liahna Babener, "Raymond Chandler's City of Lies," in Fine, *Los Angeles in Fiction,* 139. The author mistakenly identifies Helen on page 132 as a character in *The Big Sleep* rather than in *Farewell, My Lovely.*

12. Speir, *Raymond Chandler,* 42.

13. Peter Wolfe, *Something More than Night: The Case of Raymond Chandler* (Bowling Green, Ohio: Bowling Green State Univ. Press, 1985), 132.

14. Jameson, "Synoptic Chandler," 37.

15. Gershon Legman, *Love and Death: A Study of Censorship* (New York: Hacker Art Books, 1963), 70.

16. Joanna Smith, "Raymond Chandler and the Business of Literature," in Van Dover, *Critical Response to Raymond Chandler,* 190.

17. Raymond Chandler's "The Pencil" was first published as "Marlowe Takes on the Syndicate," *London Daily Mail,* April 6–10, 1959; it was later published elsewhere as "Wrong Pigeon" and "Philip Marlowe's Last Case," as well as under Chandler's title, "The Pencil." See Matthew Bruccoli, *Raymond Chandler: A Checklist* (Kent, Ohio: Kent State Univ. Press, 1968), 18.

18. Speir, *Raymond Chandler,* 111.

19. Hiney, *Raymond Chandler,* 237.

20. MacShane, *Life of Raymond Chandler,* 89.

21. *Selected Letters of Raymond Chandler,* 192.

22. Philip French, "Media Marlowes," in Gross, *World of Raymond Chandler,* 68.

23. William K. Everson, *The Detective in Film* (Secaucus, N.J.: Citadel, 1972), 101.

24. Hiney, *Raymond Chandler,* 138.

25. Leonard Maltin et al., ed., *Movie Guide* (New York: New American Library, 2000), 429.

26. Everson, *Detective in Film,* 104.

27. Leslie Halliwell, *Film Guide,* ed. John Walker (New York: Harper Collins, 2000), 273.

28. Edward Dmytryk, *It's a Hell of a Life but Not a Bad Living: An Autobiography* (New York: Times Books, 1978), 61. On Dmytryk, see also Morgan and Perry, *Book of Film Biographies,* 54.

29. Unless specifically noted otherwise, any quotations form Edward Dmytryk in this chapter are from the author's interview with him.

30. Stephen Pendo, *Raymond Chandler on Screen: His Novels into Film* (Metuchen, N.J.: Scarecrow Press, 1976), 38.

31. Clark, *Raymond Chandler in Hollywood,* 67.

32. Griffith, *Adaptations as Imitations,* 49.

33. Clark, *Raymond Chandler in Hollywood,* 64.

34. John Paxton, *Murder, My Sweet: A Screenplay* (Los Angeles: RKO, 1944), 6.

35. Dmytryk, *Hell of a Life*, 61.

36. Ibid., 59.

37. Barton Palmer, *Hollywood's Dark Cinema* (New York: Twayne, 1994), 82, 78.

38. Edward Dmytryk, *Odd Man Out: A Memoir* (Carbondale: Southern Illinois Univ. Press, 1996), 152.

39. Tuska, *In Manors and Alleys*, 368.

40. Everson, *Detective in Film*, 230.

41. Paxton, *Murder, My Sweet*, 127.

42. Phillips, *Film: An Introduction*, 248.

43. Foster Hirsch, *The Dark Side of the Screen* (New York: Da Capo, 1983), 176.

44. Geoffrey McNab, "Video Reviews: *Murder, My Sweet*," *Sight and Sound*, n.s., 8, no. 9 (September 1998): 59.

45. Frank Miller, *Movies We Love: Classic Films* (Atlanta: Turner, 1996), 207.

46. Dmytryk, *Hell of a Life*, 60.

47. Selby, *Dark City*, 164:

48. Pendo, *Raymond Chandler on Screen*, 20.

49. October 2, 1947, *Selected Letters of Raymond Chandler*, 97.

50. Tuska, *In Manors and Alleys*, 390–91.

51. Ibid., 391.

52. All quotations from Tim Zinnemann in this chapter are from the author's interview with him.

53. Royal Brown, "Modern Film Music," in Nowell-Smith, *Oxford History of World Cinema*, 564.

54. Robert Bookbinder, *The Films of the Seventies* (New York: Carol, 1993), 128. See also Naremore, *More than Night*, 233–34.

55. Crowther, *Film Noir*, 85.

56. David Goodman, *Farewell, My Lovely: A Screenplay* (Los Angeles: Avco Embassy, 1975), 8.

57. Ibid., 43.

58. James Parish and Michael Pitts, *The Great Detective Pictures* (Metuchen, N.J.: Scarecrow Press, 1990), 197.

59. Clark, *Raymond Chandler in Hollywood*, 200.

60. Goodman, *Farewell, My Lovely*, 107.

61. Pendo, *Raymond Chandler on Screen*, 180.

62. Clark, *Raymond Chandler in Hollywood*, 200.

63. Pendo, *Raymond Chandler on Screen*, 185.

64. French, "Media Marlowes," 75.

65. "Robert Mitchum: Obituary," *London Times*, July 3, 1997, 27.

4. Knight Moves

1. Frank Krutnik, "Something More than Night: Tales of the Noir City," in *The Cinematic City*, ed. David Clarke (New York: Routledge, 1997), 83.

2. Skenazy, "Behind the Territory Ahead," 112–14, passim.

3. Hiney, *Raymond Chandler,* 99.

4. Elizabeth Ward and Alain Silver, *Raymond Chandler's Los Angeles* (Woodstock, N.Y.: Overlook Press, 1987), 166–67.

5. Hiney, *Raymond Chandler,* 69.

6. Raymond Chandler, "The Curtain," in Chandler, *Killer in the Rain,* 95. Cf. Raymond Chandler, *The Big Sleep,* Collected Edition (1939; reprint, New York: Vintage, 1992), 21. Subsequent page references to the text of the novel refer to this edition and will appear in parentheses after each citation from it.

7. Peter Rabinowitz, "Rats Behind the Wainscoting: Chandler's *Big Sleep,*" in Van Dover, *Critical Response to Raymond Chandler,* 126–27.

8. Martin Priestman, *Detective Fiction and Literature: The Figure in the Carpet* (New York: St. Martin's Press, 1991), 174.

9. Legman, *Love and Death,* 69.

10. David Geherin, *The American Private Eye: The Image in Fiction* (New York: Ungar, 1985), 75.

11. Robert Merrill, "Raymond Chandler's Plots and the Concept of Plot," *Narrative* 7, no. 1 (January 1999): 6.

12. LeRoy Panek, *Probable Cause: Crime Fiction in America* (Bowling Green, Ohio: Bowling Green State Univ. Press, 1990), 147.

13. Wolfe, *Something More than Night,* 127.

14. *Selected Letters of Raymond Chandler,* 4.

15. Durham, *Down These Mean Streets,* 34.

16. Hiney, *Raymond Chandler,* 86.

17. *Selected Letters of Raymond Chandler,* 4.

18. Bogdanovich, *Who the Devil Made It,* 333, 335.

19. Leigh Brackett, "From *The Big Sleep* to *The Long Goodbye,*" in Gorman, Server, and Greenberg, *Big Book of Noir,* 137.

20. Joseph Blotner, "Faulkner in Hollywood," in *Man and the Movies,* ed. W. R. Robinson (Baltimore: Penguin, 1967), 292.

21. Unless specifically noted otherwise, any quotations from Howard Hawks in this chapter are from the author's interview with him.

22. A.M. Sperber and Eric Lax, *Bogart* (New York: Morrow, 1997), 288–89.

23. Jameson, "Synoptic Chandler," 33. Cf. Steve Swires, "Leigh Brackett: Journeyman Plumber," in *Backstory Two: Interviews with Screenwriters of the 1940s and 1950s,* ed. Patrick McGilligan (Los Angeles: Univ. of California Press, 1997), 18.

24. Raymond Chandler, introduction to Chandler, *Trouble Is My Business,* viii.

25. Sperber and Lax, *Bogart,* 288.

26. Clark, *Raymond Chandler in Hollywood,* 99.

27. Roger Ebert, "Raymond Chandler," in *Book of Film: Writings from a Century of Cinema,* ed. Roger Ebert (New York: Norton, 1996), 594–95; Michael Sragow, "Bogart's Birth as an Icon," *New York Times,* Jan. 16, 2000, sec. 2: 4.

28. Joseph McBride, *Hawks on Hawks* (Los Angeles: Univ. of California Press, 1982), 102–3.

29. Swires, "Leigh Brackett," 17.

30. See William Faulkner and Leigh Brackett, *The Big Sleep: A Screenplay,* in *Film Scripts One,* ed. George Garrett, O. B. Hardison, Jr., and Jane Gelfman (New York:

Appleton, Century, Crofts, 1971), 232–34. This published draft of the screenplay was composed solely by Faulkner and Brackett and does not include Jules Furthman's subsequent revisions, or those of Philip Epstein, which will be treated below.

31. Parish and Pitts, *Great Detective Pictures,* 48.

32. Bruce Kawin, "Hawks and Faulkner," in *Howard Hawks: American Artists,* ed. Jim Hillier and Peter Wollen (London: British Film Institute, 1997), 148.

33. Pendo, *Raymond Chandler on Screen,* 46.

34. Elizabeth Cowie, "Storytelling: Classical Hollywood Cinema and Classical Narrative," in *Contemporary Hollywood Cinema,* edited by Murry Smith (New York: Routledge, 1998), 188.

35. Ebert, "Raymond Chandler," 595–96.

36. Hirsch, *Dark Side of the Screen,* 159.

37. Joseph McBride, "Hawks: An Interview," *Film Comment* 14, no. 2 (March–April 1978): 39.

38. Bogdanovich, *Who the Devil Made It,* 335.

39. Roger Shatzkin, "Who Cares Who Killed Owen Taylor?" in *The Modern American Novel and the Movies,* ed. Gerald Peary and Roger Shatzkin (New York: Ungar, 1978), 86. The title of the essay is a humorous reference to Edmund Wilson's essay about Agatha Christie—"Who Cares Who Killed Roger Ackroyd?"—treated earlier.

40. Sarris, *"You Ain't Heard Nothin' Yet,"* 279. For a summary of Breen's censorship demands with respect to the script, see Shatzkin, "Who Cares Who Killed Owen Taylor?" 85–86.

41. Thomas, *Films of the Forties,* 176.

42. Phillips, *Graham Greene,* 34.

43. David Thomson, *The Big Sleep* (London: British Film Institute, 1997), 58–59.

44. Pauline Kael, *5001 Nights at the Movies* (New York: Holt, 1991), 718.

45. David Thomson, "Ten Films that Showed Hollywood How to Live," *Movieline,* July 1997, 61.

46. Faulkner and Brackett, *The Big Sleep,* 232.

47. Todd McCarthy, *Howard Hawks: The Grey Fox of Hollywood* (New York: Grove Press, 1997), 385.

48. Chandler, "Killer in the Rain," in Chandler, *Killer in the Rain,* 41.

49. Kawin, "Hawks and Faulkner," 150.

50. McCarthy, *Howard Hawks,* 382.

51. William Grimes, "Mystery of *The Big Sleep* Solved," *New York Times,* January 9, 1997, sec. C, p. 13.

52. Brackett, "From *The Big Sleep* to *The Long Goodbye,*" 27.

53. McCarthy, *Howard Hawks,* 315.

54. Sarris, *"You Ain't Heard Nothin' Yet,"* 404.

55. Curtis Hanson, "The Dark Side: Thrillers," *Newsweek,* Summer 1998, 62, Special Issue: A Century of Movies.

56. Clark, *Raymond Chandler in Hollywood,* 205.

57. Crowther, *Film Noir,* 35.

58. Stephen Bourne, *Brief Encounters: Homosexuals in British Cinema* (London:

Cassell, 1996), 141; Gene D. Phillips, *Exiles in Hollywood: European Directors in America* (Cranbury, N.J.: Lehigh Univ. Press, 1998), 125. See also Christopher Kelly, "Unbearable Lightness: Homosexuality in the Movies," *Film Comment* 35, no. 2 (March–April 1999): 16–25.

59. Griffith, *Adaptations as Imitations,* 68.

60. Jay Nash and Stanley Ross, eds., *Motion Picture Guide: 1927–83* (Chicago: Cinebooks, 1985), 1:200.

61. Brian McFarlane, *An Autobiography of British Cinema* (London: Methuen, 1997), 601–602.

62. Norman, *100 Best Films,* 88.

63. Tom Leitch, "*Psycho* Remade," *Short Cuts: Journal of the Literature/Film Association,* Summer 1998, 3.

5. Down among the Rotting Palms

1. Raymond Chandler, "Pearls Are a Nuisance," in Chandler, *Simple Art of Murder,* 139.

2. Chandler, "Plan of Work," 207.

3. Chandler, draft letter, 245–46.

4. Chandler, *Raymond Chandler Speaking,* 211.

5. William Marling, *Raymond Chandler* (Boston: Twayne, 1986), 35.

6. Pendo, *Raymond Chandler on Screen,* 86–87.

7. MacShane, *Life of Raymond Chandler,* 72.

8. Pendo, *Raymond Chandler on Screen,* 87.

9. Wolfe, *Something More than Night,* 153.

10. Raymond Chandler, *The High Window,* Collected Edition (1942; reprint, New York: Vintage, 1992), 9. Subsequent page references to the text of the novel refer to this edition and will appear in parentheses after each citation from it.

11. Speir, *Raymond Chandler,* 45.

12. Peter Sandgren, "Film Noir: Locating Two Chandler Films in the Noir Tradition" (Ph.D. diss., University of Connecticut–Storrs, 1991), 88.

13. Lid, "Philip Marlowe Speaking," 48.

14. Chandler, *Later Novels and Other Writings,* 1038.

15. Rabinowitz, "Rats Behind the Wainscoting," 127.

16. Speir, *Raymond Chandler,* 139.

17. MacShane, *Life of Raymond Chandler,* 98–99.

18. Chandler, "Selected Letters," 1023–24.

19. *Selected Letters of Raymond Chandler,* 97.

20. Fredric Jameson, "On Raymond Chandler," in Van Dover, *Critical Response to Raymond Chandler,* 69–70.

21. Nicholas Freeling, *Criminal Convictions: From Dickens to Chandler* (Boston: Godine, 1994), 115–16.

22. Pendo, *Raymond Chandler on Screen,* 89.

23. Everson, *Detective in Film,* 221.

24. Clark, *Raymond Chandler in Hollywood,* 29.

25. William Luhr, *Raymond Chandler and Film*, rev. ed. (Tallahassee: Florida State Univ. Press, 1991), 108.

26. Maltin et al., *Film Guide*, 903.

27. Nolan, "Marlowe's Mean Streets," 28.

28. Maltin et al., *Film Guide*, 903.

29. Jesse Green, "Pilfering Literature for the Movies," *New York Times*, May 11, 1997, sec. 2, p. 23.

30. T. Syamala, "Contribution of Raymond Chandler to American Cinema," *Indian Journal of American Studies* 25, no. 2 (Summer 1995): 77.

31. *Selected Letters of Raymond Chandler*, 80.

32. Phillips, *Hemingway and Film*, 74.

33. Hirsch, *Dark Side of the Screen*, 54. See also Orr, "Postmodernism and Noir," 66.

34. Sandgren, "Film Noir," 81–82.

35. Hirsch, *Dark Side of the Screen*, 115.

36. Thomson, *Biographical Dictionary of Film*, 82. Mast and Kawin, *Short History of the Movies*, 295.

37. French, "Media Marlowes," 73.

38. Pendo, *Raymond Chandler on Screen*, 98.

39. Ibid., 91.

40. Sandgren, "Film Noir," 92.

41. Clark, *Raymond Chandler in Hollywood*, 127.

42. Sandgren, "Film Noir," 92.

43. Clark, *Raymond Chandler in Hollywood*, 125.

44. Ibid.

45. Sandgren, "Film Noir," 85.

46. Lid, "Philip Marlowe Speaking," 50.

47. *Selected Letters of Raymond Chandler*, 89.

48. Alain Silver and Elizabeth Ward, *Film Noir: An Encyclopedia Reference* (Woodstock, N.Y.: Overlook Press, 1992), 30.

49. Curtis Brown, "The Many Faces of a Private Eye," in *The Movie Buff's Book Two*, ed. Ted Sennett (New York: Pyramid, 1977), 31.

50. Silver and Ward, *Film Noir*, 30.

6. Dead in the Water

1. Hiney, *Raymond Chandler*, 88.

2. On Chandler's cannibalizing his short fiction for *The Lady in the Lake*, see Durham, *Down These Mean Streets*, 124–25.

3. Chandler, *Raymond Chandler Speaking*, 244–45.

4. Ibid., 246.

5. Raymond Chandler, *The Lady in the Lake*, Collected Edition (1943; reprint, New York: Vintage, 1992), 209.

6. Speir, *Raymond Chandler*, 56–57.

7. Ralph Willett, *The Naked City: Urban Crime Fiction in the USA* (New York: Manchester Univ. Press, 1996), 25.

8. Hunter, "Kill Me Again," 146.

9. Freeling, *Criminal Convictions*, 114.

10. Lid, "Philip Marlowe Speaking," 48.

11. Wolfe, *Something More than Night*, 177.

12. Homberger, "Man of Letters," 10.

13. Chandler to Carl Brandt, November 26, 1948, in MacShane, *Life of Raymond Chandler*, 118.

14. Shatzkin, "Doubled Indemnity," 391.

15. Chandler to Philip Gaskell, *Selected Letters of Raymond Chandler*, 345.

16. Chandler to Gaskell, *Selected Letters of Raymond Chandler*, 344.

17. Chandler to Edward Weeks, June 10, 1957, in MacShane, *Life of Raymond Chandler*, 119.

18. Shatzkin, "Doubled Indemnity," 391.

19. MacShane, *Life of Raymond Chandler*, 119.

20. Raymond Chandler, *Lady in the Lake: A Screenplay* (Los Angeles: Metro-Goldwyn-Mayer, 1945), 195. See also Clark, *Raymond Chandler in Hollywood*, 111.

21. Luhr, *Raymond Chandler and Film*, 61.

22. Clark, *Raymond Chandler in Hollywood*, 111.

23. *Selected Letters of Raymond Chandler*, 78.

24. Phillips, *Film: An Introduction*, 105.

25. Clark, *Raymond Chandler in Hollywood*, 110.

26. Chandler to Alex Barris, April 16, 1949, in Chandler, *Raymond Chandler Speaking*, 132.

27. Clark, *Raymond Chandler in Hollywood*, 110.

28. Tuska, *In Manors and Alleys*, 379.

29. Silver and Ward, *Film Noir*, 166.

30. Muller, *Dark City*, 75.

31. Telotte, *Voices in the Dark*, 18, 15.

32. *Raymond Chandler and Film*, 140.

33. Clark, *Raymond Chandler in Hollywood*, 112.

34. Chandler, *Lady in the Lake: A Screenplay*, 13–14.

35. Pendo, *Raymond Chandler on Screen*, 76.

36. Tuska, *In Manors and Alleys*, 380.

37. Nolan, "Marlowe's Mean Streets," 32.

38. Chandler to Philip Gaskell, July 17, 1953, in *Selected Letters of Raymond Chandler*, 344–45.

39. Clark, *Raymond Chandler in Hollywood*, 110. On Robert Montgomery, see also Morgan and Perry, *Book of Film Biographies*, 118.

40. R.W. Flint, "A Cato of the Cruelties," in Van Dover, *Critical Response to Raymond Chandler*, 41.

41. "*Dark Passage*," *Sight and Sound*, n.s., 8, no. 11 (November 1998): 70.

42. Telotte, *Voices in the Dark*, 19.

7. Decline and Fall

1. Durham, *Down These Mean Streets*, 69.

2. Tom Reck, "Raymond Chandler's Los Angeles," in Van Dover, *Critical Response to Raymond Chandler*, 110–11, 114–15.

3. Raymond Chandler, *The Little Sister*, Collected Edition (1949; reprint, New York: Vintage, 1988). Subsequent page references to the text of the novel refer to this edition and will appear in parentheses after each citation from it.

4. Willett, *Naked City*, 28.

5. Schatzkin, "Doubled Indemnity," 335.

6. Henry Wessells, "Raymond Chandler and the Origins of Film Noir," *AB Weekly*, December 8, 1997, 1504.

7. Bryan Forbes, *A Divided Life: An Autobiography* (London: Mandarin, 1993), 273.

8. Corrigan, "Pens and Pulp," 38.

9. Raymond Chandler, "The Hollywood Bowl," in Chandler, *Notebooks of Raymond Chandler*, 273.

10. Clark, *Raymond Chandler in Hollywood*, 154.

11. Chandler, *Raymond Chandler Speaking*, 148, 217, 220.

12. Hiney, *Raymond Chandler*, 188.

13. *Selected Letters of Raymond Chandler*, 134, 158.

14. Babener, "Raymond Chandler's City of Lies," 133.

15. Smith, "Public Eye of Raymond Chandler," 430.

16. *Selected Letters of Raymond Chandler*, 125.

17. Wolfe, *Something More than Night*, 186–87.

18. *The Selected Letters of Raymond Chandler*, 158.

19. Raymond Chandler, "Ten Per Cent of Your Life," in Chandler, *Raymond Chandler Speaking*, 163–64.

20. MacShane, *Life of Raymond Chandler*, 152.

21. Hiney, *Raymond Chandler*, 190.

22. MacShane, *Life of Raymond Chandler*, 156.

23. Lid, "Philip Marlowe Speaking," 44.

24. Shatzkin, "Doubled Indemnity," 577, 614.

25. Nat Segoloff, "Sterling Silliphant: The Finger of God," in *Backstory Three; Interviews with Screenwriters of the 1960s*, 351.

26. Clark, *Raymond Chandler in Hollywood*, 156.

27. Ibid., 159.

28. Sterling Silliphant, *Marlowe: A Screenplay* (Los Angeles: Metro-Goldwyn-Mayer, 1968), 48.

29. Luhr, *Raymond Chandler and Film*, 156.

30. Clark, *Raymond Chandler in Hollywood*, 165.

31. Ibid., 159.

32. See Silliphant, *Marlowe*, sc. 144, p. 51, dated July 2, 1968.

33. Charles Gregory, "Living Life Sideways," in Palmer, *Perspectives on Film Noir*, 165.

34. Silliphant, *Marlowe*, 74.

35. Ibid., 70.

36. Kim Newman, "*Marlowe*," in Hardy, *BFI Companion to Crime*, 221.

37. Edward Gallifent, "Echo Park: Film Noir in the Seventies," in *The Book of Film Noir*, ed. Ian Cameron (New York: Continuum, 1992), 258.

38. Newman, "*Marlowe,*" 221.
39. Silliphant, *Marlowe,* 128.
40. Brown, "Many Faces of a Private Eye," 32.
41. Nash and Ross, *Motion Picture Guide,* 5:1884.
42. Pendo, *Raymond Chandler on Screen,* 13, 29–30.
43. Gregory, "Living Life Sideways," 164–67.
44. Marilyn Stasio, "Crime," *New York Times Book Review,* June 15, 1997, 35.
45. Freeling, *Criminal Convictions,* 117.

8. Modern Times

1. MacShane, *Life of Raymond Chandler,* 205.
2. Chandler, *Raymond Chandler Speaking,* 233.
3. Chandler, "Simple Art of Murder," 18.
4. Chandler, *Raymond Chandler Speaking,* 233.
5. E.M. Beekman, "Raymond Chandler and an American Genre," in Van Dover, *Critical Response to Raymond Chandler,* 89.
6. Chandler, "Curtain," 85.
7. Raymond Chandler, *The Long Goodbye,* Collected Edition (1953; reprint, New York: Vintage, 1992), 3. Subsequent page references to the text of the novel refer to this edition and will appear in parentheses after each citation from it.
8. Phillips, *Film: An Introduction,* 249.
9. MacShane, *Life of Raymond Chandler,* 196.
10. Ibid.
11. Legman, *Love and Death,* 68.
12. J.K. Van Dover, introduction to *Critical Response to Raymond Chandler,* 9.
13. Hiney, *Raymond Chandler,* 246.
14. Beekman, "Raymond Chandler and an American Genre," 97–98.
15. Wolfe, *Something More than Night,* 209.
16. Merrill, "Raymond Chandler's Plots," 13. See also Smith, "Chandler and the Business of Literature," 195.
17. Wolfe, *Something More than Night,* 197.
18. Robert Miller, "The Publication of Raymond Chandler's *The Long Goodbye,*" *Papers of the Bibliographical Society of America* 63 (Fall 1969): 280.
19. Ibid., 281, 285.
20. Van Dover, "Chandler and the Reviewers," 34.
21. Swires, "Leigh Brackett," 23.
22. Brackett, "From *The Big Sleep* to *The Long Goodbye,*" 139–41.
23. Houseman, *Front and Center,* 148.
24. Pendo, *Raymond Chandler on Screen,* 53.
25. Leigh Brackett, *The Long Goodbye: A Screenplay* (United Artists, 1972), 53.
26. Pendo, *Raymond Chandler on Screen,* 148.
27. Ibid., 164.
28. Brackett, *Long Goodbye,* 95.
29. Brackett, "From *The Big Sleep* to *The Long Goodbye,*" 140–41.
30. Swires, "Leigh Brackett," 24.

31. Patrick McGilligan, *Robert Altman: A Biography* (New York: St. Martin's Press, 1989), 363.

32. David O'Brien, *Robert Altman: Hollywood Survivor* (New York: Continuum, 1995), 58.

33. Jan Dawson, "Robert Altman Speaking," *Film Comment* 10, no. 2 (March–April 1974): 41.

34. Tuska, *In Manors and Alleys,* 389.

35. Pendo, *Raymond Chandler on Screen,* 148.

36. O'Brien, *Robert Altman,* 55.

37. Tuska, *In Manors and Alleys,* 391.

38. Graham Fuller, "Altman on Altman," in *Projections Two,* ed. John Boorman and Walter Donohue (Boston: Faber and Faber, 1993), 168.

39. Brackett, *Long Goodbye,* 97.

40. Tuska, *In Manors and Alleys,* 389.

41. O'Brien, *Robert Altman,* 58.

42. Dawson, "Robert Altman Speaking," 40.

43. Donald Lyons, "Seventies Film Noir," *Film Comment* 29, no. 4 (July–August 1993): 48.

44. Kael, *For Keeps,* 515.

45. Gerard Plecki, *Robert Altman* (Boston: Twayne, 1985), 64–65.

46. Swires, "Leigh Brackett," 24–25.

47. O'Brien, *Robert Altman,* 53.

48. Edward Lipnick, "Creative Techniques for *The Long Goodbye,*" *American Cinematographer,* March 1973, 279.

49. Peter Lev, "*The Long Goodbye,*" in *The Encyclopedia of Novels into Film,* ed. John Tibbetts and James Welsh (New York: Facts on File, 1999), 247.

50. Judith Crist, *Take 22: Moviemakers on Moviemaking* (New York: Viking, 1984), 4–5.

51. Swires, "Leigh Brackett," 25; "*The Long Goodbye,*" *Sight and Sound,* n.s., 9, no. 8 (August 1999): 62.

52. Brown, "Many Faces of a Private Eye," 33.

53. Clark, *Raymond Chandler in Hollywood,* 168.

54. Kael, *For Keeps,* 515–17.

55. Aljean Harmetz, "Why Don't People Go to the Movies They Don't Go To?" *New York Times,* May 27, 1973, sec. 2, p. 11.

56. Peter Biskind, *Easy Riders, Raging Bulls: Coppola, Scorsese, Altman and Other Directors* (New York: Simon and Schuster, 1999), 214.

57. Leonard Matlin, et al., eds., *Movie Guide,* 817.

58. Lyons, "Seventies Film Noir," 51.

59. Parish and Pitts, *Great Detective Pictures,* 306.

60. Naremore, *More than Night,* 204.

61. Dave Kerr, "Quickies: Robert Altman," *Film Comment* 35, no. 2 (March–April 1999): 74.

62. David Breskin, *Inner Views: Filmmakers in Conversation,* rev. ed. (New York: Da Capo, 1997), 318–19.

63. Brackett, "From *The Big Sleep* to *The Long Goodbye,*" 141.

9. Lured

1. Chandler, "Writers in Hollywood," 997, 1001. See also Benedict Carver, "Scripts Written by Committee," *Sight and Sound,* n.s., 9, no. 3 (March 1999): 22.

2. *Selected Letters of Raymond Chandler,* 101.

3. Chandler, "Writers in Hollywood," 998.

4. Pauline Kael, *For Keeps,* 614–15. See also Larry Gelbart, "A Beginning, a Muddle, and an End: A Screenwriter's View of Writing Movie Scripts," *New York Times Book Review,* March 3, 1997, 8.

5. Richard Corliss, "Still Talking: Hollywood Screenwriters," *Film Comment* 28, no. 6 (November–December 1992): 13. See also Jaime Wolf, "The Blockbuster Script Factory," *New York Times Magazine,* August 23, 1998, 32, 34.

6. Murray Schumach, *The Face on the Cutting Room Floor* (New York: Da Capo, 1975), 64.

7. Hiney, *Raymond Chandler,* 138.

8. Peter Brunette and Gerald Perry, "James M. Cain: Tough Guy," in *Backstory One: Interviews with Screenwriters of Hollywood's Golden Age,* ed. Patrick McGilligan (Los Angeles: Univ. of California Press, 1986), 127, 128.

9. Frank Walsh, *Sin and Censorship* (New Haven, Conn.: Yale Univ. Press, 1996), 187.

10. Billy Wilder, "One Head Is Better than Two," in *Hollywood Directors, 1941–76,* ed. Richard Koszarski (New York: Oxford Univ. Press, 1977), 273.

11. *Selected Letters of Raymond Chandler,* 6.

12. Ivan Moffat, "On the Fourth Floor of Paramount: Interview with Billy Wilder," in Gross, *World of Raymond Chandler,* 45.

13. Schickel, *Double Indemnity,* 35.

14. Nolan, "Marlowe's Mean Streets," 28.

15. See Brunette and Perry, "James M. Cain," 125.

16. Moffat, "On the Fourth Floor," 47.

17. Kevin Lally, *Wilder Times: The Life of Billy Wilder* (New York: Holt, 1996), 130.

18. Tuska, *In Manors and Alleys,* 370.

19. Matthew Robbins, "The Script Doctor," *New York Times,* March 14, 1999, sec. 2, p. 26.

20. Sobchack, "Lounge Time," 161.

21. Brunette and Perry, "James M. Cain," 127.

22. MacShane, *The Life of Raymond Chandler,* 107.

23. Brunette and Perry, "James M. Cain," 127.

24. *Selected Letters of Raymond Chandler,* 28.

25. Brunette and Perry, "James M. Cain," 127. See also Schickel, *Double Indemnity,* 37.

26. Moffat, "On the Fourth Floor," 48.

27. Michael Wood, "Fearful Cemetery," in *Hitchcock's America,* ed. Jonathan Freedman and Richard Millington (New York: Oxford Univ. Press, 1999), 174, 179.

28. Maurice Zolotow, *Billy Wilder in Hollywood,* rev. ed. (New York: Limelight, 1992), 114.

29. John McCarty, *Thrillers: Classic Film Suspense* (New York: Carol, 1992), 50; Pete Hamill, "Metro Retro: When Mayhem was in Style," *New Yorker,* September 27, 1999, 78.

30. Unless specifically noted otherwise, any comments made by Wilder about the film from this point onward are from the author's personal interview with him.

31. Stephen Farber, "The Films of Billy Wilder," *Film Comment* 7, no. 1 (Winter 1971–72): 17.

32. Cf. James M. Cain, *Double Indemnity* (New York: Vintage, 1992), 23–24. Subsequent references to the text of the novel refer to this edition and will appear in parentheses after each citation from it.

33. Telotte, *Voices in the Dark,* 48–49.

34. Barry Norman, *The 100 Best Films of the Century* (New York: Carol, 1993), 113.

35. Schickel, *Double Indemnity,* 39.

36. Frank Krutnik, *In a Lonely Street: Film Noir, Genre, and Masculinity* (New York: Routledge, 1991), 253.

37. Dave Kehr, "Edward G. Robinson: Always an Anti-Hero," *New York Times,* March 7, 1999, sec. 2, p. 30.

38. John Allyn, "*Double Indemnity:* A Policy that Paid Off," *Literature/Film Quarterly* 6, no. 2 (Spring 1978): 121.

39. Brunette and Perry, "James M. Cain," 125.

40. Raymond Chandler and Billy Wilder, *Double Indemnity: A Screenplay,* in Chandler, *Later Novels and Other Writings,* 964.

41. Bernard Dick, *Billy Wilder,* rev. ed. (New York: Da Capo, 1996), 48.

42. Ed Sikov, *On Sunset Boulevard: The Life and Times of Billy Wilder* (New York: Hyperion, 1998), 198.

43. Dick, *Billy Wilder,* 43.

44. Brunette and Perry, "James M. Cain," 126.

45. Brian Gallagher, "Sexual Warfare in Billy Wilder's *Double Indemnity,*" *Literature/Film Quarterly* 15, no. 4 (Fall 1987): 243.

46. Telotte, *Voices in the Dark,* 50.

47. Tony Thomas, *The Films of the Forties* (New York: Carol, 1990), 112.

48. William Marling, *The American Roman Noir: Hammett, Cain, and Chandler* (Athens: Univ. of Georgia Press, 1995), 264.

49. Chandler and Wilder, *Double Indemnity: A Screenplay,* in *Best American Screenplays Three,* ed. Sam Thomas (New York: Crown, 1995), 303. This is the first draft of the screenplay, which includes the original ending of the film.

50. James Naremore, *More than Night: Film Noir in Its Contexts* (Los Angeles: Univ. of California Press, 1998), 91.

51. See Chandler and Wilder, *Double Indemnity: A Screenplay,* in Thomas, *Best American Screenplays Three,* the first draft of the script, which includes the execution scene, 302–304; cf. Chandler and Wilder, *Double Indemnity: A Screenplay,* in Chandler, *Later Novels and Other Writings,* the final draft of the screenplay, which has the ending as it appears in the release prints of the film, 970–72.

52. Cameron Crowe, *Conversations with Wilder* (New York: Knopf, 1999), 252; Schickel, *Double Indemnity,* 64.

53. Phillips, *Film: An Introduction,* 255.

54. Chandler, "Writers in Hollywood," 999.

55. Zolotow, *Billy Wilder in Hollywood,* 121. See also Sikov, *On Sunset Boulevard,* 213.

56. Clark, *Raymond Chandler in Hollywood,* 48.

57. MacShane, *Life of Raymond Chandler,* 111, 113.

58. Harry Kurnitz, "Billy the Wild," *Holiday,* June 1964, 95.

59. Raymond Chandler, "Selected Letters," in Chandler, *Later Novels and Other Writings,* 1041.

60. Moffat, "On the Fourth Floor," 46–50, passim; Crowe, *Conversations with Wilder,* 69.

61. Jay Rozgonyi, "The Making of *Double Indemnity,*" *Films in Review* 41, nos. 6–7 (June–July 1990): 345.

62. Raymond Chandler, *Raymond Chandler Speaking,* 125–26. Brackett is identified in a footnote on 125 as a "film director"; he was, rather, a screenwriter and producer.

10. No Way to Treat a Lady

1. John Houseman, *Front and Center: A Biography* (New York: Simon and Schuster, 1979), 114.

2. Hiney, *Raymond Chandler,* 147.

3. Durham, *Down These Mean Streets a Man Must Go,* 44, 46.

4. Clark, *Raymond Chandler in Hollywood,* 59.

5. Tom Weaver, "Norman Lloyd," *Starlog,* December 1998, 72.

6. Houseman, *Front and Center,* 116.

7. James Agee, *Agee on Film* (New York: Grosset and Dunlap, 1969), 158.

8. Ibid., 131.

9. Luhr, *Raymond Chandler and Film,* 40.

10. Paul Jensen, "Film Noir and the Writer: Raymond Chandler," *Film Comment* 10, no 6 (November–December 1974): 21. Special Film Noir Issue.

11. Clark, *Raymond Chandler in Hollywood,* 51

12. Luhr, *Raymond Chandler and Film,* 75.

13. Nolan, "Marlowe's Mean Streets," 31.

14. Naremore, *More than Night,* 109.

15. Spencer Selby, *Dark City: Film Noir* (Jefferson, N.C.: McFarland, 1984), 132.

16. Naremore, *More than Night,* 109.

17. Nicholas Christopher, *Somewhere in the Night: Film Noir and the American City* (New York: Holt, 1998), 13. See also Martin, *Mean Streets and Raging Bulls,* 39.

18. Naremore, *More than Night,* 110.

19. John Houseman, "Lost Fortnight: A Memoir," in Chandler, *Blue Dahlia,* xiv.

20. Ibid., xvi.

21. Ibid., xvii–xviii.

22. Weaver, "Norman Lloyd," 72.

23. Muller, *Dark City,* 136. See also David Thomson, *A Biographical Dictionary of Film,* rev. ed. (New York: Knopf, 1994), 412.

24. Hiney, *Raymond Chandler*, 157.

25. Chandler, *Raymond Chandler Speaking*, 138.

26. Matthew Bruccoli, "Afterword: Raymond Chandler in Hollywood," in Chandler, *Blue Dahlia*, 133.

27. Chandler, *Blue Dahlia*, 113–115.

28. Bruce Crowther, *Film Noir: Reflections in a Dark Mirror* (New York: Ungar, 1989), 94.

29. Gay Brewer, "Raymond Chandler without His Knight: *The Blue Dahlia* and *Playback,*" *Literature/Film Quarterly* 23, no. 4 (Fall 1995): 275.

30. Chandler, *Blue Dahlia*, 127.

31. Rui Nogrieira, "Wendall Mayes," in *Backstory Three: Interviews with Screenwriters of the 1960s,* ed. Patrick McGilligan (Los Angeles: Univ. of California Press, 1997), 263.

32. Luhr, *Raymond Chandler and Film,* 52–53.

33. Bruccoli, "Afterword," 132–33.

34. Mike Phillips, "*The Blue Dahlia,*" in Hardy, *BFI Companion to Crime,* 54.

35. Naremore, *More than Night,* 122.

36. Bruccoli, "Afterword," 133–34.

37. Clark, *Raymond Chandler in Hollywood,* 87.

38. Bruccoli, "Afterword," 133.

39. See Clark, *Raymond Chandler in Hollywood,* 86.

40. Wolfe, *Something More than Night,* 29.

41. *Selected Letters of Raymond Chandler,* 61.

42. Thomson, *Biographical Dictionary of Film,* 484. See also Robin Morgan and George Perry, eds., *The Book of Film Biographies* (New York: Fromm, 1997), 11–12.

43. Chandler to Dale Warren, August 18, 1948, *Selected Letters of Raymond Chandler,* 123.

44. Agee, *Agee on Film,* 203.

45. Alan Barbour, "*The Blue Dahlia,*" *Films in Review* 48, no. 1 (January–February 1997), 54.

46. Houseman, *Front and Center,* 147; Chandler to Erle Stanley Gardner, March 1946, *Selected Letters of Raymond Chandler,* 70.

47. Roger Shatzkin, "Doubled Indemnity: Raymond Chandler, Fiction, and Film," 394.

48. Chandler to Hamish Hamilton, October 13, 1950, in Chandler, *Raymond Chandler Speaking,* 60.

49. Schatzkin, "Doubled Indemnity," p. 396.

50. Raymond Chandler, "A Qualified Farewell," in Raymond Chandler, *The Notebooks of Raymond Chandler* (New York: Ecco Press, 1976), 68.

51. Bruccoli, "Afterword," 136.

52. Chandler, "Qualified Farewell," 76.

53. George Marshall to Matthew Bruccoli, December 16, 1974, in Bruccoli, "Afterword," 134.

54. Gene D. Phillips, *Fiction, Film, and Faulkner: The Art of Adaptation* (Knoxville: Univ. of Tennessee Press, 1988), 29–30.

11. Dance with the Devil

1. MacShane, *Life of Raymond Chandler,* 170.

2. Nora Sayre, "In the Shoes of a Scary Stalker," *New York Times,* April 12, 1998, sec. 2, p. 12.

3. Gordon Gow, "The Fifties," in *Hollywood: 1920–70,* ed. Peter Cowie (New York: Barnes, 1977), 184.

4. John Russell Taylor, *Hitch: The Life and Times of Alfred Hitchcock* (New York: Da Capo, 1996), 214.

5. MacShane, *Life of Raymond Chandler,* 171.

6. François Truffaut, *Hitchcock,* rev. ed. (New York: Touchstone, 1985), 193. See also Muller, *Dark City,* 125.

7. Vito Russo, *The Celluloid Closet: Homosexuality in the Movies,* rev. ed. (New York: Harper and Row, 1987), 94.

8. Patricia Highsmith, *Strangers on a Train* (New York: Penguin, 1979), 30.

9. Raymond Chandler, "Cast of Characters," in Raymond Chandler with Czinzi Ormonde, *Strangers on a Train: A Screenplay* (Los Angeles: Warner Brothers, 1950), 1.

10. Jane Sloan, *Alfred Hitchcock: A Guide to References and Resources,* rev. ed. (Los Angeles: Univ. of California Press, 1995), 239.

11. Patricia Highsmith, introduction to Gross, *World of Raymond Chandler,* 5. See also Phil Hardy, "Patricia Highsmith," in Hardy, *BFI Companion to Crime,* 164.

12. Taylor, *Hitch,* 215.

13. Chandler, *Raymond Chandler Speaking,* 132.

14. Larry McMurtry, "Raymond Chandler," *New York Times Book Review,* November 15, 1981, 46.

15. Raymond Chandler, "Notes about the Screenplay for *Strangers on a Train,*" in Chandler, *Raymond Chandler Speaking,* 133, 134–35.

16. September 13, 1950, *Selected Letters of Raymond Chandler,* 222.

17. Maurice Yacowar, *Hitchcock's British Films* (Hamden, Conn.: Archon Books, 1977), 300. See also James Wolcott, "Death and the Master: Hitchcock," *Vanity Fair,* April 1999, 144, Special Hollywood Issue.

18. Robert Corber, "Hitchcock, Homophobia, and *Strangers on a Train,*" in Freedman and Millington, *Hitchcock's America,* 99.

19. Unless specifically noted otherwise, any quotations form Alfred Hitchcock in this chapter are from the author's conversation with him.

20. Pauline Kael, *I Lost It at the Movies* (New York: Boyars, 1994), 9.

21. David Parkinson, ed., *The Graham Greene Reader* (New York: Applause Theater Books, 1995), 163.

22. Jensen, "Film Noir and the Writer," 25.

23. Chandler with Ormonde, *Strangers on a Train: A Screenplay,* 32.

24. Chandler, *Raymond Chandler Speaking,* 135.

25. Taylor, *Hitch,* 215.

26. Clark, *Raymond Chandler in Hollywood,* 141.

27. Raymond Chandler, *Strangers on a Train: A Screenplay* (Los Angeles: Warner Brothers, 1950), 19. Extensive revisions to the screenplay by Czenzi Ormonde are not included in this version of the script.

28. *Selected Letters of Raymond Chandler,* 243–44.

29. Clark, *Raymond Chandler in Hollywood,* 147–48.

30. Taylor, *Hitch,* 216.

31. *Selected Letters of Raymond Chandler,* 247–48; Larry Gross, "Parallel Lines," *Sight and Sound,* n.s., 9, no. 9 (August 1999): 39–40. Hitchcock Supplement.

32. Susan Green, "John Michael Hayes: *Qué Sera, Sera,*" in McGilligan, *Backstory Three,* 175, 183–84; Frank Rich, American Pseudo: The Talented Mr. Ripley," *New York Times Magazine,* Dec. 12, 1999, 85.

33. Bill Desowitz, "Strangers on Which Train?" *Film Comment* 28, no. 3 (May–June 1992): 4; Thomas Doherty, *Pre-Code Hollywood: Sex and Immorality in American Cinema* (New York: Columbia Univ. Press, 1999), 363, 125. See also Gerald Mast and Bruce Kawin, *A Short History of the Movies,* rev. ed. (Boston: Allyn and Bacon, 2000), 303.

34. *Selected Letters of Raymond Chandler,* 245.

35. Chandler with Ormonde, *Strangers on a Train: A Screenplay,* 156.

36. MaryKay Mahoney, "A Train Running on Two Sets of Tracks: Highsmith and Hitchcock's *Strangers on a Train,*" in *It's a Print! Detective Fiction from Page to Screen,* ed. William Reynolds and Elizabeth Trimley (Bowling Green, Ohio: Bowling Green Univ. Press, 1994), 107. See also Corber, "Hitchcock, Homophobia," 113.

37. Patricia Hitchcock O'Connell, the director's daughter (who played a supporting role in the film), read an early draft of this material and felt that I had presented the creative differences between her father and Chandler accurately.

38. Robert Harris and Michael Lasky, *The Complete Films of Alfred Hitchcock* (New York: Carol, 1995), 156. For Hitchcock's further thoughts on the film, see Bogdanovich, *Who the Devil Made It: Conversations with Film Directors,* 518–19.

39. Peter Bogdanovich, "Hitchcock Remembered," *New York Times,* April 11, 1999, sec. 2, p. 15.

40. Sloan, *Alfred Hitchcock,* 368–69.

41. Patricia Highsmith, *Plotting and Writing Suspense Fiction* (New York: St. Martin's Press, 1983), 106; David Thomson, "Without Them, Mr. Ripley Would Be a Nobody," *New York Times,* Dec. 19, 1999, sec. 2: 17; Anthony Lane, "Killing Time: Mr. Ripley," *New Yorker,* Jan. 3, 2000, 130. On Highsmith's crime fiction, see Noel Mawer, "From Villain to Vigilante," in Gorman, Server, and Greenberg, *Big Book of Noir,* 291–95.

42. Schatzkin, "Doubled Indemnity," 397.

43. MacShane, *Life of Raymond Chandler,* 144.

44. Luhr, *Raymond Chandler and Film,* 75.

45. Nolan, "Marlowe's Mean Streets," 33.

46. Raymond Chandler, *Raymond Chandler's Unknown Thriller: The Screenplay of Playback,* ed. James Pepper (New York: Mysterious Press, 1985), 3.

47. Brewer, "Raymond Chandler without His Knight," 278.

48. Robert Parker, introduction to Chandler, *Raymond Chandler's Unknown Thriller,* xvii.

49. Ibid., xviii.

50. MacShane, *Life of Raymond Chandler,* 251–52.

51. Durham, *Down These Mean Streets,* 138.

52. Raymond Chandler, *Playback,* Collected Edition (1958; reprint, New York: Vintage, 1988), 116.

53. Ibid., 112–13.

54. Parker, "Crime/Mystery," 22.

55. November 10, 1950, in Chandler, "Selected Letters," 1041.

56. Ibid.

57. Chandler, *Raymond Chandler Speaking,* 126.

58. Chandler, "Selected Letters," 1041. See also Michael Sragow, "The Bizarre Conglomerate Known as Hollywood," *New York Times Book Review,* February 2, 1999, 28.

59. Carver, "Scripts Written by Committee," 22.

60. Chandler, "Qualified Farewell," 76.

61. Chandler, *Raymond Chandler Speaking,* 126–27.

12. The Stag at Eve

1. French, "Media Marlowes," 73.

2. Clark, *Raymond Chandler in Hollywood,* 151.

3. MacShane, *Life of Raymond Chandler,* 164–65.

4. Clark, *Raymond Chandler in Hollywood,* 152.

5. French, "Media Marlowes," 74.

6. Bryan Forbes to the author, May 25, 1998.

7. Michael Pitts, *Famous Detectives Two* (Methuen, N.J.: Scarecrow Press, 1991), 107.

8. Forbes to author, July 13, 1998.

9. Forbes to author, May 25, 1998.

10. Michael Gilbert, "Autumn in London," in Gross, *World of Raymond Chandler,* 109.

11. Federal Bureau of Investigation, Freedom of Information Section, letter to author, November 25, 1998.

12. Raymond Chandler, "The Mystery Writers of America," in Chandler, *Raymond Chandler Speaking,* 42.

13. Chandler, *Raymond Chandler Speaking,* 43.

14. Wolfe, *Something More than Night,* 227.

15. Ward and Silver, *Raymond Chandler's Los Angeles,* 93.

16. Ibid.

17. *Selected Letters of Raymond Chandler,* 464.

18. Ibid., 479; see also Chandler, *Raymond Chandler Speaking,* 248.

19. Clive James, "The Country Behind the Hill," in Gross, *World of Raymond Chandler,* 125.

20. Stoppard, "Stalking Raymond Chandler's Spirit," sec. 2, p. 29.

21. Chandler, *Raymond Chandler Speaking,* 70.

22. Raymond Chandler, "Casual Notes on the Mystery Novel," in Chandler, *Raymond Chandler Speaking,* 70.

23. Jon Breen, "Author Notes," in Gorman, Server, and Greenberg, *Big Book of Noir,* 328.

24. Stoppard, "Stalking Raymond Chandler's Spirit," sec. 2, p. 29.

25. Ed McBain, "Philip Marlowe Is Back," *New York Times Book Review,* October 15, 1989, 44.

26. R.Z. Sheppard, "Capering: *Poodle Springs,*" *Time,* 88.

27. Raymond Chandler and Robert B. Parker, *Poodle Springs* (New York: Berkley, 1980), 5. Subsequent page references to the text of the novel refer to this edition and will appear in parentheses after each citation from it.

28. Stoppard, "Stalking Raymond Chandler's Spirit," sec. 2, p. 29.

29. Rodney Farnsworth, "Bob Rafelson," in *International Dictionary of Films and Filmmakers: Directors,* ed. Laurie Hillstrom, rev. ed. (Detroit: St. James Press, 1996), 2:792. See also Morgan and Perry, *Book of Film Biographies,* 137.

30. Michael Barson, *Hollywood Directors: The Sound Era* (New York: Noonday Press, 1995), 608.

31. Biskind, *Easy Riders, Raging Bulls,* 176–77.

32. Hilary de Vries, "Caan's New Game: *Poodle Springs,*" *TV Guide,* July 25, 1998, 28.

33. Avis Weathersbee, "Last Nod to Chandler: *Poodle Springs,*" *Chicago Sun-Times,* July 26, 1998, sec. E, p. 13.

34. *Selected Letters of Raymond Chandler,* 483.

35. Weathersbee, "Last Nod to Chandler," sec. E, p. 13.

36. Will Joyner, "Married Marlowe and a Stretched Chandler," *New York Times,* July 14, 1998, sec. E, p. 32.

37. Weathersbee, "Last Nod to Chandler," sec. E, p. 13.

Epilogue: Endless Night

1. "Pulp Fiction," *Sight and Sound,* n.s., 9, no. 5 (May 1999): 4.

2. Stephen Holden, "Film Noir Is Back," *New York Times,* March 8, 1998, sec. 2: 15; Richard Jameson, "Son of Noir," *Film Comment* 10, no. 6 (November–December 1974): 33, Special Film Noir Issue.

3. "Mike Hodges Discusses *Get Carter,*" in *British Crime Cinema,* edited by Steve Chibnall and Robert Murphy (New York: Routledge, 1999), 118.

4. Jameson, "Son of Noir," 30.

5. Clark, *Raymond Chandler in Hollywood,* 16. See also Martin, *Mean Streets and Raging Bulls,* 79.

6. Jim Shephard, "Jolting Noir with a Shot of Nihilism," *New York Times,* February 7, 1999, sec. 2, p. 24. On *Chinatown* as neo-noir, see Martin, *Mean Streets and Raging Bulls,* 69–75.

7. Naremore, *More than Night,* 10.

8. Priestman, *Detective Fiction and Literature,* 191. See also Stella Bruzzi, "Dennis Potter," *Sight and Sound,* n.s., 9, no. 2 (February 1999): 32.

9. Shephard, "Jolting Noir," 247.

10. Phillips, *Film: An Introduction,* 253. See also Yoquinto, *Pump 'Em Full of Lead,* 75–77.

11. Kael, *5001 Nights,* 90.

12. "The Best Films," *TV Guide*, September 12, 1998, 96.

13. Donald Lyons, "The Bad and the Beautiful: *L.A. Confidential*," *Film Comment* 33, no. 6 (November–December 1997): 15.

14. David Everitt, "The New Noir: Still Deadly," *New York Times*, Jan. 23, 2000, sec. 2: 28. On Chandler and neo-noir, see Foster Hirsch, *Detours and Lost Highways: A Map of Neo-Noir* (New York: Limelight, 1999), 114-17. Hirsch writes that the Chandler films of the 1970s anticipate the full-force revival of noir in the 1980s and 1990s.

15. Hanson, "The Dark Side," 62; Schatzkin, "Doubled Indemnity," 112.

16. Baker and Nietzel, *Private Eyes*, 45.

17. Terry Teachout, "The Sensitive Shamus," *New York Times Book Review*, March 14, 1999, 19.

18. MacShane, *Life of Raymond Chandler*, 214.

19. Parker, "Crime/Mystery," 22.

20. Smith, "Quickness of Fancy," 5.

21. Louis Giannetti, *Understanding Movies*, rev. ed. (Upper Saddle River, N.J.: Prentice-Hall, 1999), 391.

22. Wessells, "Raymond Chandler and the Origins of Film Noir," 1506.

23. Nolan, "Marlowe's Mean Streets," 36.

24. Kim Newman, "Philip Marlowe," in Hardy, *BFI Companion to Crime*, 219.

Selected Bibliography

The original date of publication of a Chandler work appears after the title when the edition consulted is of a later date.

Auden, W.H. "The Guilty Vicarage: Notes on the Detective Story by an Addict." In *The Dyer's Hand and Other Essays*, 146–88. New York: Random House, 1962.

Baker, Robert, and Michael Nietzel. *Private Eyes: One Hundred and One Knights, A Survey of American Detective Fiction*. Bowling Green, Ohio: Bowling Green State Univ. Press, 1985.

Barbour, Alan. "*The Blue Dahlia*." *Films in Review* 48, no. 1 (January–February 1997): 54.

Biskind, Peter. *Easy Riders, Raging Bulls: Coppola, Scorsese, Altman and Other Directors*. New York: Simon and Schuster, 1999.

"Blood Read Type: Hard-boiled Fiction." *Sight and Sound*, n.s., 9, no. 9 (September 1999): 4.

Bogdanovich, Peter. "Hitchcock Remembered." *New York Times*, April 11, 1999, sec. 2, pp. 15, 18.

———. *Who the Devil Made It: Conversations with Film Directors*. New York: Ballantine Books, 1998.

Bookbinder, Robert. *The Films of the Seventies*. New York: Carol, 1993.

Brackett, Leigh. "The Long Goodbye: A Screenplay" (unpublished). United Artists, 1972.

Breskin, David. *Inner Views: Filmmakers in Conversation*. Rev. ed. New York: Da Capo, 1997.

Brewer, Gay. "Raymond Chandler without His Knight: *The Blue Dahlia* and *Playback*." *Literature/Film Quarterly* 23, no. 4 (Fall 1995): 273–78.

Brown, Curtis. "The Many Faces of a Private Eye." In *The Movie Buff's Book Two*, edited by Ted Sennett, 26–33. New York: Pyramid, 1977.

Bruccoli, Matthew. *Raymond Chandler: A Descriptive Bibliography*. Pittsburgh: Univ. of Pittsburgh Press, 1979.

Cameron, Ian, ed. *The Book of Film Noir*. New York: Continuum, 1992.

Chandler, Raymond. *The Big Sleep*. 1939. The Collected Edition, New York: Vintage, 1992.

———. *The Blue Dahlia: A Screenplay*. Edited by Matthew Bruccoli. Carbondale: Southern Illinois Univ. Press, 1976.

———. *Chandler Before Marlowe: The Early Prose and Poetry*. Edited by Matthew Bruccoli. Columbia: Univ. of South Carolina Press, 1973.

———. *Farewell, My Lovely*. 1940. The Collected Edition, New York: Vintage, 1992.

———. *The High Window*. 1942. The Collected Edition, New York: Vintage, 1992.

———. "The Innocent Mrs. Duff: A Screenplay" (unpublished). Los Angeles: Paramount, 1946. Unproduced.

———. *Killer in the Rain.* Edited by Philip Durham. Boston: Houghton Mifflin, 1964.

———. *The Lady in the Lake.* 1943. The Collected Edition, New York: Vintage, 1992.

———. "The Lady in the Lake: A Screenplay" (unpublished). Los Angeles: Metro-Goldwyn-Mayer, 1945. Extensive revisions of this screenplay by Steve Fischer are not included in this draft of the script.

———. *Later Novels and Other Writings.* Edited by Frank MacShane. Literary Classics Series. New York: Library of America, 1995. A companion volume to Chandler's *Stories and Early Novels.* This volume contains the final draft of the screenplay of *Double Indemnity.*

———. *The Little Sister.* 1949. The Collected Edition, New York: Vintage, 1988.

———. *The Long Goodbye.* 1953. The Collected Edition, New York: Vintage, 1992.

———. *The Notebooks of Raymond Chandler.* New York: Ecco Press, 1976.

———. "Oscar Night in Hollywood." *Atlantic Monthly* 181 (March 1948): 24–27.

———. *Playback.* 1958. The Collected Edition, New York: Vintage, 1988.

———. *Raymond Chandler Speaking.* Edited by Dorothy Gardiner and Kathrine Walker. Rev. ed. Los Angeles: Univ. of California Press, 1997.

———. *Raymond Chandler's Unknown Thriller: The Screenplay of Playback.* Edited by James Pepper. New York: Mysterious Press, 1985. Unproduced.

———. *Selected Letters of Raymond Chandler.* Edited by Frank MacShane. New York: Columbia Univ. Press, 1981.

———. *The Simple Art of Murder.* With an Introduction, "The Simple Art of Murder," by Chandler. 1950. The Collected Edition, New York: Vintage, 1988. In Chandler's *Later Novels and Other Writings,* editor Frank MacShane reprints two essays by Chandler, both of which Chandler entitled "The Simple Art of Murder." The present essay, which serves as the introduction to this volume, originally appeared in *Atlantic Monthly,* December 1944.

———. *Stories and Early Novels.* Edited by Frank MacShane. Literary Classic Series. New York: Library of America, 1995. A companion volume to Chandler's *Later Novels and Other Writings.*

———. "Strangers on a Train: A Screenplay" (unpublished). Los Angeles: Warner Brothers, 1950. Extensive revisions of the screenplay by Czenzi Ormonde are not included in this draft of the script.

———. *Trouble Is My Business: Philip Marlowe Stories.* With an Introduction by Chandler. 1950. The Collected Edition, New York: Vintage, 1992. In Chandler's *Later Novels and Other Writings,* editor Frank MacShane reprints two essays by Chandler, both of which Chandler entitled "The Simple Art of Murder." The present essay, which serves as the introduction to this volume, originally appeared in *Saturday Review of Literature,* April 15, 1950.

———, with Steve Fisher. "The Lady in the Lake: A Screenplay" (unpublished). Los Angeles: Metro-Goldwyn-Mayer, 1946. Chandler was uncredited.

———, with Czenzi Ormonde. "Strangers on a Train: A Screenplay" (unpublished). Los Angeles: Warner Brothers, 1950.

————, with Robert B. Parker. *Poodle Springs*. 1989. Reprint, New York: Berkley, 1990. Chandler's last novel, as completed by Parker.

————, with Frank Partos. "And Now Tomorrow: A Screenplay" (unpublished). Los Angeles: Paramount, 1944.

————, with Hagar Wilde. "The Unseen: A Screenplay" (unpublished). Los Angeles: Paramount, 1945.

————, with Billy Wilder. *Double Indemnity: A Screenplay*. In *Best American Screenplays Three*, edited by Sam Thomas. New York: Crown, 1995. This is the first draft of the screenplay, which contains a final scene cut from the final draft of the script.

Chibnall, Steve, and Robert Murphy, eds. *British Crime Cinema*. New York, Routledge, 1999.

Christopher, Nicholas. *Somewhere in the Night: Film Noir and the American City*. New York: Holt, 1998.

Clark, Al. *Raymond Chandler in Hollywood*. Rev. ed. Los Angeles: Silman-James, 1996.

Copjec, Joan, ed. *Shades of Noir: A Reader*. New York: Verso, 1996.

Corrigan, Timothy. *Film and Literature*. Upper Saddle River, N.J.: Prentice-Hall, 1999.

Crowe, Cameron. *Conversations with Wilder*. New York: Knopf, 1999.

Crowther, Bruce. *Film Noir: Reflections in a Dark Mirror*. New York: Unger, 1989.

Dawson, Jan. "Robert Altman Speaking." *Film Comment* 10, no. 2 (March–April 1974): 40–41.

Desowitz, Bill. "Strangers on Which Train? The Alternate Version of *Strangers on a Train*." *Film Comment* 28, no. 3 (May–June 1992): 4–5.

de Vries, Hilary. "Caan's New Game: *Poodle Springs*." *TV Guide*, July 25, 1998, 27–28.

Dick, Bernard. *Billy Wilder*. Rev. ed. New York: Da Capo, 1996.

Dmytryk, Edward. *It's a Hell of a Life, but Not a Bad Living: An Autobiography*. New York: Times Books, 1978.

————. *Odd Man Out: A Memoir*. Carbondale: Southern Illinois Univ. Press, 1996.

Dunkle, Robert. "*The Long Goodbye*: Raymond Chandler's Novel and Robert Altman's Film." Ph.D. diss., Florida State University–Tallahassee, 1987.

Durham, Philip. *Down These Mean Streets a Man Must Go: Raymond Chandler's Knight*. Chapel Hill: Univ. of North Carolina Press, 1963.

Everitt, David. "The New Noir: Still Deadly." *New York Times*, Jan. 23, 2000, sec. 2: 28–29.

Everson, William K. *The Detective in Film*. Secaucus, N.J.: Citadel, 1972.

Faulkner, William, with Leigh Brackett. *The Big Sleep: A Screenplay*. In *Film Scripts One*, edited by George Garrett, O. B. Harrison Jr., and Jane Gelfman. New York: Appleton-Century-Crofts, 1971. Jules Furthman's subsequent revisions of the screenplay are not included in this version of the script.

Federal Bureau of Investigation, Freedom of Information Section. Letter to Gene Phillips, November 25, 1998.

Film Comment 10, no. 6 (November–December 1974). Special Film Noir Issue.

Fine, David, ed. *Los Angeles in Fiction: A Collection of Essays*. Rev. ed. Albuquerque: Univ. of New Mexico Press, 1995.

Forbes, Bryan. *A Divided Life: An Autobiography*. London: Mandarin, 1993.

————. Letters to Gene Phillips, 1985–90, 1998. In the private collection of the author.

Freedman, Jonathan, and Richard Millington, eds. *Hitchcock's America*. New York: Oxford Univ. Press, 1999.

Freeling, Nicholas. *Criminal Convictions: From Dickens to Chandler*. Boston: Godine, 1994.

Geherin, David. *The American Private Eye: The Image in Fiction*. New York: Ungar, 1985.

Giannetti, Louis. *Understanding Movies*. Rev. ed. Upper Saddle River, N.J.: Prentice-Hall, 1999.

Goodman, David. "Farewell, My Lovely: A Screenplay" (unpublished). Los Angeles: Avco Embassy, 1975.

Gorman, Ed, Lee Server, and Martin Greenberg, eds. *The Big Book of Noir*. New York: Carroll and Graf, 1998.

Grant, Barry Keith, ed. *Film Genre Reader II*. Austin: Univ. of Texas, 1997.

Griffith, James. *Adaptations as Imitations: Films from Novels*. Newark: Univ. of Delaware Press, 1998.

Grimes, William. "Mystery of *The Big Sleep* Solved." *New York Times*, January 9, 1997, sec. C, pp. 11, 13.

Gross, Larry. "Parallel Lines." *Sight and Sound*, n.s., 9, no. 9 (August 1999): 38–44. Hitchcock Supplement.

Gross, Miriam, ed. *The World of Raymond Chandler*. New York: A and W, 1978.

Halliwell, Leslie. *Film Guide*. Edited by John Walker. Rev. ed. New York: Harper-Collins, 2000.

Hannah, Dorothy. "The Brasher Doubloon: A Screenplay" (unpublished). Los Angeles: Twentieth Century Fox, 1946.

Hanson, Curtis. "The Dark Side: Thrillers." *Newsweek*, Summer 1998, 61–62. Special Issue: A Century of Movies.

Hardy, Phil, ed. *The BFI Companion to Crime*. Los Angeles: Univ. of California Press, 1997.

Harris, Robert, and Michael Lasky. *The Complete Films of Alfred Hitchcock*. New York: Carol, 1995.

Hilfer, Tony. *The Crime Novel: A Deviant Genre*. Austin: Univ. of Texas Press, 1990.

Hillier, Jim, and Peter Wollen, eds. *Howard Hawks: American Artist*. Bloomington: Indiana Univ. Press, 1996.

Hiney, Tom. *Raymond Chandler: A Biography*. New York: Atlantic Monthly Press, 1997.

Hirsch, Foster. *The Dark Side of the Screen: Film Noir*. New York: Da Capo, 1982.

————. *Detours and Lost Highways: A Map of Neo-Noir*. New York: Limelight, 1999.

Hitchcock, Alfred. *Hitchcock on Hitchcock: Selected Writings and Interviews*. Edited by Sidney Gottlieb. Los Angeles: Univ. of California Press, 1997.

Holden, Stephen. "Neo-Noir." *New York Times*, March 8, 1998, sec. 2, pp. 15, 22.

Houseman, John. *Front and Center: An Autobiography.* New York: Simon and Schuster, 1979.

Iyer, Pico. "Private Eye and Public Conscience." *Time,* December 12, 1998, 98.

Joyner, Will. "Married Marlowe and a Stretched Chandler." *New York Times,* July 24, 1998, sec. E, p. 32.

Kael, Pauline. *5001 Nights at the Movies.* Rev. ed. New York: Holt, 1991.

————. *For Keeps.* New York: Dutton, 1996.

————. "*Lady in the Lake* and *Marlowe.*" *New Yorker,* February 17, 1997, 27–28.

Kerr, David. "Quickies: Robert Altman." *Film Comment* 35, no. 2 (March–April 1999): 74.

Krutnik, Frank. *In a Lonely Street: Film Noir, Genre, and Masculinity.* New York: Routledge, 1991.

Lally, Kevin. *Wilder Times: The Life of Billy Wilder.* New York: Holt, 1996.

Lane, Anthony. "Killing Time: *Mr. Ripley.*" *New Yorker,* Jan. 3, 2000, 128–30.

Lark, Michael. *Raymond Chandler's Philip Marlowe: The Little Sister.* Illustrated by Michael Lark. New York: Simon and Schuster, 1997.

Lehman, David. *The Perfect Murder: A Study in Detection.* New York: Macmillan, 1989.

Lipnick, Edward. "Creative Technique for *The Long Goodbye,*" *American Cinematographer,* March 1973, 278–82, 328–29, 334–35.

"*The Long Goodbye.*" *Sight and Sound,* n.s., 9, no. 8 (August 1999): 62.

Luhr, William. *Raymond Chandler and Film.* Rev. ed. Tallahassee: Florida State Univ. Press, 1991.

Lupack, Barbara, ed. *Take Two: Adapting the American Novel to Film.* Bowling Green, Ohio: Bowling Green State Univ. Press, 1994.

Lyons, Donald. "Seventies Film Noir." *Film Comment* 29, no. 4 (July–August 1993): 44–53.

MacBain, Ed. "Philip Marlowe Is Back." *New York Times Book Review,* October 15, 1989, 35, 44.

MacNab, Geoffrey. "Video Reviews: *Murder, My Sweet.*" *Sight and Sound,* n.s., 8, no. 9 (September 1998): 59.

MacShane, Frank. *The Life of Raymond Chandler.* New York: Dutton, 1976.

————. "Stranger at the Studio: Raymond Chandler and Hollywood." *American Film,* May 1976, 57–59.

Maltin, Leonard, Cathleen Anderson, and Luke Sader, eds. *Movie Guide.* Rev. ed. New York: New American Library, 2000.

Marling, William. *The American Roman Noir: Hammett, Cain, and Chandler.* Athens: Univ. of Georgia Press, 1995.

————. *Raymond Chandler.* Boston: Twayne, 1986.

Martin, Richard. *Mean Streets and Raging Bulls: The Legacy of Film Noir.* Lanham, Md.: Scarecrow Press, 1997.

Mast, Gerald. *Howard Hawks, Storyteller.* New York: Oxford Univ. Press, 1982.

————, and Bruce Kawin. *A Short History of the Movies.* Rev. ed. Boston: Allyn and Bacon, 2000.

Maugham, W. Somerset. "The Decline and Fall of the Detective Story." In *The Va-*

grant Mood: Six Essays, by Somerset Maugham, 101–32. Garden City, N.Y.: Doubleday, 1953.

Maxfield, James. *The Fatal Woman: Sources of Male Anxiety in American Film Noir.* Madison, N.J.: Fairleigh Dickinson Univ. Press, 1996.

McFarlane, Brian. *Novel to Film: An Introduction to the Theory of Adaptation.* New York: Oxford Univ. Press, 1996.

McGilligan, Patrick. *Robert Altman: A Biography.* New York: St. Martin's Press, 1989.

———, ed. *Backstory: Interviews with Screenwriters.* 3 vols. Los Angeles: Univ. of California Press, 1986–97.

McMurtry, Larry. "Raymond Chandler." *New York Times Book Review,* November 15, 1981, 46.

Merrill, Robert, ed. *Critical Essays on Raymond Chandler.* Boston: G.K. Hall, 1999.

———."Raymond Chandler's Plots and the Concept of Plot." *Narrative* 7, no. 1 (January 1999): 3–21.

Miller, Frank. *Movies: 100 Classics.* Atlanta: Turner, 1996.

Miller, Robert. "The Publication of Raymond Chandler's *Long Goodbye.*" *Papers of the Bibliographical Society of America* 63 (Fall 1969): 279–90.

Moscowitz, John. *Critical Approaches to Film: The Big Sleep and Other Films.* Upper Saddle River, N.J.: Prentice-Hall, 2000.

Muller, Ed. *Dark City: The Lost World of Film Noir.* New York: St. Martin's Press, 1998.

Naremore, James. *More than Night: Film Noir in Its Contexts.* Los Angeles: Univ. of California Press, 1998.

Nash, Jay, and Stanley Ross, eds. *Motion Picture Guide: 1927–83.* 8 vols. Chicago: Cinebooks, 1985.

Norman, Ralf. *Wholeness Restored: Symmetry in the Writings of Raymond Chandler and Other Novelists.* Peter Lang, 1998.

O'Brien, David. *Robert Altman: Hollywood Survivor.* New York: Continuum, 1995.

O'Brien, Geoffrey. *Hardboiled America: Pulp Fiction and Masters of Noir.* Rev. ed. New York: Da Capo, 1997.

Orr, Christopher. "Genre Theory in the Context of Noir Film." *Film Criticism* 22, no. 1 (Fall 1997): 21–37.

Palmer, Barton. *Hollywood's Dark Cinema: The American Film Noir.* New York: Twayne, 1994.

———, ed. *Perspectives on Film Noir.* New York: G.K. Hall, 1996.

Parish, James, and Michael Pitts. *The Great Detective Pictures.* Metuchen, N.J.: Scarecrow Press, 1990.

Parker, Robert B. "Crime/Mystery: Raymond Chandler." *New York Times Book Review,* October 8, 1995, 22.

Paxton, John. "Murder, My Sweet: A Screenplay" (unpublished). Los Angeles: RKO, 1944.

Pendo, Stephen. *Raymond Chandler on Screen: His Novels into Film.* Metuchen, N.J.: Scarecrow Press, 1976.

Phelps, Donald. "Cinema Gris." *Film Comment* 30, no. 1 (Jan.-Feb. 2000), 64–69.

Phillips, William. *Film: An Introduction.* New York: St. Martin's Press, 1999.

Pitts, Michael. *Famous Movie Detectives.* 2 vols. Metuchen, N.J.: Scarecrow Press, 1991.

Plecki, Gerard. *Robert Altman.* Boston: Twayne, 1985.

Price, Theodore. *Hitchcock and Homosexuality: A Psychoanalytic View.* Metuchen, N.J.: Scarecrow Press, 1992.

Priestman, Martin. *Detective Fiction and Literature: The Figure on the Carpet.* New York: St. Martin's Press, 1991.

Pyrhönen, Heta. *Mayhem and Murder: Narrative and Moral Issues in the Detective Novel.* Toronto: Univ. of Toronto Press, 2000.

Rafter, Nicole. *Crime Films and Society.* New York: Oxford Univ. Press, 2000.

Reynolds, William, and Elizabeth Trembley, eds. *It's a Print! Detective Fiction from Page to Screen.* Bowling Green, Ohio: Bowling Green State Univ. Press, 1994.

Roth, Marty. *Foul and Fair Play: Classic Detective Fiction.* Athens: Univ. of Georgia Press, 1995.

Rozgony, Jay. "The Making of *Double Indemnity.*" *Films in Review* 41, nos. 6–7 (June–July 1990): 339–45.

Sandgren, Peter. "Film Noir: Locating Two Chandler Films in the Noir Tradition." Ph.D. diss., Univ. of Connecticut–Storrs, 1991.

Sarris, Andrew, ed. *Film Directors Encyclopedia.* New York: St. James Press, 1998.

———. *"You Ain't Heard Nothin' Yet": The American Talking Film, 1927–49.* New York: Oxford Univ. Press, 1998.

Sayre, Nora. "In the Shoes of a Scary Stalker: *Strangers on a Train.*" *New York Times,* April 12, 1998, sec. 2, pp. 11, 12.

Schatzkin, Roger. "Doubled Indemnity: Raymond Chandler, Fiction, and Film." Ph.D. diss., Rutgers University, 1984.

Schickel, Richard. *Double Indemnity.* London: British Film Institute, 1993.

Shepard, Jim. "Jolting Noir with a Shot of Nihilism." *New York Times,* February 7, 1999, sec. 2, p. 24.

Sheppard, R.Z. "Capering: Philip Marlowe." *Time,* October 2, 1989, 88.

Sikov, Ed. *On Sunset Boulevard: The Life and Times of Billy Wilder.* New York: Hyperion, 1998.

Silliphant, Sterling. "Marlowe: A Screenplay" (unpublished). Los Angeles: Metro-Goldwyn-Mayer, 1968.

Silver, Alain, and James Ursini, eds. *The Film Noir Reader.* New York: Limelight, 1998.

Silver, Alain, and Elizabeth Ward. *Film Noir: An Encyclopedic Reference.* Rev. ed. Woodstock, N.Y.: Overlook Press, 1992.

Sloan, Jane. *Alfred Hitchcock: A Guide to References and Resources.* Rev. ed. Los Angeles: Univ. of California Press, 1995.

Smith, Charles. "Quickness of Fancy: Raymond Chandler's Philip Marlowe." Ph.D. diss., University of Kentucky–Lexington, 1997.

Smith, David. "The Public Eye of Raymond Chandler." *Journal of American Studies* 14, no. 3 (December 1980): 423–41.

Sobchack, Vivian. "Lounge Time: Postwar Crises and Film Noir." In *Refiguring American Film Genres,* edited by Nick Browne, 129–70. Los Angeles: Univ. of California Press, 1998.

Speir, Jerry. *Raymond Chandler.* New York: Ungar, 1981.

Sragow, Michael. "Bogart's Birth as an Icon." *New York Times,* Jan. 16, 2000, sec. 2: 4, 8.

Sterritt, David, ed. *Robert Altman: Interviews.* Jackson: Univ. Press of Mississippi, 2000.

Stoppard, Tom. "Stalking Raymond Chandler's Spirit." *New York Times,* July 19, 1998, sec. 2, pp. 1, 29.

Symala, T. "Contribution of Raymond Chandler to American Cinema." *Indian Journal of American Studies* 25, no. 2 (Summer 1995): 77–81.

Taylor, John Russell. *Hitch: The Life and Times of Alfred Hitchcock.* New York: Da Capo, 1996.

Teachout, Terry. "The Sensitive Shamus." *New York Times Book Review,* March 14, 1999, 19.

Telotte, J.P. *Voices in the Dark: The Narrative Patterns of Film Noir.* Chicago: Univ. of Illinois Press, 1989.

Thomas, Tony. *The Films of the Forties.* New York: Carol, 1990.

Thomson, David. *The Big Sleep.* London: British Film Institute, 1996.

Tibbetts, John, and James Welsh, eds. *The Encyclopedia of Novels into Film.* New York: Facts on File, 1999.

Tuska, Jon. *In Manors and Alleys: A Casebook of the American Detective Film.* Westport, Conn.: Greenwood Press, 1988.

Van Dover, J.K., ed. *The Critical Response to Raymond Chandler.* Westport, Conn.: Greenwood Press, 1995.

Ward, Elizabeth, and Alain Silver. *Raymond Chandler's Los Angeles.* Woodstock, N.Y.: Overlook Press, 1987.

Weathersbee, Avis. "Last Nod to Chandler: *Poodle Springs.*" *Chicago Sun-Times,* July 26, 1998, sec. E, p. 13.

Weaver, Tom. "Norman Lloyd." *Starlog,* December 1998, 69–74.

Wessells, Henry. "Raymond Chandler and the Origins of Film Noir." *AB Weekly,* December 8, 1997, 1501–1506.

Willett, Ralph. *The Naked City: Urban Crime Fiction in the U.S.A.* New York: Manchester Univ. Press, 1996.

Wilson, Edmund. *Classics and Commercials: A Literary Chronicle of the Forties.* New York: Noonday Press, 1967.

Wolfe, Peter. *Something More than Night: The Case of Raymond Chandler.* Bowling Green, Ohio: Bowling Green State Univ. Press, 1985.

Filmography

Films Written by Raymond Chandler

Described below are the motion pictures for which Raymond Chandler received an official screen credit as author or coauthor of the script, and which are highlighted in the text accordingly.

Double Indemnity (Paramount, 1944)

Based on the novel by James M. Cain

Director	Billy Wilder
Producer	Joseph Sistrom
Screenplay	Billy Wilder, Raymond Chandler
Director of Photography	John F. Seitz
Editor	Doane Harrison
Art Directors	Hans Dreier, Hal Pereira
Music	Miklos Rosza
Costumes	Edith Head
Running time	107 minutes
Original release date	May 1944

Cast

Walter Neff	Fred MacMurray
Phyllis Dietrichson	Barbara Stanwyck
Barton Keyes	Edward G. Robinson
Mr. Jackson	Porter Hall
Lola Dietrichson	Jean Heather
H.S. Dietrichson	Tom Powers
Nino Zachetti	Byron Barr
Edward Norton	Richard Gaines
Sam Gorlopis	Fortunio Bonanova
Joe Peters	John Philliber

And Now Tomorrow (Paramount, 1944)

Based on the novel by Rachel Field

Director	Irving Pichel
Producer	Fred Kohlmar
Executive Producer	B.G. DeSylva
Screenplay	Frank Partos, Raymond Chandler
Director of Photography	Daniel E. Fapp
Editor	Duncan Mansfield
Art Directors	Hal Pereira, Hans Dreier
Music	Victor Young
Costumes	Edith Head
Running time	86 minutes
Original release date	November 1944

Cast

Dr. Merek Vance	Alan Ladd
Emily Blair	Loretta Young
Janice Blair	Susan Hayward
Jeff Stoddard	Barry Sullivan
Aunt Em	Beulah Bondi
Dr. Weeks	Cecil Kellaway
Uncle Wallace	Grant Mitchell
Dr. Sloane	Jonathan Hale
Angeletta Gallo	Helen Mack
Peter Gallo	Anthony L. Caruso
Joe	Darryl Hickman
Bobby	Conrad Binyon
Hester	Connie Leon
Meeker	George Carlton
Jan Vankovitch	Lee Bulgakov

The Unseen (Paramount, 1945)

Based on the novel *Her Heart in Her Throat* by Ethel Linda White

Director	Lewis Allen
Producer	John Houseman
Screenplay	Hagar Wilde, Raymond Chandler
Adaptation	Hagar Wilde, Ken Englund
Director of Photography	John F. Seitz
Editor	Doane Harrison

Art Directors	Hans Dreier, Earl Hedrick
Music	Ernst Toch
Running time	82 minutes
Original release date	June 1945

Cast

David Fielding	Joel McCrea
Elizabeth Howard	Gail Russell
Dr. Charles Evans	Herbert Marshall
Maxine	Phyllis Brooks
Marian Tygarth	Isobel Elsom
Jasper Goodwin	Norman Lloyd
Chester	Mikhail Rasumny
Mrs. Norris	Elizabeth Risdon
Sullivan	Tom Tully
Ellen Fielding	Nona Griffith
Barnaby Fielding	Richard Lyon
Lily	Victoria Horne
Miss Budge	Mary Field

The Blue Dahlia (Paramount, 1946)

Director	George Marshall
Producer	John Houseman
Executive Producer	Joseph Sistrom
Screenplay	Raymond Chandler
Director of Photography	Lionel Lindon
Editor	Arthur Schmidt
Art Directors	Hans Dreier, Walter Tyles
Music	Victor Young
Costumes	Edith Head
Running time	100 minutes
Original release date	May 1946

Cast

Johnny Morrison	Alan Ladd
Joyce Harwood	Veronica Lake
Buzz Wanchek	William Bendix
Eddie Harwood	Howard Da Silva
Helen Morrison	Doris Dowling
Captain Hendrickson	Tom Powers

George Copeland	Hugh Beaumont
Corelli	Howard Freeman
Leo	Don Costello
Dad Newell	Will Wright
Hotel Tout	Frank Faylen
Heath	Walter Sande

Strangers on a Train (Warner Brothers, 1951)

Based on the novel by Patricia Highsmith

Director/Producer	Alfred Hitchcock
Screenplay	Raymond Chandler, Czenzi Ormonde
Adaptation	Whitfield Cook
Director of Photography	Robert Burks
Editor	William H. Ziegler
Art Director	Ted Haworth
Music	Dimitri Tiomkin
Costumes	Leah Rhodes
Running time	100 minutes
Original release date	June 1951

Cast

Guy Haines	Farley Granger
Ann Morton	Ruth Roman
Bruno Anthony	Robert Walker
Senator Morton	Leo G. Carroll
Barbara Morton	Patricia Hitchcock
Miriam	Laura Elliott
Mrs. Anthony	Marion Lorne
Mr. Anthony	Jonathan Hale
Captain Turley	Howard St. John
Professor Collins	John Brown
Mrs. Cunningham	Norma Varden
Hennessy	Robert Gist
Hammond	John Doucette

Film Adaptations of Raymond Chandler's Fiction

The Falcon Takes Over (RKO, 1942)

Based on the novel *Farewell, My Lovely* by Raymond Chandler and a character created by Michael Arlen

Director	Irving Reis
Producer	Howard Benedict
Executive Producer	J.R. McDonough
Screenplay	Lynn Root, Frank Fenton
Director of Photography	George Robinson
Editor	Harry Marker
Art Directors	Albert S. D'Agostino, Field A. Gray
Music	C. Bakaleinikoff
Costumes	Renie
Running time	63 minutes
Original release date	May 1942

Cast

Gay Lawrence (the Falcon)	George Sanders
Anne Riordan	Lynn Bari
Inspector O'Hara	James Gleason
Goldie Locke	Allen Jenkins
Diana Kenyon	Helen Gilbert
Moose Malloy	Ward Bond
Bates	Edward Gargan
Jessie Florian	Anne Revere
Jerry	George Cleveland
Grimes	Harry Shannon
Marriott	Hans Conried
Jules	Turhan Bey
Laird Brunette	Selmer Jackson

Time to Kill (Twentieth Century Fox, 1942)

Based on the novel *The High Window* by Raymond Chandler and a character created by Brett Halliday

Director	Herbert I. Leeds
Producer	Sol M. Wurtzel

Executive Producer	William Goetz
Screenplay	Clarence Upson Young
Director of Photography	Charles Clarke
Editor	Alfred Day
Art Directors	Richard Day, Chester Gore
Music	Emil Newman
Running time	61 minutes
Original release date	December 1942

Cast

Michael Shayne	Lloyd Nolan
Merle Davis	Heather Angel
Linda Conquest	Doris Merrick
Louis Venter	Ralph Byrd
Lieutenant Breeze	Richard Lane
Lois Morny	Sheila Bromley
Alex Morny	Morris Ankrum
Mrs. Murdock	Ethel Griffies
Leslie Murdock	James Seay
Phillips	Ted Hecht
Hench	William Pawley
Postman	Syd Saylor
Washburn	Lester Sharpe
Dental Assistant	Charles Williams
Headwaiter	Leroy Mason
Ena	Phyllis Kennedy
Manager	Paul Guilfoyle
Marge	Helen Flint

Murder, My Sweet (RKO, 1945)
(UK title: *Farewell, My Lovely*)

Based on the novel *Farewell, My Lovely* by Raymond Chandler

Director	Edward Dmytryk
Producer	Adrian Scott
Executive Producer	Sid Rogell
Screenplay	John Paxton
Director of Photography	Harry J. Wild
Editor	Joseph Noriega
Art Directors	Albert S. D'Agostino, Carroll Clark
Music	Roy Webb

Costumes	Edward Stevenson
Running time	95 minutes
Original release date	January 1945

Cast

Philip Marlowe	Dick Powell
Helen Grayle	Claire Trevor
Anne Grayle	Anne Shirley
Jules Amthor	Otto Kruger
Moose Malloy	Mike Mazurki
Llewellyn Grayle	Miles Mander
Lindsay Marriott	Douglas Walton
Lieutenant Randall	Don Douglas
Dr. Sondeborg	Ralf Harolde
Jessie Florian	Esther Howard

The Big Sleep (Warner Brothers, 1946)

Based on the novel by Raymond Chandler

Director/Producer	Howard Hawks
Screenplay	William Faulkner, Leigh Brackett, Jules Furthman
Director of Photography	Sid Hickox
Editor	Christian Nyby
Art Director	Carl Jules Weyl
Music	Max Steiner
Costumes	Leah Rhodes
Running time	114 minutes
Original release date	August 1946

Cast

Philip Marlowe	Humphrey Bogart
Vivian Rutledge	Lauren Bacall
Eddie Mars	John Ridgely
Carmen Sherwood	Martha Vickers
Bookseller	Dorothy Malone
General Sternwood	Charles Waldron
Mona Mars	Peggy Knudsen
Bernie Ohls	Regis Toomey
Norris	Charles D. Brown
Cantino	Bob Steele

Harry Jones	Elisha Cook Jr.
Joe Brody	Louis Jean Heydt
Agnes Lozelle	Sonia Darrin
Arthur Gwynn Geiger	Theodore Von Eltz
Carol Lundgren	Tom Rafferty
Sidney	Tom Fadden
Pete	Ben Weldon
Art Huck	Trevor Bardette
Cabby	Joy Barlowe
Librarian	Carole Douglas
Owen Taylor	Dan Wallace

The Brasher Doubloon (Twentieth Century Fox, 1947) (UK title: *The High Window*)

Based on the novel *The High Window* by Raymond Chandler

Director	John Brahm
Producer	Robert Bassler
Screenplay	Dorothy Hannah
Adaptation	Leonard Praskins
Director of Photography	Lloyd Ahern
Editor	Harry Reynolds
Art Directors	James Basevi, Richard Irvine
Music	David Buttolph
Costumes	Eleanor Behm
Running time	72 minutes
Original release date	May 1947

Cast

Philip Marlowe	George Montgomery
Merle Davis	Nancy Guild
Leslie Murdock	Conrad Janis
Lieutenant Breeze	Roy Roberts
Vannier	Fritz Kortner
Mrs. Murdock	Florence Bates
Vince Blair	Marvin Miller
Morningstar	Houseley Stevenson
Sergeant Spanger	Bob Adler
George Anson	Jack Conrad
Eddie Prue	Alfred Linder

Lady in the Lake (Metro-Goldwyn-Mayer, 1947)

Based on the novel by Raymond Chandler

Director	Robert Montgomery
Producer	George Haight
Screenplay	Steve Fisher, Raymond Chandler (uncredited)
Director of Photography	Paul C. Vogel
Editor	Gene Ruggiero
Art Directors	Cedric Gibbons, Preston Ames
Music	David Snell
Costumes	Irene
Running time	105 minutes
Original release date	February 1947

Cast

Philip Marlowe	Robert Montgomery
Adrienne Fromsett	Audrey Totter
Lieutenant DeGarmot	Lloyd Nolan
Captain Kane	Tom Tully
Derace Kingsby	Leon Ames
Muriel Chess	Jayne Meadows
Chris Lavery	Dick Simmons
Eugene Grayson	Morris Ankrum
Receptionist	Lila Leeds
Artist	William Roberts
Mrs. Grayson	Kathleen Lockhart
Crystal Kingsby	Ellay Mort

Marlowe (Metro-Goldwyn-Mayer, 1969)

Based on the novel *The Little Sister* by Raymond Chandler

Director	Paul Bogart
Producers	Gabriel Katzka, Sidney Beckerman
Screenplay	Stirling Silliphant
Director of Photography (in Metrocolor)	William H. Daniels
Editor	Gene Ruggiero
Art Directors	Addison Hehr, George W. Davis
Music	Peter Matz

Song "Little Sister"	Peter Matz, Norman Gimbel, and sung by Orpheus
Costumes	Jimmy Taylor, Florence Hackett
Running time	95 minutes
Original release date	October 1969

Cast

Philip Marlowe	James Garner
Mavis Wald	Gayle Hunnicutt
Lieutenant Christy French	Carroll O'Connor
Dolores Gonzales	Rita Moreno
Orfamay Quest	Sharon Farrell
Crowell	William Daniels
Grant Hicks	Jackie Coogan
Steelgrave	H.M. Wynant
Dr. Lagardie	Paul Stevens
Wong	Bruce Lee
Julie	Corinne Camacho
Sergeant Beifus	Kenneth Tobey
Clausen	Warren Finnerty
Hady	George Tyne
Pale Face	Nate Esformes
Chuck	Christopher Cary
Gumpshaw	Read Morgan
Orrin Quest	Roger Newman

The Long Goodbye (United Artists, 1973)

Based on the novel by Raymond Chandler

Director	Robert Altman
Producer	Jerry Bick
Executive Producer	Elliott Kastner
Screenplay	Leigh Brackett
Director of Photography (in Panavision, Technicolor)	Vilmos Zsigmond
Editor	Lou Lombardo
Music	John Williams
Song "The Long Goodbye"	John Williams, Johnny Mercer, performed by the Dave Grusin Trio, Jack Sheldon, Clydie King, Erno Neufeld's Violin, Irene Kral, Jack Riley,

	Morgan Ames, Aluminium Band, the Tepotzlan Municipal Band
Costumes	Kent James, Marjorie Wahl
Running time	111 minutes
Original release date	March 1973 (reissued October 1973)

Cast

Philip Marlowe	Elliott Gould
Eileen Wade	Nina Van Pallandt
Roger Wade	Sterling Hayden
Marty Augustine	Mark Rydell
Doctor Verringer	Henry Gibson
Harry	David Arkin
Terry Lennox	Jim Bouton
Morgan	Warren Berlinger
Jo Ann Eggenweiler	Jo Ann Brody
Lt. Farmer	Steve Coit
Mabel	Jack Knight
Pepe	Pepe Callahan
Vince	Vince Palmieri
Doctor	Pancho Cordoba
Jefe	Enrique Lucero
Rutanya Sweet	Rutanya Alda
Dancer	Tammy Shaw
Piano Player	Jack Riley
Colony Guard	Ken Samson
Detective Green	Jerry Jones
Detective Dayton	John Davies
Supermarket Clerk	Rodney Moss
Real Estate Lady	Sybil Scotford
Herbie	Herb Kerns

Farewell, My Lovely (Avco Embassy, 1975)

Based on the novel by Raymond Chandler

Director	Dick Richards
Producers	George Pappas, Jerry Bruckheimer
Executive Producers	Elliott Kastner, Jerry Bick
Screenplay	David Zelag Goodman
Director of Photography (in Fujicolor)	John A. Alonzo

Editors	Walter Thompson, Joel Cox
Production Designer	Dean Tavoularis
Music	David Shire
Costumes	Tony Scarano, Sandra Berke
Assistant Director, Unit Manager	Tim Zinnemann
Running time	95 minutes
Original release date	August 1975

Cast

Philip Marlowe	Robert Mitchum
Mrs. Grayle/Velma	Charlotte Rampling
Detective Lt. Nulty	John Ireland
Mrs. Florian	Sylvia Miles
Laird Brunette	Anthony Zerbe
Billy Rolfe	Harry Dean Stanton
Moose Malloy	Jack O'Halloran
Nick	Joe Spinell
Johnnie	Sylvester Stallone
Frances Amthor	Kate Murtagh
Lindsay Marriott	John O'Leary
Tommy Ray	Walter McGinn
Cowboy	Burton Gilliam
Judge Baxter Grayle	Jim Thompson
Georgie	Jimmy Archer
Roy	Ted Gehring
Commissioner	Logan Ramsey
Woman	Margie Hall
Louis Levine	Jack Bernardi

The Big Sleep (United Artists, 1978)

Based on the novel by Raymond Chandler

Director	Michael Winner
Producers	Elliott Kastner, Michael Winner
Screenplay	Michael Winner
Director of Photography (in DeLuxe Color)	Robert Paynter
Editor	Freddie Wilson
Production Designer	Harry Pottle

Music	Jerry Fielding
Song "Won't Somebody Dance With Me"	Lynsey De Paul, performed by Diana Quick
Costumes	Ron Beck
Running time	99 minutes
Original release date	April 1978

Cast

Philip Marlowe	Robert Mitchum
Charlotte Regan	Sarah Miles
Lash Canino	Richard Boone
Camilla Sternwood	Candy Clark
Agnes Lozelle	Joan Collins
Joe Brody	Edward Fox
Inspector Jim Carson	John Mills
General Guy de Brisai Sternwood	James Stewart
Eddie Mars	Oliver Reed
Vincent Norris	Harry Andrews
Harry Jones	Colin Blakely
Commander Barker	Richard Todd
Mona Mars	Diana Quick
Inspector Gregory	James Donald
Arthur Gwynn Geiger	John Justin
Karl Lundgren	Simon Turner
Owen Taylor	Martin Potter
Rusty Regan	David Saville
Lanny	Dudley Sutton
Lou	Don Henderson

Poodle Springs (HBO-TV/Universal-TV, 1998)

Based on the novel by Raymond Chandler and Robert B. Parker

Director	Bob Rafelson
Producer	Tony Mark
Executive Producers	Sydney Pollack, William Horberg, Jon Avnet, Jordon Kerner
Teleplay	Tom Stoppard
Director of Photography	Stuart Dryburgh
Editor	Steven Cohen
Art Director	Mark Friedberg

Music	Michael Small
Running Time	95 minutes
First telecast	July 25, 1998

Cast

Philip Marlowe	James Caan
Larry Victor	David Keith
Clayton Blackstone	Brian Cox
P.J. Parker	Joe Don Baker
Muffy Blackstone	Julia Campbell
Angel	Nia Peeples
Laura	Dina Meyer

Index

Tully, Tom, 113, 185
Turner, Simon, 69
Tuska, Jon, 18, 156
TV from Radio (videocassette), 226
TV Guide (magazine), 245
Twentieth Century Fox, 30, 81

United Artists, 68, 146, 158–59, 160
Universal-International Pictures, 216–18
Unseen, The (film), 183–86
upper class: Chandler's fictional treatment of, 80, 81, 90

Van Dine, S.S., 102
Van Dover, J.K., 2–3
Van Pallandt, Nina, 148
Vickers, Martha, 59, 62
Vidal, Gore, 36
violence: in *The Long Goodbye* (film), 153–54; in *Marlowe*, 129–30, 133, 135
Vogel, Paul, 107
voice-over narration, xx–xxi; in *The Brasher Doubloon*, 86; in *Double Indemnity*, 173; in *Farewell, My Lovely*, 43–44; in *Lady in the Lake*, 108; in *Murder, My Sweet*, 34–35, 37–39. *See also* subjective camera technique

Waldron, Charles, 60
Walker, Robert, 203, 204, 216
Walter Neff (character), 174, 177–78, 179
Wang, Gene, 225
Ward, Elizabeth, 92, 109, 234, 249
Warner, Jack, 56, 62–63, 64, 67
Warner Brothers, 54, 203
Warren, Dale, 29, 193
Watson, Douglas, 35
Waugh, Evelyn, 126
Weathersbee, Avis, 236, 240, 241
Welles, Orson, 9
Wenders, Wim, 216
Wessells, Henry, 118, 247

West, Nathanael, 119
Westlake, Donald E., 3
Westminster Gazette, 14
Where's Marlowe? (film), 246
White, Ethel, 183
"Who Cares Who Killed Roger Ackroyd?" (Wilson), 5
Wilde, Hagar, 184
Wilde, Oscar, 61
Wilder, Billy, 7; admiration of Chandler's writing, 80; depicted by Chandler in *The Little Sister*, 125; directing of *Double Indemnity*, 85–86, 127, 172–73, 175–76, 177, 178–79, 180; *Double Indemnity* screenplay collaboration with Chandler, 6, 9, 166, 167–70, 172, 174, 181, 182; personality of, 181; themes of corruption and, 171–72; themes of male companionship and, 178
Wilder, Thornton, 213
Willett, Ralph, 101, 118
Williams, John, 156
Wilson, Edmund, 4, 5
Windsor, Marie, 8
Winner, Michael, 68–70, 71, 72
Wolfe, Peter, 27, 53, 102, 123, 143, 144, 197, 233
Wood, Michael, 171
World War I, 14–15
World War II: film noir and, 8
Wright, Will, 190
"Writers in Hollywood" (Chandler), 165, 182
Wynant, H.M, 128

Young, Clarence, 81–82, 83
Young, Jane, xx
Young, Loretta, 186
Young, Victor, 198
Young Savages, The (film), 208

Zerbe, Anthony, 42
Zinnemann, Tim, 43
Zsigmond, Vilmos, 156–57